MW00778773

HEART
POLITICS
REVISITED

Other books by Fran Peavey

Heart Politics with Myra Levy and Charles Varon published by New Society Publishers, 1985.

A Shallow Pool of Time, published by New Society Publishers, 1990.

By Life's Grace: Musings of the Essence of Social Change, published by New Society Publishers, 1994.

Sjecam Se: I Remember:Writings by Bosnian Women Refugees, edited by Radmila Manojlovic' Zarkovic' with additional editing and introduction by Fran Peavey.

Chapter 6: 'Political Earthquakes' originally appeared in *The Need for A Second Look at Jonestown*, edited by Rebecca Moore and Fielding McGehee III, The Edwin Mellen Press, 1989.

HEART
POLITICS
REVISITED

FRAN PEAVEY

Pluto Press

First published in 2000 by
Pluto Press Australia Limited
Locked Bag 199, Annandale, NSW 2038
Website: media.socialchange.net.au/pluto

Cover design by Susan Meller and Wendy Farley

Back cover photo of Fran Peavey by Beverly Malejan Ramsey

Index by Neale Towart

Typeset by Chapter 8 Pty Ltd, PO Box 687, Marrickville NSW 2204

Printed and bound by McPherson's Printing Group

Australian Cataloguing in Publication Data

Peavey, Fran.
    Heart Politics Revisited

    Includes index.
    ISBN 1 86403 105 0.

    1. Peavey, Fran. 2. Social reformers — United States — Biography.
    3. Social change. 4. Social problems. 5. Human rights. I. Title.

303.4

This book is lovingly dedicated to my past, present and future family. Fantastic grandparents, loving parents, fun loving siblings, great nieces and nephews, wonderful lovers and partners, fine inlaws: Sophia, and Ralph, Elizabeth and Arthur, Dorothy and Tom, Ann, Art, Dorothy and Susan, Brian, Jennifer, Tom, Frank, Aaron, Drew, Sarah Beth and Jason, Fred, Tim, Pam, and Tova, Martha and Alex.

The world didn't give me this joy and it can't take it away.

African-American Gospel song

Table of Contents

Acknowledgments

THE ORIGINAL BOOK was written in 1984 with Myra Levy and Charlie Varon. This book has some of the same chapters that were included in the first book, but each chapter has been brought up-to-date. Since the initial book was written on a Kaypro computer, the revised edition has had to be completely retyped, and in that process I was able to make many changes. I am indebted to Charlie and Myra for their original organization of the material.

I decided to redo this book primarily because so many teachers in the fields of international development and social work wrote to me upset that *Heart Politics* had fallen out of print. They begged me to reissue the book. One is, of course, always happy when the product of one's labor is found useful. But I had scarcely imagined that this book would find a home in classrooms. I was especially shocked to learn of its use in business schools. I had envisioned that it would be read by people who were curious about what it looked like on the inside of social change campaigns, rather than reading about them in the newspaper. The media are rather inaccurate, or maybe it is simply that events look very different from the inside when making the event, as opposed to viewing it from the outside as the media do. In the retyping, I found that I also had erred from time to time. I will take this opportunity to mention that the mistakes in this book are all mine; no one else is responsible for them.

This book benefits from fifteen years of talking with readers, and reading the questions that people have posed in letters after reading the material. For years, I have held a consulting period at four o'clock every day, when people can come to my home to discuss their social change campaigns. I used to charge a rock, but my rock garden overflows, so now I simply offer it for the learning I get. I thank those who have brought their social change dreams to my door. In this way, I am able to know about a broad cross-section of social change work around the world.

I have also benefited considerably from Heart Politics conferences I have attended in Australia and New Zealand, as well as one in the United States. In New Zealand, there have been two since the late 1980s; and in Australia, there have been many such meetings. They are usually five-day gatherings attended by people working at the grass roots and in electoral politics, who come together to share their ideas, their deep questions, and the development of their craft with each other. I feel such an excitement being with colleagues at these gatherings, and I learn so much from them.

There are a few social technologies, ways of working in a group and organizing discussions, that help people think freshly and explore issues together. For instance, in Heart Circle, which is one of the most powerful tools at these gatherings, we use a social process given to us by the Maori people in New Zealand. Elders explained the ceremony to the members of the first gathering, and encouraged us to use it when we wanted to think and communicate deeply, or when we needed to explore difficult issues between us. Each Heart Politics gathering has added new ideas, which have continued to deepen and broaden the experience at the gatherings.

Various kinds of editing were done by Cathy Hoffman, Tova Green, Linda Hess, and Ann Wilson. Carolyn Pincus helped decide what to leave in and what to delete, and contributed as an advisor in many ways. The huge job of going through the material and working with sentences to see that they actually say what I meant to say was taken on by Judith McCullough. She was so faithful to the intended meaning that I honor her craft and have named her my "writer's angel."

For the many types of assistance, from critical reading, fund-raising and funding, to personal support, to carrying out the many chores necessary to create this work, I would especially like to thank and honor:

The Bunting Institute and all my Bunting sisters

Peace Development Fund	Judith McCullough
Rita Archibald	Susan Meller
Beverly Axelrod	S. K. Mishra
Rachel Bagby	V.B. Mishra
Barbara Borden	Naomi Newman
Lyn Carson	Caroline Pincus
Nancy Davis	Catherine Porter
Earl Eckles	Bev Ramsey
Gay Falk	Pat Roberto
Barbara Green	Carol Rothman

Tova Green
Jan Hartsough
Barbara Hazard
Cathy Hoffman
Holly Hoffman
Yishai Hope
Polly Howells
Michael Lerner
Joanna Macy
Amy Mar
Barbara Mason

Frank Rubenfeld
Lori Senauke
Gail Senecca
Carol Shein
John Steiner
Nancy Taylor
S. N. Upadhyay
Eric Werthman
Ann Wilson
Ruth Zaporah

A special thanks to the staff at Cody's Bookstore, who answer my every question and bring important books to my attention. Small community bookstores need our support at times like these, when computer book ordering and large chains are undercutting community bookstores. No .com can ever replace Cody's.

I know responsibility for my sanity rests primarily with me, and because of that I get help from time to time. I thank my therapist, Ellen Zucker, who managed to keep me going through the remembering and writing about many of these struggles.

The people at Pluto Press in Sydney, Australia, particularly Tony Moore and Sean Kidney, were a joy to work with. I have always been blessed by publishers and editors who care for the book as much as I do and make it better for that care. A special thanks to Karen Alexander, who put me in touch with Pluto when I had completely given up on finding a publisher. "People aren't interested in social change anymore," one American publisher said to me. How do I live in such a bubble that I did not know that? Everywhere I go people are interested in social change.

And finally, I am grateful to you, the reader, for your interest and patience. In this world where every minute of your life has so many things competing for your attention, that you can take time to think about social change and perhaps take what you read in this book to fuel your own dreams of action is a gift to the world. Blessings on you.

Introduction

Heart Politics Revisited

EART POLITICS is an oxymoron, like military intelligence or cruel kindness. It is the marriage of opposites. Politics is the development and exercise of power, sometimes thought of in terms of strategy or scheming. It is a word that connotes hardness or toughness and is definitely a brain word. In a traditional sense, it is a male word. Power is the capacity or ability to act or perform effectively, but in connection with politics, it is also thought of as the possession of control, authority, or influence over others.

Heart, on the other hand, is a soft word involving feelings, tenderness, questions, and openness. Heart in politics does not accept alienation in organizing and always recognizes a deep relationship of all beings. It is a female word.

Strange, fresh options arise when these two words — heart and politics — sleep in the same bed.

Please do not mistake heart politics for "feel good politics." There is a great difference (though often a fine line) between working from the heart and manipulating people by appealing to their emotions. Germans who were alive during the Nazi period in the 1930s have described how filled with emotion their rallies were. This could be confused with heart politics, but of course it would be incorrect. Politics based on feelings of pity or on appeals to our emotions only skew action in dangerous directions. In Yugoslavia in the late 1980s and 1990s, for instance, I have seen how feelings can be manipulated to create horrible consequences. Heart politics, on the other hand, is about making a deep connection with the life found in a specific place, culture, or area of land. Since the connection is with life, it is inconceivable to think in terms of organizing to kill, to punish, or destroy. To use love of a people for deadly ends is immoral and crazy as well as inconsistent.

I have been working on social change projects in many parts of this world, including my home in the San Francisco Bay Area, for the past thirty years. I've worked person to person, in community social change, and finally in countries other than my own. When I published the first edition of this book in 1985, I had only begun to sense the dynamism and value in combining these two words — heart and politics — and the concepts they represent in work for social change.

Key Concepts in the Original Heart Politics

- Working from a connection across differences deepens and broadens one's work for social change. Connectedness to other humans as well as to animals, rivers, and all life helps make the heart accountable.

- Power is not power *over* but power *with* other humans and with nature. Power is a natural state, and is only absent when it has been stolen by those who have an interest in domination.

- Arrogance, self-righteousness, and even self-confidence are not necessary components of work for social change. Shy, self-doubting, and unsure people are also needed to work from their perspective.

- Listening is an important attitude for a social change worker.

- Cultural literacy is a key skill in making social change. Without it, true collaborative action with people and cultures different from one's own is difficult.

Additional Concepts in Heart Politics Revisited

- There are ways to listen that help move individuals and groups from passivity and cynicism to action.

- Reflection is an important activity for an activist.

- We can expect ourselves to make mistakes and to change in the process of lifelong social change work.

- We do not have to be "right" to work for social change. In fact, the arrogance that comes from assuming we are right creates resistance to our goals.

- In this time of shifting and consolidating power, with millions of others we co-create history one step at a time.

- For sustained development, slow social change is usually preferable to rapid change.

- Social change workers are responsible for organizing our own support system (financial and emotional) and must take care that rest and reflection are included in our work plan.

- Working at a human scale on problems — even those with enormous roots — is important. Large-scale problems have small-scale responses in our communities, in our personal consumption habits, and in our economic and spiritual lives.

- When we ask others to work on a project for the health of the world, we are giving them an opportunity to do something meaningful in their lives.

- It is a human's right to work for social change; action is as natural as breathing.

- Action relieves despair and brings us into community. The best response to despair is to acknowledge it and to join with others moving into action. Together we will give accountability to our actions, meet other great people, and cheer each other on. Action is the best antidote to fear, anger, and sorrow.

I've examined how individuals change, how they experience change in their lives, and how they resist change. Simultaneously, I have worked in my community on social change: how to resist changes I viewed as dangerous to life, and how to build a movement to create positive change. I have come away from these campaigns and experiments with a few ideas and many questions. I have not arrived at my theories conceptually, but through my practice of looking at the ground for ways to make social change without violence. I have looked at the violence in myself, the violence in my community, and the economic violence in the way we live. I have been alive in a social sense.

This book is about sharing what I have learned in these campaigns and in my meditations on the meaning of life as a social change worker. It is about the people who work for change, and what those struggles look like from the inside. Please don't expect large theoretical models for campaigns. I'm not sure I have discovered any large answers, but I have a few small ideas and questions.

Nonviolence, which is at the heart of my work, is itself a large idea and one I am only beginning to understand.

Maybe you wonder who I am to write such a book. Well, to tell you the truth, I am nobody. To my family, my friends, and my community, I am a small somebody. Someone whom they trust to do my work, to tell them what is happening, and to guide others. To a few dear friends, I am a special person. I feel adequately treasured and honored in my context. The truth is, I am one ordinary person who has made many small decisions on her life path to do what she could to nurture life all around me. I do not aspire to celebrity.

The other day I met someone, Tom Hurley by name, who reminded me that he worked for an organization that gave a prize every year. One year, I was one of the finalists for this prize. When Tom had called me to get more information for the decision, I asked him not to consider me for the prize, as the notoriety would interfere with my work. I am like a flower planted along the road, watching as big cars, armies, big parades with flashy twirlers blowing their self-important whistles pass by my shining face. I do my best to maintain respectful relations with the other flowers, to send out a sweet smell, and protest if someone rolls over the other flowers. I work hard, think hard, and aim at honest action. I have not tried to make a mark on history, but have worked in small ways at the grass roots to encourage life-affirming change. More and more, I see that the cumulative effect of many small actions can be the powerful forward movement toward a goal — perhaps as effective as a mass movement. What I have done, many others have done and are presently doing.

In this book, you will meet other ordinary people. I have worked with street people, with renters being evicted from their homes, with and for rivers, refugees, and antiwar forces. Sometimes, in the face of war, I have only been able to find a little tenderness to bring to those affected. My gift is small, but it is what I am inspired to bring to the battlefield. I protest the use of aggression and violence as powerfully as I can. In this book, I have recorded what this life of social change has been like, what I have seen in others as I faced the horrible times of eviction, government and corporate terrorism, and violence.

This book is based on a tremendous respect for the common people in all societies who join with others to work for the common good. Sometimes they work alone for some time before others see their way to join in a campaign. The ordinary people together are usually much wiser than their leaders, so much more willing to find peace and make change.

Everywhere there is trouble, one can find people working to change that trouble. Of late, those joining together to do the work of social change are frequently organized as nongovernmental organizations (NGOs). The growth of NGOs — where people see a task that must be done for the good of the society, form a group to figure out a strategy, and then work together to fund and do the work — is a particularly striking phenomenon of the late twentieth century. In the early 1980s in the United States, such grassroots groups were called nonprofit organizations. It is entirely possible that the social energy drawn to the development of NGOs in the last decade of the twentieth century calls on the same social creativity that the labor movement did in the 1920s and 1930s.

While this can be seen as a very positive development, one cannot help but wonder if such NGOs will become as calcified and hierarchical as the labor union movement has become. The end of the cold war, as well as the growth of populations, seems to have led to an international perception that organizations outside of government are needed to make societies work — indeed, to make governments work. NGOs are like a pressure valve between government and the people.

In NGOs we find an increasingly developed sense of socially creative people using their time, energy, and talent to make things different in our social sphere. While other creative talents — in the fine arts, performing arts, and literary arts — have long been recognized as creative, workers in the social sphere have not even been seen as a genus. This skill has not been considered a talent on aptitude tests; it has been ignored when counselors advise people about jobs. Jane Adams, Mary MacKillop, Rachel Carson, Karl Marx, and Thomas Jefferson, to name only a few, were among socially creative people. They saw society as potentially different, and also saw ways to change it. We need socially creative people now more than ever, as we learn how to implement positive change in a social environment that is growing more and more rigid and self-interested.

More and more, I see that the cumulative effect of many small actions is powerful moving toward a goal — maybe as effective as a mass movement. What I have done, many others have done and are presently doing.research, and clean-up, education, and advocacy projects. But NGOs are also involved in the Aryan Nation groups that have erupted on the scene of late. They are both a positive and a negative force in society, which holds them suspended in its social fabric.

The burst of NGOs in the public sector in the last decade of the twentieth century has been stupendous. As socially creative people sharpen their vision, they often logically begin to think in terms of founding an NGO. These social entrepreneurs then set about getting a name, legitimacy for their group from their government (in the US, we file papers with the state and national government to get a 501(c)(3) tax exemption), and create a mission statement and tasks for the group.

These NGO people are almost a tribe, living thinly sprinkled around the earth, whose members recognize each other almost immediately. I am not sure how others know their compatriots, but I call them the "soft-walking people." There are indeed heel-clicking, ego-filled people in NGOs, and they are very important to the overall picture of social change, but I am primarily relating to the less driven, more balanced community people working for the common good.

I first met this nation of soft-walking people at the Earth Summit in Rio de Janeiro, Brazil, in 1992. Many NGOs were represented in the display area and received Global 500 Awards. I was accompanying Dr. V. B. Mishra to Brazil, where he received this prestigious award, given by the United Nations Environment Programme to outstanding environmentalists from all over the world. I watched as various award winners walked up to the stage to receive their awards. They walked softly up the stairs and across the stage, as if they were barefoot, with no shoes to separate their roots from the earth, as if they grew directly from the earth, but were allowed to move from spot to spot. Perhaps they wished not to distinguish themselves from those who have no shoes.

The soft-walking people may be human trees, who know the force of wind and yet live in rootedness, with a strength and steadiness that is tree-like. Their goal is to leave no mark on the earth, so that no one following them will know they have been here. These NGO people do not click as they walk, or have steel heels; they have no snap that demands attention when they move. These nationals come from all races, all political persuasions. They control nothing, but seem to have overarching control of everything around them. The soft walkers are not making history, they are history itself living in our midst.

Steely-heeled people of domination and corporate position feel almost self-conscious in the presence of the soft-walking people. The soft walkers tilt their heads when confronted by the steely-healed ones, and they keep moving. There is no resistance, only forward motion. A whole nation, softly flowing forward. In our time, it is each person's joy to find members of this nation and stand as close to them as possible, so that some of their quiet power might rub off.

Many people from my generation bemoan the loss of a movement like the one that existed in the sixties. I see a much more powerful movement rising invisibly in NGOs — these soft walkers who work for social change wherever they find themselves. They work for social goals, rather than individual or corporate goals. They work for the common good, with difficulty and with grace. They know confusion and pain, and are underappreciated in their work. But they continue.

This book is for these social change workers — or for those who want to join them. Whether you are young and learning about how things work and testing your social change wings, or thirty-five to sixty years old and stepping into leadership roles, or older and in the time of mentoring, there is lots of room in this world for more activists. As the spirit of service catches on, change workers can increasingly be found in corporate offices and in government itself. A wind is carrying this urge to do service in the common good to all corners of the earth.

The beauty of NGOs is that they allow like-minded people to get together to pursue social change goals. An individual without friends and allies is powerless to make social changes — unless she possesses the money to hire a public relations firm to bring an issue to the attention of government decision-makers. But together, these groups can have serious impact.

As I have traveled around the world, I have noticed a new, more powerful sense of identity and pride arising in the NGO community. I hear discussions of ethics, skills of the trade, and other concepts necessary for making NGO work into a vocational choice and legitimate lifetime activity.

While NGOs are helpful to make democracy work, it is important to remember that they usually do not represent a cross-section of a community; rather, they are one coherent voice of a group with some similar interest. It is important in a democracy to have a representative nature. NGOs can assist in facilitating and compelling transparency and genuine representation.

One of the hottest issues in the development of NGOs is their relationship to government itself. When government begins to turn to NGOs to carry out quasi-governmental functions, many problems arise. In many parts of the world, NGOs are, in fact, funded by the government, and therefore are often somewhat resistant to being critical of it. Government recognizes that small, community-based organizations are more suited to carry out certain activities. While this has advantages, it also means that NGOs exist at the political whims of the party in power. There are large NGOs in many parts of the former Communist world that are, in fact, indistinguishable from government.

In the United States, many NGOs are concerned about government funding of religious groups to support their services to the poor. How does it affect a church's freedom to criticize the state or city government when the food program from which the church derives many benefits is funded by a government agency? In India, we struggled with these issues; the foundation that I work with there has traveled that treacherous terrain, from critiquing the government's sewage system to proposing a better one, and then designing that system.

In the US, NGOs are funded by individuals and foundations that benefit from a tax code that encourages philanthropy on an individual basis. Every year, some tax conservatives who decry the loss of tax revenue through gifts to NGOs try to diminish or end the deductions that allow such organizations to thrive. It will be a cold day if the private funding of such groups is shut down; we must fight that development with all our might. The plurality of points of view is crucial to counter the heavy hand of multinational corporations colluding with and directing government.

For NGOs around the world, another important trend is the effort to become increasingly self-sufficient through investment, or through the production of items from which their group can benefit. Partnership between NGOs worldwide has had positive benefits in this regard. But this is an important global development.

A development that bodes poorly for the future effectiveness of NGOs is that corporations in the US and elsewhere have found that they can create NGOs that appear to be made up of local citizens, but in fact are composed of paid employees of the corporation whose purpose is to create the impression that ordinary citizens support the corporation's goals. For example, one organization called Citizens for Safe Energy is actually funded by the nuclear power industry, and the people sitting at tables in airports are employees of that industry. When industry bothers to mimic our community organizations, you know we have become a power to contend with.

One important theme in this book is how to work toward cultural literacy — that is, how to read, translate, and work with, across, and between boundaries. In the evolution of humanity, there have been relatively few instances in which people traveled sufficient distances from their own home cultures to develop the skills necessary to work effectively and respectfully with a culture other than their own. Rigid social structures kept people from moving across boundaries in their own land, and from coming to know people of a different social class or group from their own. While it was considered necessary to speak and understand the languages spoken by others, skills of cross-cultural understanding were not encouraged and did not develop.

In the 1950s, William Lederer wrote *The Ugly American,* a book in which sensitive and intelligent people read with chagrin about the antics of culturally illiterate diplomats, aid workers, and political leaders. It is now understood that cultural literacy is far more than language. It includes manners, body language, and patterns of thinking and meaning common to a group of people.

I have found it important and helpful to develop habits of humility and curiosity when approaching people of a culture different from my own. This book recounts my early explorations in developing cultural literacy, the many errors I made, and some aspects that continue to mystify me in working in cultures other than my own. When I started working in India, for example, I did not know the ways of the culture. If I handed a gift to a friend with my left hand, he would have to do an internal translation that went something like this: "She has handed me the gift with her left hand, which would indicate that the gift is an insult. But Fran is not of our culture and does not know the rules. She has a friendly look on her face. I will choose not to receive this gift as an insult, but as a friendly gesture." In other words, I was dependent upon their graciousness and cultural flexibility. As I learned to give only with my right hand, I required less understanding and tolerance from my hosts. The more I became literate in their culture, the less inclined I was to do anything that would require translation. My actions demonstrated my respect for them and their culture. Naturally, as I have developed these skills, my work has gone more smoothly as well. As change workers, it is incumbent upon us to know how our hosts analyze and receive our actions, so as not to create any unintended meaning or cross-cultural noise. As linguists and cultural anthropologists assist us in the development of cultural sensitivity and literacy, we learn to avoid cultural imperialism.

Some time ago, a woman came to see me from an ashram in Auroville, in the south of India. She was wearing a light purple dress, I remember, and had shoulder-length hair. She said she had come specifically to invite me to that ashram and to bring me a story. As we sat in my living room drinking tea, she graciously told me this story, waving her hands in the air as she spoke.

"There is a legendary bird, the huma bird, which lives its entire life flying in the atmosphere high above the earth. Never does that huma bird land on earth. When it comes time to lay its egg, it lays its' eggs in the air. The egg begins to fall to the ground, while inside the baby bird begins to peck its way out of the egg. Even as the egg falls to the ground, it is not known whether the beak will harden sufficiently to open the shell of the egg, whether the wings will dry enough for the bird to fly back up into the atmosphere to join the other members of its species. Will the bird mature in time to avoid being crushed by the ground?

"Is this not the condition we human beings are in at this time?" she asked. "Will we mature soon enough to put away our dangerous habits of ego and mindlessness in order to live sustainably on the earth?

"If this species of huma birds continues, that must mean that enough birds get out of the egg before being dashed upon the earth and fly back up into the atmosphere. If it's sustainable for the huma, maybe there's hope for our species, too."

It's just a story, but like all stories it may have a gift for us, wherever we find ourselves working — in NGOs, in corporations, in government, in our families and neighborhoods. Heart Politics Revisited is my story of trying to mature enough to be of service.

Organization of this Book

There are essentially two ways of reading this book. (Of course, there are actually many more ways than two, including reading it randomly.) One way is to read from beginning to end. The first chapter, Connectedness, is a very quick overview of some of the essential threads that weave themselves throughout the book. Chapters 2 and 3 talk about the elements of my background, ancestry, and upbringing that may have had an influence on my political practice and social change work.

In the next eleven chapters (4–14), I take a look at many of the campaigns I have been involved in and that have contributed to my thinking. (Note to people looking for a chapter on HIV: I decided not to include one here, even though AIDS work has been an important part of my work and life, especially in the years 1984–89, because I have written about it so extensively before. If you would like to see my thoughts on this issue and this work, you can read my book *A Shallow Pool of Time* (New Society Publishers, 1990), or the AIDS chapter in *By Life's Grace: Musings on the Essence of Social Change* (New Society Publishers, 1994).

The next three chapters (17–18) are conceptual chapters that pull ideas from all of the campaigns and from my background and weave them together thematically. The last chapter discusses concepts in my personal practice that sustain my social change work and contribute to it in significant ways. In this final chapter, I discuss finances, spiritual practice, family and support systems, as well as jail experiences that have occasionally been the consequence of my social concerns.

Some readers will prefer to begin with the concepts and then move to the individual campaigns. Others will become curious as to how I managed to keep working for social change, when most people leave the field as they grow older. If you need to relieve the agony of wondering how I have been able to do this work, please look at Chapter 18. To your question, "Why can she do those things and not me?" I would answer, "There is no reason. You can work for social change wherever you are, in small and large ways."

Please remember that I am recounting thirty years of work. Each campaign was done one day, one small decision, at a time. I'm sure that many of you have had or will have comparable experiences, questions, and conclusions when you are my age — in my fifties when writing this.

Various editors have fought with me to change the order that the chapters appear in; but, for me, it makes sense to go from the background to the specific to the general, and finally to the support structure that makes it all work. You may find that you want to know how I make my life work, spiritually, economically, and physically, and that questions regarding those issues are interfering with your reading. If this is the case, turn to Chapter 18.

I know from other books I have published that this book may be the beginning of a dialogue with you, the reader. I expect to have interesting interactions with many of you by letter, e-mail (fpeavey@igc.org), or in person, at conferences or presentations. I very much look forward to that dialogue. If you want to know what I'm doing right now you can check out our web site "www.crabgrass.org" for the latest newsletter.

Chapter 1

Connectedness

HUMAN BEINGS are a lot like crabgrass. Each blade of crabgrass reaches up to the sun, appearing to be a plant all by itself. But when you try to pull it up, you discover that all the blades of crabgrass in a particular piece of lawn share the same roots and the same nourishment system. Those of us brought up in the Western tradition are taught to think of ourselves as separate and distinct creatures with individual personalities and independent nourishment systems. But I think the crabgrass image is a more accurate description of our condition. Human beings may appear to be separate, but our connections are deep; we are inseparable. Pull on any part of our human family and we all feel the strain.

I grew up in Idaho, where my Dad used to have us pick potatoes in the fall with the Mexican farmworkers, "to keep us humble." And I remember being disgusted with the Mexicans when they would pee in the field. Why didn't they just go into the farm owner's house the way I did? Why didn't they go to the toilet in privacy? I thought they must be backward, primitive people who didn't use toilets. I didn't understand the difference in class between the paid fieldworkers and me. It was confusing, because I liked the young people whom I could talk with, and the relationship between the parents and children seemed warm and comfortable. But the social distance was so great that I did not get much real information about them, or their reality.

I was a Camp Fire Girl, and when I was about twelve, one of our group projects was to sew and embroider a needlework layette set of blankets, clothes, diapers, and booties for a newborn baby. When it was finished, we took our layette to a Mexican farmworker family that was expecting a baby. The family picked potatoes on the farms owned by my parents' friends. When I saw how the Mexicans were cramped together in that farm labor camp, eight people to a room, I was stunned. The wonderful Christian people I knew —

how could they let their workers live like this? It just didn't make sense to me that the same ranch owners who were so nice to me could live so well, while the people they relied on to get their crops in lived so badly. I went home and cried all night. The Johnsons and the Hennys, the upstanding people in our communities, who were in our church!

I argued with those in my family who said Mexicans were inferior. My brother and sister would call someone a "Mexican" when they did something really stupid. "That's not right," I used to say, more on an idealistic faith than real information; "they're just people like all the rest of us." But if you are washed over with any attitude for a long time, even though you object to it, some of it seeps into your skin and becomes part of you. Years later, I was to discover shadows of prejudice in myself. In fact, it has been a lifelong battle to rout out prejudice in my character; I sometimes become discouraged by how deep and resistant to new information these ideas of superiority are.

In the 1960s, I taught science at Roosevelt Junior High School in San Francisco. I had a student in one class named Roberto, who often irritated me. One day he asked, "Miss Peavey, do you think it has anything to do with the fact that you don't like Mexicans?" I was stunned. Of course, I defended myself against his accusation, but as I reflected over time I came to think that there was truth in what he said. It wasn't exactly that I didn't like Mexicans, but that I felt different from them, possibly that I knew something they didn't know (and they knew something I didn't — and couldn't), and I felt guilt and fear about that.

About ten years later, I went to Mexico during my Christmas vacation to lead several counseling workshops. People usually started telling me their problems in English, but when they got absorbed, they switched to Spanish. Since I didn't speak Spanish, I had to learn to listen closely to the emotional tone of what they were saying. I was surprised at how much I could understand.

One day, I booked a trip in a private car. When I tried to sit in the front seat to get a better view, the driver asked me to move to the back. This turned out to be a matter of class: lower-class riders were expected to sit in front with the driver, and people who had paid the full fare sat in the back. Soon, a poor woman carrying a baby got in and sat next to the driver. She didn't speak much English. After driving a while, we stopped for refreshments, and when I got back to the car, the woman was sitting there crying. I didn't know what to do — our cultures were so different. So I just tapped her on the shoulder and said, "Is there something wrong, Senora?" She turned around and looked at me. Then she got out of the car, sat down next to me, and started telling me her story.

It seems that she had given birth to thirteen children, and only two were living — a six-year-old son and this little baby. Now, the baby was very sick. She was afraid he was going to die, so she was taking him to the children's hospital in Mexico City. She told me the story mostly in Spanish. I couldn't follow the details, but as she cried I put my arm around her and listened, and I understood the gist of what she was saying.

When the baby started crying, the woman stiffened and tried to get him to quiet down. We checked the diaper and whether he was hungry. No, it seemed he was just sad. I said, "No, no, the baby's trying to get well. He's telling you how hard it is for him right now. It's all right for the baby to cry." I held the crying baby in one arm and his mother in the other, and just paid attention. As we were getting close to Mexico City, she said, "It took me two days to find the money to come here, so I didn't have time to take the baby to have the priest bless him. Would you bless the baby?" At first I was utterly embarrassed. I knew nothing about baby-blessing. But my second thought was: After all, what is a blessing? Blessing is saying, "All the power and love that I am in touch with I pass openheartedly to you."

I started talking to the little baby — about how hard it must be, but that life was really worth it; that there were people all around the world who would love him if he could just grow up, if he would just hang on. Life was really wonderful, though sometimes terrible. It was worth all the effort to stay alive. But if he couldn't, we would all understand. I started crying too, feeling how hard the baby's life was. Maybe he didn't have enough food; maybe his mother couldn't give him enough milk. Maybe he was sick and in pain. He was very sick — his skin looked green and yellow. I kept thinking how precious life — this particular life — was. I know so many people who would love this baby. Remembering the love for children in my own family and all the friends I loved in San Francisco, I thought: their love extends to you, little one. The only reason they don't love you is that they don't know you yet. They would love you if they were here; since I'm here, I represent them and pass their love to you. It seemed like a reasonable blessing to me.

When we reached Mexico City, I got her a taxi and paid the fare so she could hurry off to the hospital. I had a stamped postcard in my pocket, and I wrote my name and address on it and said, "I want you to send this to me and tell me how the little one turns out."

She said she couldn't write. I said, "Well, please find a way. I care." About two weeks later, the postcard arrived. "Fernando is well, we are home from the hospital. Thank you very much. May God bless you. Rosa Rosales, by her sister's hand. P.S. Please visit us the next time you come to San Jose Purua."

There was one black student in my elementary school. She lived in the housing project not far from my own home. Sometimes we would walk to or from school together. Then one day, she was not at school. All the classes from the school were assembled in the auditorium where the principal talked to us. "A very bad thing has happened to our school. One of our students said bad things about a Negro girl in the school. Now, she has had to transfer to the Catholic school. This should not happen in America." She said the offending student was Jim Thompson, who lived on my block. She shamed us all. I didn't ever know what he said or did, but I knew that whatever it was, was very bad, and I didn't want ever to do something like that.

As a sophomore in high school, I attended a Presbyterian conference in Iowa with young people from all over the country. My roommates there were two black girls from the South. This was my first contact with Southerners, not to mention black Southerners. All I knew about relations between whites and blacks in the South was that for some baffling reason, when confronted with blacks, white people became vicious, yelled hateful things, and formed lynching parties. I had read about such things in *Time* and *Life* magazines. And I remembered Jim Thompson. I was relieved that I seemed to get along with my roommates. But I felt shy and afraid.

I could tell there were some real differences when we all got together in our room. Timidly, I asked a few questions, but mostly I watched and listened. I was surprised and pleased that we would be cordial with each other. It gave me hope that someday, if necessary, I could get along with "Negroes."

Some months later, reading *Time* magazine, I saw a picture of one of my conference roommates trying to enroll in high school. She was tall and skinny and was wearing a plaid dress. The crowd around her was hostile. Someone was sticking fingers up behind her head to indicate that she had horns. I remember feeling cold with fear for her, and at the same time admiring her courage. I wrote her my best wishes. She was making history.

From my experience with her, I had learned that being white didn't automatically mean one had to behave in an uncivil way to black people. It was puzzling to me that other white people acted that way. But the fear lingered — fear of doing something bad — and this fear translated itself into fear of black people.

Roosevelt Junior High was halfway between Pacific Heights, a relatively rich white neighborhood, and the Fillmore District, mainly a black neighborhood, especially in the mid-1960s. Roughly a third of my students at Roosevelt were black.

It was a time when civil rights for black Americans was an active struggle. Every night on television, I saw demonstrations for voting rights, for the right to eat in public restaurants. A part of me wanted to go and participate in this history of my country. But I walked into my classroom instead, doing my best to create equality and intelligence in my classroom.

Soon after I began teaching, I realized that I didn't know anything about being black. It was 1963, and I had not been exposed to black history or tolerance training. So I went to the local NAACP chapter and said, "I'm teaching your children, and I don't have any idea what their life experience is. I hear things in the teachers' room that sound like prejudice to me. But I'm from Idaho. I don't know about Negroes." I asked them to teach me about black history; to introduce me to black scientists, so I could give my science students role models; and to teach me about the worldview of black kids. I had a lot of questions.

After school once a week, I went for my "black lessons." I hoped my fellow teachers wouldn't find out about what I was doing — it was an admission of my naiveté about black culture, and teachers aren't supposed to be naive. I wondered about the other white teachers: did they all know about black life? I assumed they had more contact with black culture, since most of them were raised in urban areas. I now think many of them were probably as mystified as I was, but camouflaged their unknowing.

My tutors, black NAACP volunteers, took me around the school neighborhood to meet people. I lived on the edge of the Fillmore District, so I also met black people in the grocery store and became a part of the community, at least a little bit.

My tutors took me to people's homes, workplaces, and churches. They would introduce me as the teacher from Roosevelt who wanted to learn about the black community. I noticed that people would warm up and talk in a way that they wouldn't if my tutors weren't there. I'd ask them what their lives were like, what they wanted their children to learn, how school had been for them, how those who were parents felt when they visited their children's schools for open house night. They pinned a lot of their hopes for their kids on the school, but felt it to be an alien institution — one where many had never felt at home. Even now, many felt intimidated by their children's teachers.

It was a great relief to be able to ask the questions that came up for me during the school week, especially in a situation where people valued my asking. One lesson was at the beauty parlor. I learned about the techniques for processing black people's hair. So one day, when I came into class with a permanent and the kids said, "Oh look, Miss Peavey's got her hair processed," I could respond intelligently and openly about the different ways each race deals with its hair aspirations. One girl asked if she could touch my hair. "Sure, if I can touch yours." She shrieked when she found out how thin and soft my hair is. I liked the touch of hers. We were a science class, so we put our hair under the microscope and examined the differences up close. We took every chance we had in that class to demystify our differences.

One week, I asked my tutors why so many black men were always standing on the street in the neighborhood. One tutor took me to visit with a few of them. Most didn't have jobs, I learned. They liked being outside, where they could see their friends and catch up on news. The street corner was their office, their meeting place. And, contrary to my assumption, few men stayed in the same place on the street all day long. Most spent a few hours and then went on. I asked a group what they most wanted from people around them, especially white people. "Respect," was their unanimous reply. I asked them to tell me more about respect. They described how white people communicated disrespect by the way they look at them, the way they look at their clothing, and how they rarely asked for opinions or ideas from black people. I asked them if they hated white people. They were uncomfortable with the question. "Not all white people," one man said. Others nodded in agreement. "But some white people who don't respect me, I do hate." I could feel the power of their sentiment. "If I respected you, how would I show it?" I asked. A flood of answers came. "Look at me." "Listen to my ideas and think about them." "You could tell me." "No, it has to come from inside. Either you respect me or you don't. There's no trick. I can smell respect." They all agreed. It had to come from the inside.

Because I was a science teacher, I made a point of meeting doctors and technicians, who told me about getting their education in the sciences. They described the difficulties of attaining and keeping their positions. I remember one inhalation therapist who told me that until recently, he had never heard of any famous black scientists besides George Washington Carver. He also told me how hard it had been for him to get his license, even though he had been working in the field for several years. He laid the blame on himself, and asserted that he would be able to succeed through hard work. After we left, my tutor explained that if I hadn't been there, the therapist might have pointed to racial discrimination as the key obstacle in his professional career. But, my guide told me, it is frightening for black people to let whites see the anger and vulnerability they feel when faced with discrimination.

I've always been grateful to my tutors for being patient with me, and for pointing out when my assumptions were based on ignorance or prejudice. For instance, I would frequently correct my black students' grammar. They would say "we was" or "I ain't gonna do that no more" — things like that. I noticed these errors were consistent, so I asked one of my tutors. "Why do they keep making the same mistakes?" She explained that just as American English is different from British English, black English is different from white English. African languages had their own syntax, she explained, and some of it may have been retained. Now it is called "ebonics." She said that while most black parents would appreciate my sharing white English with their children, so they could have a better chance at economic success, I should be careful not to *put down* black kids for the way they spoke, or to consider it wrong. That might communicate that it was wrong to be black.

I adopted a rule in those lessons that I have found useful many times since. I do not defend myself when someone points out an oppressive attitude or a racist remark of mine. What I've said may be well intended, but that isn't really relevant when it hurts another person. Of course, sometimes I feel unfairly accused or misunderstood, and often I feel confused, but what I learn from people whom I am different from is very valuable to me. It seems it is occasionally necessary to go through feelings of discomfort to learn how to live with people.

In 1966, race riots flared up in San Francisco. I still lived on the edge of the Fillmore District, although I wasn't teaching at Roosevelt anymore. One evening, I heard stones hitting my window. I was afraid the window would break. I looked out and saw people in the street shouting and jeering. One of them yelled, "We want you down here! Come down here, Miss Peavey!" It was a group of about twenty black kids, most of them former students of mine. And they were wired. I was scared to go downstairs — it felt like walking into a mob. Some friends were visiting me, and I told them, "Turn off the lights. When I go down there, stand at the window and watch. If I run into trouble, call the police." Then I went downstairs, keeping my hands out of my pockets, so the kids would realize I was totally defenseless. My friends were watching from the window. I said I was glad to see them, that I had missed them since stopping teaching. Calling them by name, I asked how they were. Walking closer, I could talk softly to them. Finally, I said to the kids, "Why don't you come upstairs? I have some cookies." So up they came, while my friends moved into the kitchen. We were scared.

My friends started making cookies — three people in my tiny kitchen made different cookie recipes for hours. They kept an ear to the door, listening to the kids' stories. I kept bringing the cookies in. I sat with them until about midnight, listening. The kids recounted their day's activities: rioting, breaking windows, looting, and getting even with the honkies, the charlies who had been bugging them for years. They told of smashing the window of a store whose owner had always treated them badly, and stealing some liquor. They were proud to be evening things out for their people. The power in that group was awesome. I felt privileged to be listening to them. Finally, it was time for them to go. I offered to take them home in my car, since "I don't want you kids to get in any trouble with the police tonight." To my surprise, they accepted my offer and piled into the car. I began to realize how separated, how isolated we had been from each other, and what the effects of that isolation had been on them. And on me.

My grandmother Carpenter used to say to me that it would break her heart if I married a black man. We would have little arguments, but nobody could ever argue much with my grandmother, because she was so beloved. And since I was not anticipating marrying a black man, it didn't seem necessary to fight about it. Like me, she had known very few black people in her life.

One year, she came from Idaho to visit me in San Francisco. There was a little grocery store on my corner that had a real community feeling. A bunch of us always stopped in around 5:00 p.m.: the garbage men, Deputy (so called because he worked in the sherriff's office), Jimmy and Louie (the two Chinese guys who ran the store), and me — I was called "Teach." We stood around and joked every night. If you didn't come by for a couple of days, they would send somebody by your house to see if you were all right, and if you were sick, they'd send groceries over. It felt like our grocery store.

If there was a rush of business, we'd go back behind the counter and bag groceries for Jimmy and Louie, and we all had charge accounts, even though officially charge accounts weren't allowed.

Deputy, a tall, attractive black man of forty-five or fifty, was behind the counter the day I walked in and announced I wanted to introduce my grandmother. In a second, Deputy was in front of us, saying, "I want to give your grandmother a big kiss." My heart stopped. What if my grandmother wasn't gracious to my friend? What if she hurt Deputy's feelings? While my heart was hovering there, refusing to beat, my grandmother gave Deputy a big kiss.

Later, when we went outside, I said to her, "I was kind of surprised, because I know how you feel about black people." She answered, "Why Frances, I'm sure any friend of yours must be a very fine person." Deputy was.

It occurred to me then that it's easier to be prejudiced against people you've never met. Fear and hatred can thrive in the abstract. But most of us, if given a protected situation and a personal connection to the people we thought we feared or hated, will come through as compassionate human beings. Although my grandmother had openly prejudiced attitudes, her human decency overcame those attitudes in the moment. The more isolated people are from each other, and the more negative the images are in the media, the more difficult it is to come together in an evenhanded way. And if the power is unbalanced, if there is fear or historical hatred, it is even more difficult.

An oral history from Studs Terkel, presented in *American Dreams: Lost and Found,* demonstrates this point. It is the story told by C. P. Ellis, who grew up in Durham, North Carolina, the son of a textile worker who died at forty-eight of brown lung disease. As a young father of four, C. P. found he was barely able to support his own family. "I worked my butt off and just never seemed to break even," he remarked. "I really began to get bitter. I didn't know whom to blame. I had to hate somebody. The natural person for me to hate would be black people, because my father before me was a member of the Klan. As far as he was concerned, it was the savior of the white people."

Ellis joined the Ku Klux Klan ("It was a thrilling moment"), and rose to become president of the Durham chapter. Then, while he was on the school committee of his community, he was thrust into a working relationship with Ann Atwater, a black civil rights leader:

> A Klansman and a militant black woman, co-chairperson of the school committee. It was impossible. How could I work

with her? … Her and I began to reluctantly work together. She had as many problems workin' with me as I had workin' with her.

… I said: "If we're gonna make this thing a success, I've got to get to my kind of people." The low-income whites. We walked the streets of Durham, and we knocked on doors and invited people. Ann was goin' into the black community. They just wasn't respondin' to us when we made these house calls. Some of 'em were cussin' us out. "You sellin' us out, Ellis, get out of my door. I don't want to talk to you." Ann was gettin' the same response from blacks: "What are you doin' messin' with that Klansman?"

One day, Ann and I went back to the school and we sat down. We began to talk and just reflect. Ann said: "My daughter came home cryin' every day. She said her teacher was makin' fun of me in front of the other kids." I said: "Boy, the same thing happened to my kid. White liberal teacher was makin' fun of Tim Ellis's father, the Klansman. In front of other peoples. He came home cryin'." At this point I begin to see, here we are, two people from the far ends of the fence, havin' identical problems, except hers bein' black and me bein' white. From that moment on I tell ya, that gal and I worked together good. I began to love the girl, really. (*He weeps.*)

Connection is never impossible, though it can look that way. Years later, in my work in the former Yugoslavia during their war, I learned about the consequences of not keeping connections clear during times of social stability. Of course, some neighbors had nurtured resentments from a lifetime of living together. Conflicts are a part of life. The lack of habits of working things out, of reconciliation and forgiveness, interferes with communication and connection. In a situation that allows people to act in brutal ways, some people will take such an opportunity to even things out when they feel the other has victimized them. Hatred and greed can be consciously generated by decisions of a leader, as in Yugoslavia, but then so can reconciliation. Connection is an important part of civilization.

I am becoming interested in the practices of social reconciliation that are developing all over the world. A leader in this development is South Africa, where they instituted Truth and Reconciliation hearings, the purpose of which was to bring the victims of violence or their relatives together with the perpetrators. The victim confronted the perpetrator with the consequences of the violence and found, through completing the circle of connection that was broken by the violent act, that his or her dignity was restored. The resentment that has been harbored flows through the transaction, and passes. Reconciliation often can be found in this act. In a social sense, this reconciliation is a three-way gift: the first gift is to the victim, in that the burden of resentment is lifted; the second gift is to the one who committed the crime; and third, the society receives a gift through the connection, on which civil society rests.

As I think about connectedness as a political principle, I realize that decency is situational. Even some of our seemingly noblest efforts have a kind of delusion embedded in them if they lack solid relationship over time. If we aren't connected to the people we think we're fighting for, there's an emptiness at the center. And if forgiveness is not at the core of our connections, we experience the same coldness that's at the heart of prejudice — the coldness of resentment and separation. It's as if stones that interfere with a clear connection are carried in the heart. I have been looking for a way to remove those stones, but first I have to be sensitive enough to notice that they're there.

Before coming to San Francisco, I'd never heard about gay people. My response upon hearing of the phenomenon of people being attracted to people of their own gender was: well, it's logical. If you flip two coins, sometimes they'll be heads and heads, sometimes tails and tails, and sometimes heads and tails. One shouldn't expect that men would love only women or women love only men. I saw homosexuality as a statistical imperative. Looking back at my childhood sexual fantasies, I had played with ideas of same gender sexual love. But that was in my fantasy world. It had not occurred to me that people did anything sexually other than what I knew my parents did. Whether I was repressed, in denial, or simply naive I cannot say.

Homosexuality became an issue for me when I was working at San Francisco State College, supervising student teachers. It was 1971, before most heterosexuals were particularly aware of gay people. One of my student teachers came to me with a problem: she had received a love letter from one of her students — a girl.

I knew I was out of my depth. So I told her the only thing I really knew about what to do in such a situation: "When you're wondering about a group of people who are different from you (or whom you are different from), find people from that group and ask them to teach you." After making a few phone calls, I went to the downtown office of the Daughters of Bilitis. They agreed to send two lesbians to our class to talk with us. The women who came to our class told us what it was like to be gay. They explained that homosexuals were a minority even in their own families, and found it difficult to find allies with whom they could explore their feelings without being ostracized. It is especially difficult to be an adolescent with a growing awareness of who you are and who you are attracted to, and to have no one in the school to talk to. To be accepted, most had to maintain the pretense of being heterosexual. This made them feel dishonest and resulted in unstable connections with other people, as well as negative feelings about themselves.

Soon after this meeting, I attended a training program for sex educators. I felt liberated seeing beautifully made films about what gay people were like, what they did sexually. I met very ordinary gay people who did not seem strange. I felt feelings within myself of attraction for women as well as for men. Connection was changing — expanding — my experience of myself. It was exhilarating.

I offered a weekend workshop on sex education for teachers. The workshop had only two learning goals: (1) sex education should teach young people to be competent lovers; (2) any sexual activity is positive, providing all participants in the act are completely willing and eager to participate. (Please remember, this was before the AIDS virus changed sex and sex education.) It included a panel of teenagers, some heterosexual and some homosexual, talking about what school was like for them. The gay kids described their experiences in school; they were isolated and lonely, without any good role models and elders with whom they could talk. Fellow students, as well as teachers, teased them. One guy told of developing a tough demeanor as a defense. Others complained of feeling excluded from social events, like dances, that were biased toward heterosexuals. They felt they had to play games with their identities and lived in fear of having their secret discovered.

After the workshop, many teachers who had attended began inviting gay speakers to their high school sex education classes. In stepping forward as allies of gay people, we found ourselves in a controversial position. Soon, my students were getting fired all over the Bay Area. I was not rehired at the college.

As the years rolled on, I found myself in several close relationships with women as well with men. It increasingly seemed to me that I was an equal opportunity lover. Each of these relationships was my personal business, and I was not very open about them.

Finally, a woman came along in 1989 who completely swept me

off my feet. I wrote to my family: "If this were a traditional situation, I would be inviting you to a marriage. But that legal avenue is temporarily not available to us. But I want you to treat her as my partner, as you would any in-law." I had been a little nervous about how my brother, Art, would respond to my loving a woman. He has been known to make comments judgmental of homosexuality. I called him before he received the letter. "Do you have any reservations about me loving a woman?" I asked. His reply was enthusiastic: "Why should I have any objection? I love a woman."

After a year of loving each other, we decided to have a celebration of love and commitment. Almost all relationships need a little social glue to hold them together. We held the ceremony in her synagogue, with a rabbi, my Protestant minister, and a friend who is a Buddhist feminist officiating. My love wore a ring of summer flowers in her hair, and a skirt and blouse. The flower girls also were adorned in flowers. I wore a tan raw silk outfit with a turquoise scarf. About eighty friends and family attended. We knew that many people had to "travel" quite a distance to get to the ceremony, but there was no judgment or rejection in evidence.

Vows were said. No one promised to obey. We promised to stay open to each other and to stay together as long as it was good for both of us. I gave her a ring; she placed a necklace made of a large jade circle around my neck. I read a poem celebrating our great and abiding love.

Friends stood to speak about love, to sing and share joy. Art stood up during the ceremony and turned to my dear one and her parents and said, "I want to welcome you to our family." Tears came to my eyes. Dorothy, one of my sisters, stood and spoke, "Take good care of Fran. We love her."

To tell the truth, we have not personally experienced much homophobia. We know it is in the world because of the votes of the people and their representatives in Congress to limit our rights. We hear hateful things said in the media about people of the same gender who love each other. We have friends who have been beaten up and experience blunt numbness or active rejection from friends when they find out about their lives. But, for example, when we toured Episcopal parishes in New Zealand, staying with ministers, while we expected to encounter some homophobia, we never experienced anything but acceptance.

As a potential target of public prejudice, it is easier for me to have empathy for others who are pushed by bigotry from the center of our society. And for some people, it seems to make them more inclined to scapegoat others. When a political leader thinks he or she can gain favor with the public by blaming the woes in our country on gay people, on black people, or any other group to be scapegoated, I know how dependent we are on the sanity of all of us. We must not target anyone — whether immigrant, black, gay, or anything else — for our troubles. Blame, especially in a social sense, is not useful. Just as a healthy individual does not sit around blaming someone for her problems, we as a society need to set about building what needs to be built.

As I look around at other societies, it does seem to be a part of human behavior to scapegoat, for a group to establish a common bond by pointing to someone outside the norm. I notice how easy it is in conversation for one person to take a position, which then is followed by group efforts to focus on the person as the problem, isolate that person, and ostracize him. Connection means staying connected and working conflict and misunderstandings out. Being the target of misuse of power when I was a child, as a woman, or as a equal opportunity lover, helps me understand racism a little, and motivates me to listen and change when someone different from me tries to tell me about an oppressive attitude I may have.

For thirty years, I have been actively trying to challenge my own prejudices. It is quite discouraging to see how far I have yet to go before I wipe away the fear I have of people different from myself. But I know this is no time to stop trying. I accept the fact that I may be a racist; I grew up in a society where white power was the norm, and without making a conscious choice, I learned some very bad attitudes. It is my choice now what kind of a racist to be. Can I work against those notions of white power? Can I make decisions that benefit the common good, rather than for my own group? Will I challenge ideas of superiority that come up within myself and in conversations with friends? I hope so.

I cannot believe that racism is a permanent stain. I am impatient with the persistent stickiness of that stain within myself. Every time I have a chance to work collaboratively with people from different racial, ethnic, or economic backgrounds, I find I learn a lot. It is not easy. It is just important to do because it is what needs doing now. I feel it is necessary (even though I don't really know how) to evolve beyond the stage of prejudice into a more power-sharing, cooperative arrangement in all institutions and personal relations. I know racism has been imbedded in my country from the beginning, and it is a complex negotiation to continue to love my country while working to change racism, particularly toward Native

Americans, African Americans and those of Mexican and Asian ancestry. I simply know we can do better than old institutional patterns, dependent upon domination by people of pink skin over those of other pigmentation. It is essentially from this pride that I work to change — improve — my own racism and the prejudice found in our institutional and governmental patterns.

I shudder when I see open hostility toward "the other" growing around me. Now that the cold war is over, the US no longer has a national enemy. Without an enemy to mobilize our efforts against, is it possible that we might need someone to focus hatred upon? I hope not, for I worked in the former Yugoslavia during the war, and I know how horrible an ethnic war is.

With each new connection I make, I feel a little less confused and lonely, and a little more secure. Usually, this security is a general feeling, but there have been times it has become more tangible. One night, as I walked to my car, a black man about my age pulled a knife on me. Just then, another guy came up behind him and said, "Hey, man, that's my teacher, Miss Peavey. You leave her alone." There stood Percy Blunt, one of my black students from Roosevelt, looking out for me.

Chapter 2

Sprouting: the Seeds of Praxis

WHEN I was young, I thought Twin Falls, Idaho, must be the hub of the world, like Rome in ancient times. My grandfather Carpenter used to say, "You can get anywhere from Twin Falls. All the roads to the rest of the world come through here." And indeed Highway 93, which runs from Alaska to Chile, passed in front of our house. So this road in front of our house was a global road. I would lie on our lawn on those hot, dry, summer days, and daydream about going down that highway. I could start walking or get on my bike and go to Chile or Peru or Alaska. Wouldn't that be grand!

But people rarely seemed to take those roads that led to the rest of the world. As I grew up, I didn't meet many people whose ideas or backgrounds were much different from my parents. Our daily newspaper focused on local events and didn't pay much attention to international news.

Now, finding myself on the streets of the former Yugoslavia or New Delhi I think: what an unlikely turn of events! Here are my Idaho feet walking on these faraway streets. Standing on a stage in Ames, Iowa, or Liverpool, England, performing comedy, or sitting in jail after a civil disobedience action, or in a refugee camp in the former Yugoslavia, I wonder how I've come so far from where I was "supposed to be."

I was supposed to marry an Idahoan. A farmer would have been acceptable, but a businessman or a professional man was preferable. I was supposed to have kids and probably be a schoolteacher, because if something were to happen to my husband I should be prepared to take care of my family and myself. Even when I was a kid, my mother could tell that I had a natural talent for teaching: after learning how to read I came home and taught my younger brother and sister. It is also reported that after my first day in school, I came home refusing to return because the teacher was not good; she hadn't taught me to read that day.

My parents expected me to go to college and get a bachelor's degree. My mother had a master's degree in drama and education. My father had done his academic work in fire engineering. I didn't know how to see any other vision of my life besides what they expected of me.

In the eighth grade, each student had to make a career notebook. I looked around at the women in my family. What should I be? One day in class the teacher asked each of us to take out a piece of paper and write our names and what we wanted to be. The teacher took up all the papers and read out each one and commented on the career ideas of each student. "Yes, Jimmy, I think you will make an excellent doctor. You should interview Dr. Oldham. He has always been very helpful in talking to students making their notebook of medicine." When she came to my paper she said, "Oh, Frances. You have to make your notebook on something else. You can't just be an interesting person." I replied in all earnestness, "Well, I think I will do many things, but mostly I want to have an interesting life. I don't want my life to be waiting for my kids to come home, playing bridge with the other women for my enjoyment, and serving on church committees." Finally, the teacher said I could make two notebooks: one about teaching and the other about living an interesting life.

I didn't know that there was such a career as activist or I might have made my notebook on being one. Most children, thinking themselves to be powerful little beings, work to change their world. One of my early disarmament activities involved hiding the butter paddle that my parents used to spank us. When we moved, I am told that many butter paddles where found. Upon finding that there were no movies fit for children to see on a Saturday afternoon, my friend Carol and I wrote to President Eisenhower to see if he could correct that situation. Misreading a sign across a street close to our school to be "Presbyterian Crossing," rather than "Pedestrian Crossing," I went to the principal complaining that my friend Carol was an Episcopalian, but she should be able to cross there, too.

At one point, when I was about ten, I decided I wanted to become a tree. It wasn't that I wanted to stop being a human being; I just wanted to be a tree. It wasn't logical. It was life. Trees are so beautiful. Solid. They blow in the wind, hold the soil in place. I admired trees as a group, and some specific trees seemed particularly spectacular. I loved trees and have been known all my life to hug them, pat them, talk to them.

On my birthday, when I made a wish before blowing out the

candles on the cake, I wished to become a tree. That summer, as I lay on the grass, gazing at the clouds in the sky, dreaming about all the things a young girl in Idaho dreams about during the great expanse of summer, I dreamed about becoming a tree. Not only did I dream, I actually started to hatch a plan of how I could achieve my dream.

With only an intuitive understanding of nuclear physics, I had the idea that a tree was made up of little pieces of tree and little pieces of "not-tree," that there were vast spaces in what looked to be solid. And using the same line of reasoning, I was made up of little pieces of me and space that was not-me. If I could get the pieces of me to line up with the not-tree, and the tree to line up with the not-me, then there would be room for us to simply merge.

All summer I planned how to get this merging to occur. When winter came, it was time to act. First, I picked a tree at the bottom of a ski slope that I thought would be good to be, that is, to merge with. I selected a quaking aspen tree, one of the most beautiful trees I had met at that young age. The trunk was white with speckles of black throughout the loose bark. In the summer, the leaves were green on one side and silver on the underside. In the wind, the leaves fluttered in a truly exhilarating and yet peaceful way. Fall turned the leaves a bright orange and red. Then, the whole forest seemed to be on fire. When we would go to the mountains in the fall, my mother would cut aspen leaves and send bouquets with us to school to decorate our classrooms. Yes, an aspen tree would be my new identity. I felt I would truly be happy as an aspen.

I went up the slope on the ski lift. I was quite excited at the prospect of becoming a tree, and so almost as soon as I got to the top, I turned around and headed down the hill as fast as I could. You see, I thought if I hit the tree at a fast speed, the me would fit into the not-tree and the tree would squeeze into the not-me. I know this sounds now like suicide. But to my youthful mind, it was not that at all. I was not choosing not to be a human being. There were parts of the plan that I had not thought out thoroughly. Somehow, I thought I would be a tree and me simultaneously. The anticipation was glorious ecstasy.

I aimed one ski on one side of the tree and the other ski on the other side. And I hit the tree hard. Very hard. But not hard enough. I knocked the wind out of me, but did not exactly merge with the tree. Little parts of my chin, nose, and forehead were left on the surface of the tree. Or at least they were no longer with me. Looking up from lying on the snow, seeing that the tree was still separated from me, I started crying. People gathered around, thinking I had hurt myself. But I was sobbing because I could see that I had not become a tree. What a disappointment!

My parents had a hard time understanding why I was so scratched and bruised when I came home. How could I have wanted to become a tree without talking it over with them? they persistently inquired. There are just some things a young girl can't discuss with her parents. They simply wouldn't understand.

I still love trees. And may come back as one in my next life if I am noble enough in this life. I told this story to a young boy recently, and he cleverly observed that I had not succeeded in merging with the tree because I had my clothes on. It's something to think about.

My ancestors came to this continent from many places. They loved people of different national origins, and made babies from that love. My father's mother's genes came from England, from Wales, and from Scotland. On my grandfather Peavey's side, they came from Italy. The name Peavey comes from Pavia, a region in Italy. The story is told that there were two Peavey brothers, one who carried all the money and the other who arrived in the new country penniless. The brother carrying all the money founded the Peavey Company in Wisconsin, and the penniless brother never got anything; we are descended from the poor brother.

The name Peavey was given to a logging crowbar that acts as a lever, with a pointed hook and a hinged hook near the end, that was invented years ago by an ancestor, Joseph Peavey. Whenever there is a logjam blocking a river, a courageous lumberjack walks out on the logs with his peavey. He finds the one key log that can unjam the logjam; he uses the peavey to force the key log free. Now, as all the logs are moving, he must run on the moving logs as fast as he can to safety. The danger involved in being a lumberjack and the bravery of loggers was part of our family story. In working on thorny global issues of environment and peace, now I often wish there was a way to find a tool that would pry loose the entangled groups in a way that allowed the life force to run free.

On my mother's side of the family — the Carpenters — there were Native American genes and genes from Scotland, England, and Sweden. Some Carpenters came to Brattleboro, Vermont, shortly after the Mayflower and helped found an organ factory to bring music to their new homeland. Growing up, I heard stories of an ancestor who came from a Quaker family, and was excommunicated when he went to fight against slavery in the Civil War. One of my great-grandfathers left his town and went out as an explorer. He met a Native American woman, married, and had children. I asked my grandfather about their home life. I expected to hear about whether they lived in a teepee or a wooden house. Instead, he told me about the laughter he remembered in their home and how happy they were. The culture from that great-grandmother is lost to me, but I treasure knowing she was here and is a part of my gene pool.

Recently, a new acquaintance told me she was Native American. I told her that the tribe my great-great-grandmother was from was Menominee. I had always heard that name, but that was all I knew; I had never seen the word. She wrote it on a post-it note and suggested I look it up on a Web site. The paper seemed very precious when she handed it to me. To her, it was most appropriate that my grandparents had passed along this part of my lineage in a non-written way. I had been a participant in the verbal tradition. I still have the piece of paper. I rushed home and looked up the Web site. But I didn't know what to say. So I am working on a letter to ask about their knowledge of my ancestors.

All of my grandparents were pioneers. They came to the West and built farms, towns, and lives in Idaho. When they came to this land, there were people from the Nez Perce, Shoshone, and Black Feet nations living on the land. It seemed to my grandparents that there was room for them to settle down.

The Indians moved from place to place and did not have the idea of ownership of the land. Instead, they felt the land owned them. My ancestors had the idea that people could own land. These different ideas about land ownership caused many wars and much heartache for everyone, especially the native people, who lost most battles. It was not only the wars that acted to destroy the lives and culture of the native people. The people who came from crowded Europe brought germs and guns with them. Being forced to live in a different relationship to the land sowed the seeds of hopelessness in the native people; it was disruptive to their way of life and their identity.

The complex history of agreements between the government of the settlers and the government of the Indians is not honorable on the part of the US government. Land would be granted in treaties to the Native Americans, and then uranium, gold, or some other resource would be discovered on it, and somehow the agreement would be broken. Or the government simply decided not to discipline the white settlers who moved onto land promised to the Indians. There seemed no way to control the hordes of Europeans who came west; indeed, with the myth of "manifest destiny" (also known as greed, mixed with racism), there seems to have been no desire on the part of the US government to control the European settlers. I do not think they wanted to control the European settlers' appetite for land.

I wish my ancestors had made agreements they could have kept. It would make it easier for me when I meet and work with native people. Sometimes in my anguish I think I can feel my ancestors reaching through the ages to me. I grew up hearing stories about shared kindness between Indians and the settlers. I also grew up hearing about wars and massacres. As we drove along the roads of Idaho, my father would tell us stories. Massacre Rocks was especially memorable. "You see," Daddy would say, "the wagon train came through this gap in the rocks; the Indians hid behind the rocks. Many people were killed on both sides of those battles."

My grandmother as a child in northern Idaho knew General Howard, who led the battle against the Nez Perce on White Bird Hill. Whenever we drove over that hill, my parents would tell the story of Chief Joseph of the Nez Perce. He was a peace-loving chief and kept his people from going to war with settlers who came into the land of the Nez Perce. The US government would promise land to the Indians, and settlers would come into that land. Over and over it happened. The US government could not, or did not, control the settlers. Fights would occur over the land or because of an insult. From time to time, men on all sides would get drunk and kill someone from the other side. Then, resentment between the people built.

One day, Chief Joseph could no longer control the younger men, who got drunk and went out to avenge the killing of an Indian man. In spite of Chief Joseph's objections, a war broke out. He said, "I would have given my own life if I could have undone the killing of white men by my people."

When Chief Joseph surrendered to General Howard, after a very bloody battle on White Bird Hill, he gave a speech that I have always loved: "Tell General Howard I know his heart... I am tired of fighting. The old men are all killed... He who led the young men is dead. It is cold and we have no blankets. The little children are freezing to death. My people, some of them, have run away to the hills and have no blankets, no food; no one knows where they are, perhaps freezing to death. I want time to look for my children and see how many of them I can find... Hear me, my chiefs, I am tired; my heart is sick and sad. From where the sun now stands, I will fight no more forever." Colonel Miles received his gun and said, "No more battles and blood. From this sun we will have a good time on both sides, your band and mine." How could he say that, after what had just happened?

My grandmother Peavey had already exposed me to pacifist ideas. Her motto was "Peace at any price." Grams was proud that none of her relatives or sons had fought in any wars. And yet, in her youth Grams and her parents had been friends of General Howard; members of my family had been part of the community that supported his values and his efforts to conquer the Nez Perce. General Howard had even given my grandmother his family's christening dress. All the Peaveys had been christened in it, and it was part of the legacy I was to inherit. Ultimately, I returned the christening dress, telling Grams that I was not proud of our connection to General Howard, and did not want a dress to remind me of the shame I felt when I thought of what he stood for. My ancestors had a direct relationship to the fact that the Nez Perce had been slaughtered, their culture driven underground. In the battle of White Bird Hill, the native people lost much of their territory and sovereignty.

Growing up, I heard stories of courageous women and men who settled the West, who worked hard "proving up" farms. It seemed that my grandparents harped on what it took to build and sustain the community that I took for granted. The Homestead Act had promised settlers that if they could improve the land (prove it up) and farm it for five years, they could own it. When the settlers came to the land, it was filled with trees, sagebrush, rocks, and "weeds." The land had to be cleared and fenced, houses and barns had to be built. Now, we may look on these acts as crimes against nature, but I wonder where we would all be, had they not found ways to grow food on the land. It was back-breaking work. The land was in its natural state because the Indians had not been farmers. They had lived on roots, berries, wild animals, and fish. Because the Indians were not so many in number, the land naturally gave them most of what they needed to live. When the settlers came, they wanted to grow plants, and raise cows and sheep. The way the land naturally was did not give them the foods they had grown accustomed to in Europe, a densely populated area.

Grams' parents had come west, leaving Wisconsin in the late nineteenth century. They had come in a large ship around the southern tip of South America, landing in San Francisco. Then, they went by wagon to northern Idaho, where the weather was supposed to be better than in Wisconsin — but not by very much. The northern Idaho winters were very cold.

Grams had been an early graduate of the University of Idaho, which was close to her family's prune orchard. She had also attended Stanford for a year of graduate study in history. My grandmother fell in love with Arthur Jacob Peavey, but her parents did not approve of A.J. They sent Grams to study at Stanford with her brother. She studied but did not take the tests at Stanford, because she could not afford the fees that at the time were paid only when you took the exams. She and her husband were married in San Francisco around the turn of the century. Their wedding license was destroyed in the San Francisco earthquake of 1906. The newlyweds set off for southern Idaho, where they hoped to live. It was her new husband's dream to build a farm there; it was Grams' nightmare.

My grandmother and grandfather Peavey homesteaded a ranch twenty or thirty miles outside of Twin Falls. My grandmother told me how lonely it was proving up a farm. It was hard, lonely work building a home and outbuildings for the animals, and setting in fences in such a desolate desert. There were no women friends for many miles; she had to talk with her children and with people who dropped by. A visitor was precious. My grandmother took care of a small post office and farm they had built in the desert. Indians often stopped by and helped my grandmother. They had friendly relationships. There was a mix of fear and gratitude in the stories. Grams took care of the elevator and post office, and Granddad did the building and farming. Such hard work was not a joy for my grandfather. Finally, he gave up the farm and decided to make a life in the closest large town, Twin Falls. Grams lived alone on the farm while my grandfather was in town building an insurance business. For several years, my grandmother took care of the farm and children, until her husband brought the family to the town, where he had built a home for the family and a growing insurance and title business.

I adored my Grams, as did everyone in the family. Surely, no one admired her sense of independence and style more than I did. She wore Levi's most of the time. She was a first-rate intellectual; she loved to read, to discuss ideas. Once she told me that her mother had advised her to always carry an *Atlantic Monthly* with her on stagecoaches, as men rarely made advances toward smart women. She read the *New York Review of Books* and advised the state library about what books she felt it should buy. Developing an intellectual relationship to community issues was important to Grams — and has become important to me.

Occasionally, Grams invited her grandchildren and our best friends over for afternoon tea parties. There would usually be three of us at each party, and the first one to ask "Can I pour?" would assume that prized responsibility. Then, we bid for the identities we were to assume for the duration of the tea. Mrs. Gotrocks was my favorite. There were also Mrs. Smythe and Mrs. Elderfinger.

Tea (fruit juice) and little cookies and cakes were served, usually on the patio, and Grams would pose a question for our consideration. It might be about a forthcoming election, the quality of our learning at school, our thoughts about the future, our philosophy of life, or what we considered the most important or difficult aspects of growing up. Then, she would sit back and listen carefully to our free-flowing discussion. From time to time, she would go into the house and come back with a book or article from a magazine. "If that's what you think," she would say, "then you should read this. I'd like to know what you think of it." Sometimes the reading agreed with one's point of view and added a new dimension; other times it presented a different point of view and made one think a little harder. She would chastise us only if we spoke without thinking through our point. "Don't you think it would help if you took a minute to compose your thoughts before going off half-cocked, Frances?"

As we grew older, the teas were replaced with less formal visits. The same sorts of subjects were explored, magazines and books dispensed, and mild criticism leveled if we had neglected the books that Grams thought "surely by now" we would have read.

Much of the acceptance in my upbringing came from my grandmother and granddad Carpenter. They were simple people who knew how to listen to and love children. My grandmother Carpenter was especially kind to me. My favorite memory of her came from regularly riding my bike into her yard, parking the bike, walking up the few steps, and ringing her doorbell. Through the curtain-covered window in the door, I could see her walk around the opening from the kitchen into the living/dining room. She would be wiping her hands on her apron, looking eagerly through the window to see who it was. "Oh, Frances," she would say, "how nice to see you. And you have just come in time to try out a new taste treat from the oven. Would you like some cookies or fresh baked bread? And how about a little milk?"

The Peavey family is prominent in Idaho. Having been early settlers in the town of Twin Falls, they knew what it took to develop a community. Grams told stories of how it was decided to plan the town so that the sewers would flow by gravity; or how the city park, with a band shell, was put in the middle of town, surrounded by churches, the county office building, and the high school. Citizens' activities were a part of my parents' life.

My father, Thomas Cummings Peavey, was a tall, thin, likable man with a good sense of humor. In general, I adored him. He was patient, kind, and sweet. My father was a successful insurance salesman, who also supervised a number of farms in Magic Valley for a Dutch land company. He was both an independent small businessman and a company hireling on a salary. He would bring me comic books from the drug store when I was home with a cold or the measles. He loved to wrestle and laugh, and told funny stories that we all enjoyed. He also had a temper, drank too much, and was exacting in his expectations. Dad loved to give lectures on how not to do stupid things. All day, people would come into his insurance office to fill in forms about accidents that had happened. My father would get to thinking, "That could happen to my children." So he would come home at night with the story and the dreaded lecture. When trying to make a point, he would shout, poke his finger in my chest to emphasize that he was talking to me, and carry on. I really hated it when he would get angry and shout. It hurt somewhere deep inside, where my most precious flowers were trying to grow.

But inevitably, he would run into some trouble while he was blowing-off mad. He would be so angry that he would step into a wastebasket and get his foot caught, would throw and break something in his rage, just when he was yelling at me about not throwing things. The trick was not to laugh in the early part of his embarrassment. If I blew it and laughed, he would only become angrier. So I learned to hunker down like a scared animal and wait for him to get over being angry, when we could have fun again. It is funny how grown-ups are. Sometimes, it seems that they are monsters; and other times, they can be so much fun and give so much love. I would just try to take care of the tender flowers inside of myself until the fun father came back again.

One time, we were having a pillow fight in a sleeping cabin at Pettit Lake, where our family stayed in the summers. Dad's family had built the cabins when they were young. Dad came upon us having a pillow fight in the large cabin. It was a lot of fun throwing pillows at each other. He didn't think pillow fights were such a good thing, and started yelling about the evils of such an act and how we kids just didn't respect this place. "YOU KIDS THINK YOU CAN JUST THROW THINGS AROUND!!!" As he said this, he tossed a pillow up into the log rafters. Somehow, blessedly at exactly that moment, the pillow got caught on a nail and tore. White feathers cascaded down upon him. We knew the anger fit was over, and we left the room laughing, as he tried to sweep up all the feathers strewn about. Needless to say, we had not broken any pillows in our pillow fight.

A few years later, my parents bought a new "Oriental carpet," which had a beautiful floral pattern and I am sure cost many pretty pennies. The first dinner at the dining room table over the new carpet, my father was well launched into the "You kids had better be careful of spilling food on this carpet, because if you so much as drop anything on it, you are going to be in big trouble" lecture in his most stern and ferocious manner.

And then — I promise you it was just this way — the roast beef that my father was carving during the lecture leapt from the platter and fell with a splat on the carpet.

As was now traditional in such situations, we looked at each other and tried to keep from laughing. Then, my father fully took in the absurdity of the situation and began laughing himself. We all roared with delight. We told the story over and over that night, laughing each time. And I knew there was a God. What other force in the universe could have had such an elegant sense of timing and drama?

My mother, Dorothy Louise Carpenter Peavey, was proud to have married a Peavey, as they were respected in the town. For her, it was important to uphold certain standards of behavior that were the Peavey standards. Peaveys did not call attention to themselves, go barefoot in public, or go downtown in pants instead of a skirt. Others could do those things — but not Peaveys. Our life was stable, respectable, and comfortable.

Mom was a very normal sort of person with little character or personality, but her sense of fairness was keen. I remember when a Mexican woman in town was held for the murder of her husband, and she took it on herself to visit the woman, and organize legal and other help. The woman had been beaten by her husband and had called the police, who had refused to interfere in a family affair. Finally, as he continued to beat her, she stabbed him with a knife. He went to the hospital to be repaired, was discharged, and stopped by a bar on his way home. He fell from a barstool, pulled his stitches out, and bled to death. Subsequently, the wife was being held for murder. This was outrageous to my mother on many levels, and she spent hours supporting the woman.

My mother struggled her whole life to keep her figure. She was a good-looking woman. It was not easy for her to accept her daughter caring less and less about her weight, the more she was exposed to lectures and motivational practices concerning dieting. My mother was proud that she was always home when we got out of school. This was her idea of being a good mother. Throughout my school days, my father and all of us children came home for lunch every day. It was a great relief from the social pressure of school to break up the day into two parts.

Mother was the primary disciplinarian of our family. Her favorite tool of discipline was the butter paddle, a small (about 8 inches long) wooden paddle with sharp ridges on one side. Little pats of butter are rolled between two paddles to make balls with decorative cross-hatching. These paddles were rarely used for butter in our house, but more often applied to our backside with varying of degrees of force.

Only once did we commit such a heinous crime that we had to pull our pants down to receive a spanking. My mother had to arrange for a party at the country club, so she left us in the car with strict instructions to wait in the car until she returned. Just outside the car window, we could see woodchucks posing on their hind legs outside their holes in the ground. It seemed that we would be able to catch one, so we got out of the car and ran over to the closest one. It jumped back into its hole before we could catch it, but we saw another woodchuck just a few feet away and went after that one. In this way, the woodchucks seduced us into wandering around the golf course farther and farther from the car. As we tried to catch woodchucks, from time to time we would find a golf ball sitting in the grass. We put those balls into our pockets until our pockets were bulging. We proudly marched into the clubhouse to return the golf balls to the manager of the golf course. We did not know that golfers had been coming in complaining to my mother about the children who were taking their balls. She was very angry and I guess must have felt humiliated. So she spanked us on our bare bottoms.

My relationship with my mother was complex, but I guess that is true of many daughters who live beyond their mother's life experience. She cooked all of our meals, and while not a good cook, she did provide nutritious meals. We liked simple food. Even Spanish rice was more complex than my father and all of us children liked.

One of mother's friends was Mrs. Duvall, who was also her singing teacher. Mrs. Duvall lived two doors from my maternal grandparents and was a part of our community, though she was probably thirty years older than mother. Mother never called Mrs. Duvall by her first name. You just didn't do that in Twin Falls.

In a small town like Twin Falls, if you have a great recipe that's easy and could be made the night before a potluck, you might be tempted to keep it a secret. Mrs. Duvall thought that keeping her recipe secret was the only way to always be asked to bring her special muffins to potlucks. Mrs. Duvall's muffins were the very best. They were sweet, with walnuts, and when hot and filled with melted butter, eating them was like eating cookies during dinner. If anyone else knew how to make them, Mrs. Duvall would be denied the opportunity to bring a dish that was universally appreciated and very easy to make. Mom had asked her for the recipe several times, only to be told that it was a secret and that Mrs. Duvall had no intention of anyone in Twin Falls getting it.

Finally, Mrs. Duvall was on her deathbed. People in town whispered that she "would only last a week or two now." Mother was never one to let ceremony stand in the way of a good recipe. As she told the story, she went to say good-bye to Mrs. Duvall — something you do in small towns. As she was sitting there talking about her gratitude for all the fine singing lessons, and the fun they had had with music in our town through the years, Mother remembered the muffin recipe. "Mrs. Duvall," she said, "you wouldn't want to die with no one in town knowing your muffin recipe, would you?" Mrs. Duvall was not sure she wouldn't regain her health and regret that she had given the recipe to Mother. She made Mother promise that she would not give it to anyone else in Twin Falls.

And so it was that Mother extracted the secret. She guarded it like a state secret for years. I eventually asked her for it, and she gave it to me only after getting me to promise never to give it to anyone else from Twin Falls. So I will give it to you now, but please don't give it to anyone from Twin Falls.

Mrs. Duvall's Muffins

1/2 cup butter
1 cup brown sugar
1 egg
Mix the above ingredients, then mix together
1 cup milk and 1/2 tsp. soda
Add milk and soda alternately with
2 cups flour
into the other mixture, then add
1 capful vanilla
1/2 cup walnuts
Let sit overnight in a covered container. Then put in greased muffin tins and bake at 350 degrees until no dough comes up when you stick a toothpick in the center.

It was important, mother always said, to have good manners. She defined character more by manners than achievements. This always rubbed against my grain. She especially tried to teach us to be "good" boys and girls. I have never been sure I wanted to be "good," especially by Twin Falls' standards. Actually, it wasn't exactly good manners. You either had "manners" or "no manners." It wasn't a matter of good or bad — the same as our family or different. It was a binary system with no gradations between the two poles.

There was a book about manners called *The Goops*. Grams had given our family a copy, and it was quoted liberally. In our family it was quoted with the same religious tones as the Bible, and possibly more frequently.

> The Goops they lick their fingers
> The Goops they lick their knives
> They spill their broth on the tablecloth
> Oh they live disgusting lives.

There were pictures of the Goops adorning each page. They were round-headed, sexless creatures, sliding and dancing around with bowls flying from their hands, splotches on their smocks, and sticky fingers. I hated the Goops. They looked as if they were having fun doing things that I was not allowed to do. They didn't have anyone quoting *The Goops* to them, I guess. The Goops were never pictured as lonely, having been sent out of the dining room, feeling punished, and with low self-esteem. No, these little guys were having fun, as all of them together had no manners. They were smiling and whooping it up, and there was a whole family of them. I never knew why their parents left them alone with their "no manners" in peace.

Of course, in this environment there was rebellion. Sometimes when our parents left us alone at dinnertime, we would put our feet up on the mahogany table, eat with our fingers, and yell "shut up!" For a little while, we could be Goops ourselves. The three older children did this from time to time when we were alone, but when the two younger children were born, we stopped, because we "didn't want to be a bad influence on the children." This is how children become like adults, and it is a little sad.

All this training was not as effective as my mother might have wished. When I graduated from high school, my uncle Frank had promised that he would bring me to New York. It was the big city, and I loved it. On the way home, I stopped in Chicago to see my Aunt Mary. She was a politician and had been invited to see the

Queen of England, who was visiting Chicago. She invited me to go along with her. We went shopping, and I got a fancy dress and shoes to match. Aunt Mary rehearsed me carefully on how to curtsey. "Right foot in front, eyes down, bend your knees, extend your right hand under the queen's and say 'your majesty.' "

I was fairly nervous the night of the reception. After all, a girl from Idaho rarely gets to meet a queen. This was the same queen I had set my alarm for some years before, so I could hear the radio broadcast of her coronation crackling over the airwaves. I remembered the hushed tones when the queen was spoken of, the intricate descriptions of her clothing, and every little thing she did. Now I, Frances Peavey, girl from Idaho, was meeting this person I was so in awe of.

As our place in the line got closer to the receiving line, my aunt drilled me once again. "Right foot in front, eyes down, bend your knees, extend your right hand under the queen's and say 'your majesty.'" I visualized doing it and did a mini-rehearsal right there. Then the magic moment came. Someone was saying "Frances Peavey, niece of Mary Peavey Brooks." Just in that moment, it all became confusion. My right foot was not in front of my left. In fact, it was the other way around. I do not know how my left foot had gotten out there in front, but it had, and that threw the plan off entirely. The Idaho natural girl came out from under all the practiced manners. I looked that queen straight in the eyes, shook her hand in the manner of a true Jeffersonian democrat, and said "hi." The queen smiled graciously and said "hi" in return.

Everyone was pretty disappointed in my manners — my aunt, my mother, and even myself a little. But we all laughed, too. I was just on the wrong foot to curtsy. Slowly, through the years, my mother conceded that I was never going to be really great in manners. It was a disappointment to her. I am always grateful that she tried, because I know what to do if I want to do it.

Now, in my life and work, the conventional manners training my mother gave me is woefully inadequate. I frequently eat with my fingers in India, where even touching the plate with the left hand is considered rude. I need more manners training about which slippers to wear in what part of a Japanese house, how to receive and offer gifts. The manners I know have little to do with how to deal with beggars in a way that honors them and their lives. The business of showing respect is not easy in the global village. Whenever I've been with people for a long time, as I leave I apologize for any unintentional lack of manners specific to that culture. "If by anything I have done I have shown any disrespect, please know that it is from my lack of awareness of the manners appropriate to this culture. These errors do not reflect any lack of respect or of high regard for you and your culture. Please forgive me."

I guess that's what *The Goops* was all about — showing respect in one narrow cultural group. Eating with people who regularly do not have enough to eat will continue to be uncomfortable, and that is appropriate. Because of my own cultural baggage, I find it difficult when I meet people from a culture that finds eye-to-eye contact disrespectful. Sometimes, manners training is a disadvantage. There is probably no nice way to reconnect with friends who have been bombed by violent elements of the American military. The awkwardness and discomfort are profound.

The land we lived on was abundant in its gifts to us. It was fertile, thanks to a neighboring ancient volcano. Originally, our area had been a desert filled with sagebrush, rabbit brush, and wild horses. The mighty Snake River, which ran through my childhood, had been dammed in several places early in the century, and the irrigation water was the magic in our valley. Many of the nation's seeds were grown in the Magic Valley, as well as potatoes, beans, sugar beets, cattle, and sheep.

About the second day after we moved into the house on Blue Lakes Blvd. (also known as Highway 93), Mr. Magle came over to see my father. Mr. Magle was a kindly older man who was our closest neighbor. We lived in a house set back from the street. Mr. Magle wanted my father to be the "water master" for our new neighborhood. Mr. Magle had been water master for many years, and now he saw a chance to pass the job on to a younger man — my father. As these two men talked on the front porch, I wondered what a water master was. It was such a grand title. We had such an abundance of water in southern Idaho in those days — the 1950s, I mean — that we irrigated the lawns on our block. Irrigated. During the summer, every eight days water would flow onto our lawn and stand there maybe four inches thick for five hours, soaking into the deepest roots of our lawn and garden. Evaporating. Sometimes we would water at night, but more often Dad would try to schedule our water days during the daytime, so we could play in the water.

At the back of our property, a small ditch flowed. It was probably only eighteen inches wide and about half that in depth. The water came from the coulee (a large ditch, about two blocks away), which came from the mighty Snake River. We couldn't go to the coulee, though. With so much water around, my parents were afraid that we would drown. An especially wonderful uncle had drowned in the Snake. The coulee was big enough to drown in, so we were not to go there without adult supervision.

There are few blessings so great in childhood as playing in water. All summer, we played around the ditch at the back of our yard. There were snails, mostly small and slimy, but well intentioned. Another resident was the water striders, the original walk-on-water creatures. As I remember, they had bumpy little bodies with very long, skinny legs that went up and out from their body and somehow managed to stay on top of the water. I imagined they had suction cups on the bottom of each foot that they used to stick to the water; and because their legs reached so far from their body, they were able not only to float on the water, but also to dart around on the surface of the water. There were other life forms in that ditch as well. Occasionally, we would have to clean out the ditch. Dad would tell me the day before, and I would organize the neighborhood kids to gather all the snails and water striders into a jar, so they would not be hurt in this major renovation of their home.

At the back left corner of the yard was the dam. This was a piece of concrete known as a culvert, inserted into the ditch, through which the water flowed. When Dad wanted to flood the yard, he would place a piece of tin, with a bent handle at the top, into the slot in the culvert. This would divert the water into another pipe and ditch that ran along the yard.

Through clever use of pieces of canvas and dirt dams, Dad could direct the water into the front or back yards. Water was especially relieving on those hot, dry, summer days. Idaho air is so hot and dry that it sucks the moisture from your nose and leaves it sore and with cracks in the skin inside. Anyway, every eight days was water day. Dad would irrigate the back yard in the morning, so that at the hottest part of the day, we would be able to play in the water when it was in the front yard. We would run and slide along the slippery grass — creating a wake of water spraying all around. We found that by using a piece of plastic sheeting as a sled, we could go farther. We could roll around in the water, push each other down, and do somersaults in the wonderful water — oh! so many joys on water days.

A few years ago, I returned to the family home to find that it had been made into a real estate office, and the front yard had been paved over for parking. The apricot tree in the back yard had been cut down. But the ditch was still there. If it weren't for the ditches, most of Idaho's population would probably not be able to live there.

Ditches and water are the base of Idaho. If you want Scotch and water as a drink at a bar, you order "Scotch and ditch."

Ditch means "water," and my father was the water master. To my child's ear, these words sounded like magic. Water master. The position sounded much grander than it really was. My father's job was simply to set the schedule for what days each neighbor could have the water, as well as get the ditches cleaned out so the water would flow.

That my father could bring water to the front yard still seems a bit magical to me. I know there must be many children, in these days of occasional draught in Idaho and so many other places, who wish there were a water master who could bring water. And still others in flooded areas, who wish the water master could direct the water somewhere else. Water has played a most significant role in my life. These early experiences with water developed in me a love for water that has propelled me into many campaigns and areas of inquiry. Water, that substance of ultimate yielding, yet great power and versatility, is a great teacher. A friend of mine and a sometimes carpenter, Yishai Hope, once said, "Think like water," when we were trying to figure out how drips were getting into a window. But I took it to a larger application, and determined that in my life I would try to learn how to think and live like water.

Idaho also has lots of mountains and wilderness. In the summers, we would travel two and one-half hours to a set of run-down cabins on Pettit Lake, in what's called the Stanley Basin. The Salmon River runs through this long narrow valley at the base of majestic mountains, the Sawtooth Mountains. We lived on one side of Pettit Lake, and on the opposite side was a sign on a trail: "Yonder lies the Idaho wilderness." We climbed mountains, swam in lakes and streams, and found comfort in this wilderness. In front of the main cabin, we had a flagpole. We flew the flag every day we were at the lake, but on patriotic holidays we would have a special flag-raising ceremony.

On the Fourth of July, everyone from the cabins around the lake gathered at the flagpole in the morning. The children sang songs like "My Country 'Tis of Thee" and the Idaho state anthem, and everyone recited the Pledge of Allegiance. Elmer Hollingsworth, the self-appointed mayor of Pettit Lake, gave a speech. Our grandparents spoke, too, about the settling of the West and what America meant. They told us the United States was a strong, great country, full of free, mostly friendly, hard-working people. We were instructed to take care of our country and to live in a way that would make our state, country, and ancestors proud. As I recall, that meant voting, not littering, working for your community's health, and not starting forest fires. Our obligation to go to war was not mentioned, because my grandmother Peavey was a pacifist. She said all wars were economic wars, and no one should get killed for others' money. Freedom was often an excuse that governments created to get people to be willing to make the sacrifices necessary for war. After the speeches, we ate brunch. Somehow, we always forgot to bring a baseball bat from home, so all afternoon the children worked at carving a bat out of a piece of pine tree. In the evening, we played baseball among the pine trees and then hide-'n-go-seek. There was a barbecue dinner, and late at night our parents shot fireworks over the lake. Uncle Elmer's dog and our dog would almost ritualistically have a fight; everyone would rush out with buckets of water to stop them. It was a beautiful and exciting day, one of the best of the year.

In history and civics classes, I believed pretty much what I was taught: that in this democratic country, the people rule. Like so many others who go through the US educational system, I became an idealist. I wanted to believe that my country was the best in the world, and that things worked as the civics books said they did.

Every four years, my father would take us to the polls. He was precinct captain and had to count the votes. I remember going there with him in the evening; he would squat down next to me and say in a hushed voice, "This is the way we elect our leaders. This is the way the people run the country. Democracy is very important." You had to be quiet at the polls — no running around. It was almost a sacred place.

My family was staunchly Republican and prominent in the local party. My father at one time was the treasurer of the state Republican committee. Aunt Mary was married to a US senator; and after his death, she was chairwoman of the Republican National Committee. Later, under Nixon, she ran the US Mint. My mother cried for three days when Agnew resigned in disgrace, but only one day when Nixon quit. She was becoming accustomed to the shame and disappointment of having her faith in leaders broken.

Before each election, both of my parents worked to get out the vote. The local election was as important as the national one, because they had definite ideas about how things should be run. Prejudice among their peer group was focused on the Mormon Church. My parents would campaign actively among the Protestants and Catholics to keep Mormons from getting a majority on the school board. Politics was something citizens did, win or lose, because it had to be done in order to have a democracy. And in a democracy, people could vote based on prejudices. Something about that seemed very wrong to me.

Life was manageable in Twin Falls. Conflicts were evident but not overwhelming. We knew our neighbors, our policemen, the school-teachers, and the superintendent of schools. Soon after getting my driver's license, I made an illegal left turn in town and was ticketed for it. I went to pay the fine, and there was Judge Pumphreys. He said to me, "Frances, it's a great disappointment to me to have you appear in court before me. I remember when you were a little girl and you had a pink dress at your aunt's wedding." He went on for a while in this vein, and then said that I would either have to spend a night in jail or pay the thirteen dollars fine "from money you've earned your-self." (I naively chose the jail time, thinking it more attractive than going home to negotiate borrowing the money from my parents, based on my promise to do some work. When I called my parents to ask them to bring my pajamas and books, I learned that spending time in jail is an offense far worse than making an illegal left turn.)

In such a small town, it wasn't hard to get things done. When our high school was being moved to a new building, my grand-mother Peavey decided that the now-separate junior high school should be named for Vera O'Leary, the retired long-time principal. My dad said he would take care of it. So he talked to the appropri-ate friends, and the school board agreed to name it O'Leary Junior High School. My grandmother was furious! From the name they had chosen, people might assume that the school was named for a man. So she and my father went to the next school board meeting and got the name changed to *Vera* O'Leary Junior High School.

My Sunday school teacher one year was the local FBI man. He wore his gun to class. I really wondered if we needed the FBI in our small town. I had read about the FBI in books and in *Time* maga-zine, and I tried to imagine what his life was like, chasing big time criminals in Twin Falls, Idaho. Were there really enough criminals there to keep him busy? When I asked him about these things, he was very tight-lipped and said a lot of his work was secret. I won-dered what kind of national secrets were buried in a small, sleepy Idaho town.

The first time it occurred to me that our government might do something wrong was in the early 1950s, when Julius and Ethel Rosenberg were convicted of conspiracy to commit espionage, and then executed. I read in *Time* magazine about people protesting the Rosenbergs' death sentences. And I took out a magnifying glass to examine the demonstrators' faces. I was intrigued by the idea of protesting, of trying to communicate something to the government and change the course of history.

My parents, of course, were opposed to Communism, and the McCarthy hearings were talked about often around our dining table. I asked my mother about Communism. She said she didn't know a lot about it, but she didn't think people worked very hard unless they had competition. "In capitalism we don't have security, so the people have to work. I looked at her and thought, "There is no competition in our home, and we get a lot of work done."

There were other stories told in the family about the government. Looking down into the water of Pettit Lake, one would see trees tied together at the bottom of the lake. The government, in its infinite wisdom, had decided that the reason we didn't have more trout in the lake was that they didn't have homes. So they had cut down trees and sunk them for homes for the homeless trout. This didn't work. Later, the government decided that the reason we didn't have trout was that the trash fish ate them. So late in the year, they detonated an explosion at the bottom of the lake and hundreds — maybe thousands — of dead white fish floated to the top. Our lake had been home to red fish, a special kind of landlocked salmon, and those never returned after the government bombed the lake. To this day, only a few trout are to be found in the lake.

The government had set all kinds of regulations for cabins located in the forest. Each one them seemed stupid, especially to my father. Forestry Department rules prohibited repairing the piers, so you should let it go and become a danger to everyone? You were supposed to paint your roof green, so it was not so conspicuous and would look like a tree — a log on the bottom and green on the top. My father felt that black roofs were less obvious and silly than green roofs. He would repair the pier or paint the roof, then go down to the forest station and tell the officers, who never caused much of a fuss. He would walk out to the car after talking to the forest rangers: "They're good Idaho boys. They agree with me. Green roofs are a city idea. No bother."

By the time I was in high school, I was tired of being a Peavey, with all the limitations and expectations that involved. My greatest goal was to leave Idaho and go away to college. My father had already decided that all of his children would go to Idaho colleges, marry Idaho spouses, and stay in Idaho, so he could play with his grandchildren. (Besides, he couldn't imagine that anyone would ever really want to live anywhere besides Idaho.) I started at the College of Idaho in 1959, but two years later managed to transfer to San Francisco State College. I moved to the "big city," which has been my home ever since, except for three years when I moved to Los Angeles to study. I value living in a city, but find the perspective of developing a community, living beyond manners, and having continuing participation in affairs of political import a way of life.

The fruit may not fall far from the tree, as the saying goes, but this fruit has floated away into many places, all connected in one large global community, where life calls for action, tenderness, and responsibility. I live as an artist, working from a pioneering cultural base to preserve and honor life and the living in all cultures — life in the water and on the land. I continue the work of my ancestors to build community wherever I am. Love of one's country is a complex affair. It can be manipulated so easily, as can hatred of one's country. The expansion of the United States and its Western culture is rampant, now that the US is so superior in weaponry and power. I am suspicious of patriotism, and yet I have those feelings. How can our feelings about our country be used to call forth more responsible and responsive behavior in the world? And how to deal with the shame one cannot help feel when people — former sweet babies and present babies — and sewage treatment plants and rivers are being bombed by the government one was born a part of?

Chapter 3
Out of Idaho

IN THE FALL of 1961, when I arrived at San Francisco State College, it was alive with political excitement. A year and a half earlier, the House Un-American Activities Committee had come to San Francisco to hold hearings about Communists in California. Thousands of people had protested against HUAC at City Hall; some had been injured by the police, others jailed. When I arrived at San Francisco State, there was still talk, inside and outside of classes, about that demonstration and about the battle to abolish HUAC.

There was another hot issue while I was there: the famous socialist Norman Thomas had been invited to speak by the students, and then the invitation had mysteriously been withdrawn. Students were furious and held a demonstration. I remembered Grams telling me that Emma Goldman had come to Twin Falls and was refused the opportunity to speak. My grandfather had been one of the men from the town who escorted her to Wells, Nevada, where they put her on a stagecoach. While Grams defended the actions of the town in denying her a platform, she wished she could have heard Emma speak. My grandfather said that the men learned a lot as they traveled the several hours to Wells with Emma Goldman.

To get from one class to another at San Francisco State, I walked past the "free speech area." Around noon, people would hold forth, espousing their causes: socialism, communism, devil-worship, the Campus Crusade for Jesus. Civil rights was the most frequent topic. Whatever the important issues of the day, people would get up and speak about them. I never did; as a shy person I did not find the gumption to pull myself out of the crowd. It was impressive to me that people had the nerve to stand up and talk about such strong ideas. I thought the forum was great: in America, you stand up and speak. This was the First Amendment in action.

A few years later, during the Vietnam War, I trained people in nonviolent action. Part of that training was street speaking. I would do the training and then send people out on the streets to practice. I was too shy to go myself, but other trainers felt it was an important skill to teach to antiwar activists. Finally, my fellow trainers noticed that I habitually found something else "very important" to do during the street-speaking demonstration, and they insisted that I "walk the walk." I agreed in principle. We went out to Stonestown shopping mall, where there was a lot of foot traffic in an outdoor walkway between two rows of shops. The acoustics were alive with echoes; sound carried all the way down the walkway. A few friends started, and then came my turn. I stood up on the stool, looked out, and burst into a roar of laughter. I laughed and laughed; I could not stop laughing, I was so embarrassed to be standing there. Others joined in the laughter. A large crowd gathered, and they laughed. Every time I almost got it together, they would roar and get me going all over again. Finally, I was able to mumble something about the war and relinquish the stool to a better speaker. But I had gathered quite a crowd. The war was so odious, I would do anything that would help stop it. The days of the Vietnam antiwar protests were serious days. Laughter was hardly viewed as appropriate.

In the civil rights and antiwar days, there were often political meetings. I was interested and felt it my civic duty to go to some of these meetings. I used to drop in and stand around the perimeter, listening. I remember meetings attended by thirty or forty people; mostly it was men who spoke. I would watch as one person after another made a point that was obviously very important to him. People would shout and gesticulate and carry on. Sometimes, fights would break out. Frequently, I could not figure out exactly what they were arguing about; small points seemed out of proportion to the noise spent on them. I was fascinated, but had no idea what was going on. For me, attending political meetings was a lot like going to the zoo.

In 1963, after graduating from San Francisco State College, I began teaching science to eighth graders at Roosevelt Junior High School. Every morning, as required, I insisted that students pledge allegiance to the flag. Often there were students — I remember especially some black students — who wouldn't say the pledge, and I had a hard time understanding that. I did not coerce them, but at first I didn't understand their resistance.

One morning it finally got through to me. I came to my first class — eighth graders, some of whom had been grouped together as slow learners — and began taking the roll. One of the kids shouted out, "What do you think about what your people did to our people yesterday?" He was referring to the bombing of a church in Birmingham — four young black girls had been killed. I'd heard about it on TV the night before, but it was not the most important thing on my mind that morning. I looked up and all the students were paying attention, which almost never happened in an eighth grade class. It was a holy moment. I knew we couldn't go on as usual; we had to address the issue immediately. I came out from behind my lectern and started talking with the students. It would be more accurate to say I started listening about it with the students, because they had a lot to say. One of them said, "And we're *not* going to salute the flag today!" I began to see what the flag meant to these young people. It represented a country that had broken its promises to them. "With liberty and justice for all? No way, Miss Peavey."

That was also the year that the NAACP arranged my black lessons. In return, I did occasional volunteer work there — collating mailings, addressing envelopes, going door-to-door to publicize the statewide Rumford ballot measure for fair housing. Some of those I canvassed didn't want to talk about the issue. Others were eager, and went on at some length about their concerns and ideas about what could be done about racial matters in our community, state, and nation. Some got mad at me and slammed the door. They called me a "nigger lover." I got so I could brighten up when they yelled that at me and beam back, "You're right. And I love white people too!" I remember pressing my views on a sympathetic white woman: "We just have to make white landlords and banks treat Negroes fairly." She wasn't sure it was possible to *make* anyone do anything. Maybe we couldn't make people change, but laws must be made and followed; and with this structural change, perhaps increased contact and respect could grow. Change needed to be made person by person; but if that didn't result in institutional and legal changes, then things wouldn't really be any different. I did more thinking about all the things in our country that need to change to promote fairness.

As the civil rights movement grew, I wanted to become a part of it, to do something besides learning about the black community and trying to be a conscientious teacher. I had fantasies of going to Mississippi to work for civil rights, but that never happened.

One day while at the NAACP office, I heard about a demonstration to be held at a downtown hotel, the Sheraton Plaza, for fair employment of black workers. I decided to go. I don't think I had ever been to a demonstration before, but I had heard of them and was interested. There were a lot of people at the hotel. I had no idea what was supposed to happen, so I just did what everyone else did and tried not to be conspicuous.

We all sang songs and listened to speeches. Then, the police came and ordered us to leave. The group refused. Somehow, I found myself being arrested with the others. This was a jolt to my idea of myself — a teacher and law-abiding citizen. But there I was in a cell with six or seven black women. Some were from our sit-in; others were more regular inhabitants of the jail. The most important memory from that experience was the singing. I loved the strong harmonies that bounced off the concrete walls. "Before I'll be a slave I'll be buried in my grave." and "We shall not be moved!" And, of course, "Down by the riverside." The music touched me in a most powerful way. People were kind to me, and I noticed how they cared for each other. I kept worrying that my family or the other teachers at school would find out I was in jail. One of my cellmates had just begun to instruct me in the art of picking pockets when we were released. Even though I was still shy and felt very different, I appreciated the culture I witnessed in that jail. When I went back to my school, I did not say much to anyone about what had happened. But my life was opened by the experience.

After the sit-in, I sporadically attended civil rights meetings and speeches — still as an observer, never saying anything. I did take some direction from the meetings, boycotting restaurants and writing letters to congresspeople. Although I didn't know how all this would result in better conditions for black people, I was willing to cooperate.

The day John F. Kennedy was shot and killed, my teaching supervisor came to tell me the news. At lunchtime, I rushed down to the teachers' lounge, where everyone was glued to the television. Parents were calling the school, asking us to tell their children about it. I went up to my fifth-period class and solemnly said, "I have to tell you that President Kennedy has been shot." Some of the students started crying. One shouted, "It's the Republicans who did it." One of the black students was really scared and asked, "Does this mean we have to go back to slavery?"

We had been looking forward to this particular Friday in this class, because we were going to do the cloud chamber experiment. Kenneth and Clement had prepared the experiment carefully, and had gotten dry ice from the cafeteria. Even though they were sorry about the president, they pressed me to allow them to go ahead with the experiment. So I suggested to the students who needed to cry and talk quietly that they go to the back of the room, and the experiment would continue in the front of the room.

At that very moment, someone on the play yard threw a stone and injured a pigeon. The best place for such injured animals was often my classroom, so someone brought up the bird; we would either set the wing in a splint or take it to a neighbor who was a veterinarian. Several students and I set about moving the rat from his cage to a smaller cage, so the bird would be able to have the larger cage. Somehow, the rat got away from the students and was running around the room. I stepped back and saw my world in front of me: the emotional students; the serious scientists; the bird flapping, being held by a couple of kids; and a group of students chasing after the rat. I especially loved teaching at that moment.

The assassination of President Kennedy was a shock for me. I had admired Kennedy's gusto, straightforwardness, and quest to make things better, but I had never idolized him. For me, the shock was that a president had been killed. I had associated assassinations with the unstable countries in South America that were having coups and insurrections all the time. Assassinations weren't supposed to happen in our country.

The shock was even greater when I heard allegations that the CIA might have had something to do with the killing. Even the possibility that a part of "our government" could be involved in such nasty things had a powerful, disillusioning effect on me.

The assassinations of Malcolm X, Martin Luther King, Jr., Medger Evers, and Robert Kennedy were further signs that there was an evil undercurrent in our society. Our democracy had not civilized us.

I first heard objections to US involvement in Vietnam in the summer of 1965, while waiting in an office at San Francisco State. A fellow graduate student started telling me that "we had to get our troops out of Vietnam." My response was to defend the United States; there must be some good reason for our government to be involved over there; maybe we don't know all the facts. She told me that the Gulf of Tonkin incident was a sham, that US ships had provoked the "attack," which was serving as the pretext for American military involvement in Vietnam.

As she talked, I began to waver in my opinion. Only a year earlier, the US had sent troops into the Dominican Republic — an action that I had considered wrong. I knew about how often the US had invaded countries in Latin America. Maybe our involvement in Vietnam was similar. I had been wondering why the US government seemed to support dictators and repressive leaders all over the world. So the conversation about Vietnam tapped into this new doubt about which Americans foreign policy served.

She invited me to come to a meeting to find out more. It was "Vietnam summer" (an early, large-scale educational and antiwar organizing effort), and such meetings were frequent at that time. I went, joining about a hundred people in a high school auditorium. That meeting raised more disturbing questions. Within six months, I decided that we had no business being in Vietnam. I further decided that I would work against the war in my spare time.

The Vietnam War convinced me that our government was doing something very wrong. On the civil rights issue, I had retained some hope that the government was, in some instances, trying to act in the interests of justice. But how did our involvement in another country's civil war serve justice? And the war was costing us a lot of lives. For what? Nobody I knew was benefiting from that war: not my family, not the farmers in Idaho, not my college classmates. In fact, friends were faced with excruciating choices involving military service. When Muhammed Ali refused to serve in the army, it was important in my thinking. It appeared that the only needs the war served were internal to the United States government. I no longer believed that fighting Communism was a paramount virtue, worthy of killing or being killed.

During the Vietnam War, I explored a wide range of political activities. I went to marches, worked on committees, and wore a red armband during the invasion of Cambodia. I gave emotional support to a man I loved who was about to be drafted and was trying to get conscientious objector status. And I worked with a group in Los Angeles to run an underground railroad for soldiers who had deserted the military. We hid the deserters, moving them from safe house to safe house. It was an intense time. Living a secret life is not natural to my constitution. I hated lying to friends who asked about the guy loafing on my sofa with nothing to do all day. The resisters had to stay hidden until their hair grew out, until they got their head straight about what they wanted to do. One night, as we were transporting two guys, the police stopped us. I walked back to the police car and asked them where Washington Street was. Almost every city has a Washington Street; this ploy gave the police a chance to be helpers, and they forgot to suspect us.

Just hearing about the war on the news every night kept me feeling angry, crazy, and sad a lot of the time. One night, I heard a story on a talk show about three US soldiers in Vietnam. As one of the soldiers walked away from two buddies, he saw a Vietnamese girl run up, take a candy bar from them, and eat it. Then, the girl reached inside her dress and there was a big explosion — the two soldiers and the girl were blown up. Her parents must have given her a hand grenade and sent her out to do this.

After hearing the story, I lay in bed and cried. What must it be like for the Vietnamese family? I pictured them teaching their daughter how to set off the grenade. Or had some other trusted person abused the girl's trust to have her do this devastating act? How much desire to defeat the Americans lay behind the willingness to sacrifice this child? Why had they chosen a girl? And the US soldiers — what was it doing to them to know that they couldn't even share a candy bar with a child without fearing for their lives?

About the same time, it started coming to light that the food we were eating contained dangerous additives and chemical residues. Tests would indicate that a particular preservative increased the possibility of cancer only by some infinitesimal amount, but a body does not take in only that one dangerous substance. Over a lifetime — however long that is — the cumulative effect could really get you. I asked people, "Why would Kellogg's allow poison in their cereal? If they did, we would die, and we wouldn't be able to buy their product." For a long time, I refused to believe the "quacks" who said BHA and sodium nitrate and DDT were bad for us. When someone finally convinced me that our food could be dangerous, all kinds of other beliefs crumbled. The food issue was a major step in the breakdown of corporate credibility. Decisions were not logical. Big businesses weren't thinking about my needs, about my body's long-term survival. And I had trusted them to do that! They were thinking only about the shelf life and appearance of their product. Like the government, they seemed to be mesmerized by their internal needs — in this case, maximizing short-term profit. More and more, it seemed I would have to think for myself about everything.

Just about the time my generation was getting ready to be responsible adults, the definition of responsibility changed. It was no longer enough to make a living, vote, pay the bills, and prevent forest fires. Now we had to read the ingredients on every food package, and comprehend the intricacies of foreign policy when all the facts were not on the table. And voting was no longer an adequate way of participating in the political process. Politics seemed to require working constantly to inform ourselves and others, and together to press for change.

In the late sixties and early seventies, I saw my society shift. Even some of the most vociferous supporters of the war changed their opinions. Over and over I heard parents say, "My kids finally convinced me that the war was wrong." Friends would tell stories about encounters with their parents when they went home for visits. At first, the parents would be angry about their long hair and their radical ideas. But often, if the kids kept the dialogue going, the parents would begin to listen.

Getting the United States disengaged from the Vietnam War was a slow process. In the early stages, ferociously determined young people monopolized antiwar sentiment. A subculture developed — — we could tell who was "us" and who wasn't, based on length of hair and style of clothing. The movement was a tremendous force in our lives; we defined ourselves in relation to it.

Gradually, the concern spread. The complexity of what we saw as wrong spread to the inadequacies of our educational system, inequality of opportunity for racial groups, a repressive sexual environment, unequal rights for women, and the utter senselessness of the materialistic world. For many people, including me, the turning point was in 1970, with the killing of student protesters at Kent State University and Jackson State University. This showed the corruption of life in the United States. Ultimately, the battle against the Vietnam War was fought on every front in the country: in board meetings, classrooms, and workplaces; in courtrooms and congressional hearings; at dinner tables and cocktail parties. And, of course, the Vietnamese people fought across the ocean to defeat the US military forces. That's what it took to shift the ground from which our Vietnam policy grew. And this shift set changes in motion elsewhere: old assumptions about education, authority, women, sex, and family were all being challenged.

Having seen the movement against the Vietnam War from almost the beginning through to the end, I find it a cornerstone in my understanding of how social change occurs. I am humbled by the errors in analysis and strategy made by antiwar forces. Yet it gives me confidence that citizens can make a difference, not just in reforming existing institutions and processes, but in making more substantial changes as well. It is not enough to make changes one person at a time; we must change institutions and systems of thought and behavior — but that work is done one person at a time. At the same time, we found that our spiritual values had deepened and changed. We made changes and we were changed. It goes that way. The later attachment of my generation to selfish materialistic values and greed was a shock to me.

Although I am still proud of the work we did to end the war, a lot of what I learned was how *not* to make change. Seeing the news on television every night filled our lives with pain. We couldn't bear to have our country doing those terrible things in Vietnam. We were desperate to stop the madness, and as a result, our work was often poorly planned. We had a lot of rhetoric, but little coherent theory and systematic analysis. We hadn't seen enough history to have much confidence in what we were doing. We made up for all we lacked by our energy, creativity, and spontaneity.

We often treated each other with the same desperation we felt about the war itself. Meetings were filled with confrontation and accusation. Shouting matches and fistfights broke out, as we tried to agree on "principles of unity" for a rally.

Black students were coming into their power, so there were many struggles about racism among us. People were thrown out of meetings for being racist. We weren't very much aware of the issues between women and men, so the men controlled the decision-making and did most of the talking.

I remember going home from antiwar meetings thinking, "This is hopeless." But I kept going because of my shame about my country and the war. I had to do something about it, and those meetings seemed to be "the only game in town." A group of us formed nonviolence training teams, and we worked to keep violence down in the massive demonstrations against the war. There were those on "our side" whose analysis included destroying property or taking the demonstration into violent tactics. We felt that if people could not count on an announced nonviolent demonstration remaining true to the plan, they would not come out for future actions.

In the years since the end of the Vietnam War, social change has become my life's work. I studied innovation theory and technological forecasting at USC. I set out looking for an interesting life, and I have achieved that goal. My path has comprised many small, often barely perceptible choices. I just did the next logical thing, and have often felt life pulling me along. Each step has seemed to follow naturally from the previous one. I have never lost my love for the United States and Idaho. Even during the Vietnam War, when patriotism was unpopular, I still sang patriotic songs when I drove over the foothills and saw Magic Valley in Idaho stretched out before me. Burning the flag at demonstrations always bothered me. I didn't want to burn our flag; I wanted to cleanse it. An important element of my patriotism is the capacity in our country to protest, to work together to make change.

I have always felt that my work for social change was patriotic. And I have seen in Yugoslavia and Utah how patriotism can be used against a people and their own highest interests. I want my country to be a better place, to be more responsive to the needs of all life, to work for the common good of the people and the earth. I long for a country that actively encourages all of its citizens to develop their potential, and to care for the earth. My criteria for a successful economy are not measured by the stock market, but by the health of the poor. Are things getting better for them? I have come to see that love for my city, my country, and my world need not be mutually exclusive. I've begun to feel patriotic about this planet. And I work in the interests of the weaker, poorer sectors of the country and world.

People in other countries frequently ask why I don't move where life could be easier. Maybe New Zealand is committing fewer crimes in the world. But it is important to remember that New Zealand and Australia fought alongside US soldiers in Vietnam. In fact, every country seems to have its shame.

I know my country is the most dangerous country in the world. The love and worship of power, and the willingness to pay any price, including murder, to grasp and sustain that power and control, is a dominant force in our culture and in many of our leaders. It's a complex issue, because America is also a land of much greatness and many opportunities.

My answer to the suggestion that I live elsewhere is that I must stay where my bones came from. I am part of the land that is North America. That land has come to be me — through eating the food and drinking the water from that land — and I must work to "make it right. For the life of the people and of the earth." It is because I love my country that I can work to find ways for the US to improve. The United States cannot go about dumping garbage, building nuclear weapons, killing rivers and people. My America will find our way out of these deathly habits — someday. All of us together will stop her.

Campaigns

Chapter 4

The International Hotel:
Tenants Rights, 1976–79

I F YOU GO to the intersection of Kearny and Jackson Streets in San Francisco, you'll see an empty lot. That's where the International Hotel used to be, a place where thousands of people came in the late 1970s to help elderly tenants in their struggle to save their home. I was one of those who came to participate.

The International Hotel was an old four-story walk-up in the heart of what used to be Manilatown. Rooms in the hotel averaged eight by ten feet. About one hundred tenants lived there, most of them older Filipino and Chinese people. Many had lived in the hotel for twenty or thirty years. Some tenants had chosen to live in a low-rent hotel so that they could send money to family remaining in "the old country." There was a real sense of community in the I-Hotel.

Developers had been tearing down many of the older residential hotels in the area in order to put up office buildings, hotels, and condominiums. It was unclear what the developers who bought the I-Hotel would do with the property, but it was clear that they wanted the tenants evicted. It was also clear that what they planned for the future did not include any low cost-housing.

The ten-year struggle for control of the hotel began in the mid-sixties. It was a complex drama involving many players: tenants, developers, lawyers and judges, a coalition of liberal and left-wing groups supporting the tenants, the mayor of the city, and the county sheriff. I helped organize the tenants to resist eviction, and to develop a democratic decision-making structure to plan strategy. During the last year before eviction, I lived at the hotel for weeks at a time.

Supporters contributed to the campaign in many ways. Each time eviction appeared imminent, thousands came to defend the hotel. As the empty lot dramatically demonstrates, the tenants were eventually evicted. In the end, nonviolent resistance was met with violence from the sheriff's men and the police. And the hotel was demolished.

But what happened at the International Hotel is much more than a landlord-tenant battle. For me, it is a story of heart politics. At the I-Hotel, I began to feel what it's like to work for change from the heart, and to understand how different that is from working for an abstract principle.

It was because of a principle, though, that I first went to the hotel. During a four-week trip to China in 1974, I had been deeply impressed by one of the guiding principles there: "Serve the people." For me, this meant that one criterion for my social change work is that it be for the poorest sectors of the society, in their interest, rather than that of the most wealthy and powerful. While critical of other aspects of Chinese society, I admired the ideal that to live the good life was to serve the people, to work for the common good. So when the people at the I-Hotel put out a call for help, I went.

I joined the Internal Security Committee, which was in charge of supporting and organizing the tenants. Immediately, I began not just to serve, but to develop a strong bond with many of the people there.

Wahat Tompao, a wonderful, kind man in his mid-seventies, had lived at the I-Hotel for many years. He was from a mountainous area in the Philippines. During World War II, he worked for the US Army as a guide in the central Pacific. Wahat had a tremendous dignity about him, as well as a fine sense of humor. He loved to tease us. He would say, "I'm from the mountains, where people eat dog!" Then he would laugh at how repulsed we Americans would be.

Felix Ayson always felt he was close to death. A deaf man and a determined Marxist, he was always sitting with his cane in the sun in front of the building, teaching the organizers around him, sharing books and wisdom, and sharply criticizing anyone whose actions were based on a narrow political analysis. Felix's room was full of books, and he had a cat who notified him when someone was at the door. Felix died a year after the eviction.

Mr. Yip was a spry Chinese alcoholic who walked in and out of meetings and was not much involved in preventing eviction, but did what he could.

Alfredo and Luisa Delacruz were a quarrelsome Filipino couple. Mr. Delacruz had been a seaman, but couldn't work much anymore because of a mental disability. Mrs. Delacruz was one of the most powerful and respected tenants. Only her closest friends at the hotel called her Luisa; she was "Mrs. Delacruz" or "Mama D." A strong and proud woman, she worked as a master fabric cutter in a shop that made jewelry display cases. In the Philippines, she had participated in union drives at American-owned brassiere plants.

Emil DeGuzman was a young Filipino community organizer whose father had lived in the hotel. It was easy to love Emil, a humble, yet strong-willed leader, who was devoted to the residents of the hotel. His work and his understanding of strategy had drawn him further and further into the campaign until he was living at the hotel and working there full-time.

Filipe Daguro, a longshoreman, wore nickels inside his ears. On his payday, he would press money into my hand to help with the organizing.

King San, a charming four-year-old, roamed Kearny Street in total safety. He was the son of a Chinese couple who ran a second-hand store on the ground floor of the hotel. King San spent most of his days bumming quarters from tenants so he could buy sodas.

As I got to know the tenants, I grew to love many of them and appreciate the community they had built. The I-Hotel was more than simply a shelter for its tenants. For decades, it had been a cultural center for Filipino and Chinese people. A number of the tenants were seamen, as the rent was low enough that they could maintain a room while working out of town for months at a time. Filipino migrant workers rented rooms while working summers at the crab and salmon canneries in Alaska, or picking grapes in California's Central Valley. Like the seamen, they could leave their belongings in place and have a home and friendly neighbors to return to. The hotel was a place to get mail, and to hear news from the Philippines. Emil remembered going to the hotel as a boy and seeing fifty or a hundred people standing outside talking. Tenants ate holiday dinners together and invited lots of neighbors; they shared their celebrations and their funerals.

The kitchen was one of the centers of the community. Most people who live in residential hotels have to eat restaurant meals (which are usually expensive) or cook in their rooms on hot plates (which are illegal). The I-Hotel was one of the last residential hotels in the city where people could cook in a kitchen. The kitchen, on the second floor, had an eight-burner stove and a sink. And somehow, the seventy or eighty people who used it managed to avoid kitchen squabbles, which was incredible to me. If someone came in and all the burners were in use, he would simply come back later. Often people cooked for each other, especially for those who couldn't take care of themselves.

The International Hotel campaign offered outsiders many chances to work directly with the tenants. Some supporters, like those of us on Internal Security, got to know the tenants by organizing a tenants' association (the IHTA), going door-to-door in the hotel, sharing news, and finding out what they thought should be done. We had brunches every Sunday to talk with the tenants about new developments and to hear their thoughts. When eviction was threatened, hundreds of volunteers would sleep on the hotel floor, taking turns doing night watch duty, and then going off to 9-to-5 jobs in the morning.

Doctors, nurses, and paramedics got to know the tenants through their work on the Medical Committee. Facing eviction is stressful, and some tenants worried about what the strain would do to their health. The medical people gave the tenants regular checkups, kept records on their health, and taught us all CPR in case someone had a heart attack. Probably the most important thing the medical team did was talk with the tenants about their health, so they did not feel alone with their concerns.

People from political and community groups supported the campaign by sitting security watches. We always had two people by the front door watching who went in and out of the hotel. Sabotage and arson were constant threats. A fire set in the I-Hotel three years before had killed three people; while I was living at the hotel, another hotel around the corner was torched. During the day, tenants stood many of the watches; at night, community groups took over. One of the two night watch people had to walk through the hallways every hour, see that everyone was okay, and make sure the fire extinguishers were in place. The tenants knew that if they felt anxious in the middle of the night, they could come down to the watch station at the front door and talk to the security watch. The tenants came to trust the Internal Security Committee, thanks in a large part to these night watches.

When rumors were started in the city that we had guns in the hotel, security watch people were stationed in front of the doors, frisking people and going through all packages. We knew we did not have weapons — maybe a couple of tenants had personal guns in their rooms. We debunked that rumor. This turned out to be an important organizing idea. On these four-hour security shifts, supporters got to know and like the people they were fighting for; they began to fight for reasons beyond ideological ones.

Not all of the contact with the tenants was pleasant, of course. Every week, someone from Internal Security had to take Mrs. Knowles to the grocery store. Mrs. Knowles was an elderly white tenant who needed help with her shopping. She had quite a few cats and liked to complain a lot. Taking Mrs. Knowles shopping really tried one's patience, but it had to be done. That was part of our political work.

Then there was a tenant who wasn't able to control his bowels. Every week, an Internal Security member had to clean his room and wash his sheets and clothes. Sometimes people would feel sick for several days after this job; I used to throw up after cleaning his room. At first, I thought we should throw him out of the hotel, and even said so in meetings. But later, I realized that we had to work out our relationships in a way that didn't exclude him, because we shared this world. We can't dispose of people just because they displease us or have a habit we don't like. The issue of control is very important in social change. He was an alcoholic and did the best he could. Cleaning him up was part of serving the people. The medical committee worked to get him treatment, but he was resistant.

As I became more deeply involved at the I-Hotel, I had more opportunities to serve the people. One night, someone from the security watch called me out of a meeting to tell me that Mrs. Delacruz was threatening her husband with a knife. When I reached the manager's office, Mrs. Delacruz was sitting staring at the TV and clutching a knife. Mr. Delacruz wasn't around. I sat down and watched television with her until she seemed more composed. When her breathing returned to normal, I asked her what was going on. She told me that her husband had insulted her, and she was going to kill him. I asked her to give me the knife; then, we would go find him and work this out. She refused, bolted for the door, and ran downstairs to the recreation room, where Mr. Delacruz had gone. I got in front of the door, and insisted that she either give me the knife or allow someone to go in with her, to keep her from hurting him. She threw several chairs at me. I caught them and set them down calmly. Tenants and supporters were peeking down the stairs, ready to help if I got in real trouble.

When Mrs. Delacruz finally got into the recreation room, I was with her, and Mr. Delacruz had a man with him. Conflict in Filipino society is frequently dealt with through intermediaries. I didn't know what to do, so I followed the lead of my Filipino counterpart. By the time Mrs. Delacruz and I left, she and her husband had reached a settlement: he agreed to sleep on the recreation room sofa for a few nights, and she, in return, agreed not to kill him.

The next day, Mrs. Delacruz asked me to dinner to thank me. "I want you to call me Luisa," she said. "I like you. You don't let me become a criminal."

Members of the I-Hotel community also connected with other people and their struggles. When a coalition of groups occupied the Federal Building in San Francisco, demanding legislation requiring that public buildings create access for disabled people, some tenants joined them. Some tenants went to Sausalito to help save houseboat residents from the sheriffs and bulldozers. Urban poor people were fighting for hippies! I remember Wahat going up to an older man in the houseboat group and advising him about how to resist. "Use the old men, " he said. "Old people are good to put on the front lines. Young people should stay behind us."

The tenants even felt connections with tenants portrayed in a movie. During the times when eviction seemed imminent, we often showed the movie *Salt of the Earth*. In one scene, the sheriff who has come to evict a family carries their belongings out the front door; the women carry them in again through the back door. The tenants loved this scene. They stood up and shouted, "Go! Go! That's what we're going to do!" They were animated for hours afterward. It meant a great deal to have a mental image of what eviction might be like, and what we could do. Sometimes, responding to shouts of "Show it again!" we ran the movie twice in a night.

As the I-Hotel campaign progressed, people with all sorts of talents came forward to help. Welders made special brackets to brace the doors. Telephone installers put in an internal telephone system and debugged the regular phones. Someone from the squatters' movement in England showed us how to use bedsprings to barricade doors and keep the sheriffs out. The Food System, a network of cooperatively run businesses, pledged hundreds of dollars worth of food, so that if we were able to resist eviction for several days, people wouldn't go hungry. On particularly tense nights, entertainers came in and lightened our spirits with juggling, singing, and comedy.

Whatever we needed, we put the message out through the phone tree, the network we set up to transmit information to supporters. When we were fortifying the hotel, an elderly Chinese tenant, Mr. Chung, was reminded of his experiences during the Russo-Japanese War. "We had to keep the Japanese from coming upstairs," he said, and he showed us how to barricade the stairs using plywood and two-by-fours. We put out our need for wood through the phone tree. And the wood came.

Thousands of people were on that phone tree, which was used to get materials, find people with special skills, and announce demonstrations. When we were threatened with eviction, known as "code orange" time, supporters had to tell particular contact people where they could be reached. On a trial run one evening, we were able to get more than a thousand people to the hotel in an hour. Supporters gave the hotel a high priority. I often overheard people make plans with friends and then say, "I'll be there if they don't need me at the hotel."

Although resistance to eviction was our most visible strategy, a number of complementary efforts were going on simultaneously. Lawyers worked on eminent domain — a plan for the city to buy the hotel from the landlord and turn over management duties to the tenants. Others worked on a buyback plan — the hotel would be bought with federal funds, and the tenants would buy it back over the years through their rent. And there was a campaign to have the hotel declared a historic landmark.

On Saturdays, we often planned strategy, discussing which forces were for us, which were against us, and how to turn the situation to our advantage. We identified various objectives and all the possible ways of attaining them. Then, we focused on how to achieve our most immediate objectives. By analyzing why different groups and individuals in the city had chosen to support us, we developed ideas of how to appeal to others less favorably disposed.

Working from the heart, I found, does not make politics clear or simple. The I-Hotel situation was complex, often confusing, and continually shifting. Our campaign was full of dissonance and internal problems. As we fought to save the hotel, I was often unsure what was the best course of action.

The deepest internal conflict centered on the manager of the hotel, Joe Diones, a Hawaiian-born Filipino and a well-known figure in the community. Joe was a short old man with a bulldog face, a former longshoreman who had been involved in labor organizing in Hawaii. Now, he owned a nightclub in San Francisco. He had named himself manager of the hotel in 1969, when the tenants had begun to manage the hotel themselves. He collected the rent from each tenant and put it in an escrow account, which would be settled when the ownership of the hotel was changed.

Diones had been working against eviction, but he wanted to have all the authority himself. He didn't want a board of directors or a tenants' association that made decisions on a more democratic and transparent basis. He withheld financial records. And he threatened tenants and abused them. He kept a baseball bat in his office as a weapon, and he had two big "goons" who intimidated the tenants. In private, the tenants complained about him and wished him gone.

The Internal Security Committee decided the best way to stop eviction was to form a strong tenants' association. So, much of our organizing effort was put into building democracy within the hotel. Residents were slow to endorse a tenants' association — they disliked Diones, but were afraid of him. We had to have our organizing brunches on Sundays, when Diones regularly went to Reno to gamble.

Eventually we took a vote, which the tenants' association won. Joe Diones decided he wanted to be president of the association. While his goons walked menacingly around the meeting room, he threatened to resign if he wasn't elected. Diones was elected by a one-vote margin. The night of the election was very tense. I found out later that one of my colleagues on Internal Security had brought a gun with him to the meeting. I was shocked. He was part of a political organization, whose members were opposed to his action as well. I worked to get agreement that this would never happen again.

The tenants eventually threw Diones out of the hotel. It happened because one day he went too far. Very early that morning, sheriff's men had gotten past the security watches, entered the hotel, and posted eviction notices on all the doors. (Posting notices is a necessary legal step in the eviction process.) The tenants came out of their rooms to see what the commotion was about. They saw Joe Diones ranting and raving, blaming the watches.

But privately, Diones told a tenant named Moonding, "I knew the sheriffs were coming." Now, Joe may or may not actually have known; he may just have been trying to show Moonding he was in control. Moonding did some janitorial work for Joe and was somewhat dependent on him. But when he heard Joe say that, Moonding turned against him. He yelled to everyone, "Joe knew!" And when Joe went out for breakfast, Moonding grabbed some rope and tied the front door closed. When Diones returned, the tenants unanimously refused to let him in.

After he had been kicked out, Diones went to many liberal leaders in the city who had previously supported the I-Hotel tenants. He told them that young radicals and communists had taken over, that no old people were left in the hotel. Neither charge was true, of course. It was not the supporters who took over; there were few supporters there the day the tenants rose up. I was there. I watched awestruck at what it took for the tenants to rise up against Diones.

They had endured all kinds of abuse from him, but when he appeared to be colluding with the forces for eviction, they couldn't put up with him any more. It was like a tide that rose, without a vote or even much discussion. He had stepped beyond the bounds of acceptability, and he was gone.

As to the second charge, all but one or two tenants stayed right through eviction. But city leaders tended to accept Diones' story. It served their own interests, as they were increasingly under attack for their support of the tenants, and Diones gave them an out. The news media, too, tended to believe Diones' story.

Another source of internal conflict was the continual bickering among political groups. The key groups in the I-Hotel coalition were the I Wor Kuen (IWK, a Maoist group), the Karipunan ang mga Demokratikan Pilipino (KDP, Filipino Marxists), the Revolutionary Communist Party (RCP, riddled with CIA/FBI plants), and the anarchist-oriented Food System. Half a dozen community and religious groups also participated in the coalition, including the Human Rights Division of the Catholic Archdiocese, the American Friends Service Committee (Quakers), and Jim Jones and his People's Temple. Mini-coalitions formed around different points of view. Some groups wanted this to be a housing campaign; for others, it was an antiracist struggle. For me, it was a fairness campaign, and a campaign for the kind of city I wanted to live in. I was known as one of the "honest people." In political lingo, that meant that I was not allied with any group or political line. I worked for the tenants' association and took my direction from them, rather than from an outside group.

Arguments focused on how to define the I-Hotel campaign. Each of the sectarian leftist parties had a different line, based on its own political analysis of the situation. IWK's line was, this is a Third World struggle. KDP's line was, this is a housing struggle. RCP had another line. The groups fiercely debated what our chant should be: "Third World communities unite!" or "Everybody needs a home!" We managed to resolve the issue by giving equal time to the different chants. I preferred a holistic approach: "Save the hotel. It is a community and a bunch of fine people living in peace," but that didn't make much of a chant.

The competitiveness baffled me. Weren't we fighting for Third World people and for housing? Each group's Marxist dialectics had led it to its own "correct" analysis, and analysis affects strategy. The IWK tried to convince everyone to concentrate on organizing support for the hotel in Third World communities. The KDP wanted everyone to organize among other tenants' groups. Neither group could entertain the possibility that two different analyses can be equally true and important at the same time.

My position was that we should proceed on every level, and that if anyone should be in control, it was the tenants: the people who have the most invested should have the greatest say.

Which brings me to my greatest internal conflict. Early on, I had been given the job with Luisa Delacruz of developing the tenants' plan to resist eviction should the actual event occur. If the sheriffs, the police, or the National Guard came to evict the tenants, what should we do? I guess nobody else wanted to think about that. But having grown up with an insurance man for a father, I've always been preparedness-oriented.

We went about the job with gusto. We formed a Tenants Eviction-Resistance Committee and polled people about strategy. I worked with the tenants on an alert system and barricades. But the first time eviction seemed imminent, I realized too much power was in my hands. Luisa wanted to be with the people on her hall, so she was a floor captain. I was the liaison with External Security, and the center of communications for all floors, the outside, and all supporters. It was too much. Every decision was checked with me. I couldn't even go to the bathroom without someone running up with a question. I, who advocated that the tenants should be in charge of their own struggle, was in the position of controlling everything!

I don't know when I've ever felt so stretched, so tired, so alone, and so despairing. During the first eviction scare, I lived in fear for three days straight; working with little sleep, solving problem after problem, I lost perspective on the situation and became totally drained.

This experience taught me that it's not enough to translate a heart connection into commitment and hard work. You have to translate it into *appropriate* work. The situation called for me to share power, to trust people more, for my sake as well as the campaign's.

A court order delaying eviction gave me time to figure out how to delegate much of my authority. By the second eviction period, we had floor captains and area captains, all tenants. We redesigned the communication system so Luisa and I could talk together more easily. We were all able to consult among ourselves from our different stations in the building, using the internal phones. We redesigned the phone system, so each floor had an open line to all the other floors and to the outside of the building.

Finally, in August 1977, the legal and political obstacles to eviction were exhausted. On August 4, the indicators started coming in; eviction was about to happen. We had scouts watching all the police stations, people roving the city with CB radios, informants in the jail, city bus and taxi drivers ready to report on the movements of the police. Now, all of them started calling in. Internal Security went on red alert a couple of hours earlier than External Security. We wanted to have our people inside before the blockade closed access to the doors. Supporters started pouring into the area from all over the Bay Area. In meetings, concerts, and movie theaters, announcements were made that the I-Hotel was on red alert, and large numbers of people stood up and rushed to the hotel.

Supporters knew that they could get up-to-date information by listening to KPFA, a local progressive radio station. KPFA started broadcasting from the third floor of the hotel at seven o'clock that night. We would give the announcer messages: "We've just had a call that the Washington Street freeway off-ramp is closed. Please reroute and come to the hotel immediately. You may park at [such-and-such a place]."

Early in the evening, we had a tenants only meeting. It was very quiet, a little like a funeral. The Tenants Eviction-Resistance Committee announced that eviction seemed to be imminent. A tenant captain handed out a prepared paper explaining what tenants should do with their valuables. There were a million questions in everyone's mind. Some people cried; everyone was filled with fear. What would eviction be like? What would we do if police entered the building? Would people be hurt? We knew we were in for a long night. Mr. Chung got drunk early.

The medical committee took each person's blood pressure. People insisted that I get in line. The medic called out my blood pressure: 120 over 80! I always used to have the same blood pressure. Everyone shouted, "120 over 80!" They seemed to draw courage from this steadiness. I didn't.

We adjourned the meeting with lots of hugging and back patting. Tenant captains checked that every tenant who wanted a supporter had one in the building. Then came the onslaught of the media. We had given passes to certain media we did not find too obnoxious. They rushed Luisa and me; would we please announce for the cameras that we were going on red alert. We refused. This was for real, not for the movies.

By 10:00 p.m., three or four thousand people were waiting in front of the hotel, with their arms locked together and hands clasped. Another four hundred were inside. From the fire escape in the front, we watched the first police arrive, in full riot gear. Suddenly, a contingent of one hundred supporters on our front lines just walked away. The rest of the supporters were confused: why had that group pulled out? They had no way of knowing that the people who left were from the Revolutionary Communist Party. The RCP apparently had a plan, kept secret from the rest of the coalition, to walk away when the police arrived. I always figured they could not afford to be arrested and have their FBI/CIA covers blown. People from the other groups held their ground.

Bus drivers called in to report that police were heading toward the hotel on horseback. At one strategy meeting months before, we'd considered purchasing marbles — which horses can't walk on — but the idea was never followed up. We didn't think they would really bring horses to break through a nonviolent line. But soon we could see the mounted police approaching, and we realized we had underestimated the of cruelty the police.

Earlier in the evening, the captain of the roof team asked me if I would come up and talk to their team and check their placements. I had never been on the roof as I am afraid of heights. I had reliable people climb up and give me descriptions and the photos they took. I trusted the strategy they had come up with. But now, I was face-to-face with a scared captain who made a reasonable request. I gathered all my courage and climbed the vertical ladder. My hands were sweating so that I could barely grasp the rungs. A group of friends went along to catch me if I fell. We had constructed poles with large hooks to keep the hydraulic fire ladders from landing. Teams demonstrated their technique for stopping the ladders. The teams most committed to nonviolence, from the Human Rights Division of the Catholic Archdiocese and the American Friends Service Committee, were assigned to the roof, as it was the place from which the police most feared guns being directed at them.

Later in the night, when I made it down from the roof, I looked up from a catwalk that went from one wing to another and saw a spooky sight. I saw police on the roof in riot gear, carrying big guns. They had used a Fire Department hook-and-ladder to land. Our poles had not held.

The four hundred police officers in front of the hotel had no idea how hard it would be to get through our lines of supporters. Even with their nightsticks, they couldn't get through. The locked-arms technique was effective. And it minimized the urge to fight back rather than hold tight. Finally, the police had their horses rear up and come down on people. Blood began to flow. One outraged man broke loose from the line. He was bleeding from the head. He raised his hands and backed the horses away from the line. He was shouting about this city and the preciousness of life. Years later, I saw his spiritual brother courageously standing, backing up the tanks in Tiananmen Square. But the horses in front of the hotel stopped only a moment to get their bearings and then launched more attacks.

Throughout the campaign, the tenants had said that the most important thing in fighting eviction was that no one should be hurt, that no harm should come to their supporters or to the police. They had clearly said, "If people start getting hurt, we want to call off the blockade." Wahat had taken an especially firm stand on this issue. But now, when External Security captains asked supporters to move, they refused. The earlier, unexplained departure of one hundred fellow supporters and their leadership betrayal had caused the other supporters to lose faith in the leadership. "We came here to fight for the tenants and we're not leaving."

I saw Wahat standing at the window looking down at the thousands of supporters and the police pounding them with horses and battering them with nightsticks. His face was ashen. He said, "Call it off. Tell them to move, we'll leave. We don't want anyone hurt." A little later, someone found him in his room, trying to hang himself. Floor captains moved all the tenants to the first and second floors so no one was alone.

Outside, the police violence continued. Our supporters were entirely nonviolent. Even if you wanted to fight, you couldn't with your arms linked to those on either side of you. By the next day, about seventy-five of our people had reported to the hospital with injuries. None of the police or sheriffs were injured.

It took the police three or four hours to get through the crowd. At two o'clock in the morning, the sheriffs came into the building. The calmest, jolliest guy was the first sheriff to climb in the window on the second floor. Looking at his face, I knew he was a good person. He was probably a loving father and worked in Little League. But I also knew he was doing something that wasn't right. I had never thought much about chants, but a chant came to me in that moment: "Where are you going to live when you're old?" As we took up the chant, I realized that's also what we were fighting about. In addition to the Third World and low-cost housing issues, this was a fight for old people.

They broke my tailbone. I did not go willingly. There are those who claim my largeness is part of my nonviolent strategy. It is not.

Emil and I were the only two people on Internal Security who were injured. We were also the only Internal Security people whose pictures had been in the newspaper. I was dragged by my feet, boom, boom, boom, down the stairs; and every time I landed on my tailbone, I knew it wasn't helping any. As I was dragged out the front door, the undersheriff called out, "Take it easy, Fran." I hated that he knew my name. But then, I knew his.

After we had been removed from the hotel, we were led outside the police cordon a block away. Unlike the movie we had seen, there was no chance to sneak in the back door of the hotel. Standing there, looking at the hotel, was one of the saddest and loneliest moments of my life. We had given it our best, and had lost.

We waited there, greeting the tenants and supporters as they came out, hearing each of their stories, learning the latest details of what was going on inside the hotel. The supporters from the roof were the last to come out. They showed us their bruises and told a horrible tale. Ultimately, it was these people who sustained the most injuries inside the hotel. Out of view of the media, police officers had run amok, beating up the thirty unarmed and nonviolent members of the roof team. They focused their violence especially on the young Filipino tenant who was captain of the roof team. He was hit over and over in the ribs by police batons. For some time, I considered whether we should have left the roof undefended. Now, I think that was an important defense, and we should have asked media to go there, too.

My tailbone hurt so much that I couldn't sit, so from time to time I lay down on the sidewalk. We were all exhausted; most of us hadn't slept for twenty-four hours. Then it struck us — our denial that eviction would really happen had kept us from making plans for what to do afterward. The city had arranged for hotel rooms scattered all over the city, still failing to recognize that this was a community, that the tenants needed to be together, especially during this difficult and disorienting period. They knew how to take care of each other. The city had little interest in keeping this trouble-making bunch where they could draw strength and comfort from each other.

Someone had the idea of parading through Chinatown and holding a press conference in St. Mary's Park. So we did that. I stood on the edge of the crowd with many of the tenants. It was 6:00 a.m. by now, and there were only a few hundred of us left. We were a ragtag group. I looked at the faces of the tenants, thinking how I felt about them, what I knew about what they had been through, and what their lives might be like now. Wahat spoke, dignified as ever, defiant and proud. I remember him standing on a ledge, his silver hair blowing in the breeze. He said, "I don't know where we are going or what is going to happen to us. We are grateful to all of you who stood by us and helped us. There are many who don't understand why the hotel is important to us, but we know and we will always know." Some people cried. I didn't. I was too tired to cry, too shocked at being out on the street instead of inside the hotel with my friends.

An as-yet unopened drug rehabilitation center in another neighborhood offered its quarters to the tenants, and they went there in supporters' cars. They lived together for a few days and then dispersed, a number of them moving to the Stanford Hotel back on Kearny Street, three or four blocks from the I-Hotel.

Our last hope was that through court action the hotel would be given back to the tenants. Soon that hope was gone, too. Several months after eviction, a man hired by the developer rammed a bulldozer into the hotel, leaving a gaping hole. This action was illegal. The developer didn't have a valid demolition permit, and by now the hotel was listed on the National Register of Historic Places, which supposedly provided temporary protection.

A few weeks after the bulldozer incident, a group of tactical leaders from External and Internal Security met at Clown Alley, a famous hamburger joint with a good view of the hotel. We were all sitting there when a police car pulled up at a stop sign. Someone came out from the shadows to tie a thick rope to the bumper of the police car. Another person asked for directions and kept the police distracted. Then, the police car did what we knew from so many security watches it would do — gunned the gas pedal to get across the street. The other end of the rope that was tied to the bumper had been attached to the scaffolding around the hotel. The bumper flew off. All of us felt some kind of release. After all, we had just been sitting there. While it was an emotionally satisfying moment, I no longer think it was a good idea. We had always tried to have open relations with the police — this is a key value in nonviolence.

In the period of healing and reevaluation after the eviction, I even questioned nonviolence. I began to see how terrorists are bred — from frustration at the defeat of legal and nonviolent work. But the tenants I discussed this with straightened me out. How could they possibly live in a place that had cost someone's life?

Even toward the end of the campaign, some people had believed that eviction might not happen. I had always thought it might. Even though the hotel was bought with smuggled money from Thailand, even though the tenants had enough money in escrow to make a respectable down payment, the legal and political system is very attached to the supremacy of private property. For me, the most important thing was that the resistance to eviction be done well, that people not be hurt, and that it be a lesson in what it means to take a stand with poor people from diverse backgrounds. It was an opportunity for our community to think about private property used for the common good, rather than for a corporation's profit. If we have that mental image, then we can do it again and again. For the most part, it worked. Hundreds of white people grew closer to poor Filipino and Chinese people, and the feelings were reciprocal. After long years of isolation from one another, we had begun to make connections.

But people had gotten hurt. We had been lied to by the Police Department and the Fire Department. We had been betrayed by the Revolutionary Communist Party. The mayor, who had once promised he would not permit eviction, was on vacation in Hawaii when it took place. The sheriff, who had previously gone to jail rather than evict us, ended up presiding over the eviction, smashing in doors with a sledgehammer with gusto. And we lost the hotel. The tenants had been displaced. A community had been shattered.

Postscript: the Bottom Line

Twenty years after the eviction, the I-Hotel site remains vacant, its future uncertain. From time to time, something appears in the newspaper about an agreement between the developer, the city, and community groups for construction of a mixed-use building. There will be some low-cost housing for senior citizens, some offices, parking, and a few floors of hotel. Emil and I talk about getting on the list for a room in our old age. Priority for occupancy will be given to former I-Hotel tenants, although how many of them will still be alive, reachable, or willing to move when the building is completed is anyone's guess.

There are those who say that the real victory of the I-Hotel was for the other single room occupancy hotels in the city. They had been prime targets for development prior to our campaign. Now, people in the city had been educated about the necessity for such hotels and their destruction slowed.

A large hole is the reminder of what once existed there: a community of living, breathing people who didn't fight about the kitchen. It is a gash in the side of the city. A visible wound of a stabbing in the body of a great city. The net loss to the community of Filipinos and Chinese and to the city of San Francisco is great. The net loss to the developer must run into millions of dollars by now, in taxes and expenses. The eviction of those tenants did not serve the common good.

Chapter 5

Sixth Street Park: A Place In The Sun For Street People, 1979–81

E VERY community has its poor people — its untouchables. The rest of us tend to look away when we see them, trying to convince ourselves that their lives have nothing to do with ours. But this sense of separateness is an illusion. Untouchables are part of our world, and we are part of theirs. When I call them "untouchables," I am remembering the tears of one man in despair about his condition, "No one will even touch me, I'm in such bad shape."

Among the untouchables in the United States are the poor people, alcoholics, and addicted people who live on the street. In San Francisco, many such people congregate on Sixth Street, an area of rundown residential hotels, small liquor stores, and pawn shops. I worked with a progressive church, Glide Memorial United Methodist Church, to build and organize a park for the street people on Sixth Street.

In the three years of working at the park, I tested many of my assumptions about social change. I grew close to people at the bottom of our society — and the bottom of their lives — whom I never expected to know. Most of what I learned has to do with the relationship of a society to its untouchables. Issues of race, class, and violence figure prominently in this relationship.

Like the International Hotel, Sixth Street Park is now no more than a vacant lot. Because it was a reminder of a painful situation, the park became a scapegoat. Eventually, real estate interests, politicians, and journalists attacked it; the church retreated from its commitment; the park was bulldozed.

The painful relationship between the untouchables and the rest of society continues. Whether we acknowledge it or not, whether we try to improve it or not, it is there.

When I used to drive along Sixth Street, I would see run-down residential hotels, men standing around talking, a lot of litter. But I did-
n't spend much time thinking about the situation there.

In 1978, my friend Michael approached me about the idea of
buying a small vacant lot on the corner of Sixth and Minna Streets
and turning it into a park for the street people there. Michael was
working as business manager for Glide Church, which was backing
the project. The vision that emerged was a park that would honor
street people and their problems. It would be a place for those who
had no place. No pressure would be exerted on people to stop
drinking; in fact, since the land was privately owned, people could
drink there without being hassled by the police. (Laws against
drinking on the street, in effect, discriminate against those who have
no home to drink in and who cannot afford to drink in bars.)

In thinking about plans for the park, I had to tune in to the situation on Sixth Street. In my black lessons, I had learned a little
about the street life of unemployed black men. In poor, urban black
culture, the street is a newspaper, a soap opera (for personalized
drama in life), a bar (where the cheapest wine is shared), a place of
business (where drugs, sex, and stolen goods are sold, and where
contractors can find cheap labor), and a bank (where money is lent,
given, or stolen). The street is also a therapist's couch, where people
help solve each other's problems, recounting troubling experiences
and information over and over until they make sense of it.

I remember going down to Sixth and Minna for the first time with
Gene and Alvin, two black men we'd hired to help plan the park. A
small crowd of street people was gathered around us. Out of nowhere,
a big man came up to me, took my arm, and said, "Come on baby, let's
go." Bewildered, I told him I wasn't going anywhere. "But I already paid
for you," the man said. "I paid that guy, and he said you'd come up to
my room with me." All this time, he was trying to fondle my bottom. I
kept moving and finally realized what was going on, and told this
would-be john that I was not for sale and that he should get his money
back. He hurried down the block, shouting after "my pimp."

I felt afraid of the people on Sixth Street. Would they want my
money? Would they hurt me? I found I was reluctant to love people who were in bad shape. And I felt guilty, because I suspected that
I'd had more opportunities in my life then they've had in theirs.

Gene and Alvin interviewed the street people hanging out in this
particular neighborhood to find out what they wanted in a park.
And you know what they wanted? Garbage cans. Toilets. Grass. And

showers. One of the first things we learned was that these poor street people want to improve their lives. We commissioned three designs for the park, and Gene and Alvin took them back to the residents of Sixth Street for comments. The final design reflected the lives and wishes of the park's users.

With the help of young people from the California Conservation Corps and volunteers from the street, we built a park on the 25-by-125-foot lot. It was the most compact park in the city, no bigger than the front yard of a modest suburban house. Walking into the park from the Minna Street alley, you'd see men gathered around a metal barrel with a fire burning inside. They'd be cooking stew on a grate atop the barrel, or just keeping warm. Next to the barrel was a small shelter with a corrugated metal roof and two walls — the kitchen area, complete with a picnic table and a nearby sink. The shelter also served to protect people from the wind and rain; often you'd see someone sleeping there. Beyond the shelter, steps led up to a small grassy knoll, which was far enough off the beaten path that grass could survive. In the main area of the park, a few young trees and scrawny bushes clung to life.

Throughout the park, you'd see groups of men talking, eating, drinking. Some would be playing dominoes at one of the half-dozen picnic tables; others would be sleeping on benches specifically designed to be wide enough to accommodate the weary. On the Minna Street perimeter were two chemical toilets, a tool shed, and an open dirt area with a basketball hoop. The court was used regularly. We defined the Sixth Street side with large jagged boulders, so park users would be less likely to sit there and harass passersby. In the center of the park was a water fountain; and nearby, set into the brick floor, we installed a bronze plaque honoring famous people who were alcoholics: Winston Churchill, Ernest Hemingway, W.C. Fields, Judy Garland, Ulysses S. Grant, Betty Ford, and so on.

Unfortunately, the logistics of installing a shower made it impossible. For a time, we had "sleeping tubes" in the park — long corrugated-steel culvert pipes, four feet in diameter, with wooden platforms built inside. One year, during our annual park renovation, we installed a mural painted especially for the park. It depicted various aspects of life there: people sitting around the fire, staff meetings, a guy with a bottle staring off into the distance, people dancing and playing basketball.

During the six weeks we spent constructing the park, I began to see how hard life was on Sixth Street. I worked there from 8:30 a.m. until 4:30 p.m., and every day at least one disaster occurred within two blocks of the park. A car crashed into the building next door, or a woman was run over, or someone was found dead. Police officers made arrests all the time.

Around me, I saw men of all ages, sitting, standing, passing the bottle. In the early morning, they were alert; their eyes caught everything that was going on. Some approached us to give advice and offer help, others to flirt with women on the construction crew. But by afternoon, with a day's drinking and social interaction behind them, they were less coherent. Me, too. I went home and collapsed on the sofa.

I continued to feel bad about the situation there. The dirt and the lice bothered me, and the lives that seemed to be passing without consequence. I kept wishing they could live more secure, fulfilling lives. Maybe some of that is my "stuff," but some of it we shared.

But I had to examine my discomfort in light of my culture and my values. Was it fair to assume that my kind of life was the one the men on Sixth Street would want to choose? Or that they would be able to choose it if they wanted to? Probably, there were certain aspects of my life that they'd adopt, and others that would seem totally inappropriate to them. It wasn't for me to decide how they should live.

But to be able to work effectively on Sixth Street, I had to come to some understanding of why those people were there, doing what they were doing. Blaming either the street people or the society for their problems didn't help me. It only left me feeling bad about their situation, without having any ideas about what might improve it. I continued to ponder: Why are they there? How have any of us ended up where we are?

An early hypothesis was that the street people had chosen this way of life. But the more time I spent on Sixth Street, the more tentatively I held this hypothesis. I kept wondering: Could they have chosen otherwise, given the doors that had been closed on them by family abuse, racism, poverty, and their consequent feelings of worthlessness?

Although we didn't want the park to be controlled by Glide's employees, we did have a few ideas we felt strongly about. We wanted the park to be kept clean, and we knew that value was shared by the people using the park. We also wanted a volunteer staff made up of people who used the park, who would take care of it and each other. As we got to know people on Sixth Street, we'd invite them to a staff meeting. Whenever someone would complain or make a suggestion, we'd say, "Come to the meeting." Anyone who regularly used the park could belong to the staff and come to the meetings.

An early concern in our meetings was that staff members were bullying people and collecting rent on the sleeping tubes. Another big issue was getting people to use the toilets instead of peeing on the flower beds. Park users were also pulling up flowers, leaning on fledgling trees, and using the tree stakes and parts of the underground sprinkler system as weapons. We worked on all these issues, but before we could resolve them, the potential weapons had been used up and the most vulnerable plants had died. The most frequent concern brought up by the park staff was violence in the park. Almost all the issues were brought up by the park staff; rarely did church staff bring up an issue.

After about six months of staff meetings, we had a solid group.

Ben was a strong black man with a dignified manner. He often volunteered to chair meetings, and would come in early to set the agenda ahead of time. He usually initiated park clean-up in the mornings. He was physically strong, though his bouts with alcohol took a lot out of him. He was nonjudgmental in nature, and frequently came with ideas for how to organize economic development schemes.

Askew was a bearded and graying man who walked with a cane. A grant writer who had quit the 9-to-5 world, he talked slowly and ponderously — eloquently when he was at his best — and saw himself as a leader.

Godfather was a tall, slender man, a sometime-artist who always wore a cowboy hat and boots. Formerly a gardener, he began to care for the plants of the park.

Tony was a young guy from Louisiana who was, among other things, a mugger. During park construction, he had been seen knocking over an old woman and taking her purse.

Bird was a tiny fellow who looked like a sparrow. Because he was always threatening people, he had been barred from all the institutions in the city that help poor people and alcoholics. Bird and Tony were buddies. A street drunk, I learned, almost always has a buddy, someone to watch out for him, to make sure he isn't attacked or robbed when he's asleep.

Hogshead never came to meetings, but was sort of on the staff anyway. He was the wood gatherer. Hogshead was one of the ugliest people I've ever seen — his face was distorted, he was usually filthy, there was always slobber and food in his beard. Twice he vomited on me. It was an act of courage for me to shake his hand.

Extending his dirty hand in friendship was a money-making scheme of Hogshead's. When people would refuse to shake his hand, he could count on them to give him some "spare change" as guilt money. The park staff would often report, "Well, we cleaned up Hogshead today." That would be a victory. They would have taken him up to someone's hotel room, bathed him, and gotten him some clean clothes somewhere. Often, they had to delouse him. That took a special kind of commitment.

Occasionally, women and families would take up temporary residence in the park. Jan was a white woman who was romantically involved with Ben. She lived off a trust established for her by her family. When the reporter from the *Wall Street Journal* visited the park, Jan talked with her about inside tips. Tris was the daughter of my next-door neighbor in Bernal Heights. She would get kicked out of her house with her three children, and would land at the park. She would stay a few weeks, and then find her way back into her family.

Early on, the park staff trained me to respect their authority. My inclination was to walk into the park, say hello to everyone, and meander. The park staff made it clear that when I arrived, I was to report to them first — to see how things were going and find out if there were any problems. After about six months of staff meetings, I asked Ben to put on the agenda how the staff planned to deal with me when they felt I was acting inappropriately or in a racist manner. I sensed they were hesitant to challenge me and I wanted to call it out. I sat listening as they discussed the issue. We concluded that I was open to requests for change, that I knew I had not chosen racist attitudes, but had absorbed them in my upbringing. I did not want this handicap to interfere with our work together and was trying to learn to change. They offered to keep me posted when it came up and work it out with me. This precipitated about a month of individual discussions about this subject as I walked through the park, and enabled several important discussions later on.

Glide Church never paid anyone to clean the park. The people who used it kept it clean, though sometimes it took some prompting if they had let things slide for a few days. Once in a while I'd come in and say, "Oh, my, the park doesn't look so good today. Do you think you guys are going to — ?" and they'd say, "Oh, we haven't started yet today! All our workers aren't here yet!" And if I picked up a shovel or a broom, somebody would just come and take it away from me. How would you feel if somebody came into your house and said, "Oh, I don't think your house is very clean, I'll just get to work and clean it"?

Different issues concerned the staff at different times. An early one was territoriality: some people had started pitching tents and others had been camping out in the sleeping tubes. We'd intended the tubes for transients, not full-time occupants, and so we decided to remove the tubes altogether. (There had also been public pressure against them; they were a disturbing monument to homelessness.)

But the biggest issue was always violence. How should it be dealt with in the park? A staff member would say, "I got hit on the side of the head when I was trying to break up a fight." Or a staff member had been seen instigating violence; what should be done? So we'd reenact the situation, with staff members taking the different roles. We also used role-play to explore other potentially violent situations. The staff concluded that when there was trouble, they had to stick together; they *all* had to go to defuse the situation. For me, it was wonderful to see some of the people who had perpetrated violence listening to concerns about that violence in a problem-solving atmosphere, and learning nonviolent techniques for resolving conflict. And the rate of violent crimes on that block actually went down during the tenure of the park.

Before the park existed, people had congregated on Sixth Street without any collective purpose. Our job as organizers was not to define their purpose but to help it emerge. We tried to create opportunities for them to develop their collective power and purpose without controlling them, to trust that they were more knowledgeable about their own lives than we were. We viewed ourselves not as the people with the answers, decisions, or solutions, but as facilitators, enthusiasts, support people. At the beginning, I filled this role with Gene and Alvin; but after six months, they were assigned to other work.

Traditional social change organizing assumes that the organizer is the resource — the person who makes things happen, solves problems, doles out the "goodies." At the park, the organizer's job was to help people look at their own resources, to look for the common resources available to deal with any need. "Whom do we know in our network who can help us with this?" was a frequent question. The organizer was a mirror, reflecting back to them what was presented, and helping them figure out how to get things done that *they* wanted done.

Because the people felt it was their park, they took control and always made suggestions to improve it or to solve problems. When we were building the park, street people helped out with work and advice. "Listen, I used to mix cement for a living — let me show you how." During one of the spring refurbishings, the clay we put down on the basketball court got lumpy. We tried everything, but couldn't figure out how to fix it. A park newcomer came over and said, "I know a little about this. Could I have a rake?" He smoothed it out (and later joined the staff).

Staff members took their work more and more seriously, and after working together for many months, they decided that members could not come to meetings drunk. There was no single incident that led to this decision; it had become apparent that disruptions and irrelevant digressions were instigated most often by members who were drunk.

When people take on a responsibility, they see themselves in a new way. A street person joined the staff of Sixth Street Park and became responsible for a corner of the world. She agreed to help keep the park clean, to take care of sick people, to break up fights. We helped this self-consciousness evolve by celebrating staff members' birthdays in the park (complete with cake), by giving out official staff jackets to members each year, and by issuing park staff I.D. cards.

There were also park membership cards for other park users. Staff members alone were authorized to hand these out and sign the member's card. These cards were a vehicle for bringing the park rules to everyone's attention. Those rules, set out by the staff and printed on the cards, were:

> No violence in park.
> No openly visible weapons.
> All garbage in garbage cans.
> No gambling.
> No fires except in the cooking area.
> No shooting up or sale of drugs.
> Curb your dog.

While it lived, the park played an important role in the city and the world; it was a point of connection with the down-and-out. It allowed outsiders to bring their resources directly to street people. I was amazed at the number of people who'd drive up and drop off a case of milk, or a bunch of sandwiches, or a load of wood for the fire. From time to time, someone would drop by to sit in the sun and talk about their memories of being down-and-out. They would often bring a bottle of wine, some fruit, or something to eat. One day, a young career woman, dressed in a suit and high heels, stopped by to drop off some homemade brownies in a box tied with a ribbon. Around Christmas one year, there was a story on TV about the park. A few days later, a big box of sleeping bags arrived from Los Angeles. Someone had seen the story, felt a connection with the people in the park, and made an appropriate contribution. That anonymous person's thoughtfulness made winter more bearable on Sixth Street.

Relations between street people and the police also improved somewhat. Captain Forni of the district police station came to a staff meeting and listened to complaints about a new beat cop who would go into the park, ask for winos' bottles, and pour their wine out on the ground. Captain Forni agreed to explain to the cop that drinking was legal in the park. It was a friendly meeting — there was even talk of a softball game between cops and street people (which never happened), and I remember Bird asking Forni, "If I get arrested, can I call you and get out?"

At another meeting, I asked the staff what they thought about nuclear power. Everyone spoke against it. So I invited them to a rally outside Pacific Gas and Electric headquarters in San Francisco, to protest the Diablo Canyon nuclear plant. We all had a wonderful time.

Sixth Street Park opened up new possibilities in the relationship between a society and its untouchables. This excitement was picked up in early stories on the park in the *Los Angeles Times, New York Times, Wall Street Journal,* and many television shows. For all our hopes, the park did not, as some might have wished, solve the problems of the people on Sixth Street. It was no panacea. What was happening in the park was not so much a solution as progress. The realities of life on the street stayed pretty much the same for the people.

Because of the construction of a huge convention center in San Francisco, many poor people were forced to move from Third and Fourth Streets to Sixth Street. They will probably continue to be moved as real estate values in the central city climb. Many street people had grown up near the park — the neighborhood was their home turf. Others had come from out-of-town and made friends at the park. About half of those who frequented the park were on welfare or received some form of government assistance. Many could not receive aid as they had no address.

Many were shockingly young — in their twenties and thirties, though their faces looked much older. Quite a few park regulars were Vietnam veterans who had not been able to put their lives together after the war. For some men, there had been a major disappointment in family or work, and they had not landed on their feet. Families were a part of the park, too. It seemed that many of them had hit hard times and decided to come to California to escape creditors, angry family, or very painful situations. A few said that the death of a child had forced them on the road to escape memories. Then, something had happened; they had not brought enough money for the deposits and rent of an apartment. Cut from their social roots, they did not know where the resources were in their new community.

Some lived in residential hotels, but many slept on the street. If you don't have a place to go, rain is a real problem. And cold. And where do you get clean? Where do you cook? Where do you have sex? These are the kinds of problems that people deal with when they have no place to live. And there are more and more people who live this way in our cities.

Why are people homeless? I am not sure how the people who are poor came to be known as homeless people. Homes are not so much the problem as is poverty, and specifically the systematic racism that dries up hope and confidence and denies opportunity. This is the primary cause of people living on the streets, swept up by numbing alcohol and drugs. But in terms of the housing issue, there aren't many vacant living spaces, and those that do exist are expensive. Even a small room in a residential hotel cost $200 to $250 a month in the 1980s, and costs even more now. Street people don't have money for both housing and their addiction. Getting drugs or alcohol is a more pressing moment-to-moment need, allowing them to obliterate their sensitivity to the cruelty in the world, so that it's somehow tolerable to sleep outside. It's a self-perpetuating cycle.

Being poor is a full-time job. You spend your days traveling to the soup kitchen and waiting in line, often for hours; trying to get welfare and food stamps — more long lines. If you don't have a birth certificate and an address, you can't get welfare. You are always looking for something that will keep you going for another week or another day — a safe place to sleep, a few dollars you can pan-handle or steal.

If people at the park were representative, street people have a par-ticular difficulty holding on to money. They do not have the talent for hoarding. Of course, they don't have much to begin with, but they seem unable to put their own needs above others'. If a street person has only a dollar and a friend comes up and says, "I need a dollar," and has a good reason, he'll more than likely give her the dollar. Since they're in a situation where need is common, they're always broke. And yet they're sustained by each other. Multinational corporations make more by pooling their money. At the bottom, it's exactly the reverse: street people pool their non-money, and all have less. And they steal from each other more often than they steal from outsiders. People become increasingly desperate toward the end of the month, as money from welfare and disability checks runs out.

Bea, one of several women who were park regulars, had continual problems with money. A gutsy, middle-aged black woman, Bea was strikingly good-looking when she was healthy. For a while, she kept her money in a metal box, which she held under her arm. But when she'd fall asleep, someone would inevitably take the box. Then, she put her money in her shoes, but they started taking off her shoes. There was really no safe place for her to keep any money.

But the despair isn't only economic. At its center is a hopelessness about life, which has become painful, degrading, out of control. Bea was always saying, "Things are getting worse" — that was almost a mantra for her. She was in the hospital on her birthday and was struggling with the question of whether she wanted to live. The doctor had told her she would be dead within a year if she didn't stop drinking. And she was about to go on trial for robbing a police decoy in the park. Getting sobered up looks good on your record. So she stopped drinking, then started again, and finally went into detox. It's a familiar cycle.

The hospitals play a central role in the lives of street alcoholics. Many go into the hospital around Christmas time, because they know they'll receive some attention there, get a chance to get clean, be out of the rain and cold, and get fed decently. Sometimes, the boost from a stay in the hospital can help an alcoholic change his life.

Street people experience sharp ups and downs in their lives. When they are up — a little chunk of money, a barbecue — they are really up. And when they are down — arrested, beaten up, very sick — they are really down.

And death is always close by. One day, I heard that Godfather had left the hospital against the doctor's wishes and had come back to the park to die. I found him in a chair by the fire, slumped over, sleeping. The people sitting nearby explained that several weeks earlier Godfather had burned his leg at the fire. Gangrene had developed and Godfather had gone to General Hospital to have it looked at. They prepared to cut off his leg. Godfather was not in agreement about the amputation. They told him he would die if the leg wasn't amputated. It was at that point that he chose to return to the park to die, whole, among his friends.

Both the park staff and the church staff struggled with the question of responsibility. What should our position be? My own inclination was to try to talk him into going back to the hospital. But the park staff convinced me that we should respect his choice and help him live his last days in the park as he wanted to. I contacted the people at the neighborhood health center down the street from the park, and they agreed to visit Godfather once a day and to change his dressing.

The staff had to have extra meetings to plan for Godfather's care. In one meeting, they got to talking about how much they loved Godfather, and how they would miss him if he died, and several of them started to cry. Godfather stayed in the park all day and all night. Park regulars and staff covered him with blankets, coats, whatever they could find to keep him warm. They hustled up food from one of the free food places and cooked for him on the open fire. And somehow, with all this intensive care, Godfather recovered. He retained his leg, and he roamed the Sixth Street area for another three years, until he died in his sleep in a residential hotel room.

There are deaths on Sixth Street. There are shootings and stabbings, but more common are the deaths from cirrhosis and other ailments resulting from alcoholism and life on the street. When I got back from blockading the nuclear power plant at Diablo Canyon in the fall of 1981, I found out that Hogshead had just died. We had a funeral for him at the park. Glide ordered a spray of flowers, and we put it in the raised part of the park. Street people made a semicircle of empty Thunderbird bottles, and put a full bottle in the middle. In front was Hogshead's cup — he always drank from a cup. People made short speeches. One said, "It's going to be colder around here, without Hogshead to get our firewood." Someone else hoped that wherever Hogshead was, he was in a happier place than he'd been on earth. For a long time after the funeral, when they passed the bottle, they'd pour a little in the flowers for Hogshead. Those flowers seemed to last forever.

Hogshead's official name was Clarence Thigpen, and years before he had been a jazz pianist; I heard he'd played with Miles Davis's quartet. People used to say, "Hogshead would get his life together if only he could play." One day, someone brought a piano to the park. Hogshead sat down at the piano, and he couldn't play anything. He started crying and said, "I'm too far gone. I'm never going to be able to play again."

I base my work on the assumption that people are more likely to allow the helpful, socially responsible part of themselves to emerge if they are treated with respect and confidence. But it will rarely emerge when people are under attack or in deprived situations. When people are downtrodden and everything around them is bleak, reflecting poverty and misfortune, the spark of hope inside them doesn't receive the fuel of outside confirmation.

Sixth Street Park nourished that spark of hope. It was designed to be a beautiful environment in a desolate neighborhood, a place where street people could work together for the common good. The park became its own subculture — an alternative context where our society's outcasts could articulate to each other their caring; could notice and appreciate their socially responsible behavior; and could call forth the best from each other. It was a context that increased the odds that people would act from their dignity, rather than from the violent, desperate part of themselves. But it only increased the odds; it didn't eradicate violence and despair.

It was exciting to watch people at the park take on important work for the common good. Bubba was a big, tough bully when he came to Sixth Street Park. He joined the park staff after the staff had talked to him about not being violent in the park. And he began to use his size, his street smarts, and his hidden gentleness *for* people. He loved cooking for others in the park over the fire, started working on a place for park people to get mail, and became a self-appointed social worker for people looking for clothes, housing, or jobs. One night, Bubba saw a man stabbing a woman in the parking lot next to the park. He started shouting in a pained voice, "Ooh! Ooh! That's too much stabbing — too much!" This broke the concentration of the attacker, who took off; his victim survived.

Mickey was a merchant marine whose commitment was to clean up fleas, lice, and venereal disease. He would take people to a hotel room near the park, put them in the bathtub, and clean them up. The local health center gave him a gallon of delousing shampoo every now and then. He also washed people's infested clothes. He was an alcoholic, in no better shape than the others, but he made a contribution to improving the world around him.

At one meeting, I learned that the park staff had been taking care of a six-month-old baby. His father had brought him by and asked them to care for the child. So someone at the park who was squatting in the nearby Pontiac Hotel cleaned up a room for the baby. The staff pooled their money to buy food, and they had developed a wild fantasy of raising the child themselves. So far, they'd taken care of him for three days; the reason the issue got on the agenda was that they were worried the baby might be sick. I went to the park, where the baby was lying in the sun. He was a charming, bright-eyed baby. The two who took the most interest in him were Bird and Tony — the toughest, "baddest" guys in the park, the two I thought the least likely to have a soft spot in their hearts. When a nearby drunk made some profane remark, one of them hissed: "Not in front of the baby!" After considerable discussion among the staff in and outside of the meeting, the child was returned to his father within a few days.

A particular event crystallized in my mind why this park was useful for the society at large. One day, outside the park but within view, a mugger tried to rob and beat up a woman. Someone in the park, one of the less regular visitors, saw the crime in progress and went out and broke it up. The mugger was not happy about this interruption of his economic activity. He went across the street to the liquor store and bought some toilet bowl cleaner. Then, he returned to the park and threw it in the face of the man who had interrupted his crime. The lye burned the man's face, blinding him. The park staff called an ambulance, and he was taken to the hospital.

This event had been seen by several members of the park staff, and one of them, Tony, had gotten some acid on his sleeve as he tried to break the fight up. The culprit was arrested, and the district attorney wanted members of the staff to identify the acid-thrower at a hearing. This posed an ethical dilemma for the staff, especially Tony. Although he was very upset about the incident, coming forward as a witness for the state was another matter. Tony was a parole violator, and appearing in court could expose him to penalties — including more jail time. The staff discussion went on all morning; all the rights and wrongs were examined. Listening to it, I thought that this was one of the best and most unlikely places in the city for such a scrupulous ethical discussion. Tony finally decided to testify, and the group went along to support him (also to make sure he didn't chicken out, I suspect). Tony was very proud of his civic-mindedness, and as it turned out, they didn't check his record.

I would like to be able to tell you that Bubba, Mickey, Bird, Tony, and the other staff members never did another cruel thing, never mugged another passerby, never beat up another fellow street person — but this is not so. The park supported socially responsible behavior and raised ethical issues; but the situation on Sixth Street was still desperate. And much of the despair became manifest in violence.

Although violence is a part of all our lives, it's more apparent on Sixth Street, where the anger and hostility of people at the bottom of society are always in the air.

I had few direct brushes with violence at the park. The class differences between the park people and me were always evident, and they caused a lot of pain all around. Frequently, people tried to hustle money from me; my standard response was, "Do I look like the Bank of America?" But sometimes my relationship was such, and the need for the money so important, that I would slip something to the person asking for the money out of sight of the others, or make arrangements for help from Glide, the church that sponsored the park.

One day, I was talking with a bunch of guys in the park, who thought that I could help them out of their difficulties. I told them that I believed in them, in their capacity to move their lives in a positive direction. "But, you know," I added, "if I sold everything I have, and gave you all the money, things wouldn't be significantly better here." And I told them how it pained me that things were so difficult for them.

When the discussion was over and I had started walking away, Bird stood up and said, "What if I pulled this gun out?" When he said that, his tone changed. Bird's hand was in his pants pocket, and I could see a small gun outlined there, its handle poking out. On some level, this was the moment with Bird I had been dreading. I had heard from social workers in the area how he had threatened them, and scared them to the point that he was prohibited from coming into their buildings.

"What would you do *then*?" I asked forcefully.

He said, "Put it back in my pocket."

And then I said, in my best schoolteacher voice, "Well, then, just *leave* the gun in your pocket!" I turned my back and started walking casually to my car, all the time thinking: He's going to blow me away.

I got in my car, started it up, drove around the block, and parked. And then I just shook and cried, I was so scared.

Another time, someone pulled a shiv on me. A shiv is a piece of metal sharpened on both sides, and it was right at my neck — I could feel the cold metal. The guy holding it, someone I'd never seen at the park before, was saying in his toughest voice, "I could use this on you, or anybody, at any time."

And I — again the schoolteacher — said, "Oh, you should give that to me. We can't have knives in the park." Nothing happened for an instant, and then, taking the shiv away, I said, "I'll just put this in my pocket." And I did it. I stood there for a long time, just chatting, as if taking the shiv had been the most natural thing in the world.

But I was very conscious of the weight of the cold metal in my hand in my pocket.

I think that if I had acted afraid — either with Bird or with the shiv man — I might have been killed. They were taking a certain posture ("I'm the baddest of the bad"), and if you take the complementary posture ("I'm afraid of you"), then they may well kill you. You have confirmed the role they're playing. But if you take the position of being absolutely in control of the situation — that this is *not* to happen — then you kind of out-authority them. Sometimes, this works.

This dynamic is at play all the time. When you're afraid, people sense it. Imagine how it makes them feel. If you walk into the park and I see that you're afraid of me, then who am I? Someone to be afraid of. You've confirmed my self-image; therefore, give me your wallet.

We must be very clear about this transaction. Each player in it is displaying only one aspect of himself. The postures we take toward each other do not only speak about us as individuals; they also express the interaction between us. We are always signaling to each other: this is who I am; this is who I think you are to me. This is my intent, and my expectation of your intent.

So before going to the park, I would always check to see whether I was disturbed, preoccupied, or distracted. In those states of mind, I was more vulnerable, more likely to be a victim. Going into the park could also be more dangerous if I had unresolved difficulties with anyone. Once, early in the park's history, I had asked Tony to stop collecting rent on the sleeping tubes, and to stop dealing drugs in the park. Our discussion degenerated into a screaming argument. Realizing later that losing my temper had been a mistake, and that violence was one of Tony's few options for retaliation, I decided to stay away from the park for about a week to let the situation cool off. And occasionally, I intuitively sensed I shouldn't go to the park; I felt danger lurking. But when I had my wits about me, I almost always felt safe in the park, even at night, when I would occasionally swing by to see how things were going around the fire. I came to trust that the staff would protect me. They wanted the park to survive, and violence would jeopardize that.

After Bird had threatened to pull the gun on me, I told Glide's minister, Cecil Williams, about the incident. The following day, Cecil dropped into a park staff meeting and took Bird aside for a few minutes. When the meeting was over, Bird came up to me and said he wanted to talk with me. He took me around the corner, into a hallway, and I saw tears in his eyes. Bird said he was sorry that he had frightened me; he would never do that again. And he asked me to forgive him.

I think things had just gotten away from Bird that day. He had gotten overwhelmed and was grabbing at any straw to solve problems. Maybe it helped his feelings of helplessness to reduce another being into that same state. When he apologized, he said, "I didn't mean to hurt you." I know that's true. Even if Bird had blown me away — which I've always considered was possible — he wouldn't have wanted to hurt me.

Many of the people at the park stopped drinking for short periods, but only a few sustained their sobriety. One successful quitter was Ben, a soft-spoken, physically strong man with tremendous integrity and leadership ability. He had been a professional clarinetist. Ben came to see me when his sister died. We talked for a long time, and he cried. The fact that his sister had died from an alcohol-related disease scared Ben enough to stop drinking.

Henry, Ben's buddy, was already on the wagon. A rotund, pleasant-faced man, Henry would sit in the park, silently watching everything that went on. Nothing escaped his vision; his presence had a way of pulling people to a higher standard of honesty. Henry came to be known as "Buddha."

Then, Askew went into the hospital, and he decided to quite drinking, too. As he told it, "I thought about the park. I knew I had my work to do, and I couldn't do it if I was drinking as much as I was."

So Ben, Henry, and Askew stayed at the park, and their drinking friends agreed to support their abstinence. But sober, the three of them saw the park differently. Ben said, "I used to use alcohol to numb myself. Now that I'm not drinking, I see the pain of this place, and it's killing me."

So we started an irregular group for people who were feeling the pain of the park. This "sensitives group" included Ben, Askew, Henry, Karen (the new park organizer), and me. We used the sensitives group sometimes to talk with other staff members, if they were behaving badly at the park, and sometimes to provide personal help (Henry needed support to stop eating candy bars and ice cream). But mostly, we talked with each other about how hard things were on Sixth Street, and what we felt we could do. Ben, Henry, and Askew felt stuck. They were drawn to the park and to their friends, but it was cold and rainy there, and painful. Bea and Godfather were in especially bad shape. I began to understand how complex the change was for the three guys on the wagon. They had stepped outside of their old context, and seeing it from the new vantage point was excruciating. They wanted the situation to change for everyone at the park.

When you outgrow a situation, you sometimes have to divorce yourself from it to consolidate your gains. In the sensitives group, we discussed the idea of offering a clear conduit out of the park for those who needed it. But as a group, we decided that their leadership was important, both for themselves and for the park.

By its very existence, the park made the same pain that the sensitives felt accessible to the larger community. In July 1982, a reporter for the *San Francisco Examiner* wrote a long exposé attacking the park. He was so comfortable attacking the park that we considered that some people at Glide may have asked him to begin a process that would allow the church to put the park down. The story was primarily an expression of the reporter's own anger and frustration with the plight of poor alcoholics and street people. The problems he described — violence, drug dealing, alcoholism, and illness — had existed on Sixth Street before, but the park made them more visible. It became easy for the *Examiner* and for politicians and city officials to blame the park, to make it a scapegoat. The *Examiner's* large office was one block away from the park. While crime had gone down on our block, it had gone up on the *Examiner's* block. Did anyone suggest that the *Examiner* be destroyed because of this fact?

Perhaps we had been set up for the attack by all the glowing newspaper stories that had come out when the park opened. These stories had reflected journalists' desires to get connected with street people, with untouchables, and to know that their situation was finally being attended to. What a relief! Street people are real people, and this park is going to take care of them! We played along with the media hype, thinking positive publicity could only help the park. But it created unrealistic expectations.

Our failure to articulate clear and realistic goals for the park was a major mistake. We could have set as a goal a small reduction in crime in the area, rather than standing silently by, while reporters projected their magical thinking on the park. We could have publicly acknowledged that alcoholics on Sixth Street would continue to die. And we could have used the early newspaper articles to demonstrate how difficult and often miserable life on the street is, rather than allowing a romantic "Aren't street people wonderful?" attitude to prevail.

Another major mistake was our failure to develop strong support for the park — including financial support — outside of Glide Church. Because it was under Glide's wing, the park was always dependent on the man at the top of the church hierarchy, Rev. Cecil Williams. And seeing life on Sixth Street was very painful for Cecil. In fact, he rarely went to the park. When he did, he saw people much like himself — middle-aged black men — and they were in very bad shape. One could especially come to that conclusion if one weren't with them day-to-day, seeing also the small and sometimes subtle victories.

Cecil would often say, "We can't absolve our guilt by going down there." I personally think that while guilt is useful to keep us from doing bad things, doing anything on the basis of guilt is bogus. For a sensitive man like Cecil, the park must have brought up feelings of helplessness.

But the key to the park's demise was political. In the fall of 1982, after the *Examiner* article had been published, the park came under increasing attack. The surrounding neighborhood was beginning to be "cleaned up" for the 1984 Democratic convention, and a rumored large office complex, which still, in 1999, has not emerged. Mayor Feinstein wanted the vice-presidential nomination. She asked Cecil to get rid of the park, which would make the existence of street people visible to the Democrats visiting the city. Cecil caved in to her request — I don't know what he was promised. He offered jobs to Ben, Henry, and Askew. When any argument developed about closing the park, he would say, "Why are you listening to this white woman? What kind of black men are you?" Staff members were confused and felt betrayed; they did not want to lose the park, but knew no way to fight it. I, too, felt deeply disappointed. But looking at all the factors involved, I concluded that the park couldn't be saved, that it was too late to organize the park as an autonomous entity.

The park was fenced off, and all the tables, the shelter, and the drinking fountain were bulldozed. The destruction of the park took only one day. It is now a parking lot. The community ethic and sense of confidence that we had so carefully nurtured were destroyed. A place of beauty and dignity on Sixth Street was gone.

As I look back on the work we did at Sixth Street Park, I think about the street people, who at first seemed to me so different from people I knew. They are alcoholics in a society filled with alcoholics, many of whom work in the high-rise office buildings not far from Sixth Street. They are people prone to violence living in a violent society, a society that does violence to them daily. I do not know what keeps poor people from killing rich people en masse. The rich and the poor remain separate; they only *seem* unconnected.

Sometimes, I worried that in making my peace with the life on Sixth Street I had settled for less than was possible. Mind you, I was always thinking about how to make structural changes that would release these people from the poverty that held them down. But Askew, for instance, had left his wife, family, and a 9-to-5 white-collar job. Even though his present life didn't seem the kind I would want to live, I came to accept his choice. Someone else might come and save the people on Sixth Street. I was there to honor who they were and help them solve the problems *they* perceived in their lives, not the problems *I* had with their lives.

Friends would often ask me, "Isn't it hard to work at Sixth Street Park?" or "Isn't it painful to be around those people?" Certainly, it was hard. Certainly, it was painful. It was painful to see the illness, the addiction, the people out in the cold and rain. But what hurt most was to hear people say that they felt useless to their families and to the society. I think that was why they thrived on staff, wearing their staff jackets. They had an important role.

The pain of working at Sixth Street Park was the pain of connection, the pain of living people. Before I worked there, I had felt a different kind of pain — the pain of separateness, of being cut off from a whole group of my neighbors. That is perhaps more of a numbness than a pain. And now that I no longer work at the park, I feel a third kind of pain — the pain of a broken connection. Of course, I still meet friends from the park on the street from time to time. And when it starts to get cold in November, I know they are out in that cold. I am still connected to them in many profound ways.

Since the demise of the park, most of the leaders among the staff have gone through rough times. Ben has been in and out of mental hospitals, with drug problems. Askew and Henry have taken up drinking again. I've lost touch with Bird, Tony, Bea, and the others.

I have heard about several parks designed on the model of Sixth Street Park: in Oakland, Los Angeles, Oklahoma, Sweden.

But although there are increasing numbers of poor people in our country, their concerns are often disregarded. And I continue to wonder: How will we as a society learn to respect our untouchables? How will we create a context where they can respect themselves? When will we overturn our caste system? It seems we are moving in the opposite direction just now.

Chapter 6

Political Earthquakes: Peoples Temple and the Moscone–Milk Murders, 1978

THE ATOM BOMB ushered my generation into this world. Albert Einstein said, "The unleashed power of the atom has changed everything save our modes of thinking..." We knew ever since adolescence that we were the generation that must create new ways of thinking.

We came to our adulthood in the 1960s, knowing that we were not safe if our challenge to the status quo of the US government became too powerful. Members of our generation in other Western countries had the same experience. We saw what happened to John and Robert Kennedy, Martin Luther King, Malcolm X, the students at Kent State and Jackson State. It was a paradox: we had to change our way of thinking; and yet if we did, we would put our lives at risk. It was an excruciating environment — filled with conflict — in which to grow up.

Like many of my peers, I was looking for answers to profound social questions. It was easy to see that new ways of living and adapting to change were needed. Looking for models of change, and for ways of developing community, I studied utopian communities in the US I looked abroad for models, too. I studied Chinese education, and was engaged by the idea of mixing hard physical work with intellectual work. In the early 1970s, I traveled to rural and urban communities in China, where I saw communities experimenting with different ideas of social cohesion and change. I tasted the fear of experimentation and change in China, as well as the enthusiasm. I never knew how genuine that enthusiasm was, given the pressure people were under when talking to visitors. I also investigated interesting experiments in education and change in Mexico. My imagination was challenged to think about new ways in which our own society could change.

After observing many of my generation having fallen into political, spiritual, psychological, or lifestyle experimental groups, I wonder why I did not join the Moonies, Synanon, or a spiritual living group. I asked a friend who was in one such group, and she said she thought I was too stubborn and independent-minded.

I participated in a psychological group process for a while, and saw up-close how having a single powerful teacher, with no open elective process, could harm individuals. From that negative experience, I determined that three things were important to me: democratically elected leaders, respect for dissent and those who disagree, and how gently people are allowed to enter and leave a group. Also important is how a group "thinks together" and makes decisions about policy or action issues. Voting is not the only thing about democracy that I treasure, but also the openness of the decision-making process.

Upon returning from China, I was curious about communism because of its lofty concern for equality on both racial and class lines. However, in the I-Hotel I had a chance to see the practices of these groups, and they seemed oppressive to me. Truth-telling did not seem to be a high priority. How these groups hassled each other, how they found it convenient to be critical with little supporting evidence, kept me away from many feminist and progressive groups. I ended up staying close enough to know what the key issues and developments were, but not so involved that I had to subject my entire life to intergroup warfare.

San Francisco, my adopted home town since the early 1960s, is one of the areas in the US where social experimentation is an ongoing affair. I watched for groups to emerge that had alternative visions, and that put their lives behind social experiments. I wondered if I would find a group that would inspire me to see a different way that social networks could be organized to challenge the stagnant social structures I saw all around me.

So I followed with interest, in the early 1970s, newspaper articles about Peoples Temple, which painted a picture of a social movement aimed at helping the poor and challenging people to live beyond the isolation of race. I had first read about Peoples Temple several years earlier, when the entire church in Indianapolis moved west to Ukiah, California, to avoid radiation fallout from an anticipated nuclear war. I thought it strange that these people really believed they could be safe anywhere in a nuclear war.

I have long been interested in the use of social fear and insecurity to manipulate people into doing things they would not normally do. In my adolescence, reading about how Nazis used fear to get people to do things they would normally reject propelled my interest in social insanity. At the root of this kind of insanity is apocalyptic thinking, one of the crazy chips in our social motherboard. I smelled the potential for social insanity as I observed how Jim Jones used fear about nuclear war to get a whole church to make such a major move.

Social insanity was at the root of Nazism and is often involved in the creation of wars, riots, and ethnic violence. In the 1990s, the root cause of the social insanity that is buried in the overdeveloped countries is the fear of loss of pleasure and comfort. Through our fears, we are manipulated by our society into doing things we would not normally do — work too hard; endure a very narrow spectrum of ideas in our media; allow our government to go to war, diminish our civil rights, and cut government services.

One of the first signs of social insanity is the lack of open information systems and the limitation of genuine participation in group decision-making. It seemed to me from what I read about Peoples Temple that democracy was not present in the group's decision making. In normal times, social insanity is latent in a well-functioning society. But it does not take much to spark it into a raging fire, as we have seen in Yugoslavia.

I distinctly remember the day the Peoples Temple newsletter, *Peoples Forum,* was pushed under my door. I read it with genuine interest. They seemed to be doing great things in health care and education. The idea of black and white, young and old, poor and middle-class people working, living, and learning together was most attractive to me. I am white, although I prefer to think of myself as pink, and since becoming an adult I have longed to be able to connect with people who have values and traditions different from my own. It is frustrating that this is so difficult to achieve.

On the basis of what I read in the newsletter, I thought I would check out Peoples Temple. Before I went, I consulted my friend Faye, who I knew had been involved with the Temple. Perhaps she would accompany me, or at least advise me how best to approach it. Faye ran the corner launderette, and one day while doing my laundry, I mentioned to her that I was thinking of visiting the Temple. An ominous look flashed across her black face and she shook her head. "I wouldn't," she said, and mumbled something about having left the Temple. She was reluctant to talk further. The naked fear in her eyes was sufficient warning. I never went.

It turned out, however, that as a leader in the International Hotel struggle, I had ample opportunity to work with Jim Jones, the leader of Peoples Temple, and to see other Temple members in many public settings. Jim Jones was at this time a member of the San Francisco Housing Commission and participated in a number of decisions and campaigns involving low-cost housing, including the I-Hotel. He had gained political clout in San Francisco as a result of being able to deliver a crowd to any meeting or rally. Once, at a Housing Authority hearing devoted to the I-Hotel, over 200 members of Peoples Temple came to fill the audience.

As we fought in one of the most intense housing struggles in the history of San Francisco, Jim Jones made several passionate and compelling speeches. He spoke of his commitment to the hotel and of the just nature of our cause. Indeed, his commitment seemed real, because he repeatedly bussed Temple members to the rallies we staged; over 2,000 people from the Temple attended one rally. I looked at the faces of these people as they marched around the hotel with us. There were elderly black women and men, who looked as if they had known plenty of hard physical work, and young African American and European-descended middle-class idealists. It felt deeply satisfying to have so many black faces joining the primarily Asian and white faces in our demonstration. It was easy to identify the Temple members, because each carried the same size brown bag lunch. But when I asked members whether they were from the Temple, each responded as if programmed, "I am just a concerned citizen." This puzzled me, and though I continued to question them, I could not get any of these people to open up. And we were supposed to be allies!

Jim Jones sent representatives to several high-level meetings we held. We were told that he only sent his most respected leaders to deal with us. "I'll send you my right-hand men," he told us. It seemed odd to me that Jim Jones always sent white men. Where were the right-hand women? And where was this great interracial leadership structure? These men told me that there were many female leaders, and black leaders too. But I never dealt with one. Another odd thing was that the representatives were always falling asleep in meetings. When I asked them about it, they bragged in macho tones tinged with martyrdom, that they worked all night and regularly got only two or three hours of sleep. One thing was consistent — they were always passionate about how much they cared about us, and about all poor people struggling in the world.

Jim Jones was one of a small group of ministers from liberal churches in the city on record as supporting our cause. There were several periods when the sheriff legally could have evicted us. During one of those periods, a group of ministers — Jim Jones, Glide Church's Cecil Williams, and several others — swooped into the hotel late at night, saying they had heard that the sheriff was coming and they wanted to be with us. These ministers seemed to think that we could not do our work without their help. However, we had our own sources of information inside the sheriff's office and the police station; we had an evaluation system that allowed us to know when the sheriff was, in fact, coming. At the time, I guessed they were conducting a dry run to see how we would react. We calmly told them that our information was contrary to theirs, that we did not expect the sheriff that evening, and we did nothing. As Jim Jones left, I remember him pressing each of our hands with both of his big hands, earnestly saying, "I will be with you." Four hundred police officers did come in the middle of the night, on August 4, 1977. On that night, Jim Jones and Peoples Temple supporters were not with us.

Several weeks after the I-Hotel eviction, at a rally against the death penalty at San Quentin, I met two women I recognized from Peoples Temple. An article had come out in *New West* magazine about certain "strange practices" in the Temple — physical abuse and punishment, "bizarre sexual rules and practices." The article was critical of the treatment of children who had been adopted by the Temple. In the *New West* article, and later in the *San Francisco Chronicle*, there were rumors that a sizable proportion of Peoples Temple was moving to Guyana, South America. Never one to trust the press completely, I jumped at the chance to ask the women at the San Quentin demonstration what was really happening in the Temple.

One woman was black, the other white. I directed my questions to both women with my eyes, but no matter how hard I tried to have a three-way discussion, the black woman deferred to the white woman. I finally asked the black woman directly if she was under instructions not to talk. She said that it was not up to her to answer these questions. I felt suspicious of the racist dynamic in that conversation, and, as I looked back on my dealings with only white leaders, I wondered about the rosy picture of the races working together in equality in Peoples Temple.

My experiences with the Temple did not convince me that this organization was truly committed to honoring and integrating cultures. But, had I been a member of the Temple, I think I might have overlooked many things wrong with the community if I had seen different races and classes trying to work together. I could see myself having said, "Sure the Temple is messed up in a lot of ways, but there are some things that our community is doing better than the entire American society. We have our weaknesses, but we are just learning to challenge racism. Cut us some slack."

Simultaneously maintaining a supportive yet critical perspective of an institution is very difficult. For the most part, our society is unconscious of the nature of power. In a true democracy, everyone's opinions are voiced, recognized, and considered equally in the decision-making process. We understand democracy as a right to vote for people or issues that affect our lives directly. More importantly. I believe, is the ability of most people in a group or society to know how to participate in making changes; a transparency of decision making process. But democracy is so much more than voting.

Growing up in the US, we have little direct experience with participatory democracy in our family, our schools, or our workplaces. We have no experience of economic democracy. In school, we do not learn about class and race. Rather, the forces that really control our lives are large multinational corporations and banks, where democracy is unknown. The macro-decisions are made out of our view, and only the consequences are subject to public view. So, even though there is discussion of how to manage the consequences of the macro-decisions, there is only frustration and unempowerment, because we do not see, understand, or have a voice in controlling the base institutions and issues.

It seems this was also true in Peoples Temple. Jim Jones decided the larger issues. His decisions were not up for discussion and group decision-making. He espoused positive aspects of socialism and communism, linking them historically to the communal values of early Christianity. He did this in an extremely charismatic manner, but mixed with an odd, prurient relationship to sex and physical punishment.

One of the most common ways to reclaim individual power is to share one's experiences and opinions. This was not encouraged in Peoples Temple, nor was the institution structured to allow this exchange. It is common in progressive circles to experience organizations where individualism reigns, the center does not hold, and the group flies off into many factions. But in the case of Peoples Temple, the center held too much power; not enough was retained by the grassroots members. They did not select their leadership structure, members did not have enough information about the issues facing the organization, and there was no check on the power of Jim Jones himself.

But, I continue to wonder how the Temple members could have relinquished so much of their power to a leader like Jim Jones. I can only conclude that he focused the collective attention on the wrongs of US society as a whole, while the shadow within the Peoples Temple community remained unchallenged.

I heard little about Peoples Temple after everyone moved to Jonestown, Guyana. Every now and then, something would appear in the newspapers about the Concerned Relatives group, which worked in opposition to the Temple. And occasionally, an article or a program would discuss the "wonderful things happening down there." I fantasized about going to Guyana; what it would be like working to build a new community, a new farm, a new way of living. This romantic vision occasionally played across my mind. I did not act on these fantasizes, however; I had enough ambivalence from my own experiences with people from the Temple.

Then, the catastrophe struck. Congressman Leo Ryan and a few others had gone to Guyana to investigate charges of people being denied permission to leave Jonestown. He was concerned about treatment of the adopted children, as well as the condition of others who had been part of child custody fights. As he prepared to leave Jonestown with damning evidence, members of the Temple killed him; and this evidently prompted Jim Jones to call for each member to drink poisoned Kool-Aid.

Headlines in the newspapers screamed out increasingly higher numbers of people involved in the mass suicides in Jonestown. Eventually, over 900 bodies were counted and brought home in plastic bags.

What horrible days those were for me, for everyone I knew, and for my city. San Francisco that week, and for weeks after, was a city with death on its mind. The news didn't come to us in one fully developed blow. Each day's headlines were worse than the previous day's. Every day, like a wave of churning water, the news would knock me down and drag me into the depths. The numbers of dead mounted for days. Bizarre aspects of the Temple were reported in lurid detail, with emphasis on the sexual details of the drama.

The story began on Sunday, November 19, 1978. I remember that day particularly well, because I was preparing for a comedy show on the following Saturday. An important part of my performance is reading the newspaper and finding the subtle comedy in the human predicaments reported. "The newspaper is still your best comedy buy" was one of my mottoes.

As a professional comedian, I have never had a more difficult task than preparing and performing that particular show in San Francisco. I was at a loss trying to do the newspaper piece for Saturday night, November 25. I made some brief introductory remarks about how hard the week had been and focused on a few articles I had read in the newspaper.

One article, buried in the drama about the Temple suicides, was on the resignation of "the crazy supervisor, Dan White, who resigned from his position on the Board of Supervisors [which runs the city] and now wants to un-resign. We'll be hearing more about this story," I predicted, entirely too accurately.

My personal world turned upside down that week, and it really has not righted itself since in some important ways. I have tried to understand how this human disaster happened, and have found all my models of human nature and mass psychology totally unable to address the events in Jonestown. Did these people blindly commit suicide? And if so, how could they have done it? They were not crazy. For the most part, they were people much like my friends and family — people with high ideals, willing to work hard for a better life, risk takers who loved other people and cared very deeply about justice. How were the million choices made in each person's day-to-day life in Jonestown that ultimately allowed them to follow insane orders? How had they so given away their hope, their freedom, that they felt it better to kill their children than to fight for a better life for them? Had their own personal identity become so merged with the group identity that they could not extricate themselves at any single moment into the silence of aloneness? I could not comprehend the events behind the headlines.

One Peoples Temple practice I read about kept invading my thoughts. It seems that on several occasions, citizens of Jonestown were asked to practice the cyanide suicide drill to prove their loyalty to Jim Jones and his vision. It was a loyalty test, a game. These practice drills served to address individuals' objections, and ultimately to exorcise them when the ritual became reality. Actually, the final drinking of Kool-Aid must have been a small step in a very long march of de-individualization in each person's mind. Loyalty in excess is dangerous.

Playing with dangerous phenomena is something that has become commonplace in our age. Sometimes it is called risk-taking, sometimes facing a challenge. On the national and international scales, we play with nuclear weapons and chemicals that threaten not only our environment but also all life on the planet. The United States continues nuclear testing long after others have given it up, in part because the resistance would be so great if the government stopped and then decided to start again. Indeed, our government practices launching nuclear weapons partly to desensitize the people whose fingers activate the buttons. These people are conditioned to stop thinking the individual thoughts that might prevent them from performing an inconceivable act. Once individuals begin to think for themselves, they cannot act in accordance with crazy requests. Instead, they become "whistle blowers," and utter mutinous words in ways audible to those inside the system as well as outside. This is a step in reclaiming one's individual power.

The real challenge of our times is whether these words of resistance are uttered only in the private spaces of the confessional — religious or therapeutic — or whether they are expressed in places and ways that affect actual policies. People want to be clean, but not to pay the public price for that cleanliness; so they confess in private, and continue to commit the acts, trying their best to do the least harm.

Temple members had little experience thinking for themselves as individuals. The structure of the community did not allow them to think critically or to disagree with any aspect of the program. I understood from talking with Temple members that they lived in cramped quarters, and had little time to be quiet or to think. They had little sleep time during which to dream. How could they have been reflective about their situation when they had so little access to experiences that nurture human thought? On the radio, I heard the tape recording that was made in Jonestown as the suicides were happening. One woman spoke out strongly against the suicide act. She had not become the automaton that ritualized rehearsal creates. She was still thinking, reaching for her own power. But even for her it was too late. She was ignored.

As the news bombarded me with the tragedy that had occurred in Guyana, I speculated about the nature of leadership in Peoples Temple. Jim Jones had created a community in which he was the central, and sole, leader. He was surrounded by sycophants whose power was determined by how close they were to Jones. It must have been difficult for Jim Jones to maintain a realistic sense of himself in that context. Temple members called him Father, a role he played, unchallenged, in the family he had created.

Once Jim Jones moved to Guyana, he had no peers whom he could ask for advice, no one from outside his system who could question his decisions. There were also powerful drugs given to Jones by the Jonestown doctor, who had suspicious connections to the CIA. Did these drugs allow him to be manipulated himself? And was his weakened physical condition a reason why people around him did not powerfully challenge his distorted ideas?

I believe it would have been liberating for Jim Jones if others in Peoples Temple had reclaimed their power and challenged him. Jones might have fought hard to maintain his position as patriarch, but the challenge of more powerful leaders would have made the group dynamic healthier. And this would have created healthier individuals. To habitually ignore abuse is a disabling habit.

What in the system and in their own make-up prevented them from insisting on more accountability and democratic participation in decisions? What was it about the Temple members' experience in the US, and San Francisco in particular, that eroded their confidence in their responsibility for participating in the creation and maintenance of freedom? Because control is often so invisible in the United States, were they unable to discern Jones' manipulations and abuse. Or was it a relief to live under overt control after being so damaged by invisible manipulation? Did Jones use their self-hatred as a way of disarming resistance? I heard him rant and rave about his hatred of the United States. But I never heard that hatred mixed with any love for the country, the land, and its people. I do not remember him speaking with compassion for the struggle for freedom we fight in our land.

It is important to remember that when we fight for freedom, we fight for life itself.

I went to several political meetings that first week after Jonestown. Cecil Williams, a close acquaintance of Jim Jones', spoke out. Obviously in shock, he had little of substance to say; he could not say how close the two had been as political allies. No one dared to speak good words about Peoples Temple. It was now in vogue to discredit the Temple, no matter what one's relationship had been with it and with Jim Jones before the catastrophe. Before and after these meetings, people huddled together speculating that the US government did it because the Temple was getting ready to move to Russia, or that Jim Jones had been given mind-altering drugs, or had himself been brainwashed. Could there have been an agent provocateur? Many people concluded that radical thought isolated from its social context is dangerous to everyone involved, including the society from which the group comes. But there were so many questions, and we were so deeply in shock, that it was impossible to reach any conclusions.

Politicians who had engaged in mutual political backscratching with Jim Jones had started stepping away from him after the *New*

West article. Now, they ran for cover. To hear them talk was disgusting. Did these people think we had conveniently forgotten their connections with Jones? Now, they pretended they had never supported him, had never seen any merit in him or his work, lest any of the blood from the disaster contaminate their capes of power.

I remember stopping at a traffic light downtown one day after the tragedy; I watched the crowds of people cross the street in front of my car. Their faces seemed lost in thought; talking quietly, they shook their heads in disbelief. No one was smiling or talking animatedly. San Francisco had become an oversized funeral parlor. It was the Christmas season, yet people walking on the streets were not carrying packages. Shopkeepers reported a sharp drop in sales. How could you shop when there had been a death in your family?

Most of my friends in politics knew someone in Peoples Temple; most knew someone who was dead. For us, it was not just a tragic headline in the paper, about faceless "others" to whom we could ascribe insanity or whom we could describe as evil incarnate. No. These were people we had known and in some ways admired. They had put their values on the line. Rather than talking about how they hated poverty and racism, these people had taken on these issues in real ways in their lives. They had moved to Guyana with high hopes that in this new land they could build a more just society. There, they would be able to farm and live in peace. Now, only five years after the experiment had begun, they were dead — the work of their own hands?

The search for a place to bury the bodies took far too long. I was embarrassed that my culture could deny fellow human beings a decent place in the earth to lie in death. No one wanted any connection with this catastrophic event, with this group, or with the people who had lived and died for values in which they believed. Everyone washed his hands of the Peoples Temple blood.

Several other events in the aftermath of the catastrophe are an important part of my memories. I was building a home at the time of the suicides and was without a shower for a few months. I made arrangements to bathe down the street from my home at Synanon, another experimental, utopian community. Synanon had begun in San Francisco as a drug treatment program, but soon expanded to include all kinds of people. I remember meeting former Peoples Temple members from the San Francisco office who turned to Synanon for help following the suicides. I met the Temple's former public information officer there, and told him that I had considered sending a sympathy card at the time of the suicides, but had not. He said wistfully, "It would have been nice. No one sent anything very kind." The weekend following the suicides, I walked into Synanon's house on Potrero Hill to find everyone gathered in the living room, in a state of panic. An anonymous caller had informed them that a thousand drunken vigilantes were coming to storm Synanon. The wave against cults was so strong at the time that the members of Synanon obviously believed the call was real. Isolated in their own paranoia, they were terrified. Nothing actually happened, but I was not surprised when the group left the city within two years. Several years later, the bulk of the organization defected. Friends tell me that they gather from time to time and ask themselves about their time in Synanon. They can now say out loud that they lied in court, that they knew of illegal acts committed by members, which were denied publicly. They recognize the immorality of their collective acts and wonder how intelligent and well educated people could do such things. Our capacity as human beings to believe and follow wrong leadership is astonishingly real. We must always be wary about that.

The experimental communities in the city were not unique in feeling pressure at this time. Members of the city government and other leaders in San Francisco were also feeling exposed for their own connections with Jim Jones. He had attained political clout by helping liberals get elected and by delivering crowds to every cause in the city — all progressive and liberal leaders had been connected with him in one way or another.

The horror of Jonestown plunged all of San Francisco into emotional turmoil. Indeed, the existing system of values and ethics was completely disrupted. One friend, a psychologist, said it was as though the whole city had become "situationally insane." Everything was coming unglued. No one knew what to believe or why. It was a time of confusion, fear, and change that affected the whole city.

Other news continued to surface about "odd" things that had occurred in the Temple — physical punishment, Jim Jones' extramarital affairs, brainwashing, socialism, and homosexual practices. The newspaper also explained how fear of nuclear war and paranoia about US government repression was used to control people inside the Temple. It was a mixed bag: some of the reported experimental ideas seemed outrageous and cruel; but others, such as open relationships, creative sexual practices (heterosexual and homosexual), and socialism, were practiced and accepted by major sectors of the San

Francisco community. But such behavior and ideas intimidated other, more fundamentalist populations in San Francisco, because they conflicted with their own beliefs. As disorienting as the moments were for those of us who knew the situation, who could try to put the newspaper headlines into some human perspective, it must have been even more disturbing to those for whom the newspapers seemed like tabloids, appealing to their constricted, prurient side.

San Francisco is a city known for its freedom. A cosmopolitan city, it is proud of its tradition of tolerance of differing cultures, differing sexual lifestyles, and experimental ideas. One thing about tolerance — it must by nature be tolerant of intolerance. This is the contradiction built into tolerance.

Supervisor Dan White was one of the intolerant ones. San Francisco supervisors at this time were elected by district. Supervisor Dan White was elected from a working-class neighborhood composed primarily of families in single-family homes. A traditional family structure characterized his neighborhood: the father, the unquestioned head of the family, stopped at the corner bar for a beer on his way home from work; secrets were carefully guarded by the family code of honor.

Dan White was a native son from an Irish Catholic background. He had attended Catholic schools in San Francisco, fought for his country in Vietnam as a paratrooper, and served his city as a police officer and most recently as a firefighter. All his life he wanted to be "a good man." He was a civic-minded man who believed in the old-fashioned American way — its traditions and its conventional values. Homosexuality, socialism, interracial living, and experimental living were incomprehensible to him and to many of his constituents.

Prior to the week of daily news battering about Peoples Temple, Dan White resigned from his position on the Board of Supervisors. He had felt overwhelmed by the financial burden of supporting a growing family on a supervisor's salary. It became clear that his wife was suffering from exhaustion from caring for a new baby and working long hours at their fast food stand on Pier 39, a local tourist trap. White knew his salary as a supervisor would not cover his financial crunch, so he resigned without considering alternatives to or political repercussions of his action.

Dan White had little experience in the give-and-take of political life. The issues he was accustomed to addressing in his law enforcement, military, and firefighting careers were black and white. The gray of compromise, the two-way exchange of backroom decisions in City

Hall, were foreign to Dan White. Deep down, he felt they were wrong. Indeed, the morals not only of City Hall, but of the whole city, seemed to Dan White to have decayed. He complained that the new values he saw discussed in the newspapers were attacking his personal values. During this crazy, insane period, after his resignation and during the suicides in Jonestown, I think he felt his heterosexual, Boy Scout, nuclear family values betrayed by his community. In fact, he must have felt surrounded by an orientation he could not comprehend or control; an orientation he felt was epitomized by liberal mayor George Moscone, and gay activist Supervisor Harvey Milk.

White's resignation created havoc among his constituents and others who supported him: his buddies from the fire and police departments, his church, and his neighborhood. They had funded his election, worked for him; and now, when their mutual value orientation was under fire, he was deserting them. White was heavily pressured by his social context to reconsider his decision. Eventually, promises were made to help him with his financial problems if he returned to his position. Four days after he resigned, Dan While announced that he wanted his seat back.

Because Dan White often voted against the liberal political agenda, Mayor Moscone was not eager to reappoint him. Moreover, Harvey Milk, an openly homosexual supervisor whose opinion was respected by Moscone, made it clear that he opposed the reappointment. Rather than making an immediate decision, the mayor decided to seek legal counsel of the district attorney: could Dan White simply recall his resignation? The district attorney said the resignation must stand; however, the mayor could reappoint White to his old seat if he wished. So, the decision was returned to the shoulders of the mayor, who promised to think about his decision over the weekend. For most of us, the story of Dan White's resignation, though puzzling, was lost in the news about Jonestown.

Dan White received a call from a reporter on Sunday night informing him of the mayor's decision not to reappoint him. To White, the mayor's decision symbolized the final evil caused by a decadent society in which his moral values and conventional lifestyle had no place. The next day, just eight days after the initial shock of Jonestown, Dan White put his gun in his pocket and went to City Hall. In an insane city, Dan White acted out that insanity by eliminating those people attacking his way of life. He climbed through an open window in City Hall to avoid the metal detectors, walked into the mayor's office, and shot him.

I do not believe Dan White killed Mayor Moscone simply because he wanted his position back. I believed that in his own mind White had become a crusader for the values he understood and espoused. Continuing down the hall in his warrior pose, White killed Supervisor Milk. Through this action, in his personal war, Dan White dealt a severe blow to the liberal ideas he saw controlling the city.

I remember that Monday clearly. My work life at that time included designing furniture. That day, I was working in the furniture store when a friend called with the news that the mayor and Harvey Milk had been shot — by Dan White! I accused him of joking. Surely the world could not be any more insanely chaotic. But no! We turned the radio on and discovered that it was not a joke. I was stunned. With a certain resignation, I went upstairs, and in the privacy of my office, I put my head on my desk and wept. I cried for the horror of the past week — for the mayor, for Harvey Milk, for Peoples Temple, and for my city. We closed the shop and all the workers went to City Hall. There would have been no business that day anyway.

A quiet crowd stood numbly outside City Hall beside the pile of flowers accumulating on the steps. I needed to see firsthand what was really happening, so I entered the building and continued to the hallway outside the mayor's office, where several police were stationed. The place was familiar, because I had often been there to meet with the mayor while working on the I-Hotel. But this time, the atmosphere was thick and confused. People with grave faces, including the chief of police, went quickly in and out of the mayor's office. In the pressroom, I saw shock on the faces of the reporters I knew. Some smoked one cigarette after another as they gazed into space. Others just shook their heads, wrote, or talked softly.

Later that evening, together with thousands of other San Franciscans, I walked holding a lighted candle from Castro Street up Market Street to City Hall. The march was quiet, yet occasionally, above the nose blowing and sniffing, I heard singing, too. There had been too many deaths, and the dying was getting closer to home. It was a sad time for us all; hundreds of our fellow San Franciscans had died in Guyana, and now two others had died in City Hall, killed by one of the city's leaders.

The police who arrested and questioned White recognized him as a warrior fighting for "their" America, and for their values, which they believed had been overpowered by liberal ideals and strange practices. Agreeing on some level with Dan White's mission, they did not subject him to severe questioning. Even the justice system gave White an unreasonably light prison sentence: seven years, eight months for killing two public officials. Pent-up outrage exploded when the sentence was announced. Thousands of people rioted, burning police cars and smashing windows. In a strange and tragic turn of events, seven years after the Jonestown suicides, Dan White himself committed suicide after being released from prison.

Liberals in the city, and perhaps throughout the country, have never recovered from the one-two-three punch: Peoples Temple, Moscone, Milk. All dead, all killed incomprehensibly. My city, San Francisco, has become a more conservative city, a more serious city in the intervening years. It is still a city of innovative ideas, and a beautiful place to live and breathe. But I know few people who have many friends of a race different from their own, and fewer institutions whose mission is to create experimental communities to replace our isolation from each other and from consumer-driven capitalism. Other utopian living groups, such as Synanon and the Gurdjieff group, left the city for easier social pastures.

The new replacement mayor, Dianne Feinstein (who later became a US senator), announced that psychiatric help was available at Langley Porter Hospital for people deeply disturbed by the Peoples Temple catastrophe. Anyone suffering could go there. Still confused and plagued by nightmares after several months, I went for help. I thought if anyone had figured out the consequences of this disaster on our ideas about human nature and social psychology, it would be the therapists at Langley Porter. They would help me answer my questions, questions not only about what happened to those people, but about self-identity and human dignity. The people in Jonestown were in so many ways similar to my friends and me. If they could do this, what would my friends and I be capable of doing? Could we drink cyanide-laced Kool-Aid, too? What is a human being? Who am I? When I went to the hospital for help with these questions, however, the receptionist said they were only able to care for families of victims. Did they really think the rest of us weren't profoundly affected as well?

I wish I could have a nickel for each time I have sat in a car with progressive friends when the talk drifts to Peoples Temple. These discussions never come during the day, but late at night, after a few beers lower our guard, and we feel safe and close to each other. Quietly, tentatively, the questioning begins. What do you remember? Why did it happen?

The ramifications of our unanswered questions on our political ideas are hard to calculate, but I believe they are considerable.

Distrust of leadership is very high, which may account for the lack of visible progressive leaders in the city. Now, any group interested in alternative values is suspected of being a cult. Many secrets are still buried in Congress, in Guyana, in the recesses of the survivors' minds. Who killed Jim Jones? Why were so few bodies autopsied? Real fear exists of unearthing these secrets in order to suggest new answers — fear of opening old wounds, of finding the new answers unpalatable, or of finding no answers at all. The old answers and unanswered questions, however unsatisfying, were so painfully integrated into our lives that it seems easier to leave them alone.

Four years after the suicides, I was working in Sixth Street Park with an African American man named Ben. He was a street person and one of the most responsible people I have ever known. One day, after we had known each other for some time, our conversation turned to the Peoples Temple. When the subject first came up, he said, "Those people were really stupid." I replied that I had known some of them, and they had not appeared to me to be stupid. They had been idealists, who tried to do something important. He got quiet and replied, "Yes, I had a sister and a nephew down there. They weren't stupid. I just don't know what happened." He buried his head in his hands and sobbed. He had loved them so much, and had himself almost gone to Guyana because of what his family told him about the Temple. I think he was suffering from a form of survivor guilt. Why had he lived and not his relatives? He said his family just did not talk about it. They could not. It was too painful.

I understand. No one talked about it in my family of friends any more either. Talk stopped soon after the suicides. People just seemed to want the memories and questions to go away. It was as though a giant earthquake had hit, but clearing the rubble and rebuilding the structures had never happened. In fact, when the Loma Prieta earthquake occurred, we talked about it for months afterward, as we tried to make sense out of the event in our lives. We still talk about the earthquake. But the day the social earth moved in our lives is lost in silence. So, we are left with all the rubble of unasked and unanswered questions in the streets of our community memory.

What is it about our own life in the United States that encourages ordinary people to seek out leaders to follow into death? What role did government agencies play in the creation of Jones' insanity? How can institutions outside an insane group relate to it in a way not to encourage martyrdom? Even more important, how can we find healing and liberation in healthy groups and institutions?

How can we experience functional and dynamic democracy in our communities and economic institutions, so that we give birth to a citizenry knowledgeable about power and able to make things work in their lives? How do we create a flexible, open political culture, rather than fixed, rigid, and closed expectations?

In the days approaching the twenty-first century, there are few viable alternatives to rampant capitalism. Frankly, I miss having contending alternatives. How can each of us step outside of the blinding reality of an insane context and become dissidents without becoming vulnerable to rip-off leaders? What makes ordinary people follow bad leadership and do insane things? How can we hold what we believe in a life-affirming way and deny any belief that would call us to participate in death — our own death or that of any other life form? What is it in a social context that allows people to ask honest questions that liberate people? Ask yourself questions. Create new answers for yourself. Keep your questioning mind alert.

Chapter 7

The Hidden Member Of Our Family: Our Relationship to Nuclear Weapons, 1978–85

W HEN YOU BUILD a house yourself, it always feels a little more fragile than other buildings you visit. You look at a wall and see the individual two-by-fours and sheetrock. You know what's keeping the windows from falling out, how the siding is nailed in place. You remember pushing that wall up. This is how I felt about the house I built and lived in on Potrero Hill in San Francisco.

One day in 1980, I was sitting in my living room reading the newspaper. President Carter was threatening the Soviet Union with nuclear weapons, because the Soviets had invaded Afghanistan. I felt cold and afraid. It started to sink into my consciousness that the nuclear threat was serious and close, that our president was really thinking about using those bombs we had been building for years. During the Cuban Missile Crisis, I'd felt certain that neither side would be stupid enough to use nuclear weapons. During the Vietnam War, some people worried that the United States would use nuclear bombs. Not me. Even while protesting against nuclear power in the late seventies, I didn't give much thought to the other nuclear menace. But the way Carter was talking scared me.

Then it happened: there was a loud boom and the house rattled. It was a sharp jolt, and I knew that a nuclear bomb had exploded — over in Oakland, I guessed. In panic, I dived to the floor below the window. As I cowered there, everything I had ever learned about nuclear bombs came into my mind. Don't look at the explosion or your eyes will melt and run down your cheeks. The concussion will be coming soon, then the wind and firestorm. My poor house; poor me! I waited and waited. How would I know how long to keep from looking out? After what seemed an eternity, I poked my head up to the window and peeked out between my fingers. Where was the mushroom cloud? I looked again, went outside, and climbed up on the roof, but the sky was clear. Back inside, I turned on the radio and found out that we'd just had an earthquake.

In those moments, I had literally been shaken out of my nuclear denial.

Shortly after this event, a man I had met in a political group asked to come see me. David Hoffman arrived for the appointment, and I knew this was a different kind of political activist. He swore me to secrecy. What he wanted to tell me about was such an important idea that I must not discuss it with anyone. Would I agree to such secrecy?

Now, I am not very good at secrets of this kind. Political secrets I almost always think are dangerous — politically dangerous and dangerous to the political animal that I am. Secrets weaken an organizer. I am a teacher, a natural sharer. My mother said that as a child I would learn something at school and rush home to teach it to my sister. Openness is an important value to me.

Ultimately, I agreed to the secrecy, and at a following meeting David and his friend, Bob Fuller, told me of an idea Bob had had while driving across the country. Bob was trained as a nuclear physicist and had been president of Oberlin College during the civil rights days. Reflecting on his experience, he realized that he was exhausted from thinking about how to stop nuclear war. In his weariness, he let down his guard against thinking that nuclear war could happen. What if it did happen? What would it be like?

As his thinking penetrated his denial, which was founded on the belief that nuclear war must never happen, he noticed that his whole position changed. Now, standing on the other side of nuclear war, he saw police, firefighters, doctors, parents — virtually everyone in our society responsible for taking care of disasters — stretched beyond their capacity to respond. What was needed was to help people prepare for what it would take to deal with nuclear war; this would release enough energy to force the government to stop producing these weapons of destruction.

This was the aikido approach to antinuclear weapons organizing — taking the energy of the nuclear threat and using it against the threat itself. Almost immediately, I agreed to be part of this campaign. We planned to go around the world training firefighters, police, doctors, and health and other professionals to deal with the aftermath of a nuclear attack. Once these service people moved out of their denial and experienced how awful nuclear war would be, we reasoned, the international will to stop the arms race would be aroused.

Bob's wife, Alia, a poet and counselor; John Steiner, a philanthropist and healer; Joanna Macy, creator of a workshop called "Despair and Empowerment Work"; and Chellis Glendinning, author and philosopher, were each brought into the campaign. Convinced that this was the approach that would prevent nuclear war, we begin meeting every day to prepare ourselves to lead these training programs. Hour after hour, day after day, we pored over technical material on the human and environmental effects of nuclear weapons, watched government films on bomb tests and civil defense procedures, read analytical essays on deterrence and defense strategies. We immersed ourselves in nuclear war.

The process we went through now appears similar to the invention of homeopathy. When homeopathy was being developed, researchers experimented with consuming small amounts of toxic substances and watching their bodies' response. We began to take the nuclear poison into ourselves. As we did, we noticed that our responses fell into several categories:

1. Persistent denial and numbness. We were all reading *The Effects of Thermonuclear War*, a grisly and detailed book put out by the US government's Office of Technological Assessment. Although I was accustomed to whipping through technical information, I couldn't get through this book. After a paragraph or two, my eyes would stop moving and blankly stare; I would begin daydreaming.

For a while, we all pretended we were reading the book, but finally we sheepishly admitted we hadn't been able to. It was as if our minds had overload switches, as if the unthinkable (using nuclear weapons) were really *unthinkable*. Could it be that our species had evolved a technology beyond our human capacity to comprehend, unless major parts of our consciousness were turned off?

2. A semihysterical mental flailing ("We've gotta do something!"), always followed by a hollow question ("But what will really work?").

3. Absolute bewilderment about how we got into this mess as a human family. ("If I am going to be blown up in an instant, I want to know what happened.") Where did our ancestors go wrong? What in our culture allowed us to create a crisis with such high stakes?

4. Fear of losing our dear ones in a nuclear war, and feelings of deep love and connection to all creatures who must live under this terrible threat.

5. A sense that small tasks were overwhelmingly meaningless in the face of the nuclear threat. "Why vacuum the floor if all life is going up in dust anyway?" This would be followed by: "Why do anything?"

6. Plotting, in some dark corner of the mind, how to survive a nuclear war. Investigating civil defense, I was relieved to realize that I lived in the shadow of a hill that might deflect the concussion following a nuclear explosion. If they bombed the weapons storage facilities in Oakland, maybe I'd be safe. But if they bombed the defense industries to the south, I'd be done for. I found myself wondering whether my basement would provide any protection from the blast. I felt glad about all the earthquake preparations I had made.

7. Rage about the nuclear predicament, often directed at military people or governmental scientists. One weekend, feeling profoundly disturbed by the nuclear threat, I went to Berkeley, sat in coffeehouses, walked in the woods, and wrote angry poetry:

Whoever of us remains, let us make a pact
    whoever comes out of the shelters whole and is able
        we swear to all the dead others
we shall go and find them — the men in the brass stars
    and tin smiles
        and tear them limb from limb.
They shall not survive the wrath of the survivors.
    I know I can count on you.
Set your jaw,
    narrow your eyes,
        walk straight in there and shout:
"The rent on the planet is due, and it's *you*."
Go for their eyes, their throats
    and when they are gasping for breath
    shove it to them in the stomach
        for the kids and the musicians and the basketball players, and the
farmers, and their cows and chickens, and the mothers and
fathers and grandparents, and the secretaries, and the machinists,
    and the soldiers and the
        teachers and the interior decorators and
for all our softer tender selves ...
And know that I am proud of you
Wherever I am ...

8. Gratitude to the bomb for what it can teach us. By threatening us all, the bomb shows us our commonality and connections. All beings around the world have a common interest in making sure that nuclear war doesn't happen. I hope this lesson is not lost on us. Maybe as a way of acknowledging this global commonalty, we could start a new year-numbering system. Starting with the year 1945, when the nuclear bomb was detonated on Indian land in New Mexico and the whole world began to be under threat — we could name that "year 1." The year-numbering system used in the West is based on a date relevant only to a portion of the world for whom the birth of Jesus is important, where-as the date of the bomb is relevant to all religions and all people.

9. Curiosity about Soviet people who have their bombs aimed at us. I wanted to go to the Soviet Union (or at least the Soviet embassy in San Francisco) and ask people their views of the nuclear predicament. I wanted to meet some ordinary Soviet people. But I was afraid of harassment by the US government officials watching the embassy: would I be suspected of selling secrets? And I noticed my shyness, too, about meeting Soviet people. What would I say? How could I ask the real questions I had in my heart — about how we could work together to get our governments to stop this mad-ness of buying more and more nuclear weapons?

10. Repeated questioning about strategy. Is there a way to allow nuclear weapons to be used as a threat, but not for killing? If a few nuclear weapons are used, can all-out nuclear war be prevented? If global nuclear war is inevitable (after this introductory clause, there would be a half-hour digression about whether in fact it was inevitable), then what should we do in the time we have left?

After meeting for several months, the group decided to spend four full days together to explore the nuclear threat even more inten-sively. We went to Forest Farm, a beautiful seminar center in Marin County. Fortunately, it rained the entire time, so the swimming pool and lovely hiking trails didn't seduce us.

We confessed our fears about exploring the nuclear land inside us; it felt like the back forty acres of our hearts and minds, wild, out of control, a tangle of overgrown weeds, thistles, and discarded rub-bish. Who knows what monsters lived in that morass? We saw sev-eral films about nuclear war, borrowed from the army post at the Presidio. Bob gave us a lecture on the history of nuclear weapons — how they were originally thought of and built, and how they work. It didn't seem that hard to create a nuclear explosion, espe-cially if plutonium could be stolen from a nuclear power plant.

The more we learned, the worse the situation seemed to us. And as we shared that truth with each other, we felt more vulnerable. Sometimes, we found ourselves wishing "they" would do it quickly and get it over with. Other times, we wondered whether we were ruining the time we had left with our obsessive research. We felt empathy for the fanatical hobbyist who escapes into a tiny niche to avoid looking at the big, frightening picture.

John suggested we take turns telling our "nuclear stories" — our life histories as seen through the nuclear prism. I didn't like the idea. What would we say? What would I say? What did nuclear weapons have to do with me?

The nuclear stories turned out to be the most revealing and powerful part of our retreat. People reported having been fascinated with explosives and power, having nuclear nightmares that had left them helpless for days, having surreptitiously made decisions about where to live based on anticipated fall-out patterns. In revealing our secrets, we discovered that several of us had friends or relatives who had helped develop the bomb, assembled nuclear weapons, transported or maintained them. And we had all been paying for them through federal taxes. Nuclear weapons were a hidden member of our family; in income tax terms, they were dependents.

Deep in our barely conscious minds, we had been facing nuclear destruction for years, and it was eating us up. Now, facing the beast together, we felt immeasurable sadness, anger, terror, and hopelessness. It was as if the bomb were going off inside of us, as if we were already nuclear victims. The bomb had exploded in the quality of our lives, threatened our relationships and our confidence in the future. Some of us noticed a greed response; we wanted to acquire a lot of money, so that our family would have the best options should a nuclear war come. Others' response was to work very hard, so they could think they had done their best to stop it. This was a very expensive weapons system indeed!

One night, it was Alia's turn. In her nuclear story, she talked about how it was so hard for her to come across the bay to meetings in San Francisco. She was afraid that if there were a nuclear war, and her children were horribly injured, the baby-sitter would not love her children enough to put them out of their misery. Her sharing was the most gruesome thing we could think of. Should we keep poisons or a painkiller with us at all times? In the event of a nuclear war, how would we decide whether to use them? We sat together for a long time, crying, talking about our deepest fears for the future.

Then, something happened. We started laughing. From deep inside us, a roar erupted, as we began to wildly burlesque the situation. We invented nuclear laxatives (to really get things moving). We played with the idea of packing little pieces of nuclear weapons in cereal boxes for children to collect, so that by the time they grew up, they could have their own bombs. We considered personal uses of weapons, like nuking your neighbors for parking in your driveway, or for starting their lawnmower at seven o'clock on Saturday morning. As we stood in front of the biggest beast and roared with laughter at its absurdity, our hearts and minds came alive. We had gone through our numbness, we had hit rock bottom, and now we were bouncing up. We stayed awake until 2:00 a.m. Our muscles were weak from laughing.

We awoke the next morning with a new perspective and a sense of renewal; we felt transformed. After months of tiptoeing around the edges of our nuclear darkness, we had faced the terrible truth. And at the core of that truth, we had found a part of our humanity that had been choked by our fear. By saying how deeply we feared nuclear war, we had told each other and ourselves how much we loved life. We had said, in effect: "We are passionate human beings. We care about life! These weapons cannot have our lives!"

There is something about the nuclear threat that says, "You will be destroyed if you face this." Somehow, we had walked through that jungle of terror — and we had survived! The experience filled me with an inner calm and determination. I knew that I had the internal resources to keep going, to do what was needed to help prevent nuclear war, to do my small part no matter what my fears.

After the retreat, we all began working very hard for human survival. I developed nuclear comedy sketches with my friend Charlie, traveled around the world to see how people in other cultures viewed the survival crisis, and led workshops similar to the one we had designed for ourselves at Forest Farm. We did those workshops in communities across the country.

We found medical personnel particularly responsive; anyone who bore civic responsibility felt vulnerable in ways they could not figure out how to "fix." Parents had a special concern. How can I face my children when I cannot protect them from this fear. We consulted child psychologists, and they said: Tell children you are afraid, too, but you will do your best to be there with them, and will go through whatever you have to together. It will help if you can face your children with the commitment that you are working to stop such a disaster from ever happening.

I have now listened to hundreds of people tell their nuclear stories, speaking of their fear, anger, and hopelessness, and of their intense passion for life. I see all of us struggling to tell the truth about living in the nuclear age and, by doing so, to reclaim our lives and the consequences of our collective actions. For if we acquiesce in the death of our planet, then who are we?

A fifteen-year-old student in western Massachusetts eyed me squarely as she said, "I don't have a very long nuclear story, but I want to know one thing. When I dream about nuclear war, why is it always in black and white, and silent?"

Another student told about a dream of the moments just before a nuclear attack: She remembers that a Russian woman lives at the bottom of the hill. Not wanting her to face this alone, she goes to be with her.

A third student reported a dream in which the Soviet premier is awakened from a drunken slumber with some news and, without really thinking it through, orders Soviet missiles to be launched. Then, realizing what he's done, the premier shoots himself.

A woman in Colorado said, "I want to promise my children that I'll protect them, and I can't."

A farmer in California's Central Valley broke down sobbing. For him, it was almost a sacred duty to feed his fellow citizens. "If my land and water are ruined," he said, "what will I do? How will I grow anything?"

A Jewish woman who left Germany just before World War II said: "We know that the worst *is* possible."

One day at Sixth Street Park, as Ben and I discussed the nuclear threat, a hurt look came over his face. "They wouldn't really do that, would they?" he asked.

We each have a direct, ongoing relationship with the survival of the planet. Just as we have family lives and work lives and sex lives, we have "planet-survival lives." With the demolition of the Berlin wall and the ending of the cold war, we can see what environmental destruction has occurred in Europe. Neither communism nor capitalism as economic systems seems to have put the health of all species as a priority; where there is participatory democracy, capitalism has sometimes had to bend to public pressure to cease some dangerous habits.

Of course, it is not just radiation, not simply nuclear weapons that threaten our lives on this planet. Radiation is combined with other toxic substances. The extreme changes in the weather are significant. The loss of birds is a very important indicator that important parts of life are already dying; many species are being lost each year. I burn to understand what has gotten us into this situation, what will help us get out, and what part of that work is mine to do. I want to be able to hold these questions so easily and gently — and so compellingly — that my creativity can address them continuously.

I found the articles I read about the causes and degree of threat to life on the planet pretty confusing. Evidence and testimony are often contradictory. The confusion and sadness about the future of human life on earth is not accidental. Scientists funded by polluters, weapons designers, and manufacturers put out all sorts of information about how key toxic and radioactive substances are not disturbing the ozone layer or affecting life. Vested interests hire lobbyists to add confusion to hearings about the factors influencing water, air, and weather quality. It is important in a democracy that the people not get aroused about their safety, or they will exert pressure on the government to do something. And that might put someone out of business.

The way we have organized our energy production enables nuclear producers to fund decision-makers to protect their industry. And the jobs that are created by nuclear weapons also makes it difficult to shut this industry down. But surely there is more to life than a specific job.

I notice that my planet-survival life goes in cycles. There is an "outward" part of the cycle, when inspiration is at hand, the focus of my work is clear, and I feel powerful and passionate, ready to call forth all possible resources to increase the odds of human survival.

During the "inward" part of the cycle, denial, powerlessness, and confusion take over. I feel smaller, more overwhelmed, more in touch with suffering — my own and that of others. Some weeks, despair seems to be on every plate, in every dream, in every wrinkle of the fabric of life. I need to sleep more, rest (or hide) from the struggle, and notice what I'm avoiding thinking about. I read, examine my work, doubt myself. I talk with my friends about what I'm experiencing. I've come to see this part of the cycle as a time of seed planting. I try to be patient, to value these explorations, to know that in time they may flower into action.

In both parts of the action cycle, I see flashes of possible extinction and flashes of life's glorious power. A loud plane overhead sends a chill through me. Driving, I see the panorama of my city and imagine it gone in an instant. Walking among redwood trees that are hundreds of years old, I'm filled with the terror of extinction. I wonder: Do the trees know that their species is threatened *right now?*

The next moment I am fully occupied with the trees' beauty. The possibility of nothingness reminds me that at one time there was nothing. All of earth came from a swirling fermament — and wonder of all wonders, life in all its beautiful complexity emerged! It makes me feel entirely alive and allied with life. I watch with awe and appreciation as my chickens lay eggs, tomato plants grow in the garden, a fellow human being tells a heartfelt truth. Like someone sanding her fingertips to make them more sensitive to braille, I sand away my nuclear denial and become more sensitive to the powerful pulls of life and extinction. Yet, it is important that I not become attached to apocalyptic visions. Do we as a species need such an immediate and terrible threat in order to value and honor life? I am attached to life and its continuation.

Can we actually un-invent something like nuclear weapons? I read with interest about Japan's successful ban on gunpowder in the seventeenth century. But it seems that the ban resulted in a militaristic counterreaction that, in the long term, may have been worse. Often, great ideas in one generation have unexpected negative consequences in later generations.

What are the effects of nuclear proliferation? Might the mere possession of such powerful weapons make a leader or a nation more cautious or mature? As less wealthy countries get nuclear weapons, might they gain a more equitable share of the world's power? Have we finally invented something so inconceivably horrible that we will have to learn new ways to share power and resources?

Why has war been developed? Is it the result of the attachment to novelty? The need to trade in order to satisfy insatiable desires for variety has caused a lot of trouble. Do wars stem from some countries meddling in the affairs of others, so as to get reliable supplies of resources at artificially low prices? Is it possible to reverse that trend, to reduce the number of things in our lives that come to us at other people's expense? What if we gave up bananas grown on US-owned plantations in Central America? Might that help keep our government from interfering with the people there? I really love bananas. Would I be willing to give them up if that would reduce the risk of war and put more food on a Central American table?

Are there kinds of international trade that could mitigate against war? The interlocking trade agreements (NAFTA, GATT, WTO, etc.) and the development of global multinational corporations have not stopped business from meddling in internal policies of developing countries, in order to gain access to resources such as oil and agricultural products.

Now that the US is the superpower in an unbalanced world, the role of our government is crucial. Other countries seem to have some expectation (where did that come from?) that our military will sort out conflicts all over the world. Since our "national interest" is usually really "our industries' interest" in a region, the pressures to use the US military are complex. Did we mobilize our forces in the former Yugoslavia (but not in Rwanda!) to stop genocide, or to protect certain oil interests in the Gulf? What can we do about the use of "depleted" (still very much radioactive) casings for bombs — used in Iraq and the Balkans — to make the bombs able to penetrate tanks "like slicing butter"? Oh, the mind spins!

All this pondering about war, about massive weapons, helps me to make choices in my life and work. I often work with peace and social change groups to plan strategy. I spent two weeks in jail for participating in a blockade of the Lawrence Livermore Lab, where nuclear weapons are designed. I expect to be fighting nuclear weapons for the rest of my life, and I hope that's a long time. I now think that it may take four or five generations for our species to learn to make change without war and violence. I am still asking questions about this issue and am not satisfied with my current answers.

War is a profound experience in the defining of a people. It allows people to put aside petty differences and join an effort larger than themselves. Having gone through such a difficult sacrificial experience, they are bonded together in a common purpose. Historically, that has been one effect of war. One of the exciting things about the nonviolent struggles in India, the Philippines, China, and Russia is that a new way is emerging to bring people together for *nonviolent* change.

Often, I think about these things while sitting on the toilet. In the Renaissance, I sometimes imagine, there must have been a woman a little bit like me, trying to make sense out of a very confusing time. What did she think about the new ideas being discussed in her home? What were her questions? My grandmothers must have been wondering how to settle the land in this country without war. Or, I imagine a woman in Iraq wondering how to get out from under the crushing burdens resulting from the Gulf War. Or a woman in the Ukraine thinking about the nuclear weapons left over from the Soviet Union. Surely, she must want to get those weapons out of her land.

I think of a woman in the future, thinking about the world. What are the questions on her mind as she sits on the toilet? What weapons is she working to stop? Has she learned new ways of thinking, of living, and of feeling that allow people to live together, working to learn from conflict, rather than die from it?

I believe that the combined acts of kindness and tenderness that we experience from childhood through old age have something to contribute to our learning to disarm ourselves in the many ways we will need to if we are to move toward a peaceful, healthy world. As an old boyfriend used to paraphrase a popular song: "Let there be peace on earth, and let it begin with Fran Peavey." I know he deeply hoped for that — and I do, too.

Chapter 8

How Can I Keep From Laughing?
Comedy in Hard Times,
1979–88

I READ THE newspaper every day. Sometime ago, I realized that the way I was reading the paper wasn't working for me. I really wanted to know what was going on in the world, but all the stories about horrors and disasters only left me feeling numb and helpless. I wanted a transparent newspaper, which I could look through to see how ordinary people in those places were dealing with those events, what could be done, and even more significantly, what was being done. Watching the news on TV was an even more pacifying, disempowering experience. It almost seemed as though the newspaper publishers and TV broadcasters were programming us to look to the ads for relief from the news, to buoy up the consumer world. "The world may be falling apart, but you can fix yourself up at Macy's."

I started experimenting with less passive ways of absorbing the news. I talked back to the television set, ripped up the newspaper, and finally began to develop a comedy act about the news. Comedy seemed a natural medium for me. I had grown up in a pre-TV family; we spent many nights laughing together at the absurdities of life and at each other's funniness. I have always enjoyed telling stories and laughing with people.

I got up on stage at a coffeehouse in San Francisco and began to explore current events with the audience. I read choice items from the *San Francisco Chronicle,* our local comedy newspaper, personalizing the news. I developed a chant that continues to be a favorite: "The people, united, will sometimes win and sometimes lose."

One of my big shows, planned months in advance, occurred a few days after the People's Temple mass suicide in Guyana. I didn't know how I could do the show with my heart so heavy and my mind so confused about the tragedy. So, I mixed a little reality in with the comedy, and people seemed relieved to have that balance. I started wondering whether there could be a social form, a niche in our community life, called "realedy" — neither comedy nor tragedy but a lively mix of the two. I envisioned a forum where we could talk about our lives, what was happening in the news, and share the absurdities around us. Realedy would serve as a vehicle to help us come out of the closet with what was really happening in our world and in our hearts. I hoped we would get beyond opinions, to questions and feelings about our public affairs. Maybe we would work our way to what needed to be done to activate each of us to work to restore normalcy to the situation.

One day while I was preparing for a show, the idea of doing a ventriloquist act with the American flag occurred to me. I had already experimented with the flag standing next to me on-stage; I would nudge it and talk to it as I read the newspaper. Now, I wanted the flag to have a voice of its own. Since I wasn't a ventriloquist, and did not know how to learn the skill, I asked my good friend Charlie Varon to play the voice of the flag. I bought a small flag and sewed a piece of cloth on the back of the stars. I would put my hand inside and move the flag's "mouth" while Charlie spoke his lines offstage.

The character we began to develop for the flag was a crotchety guy with a lot of problems: memory problems (he couldn't remember whether the mission to rescue the US hostages from Iran had succeeded or failed); hearing problems (he heard "erection" for "election"); ego problems (he worried that the Soviet Union had bigger missiles than he did). He was not a malevolent guy, or inherently evil. But he did make mistakes and often failed to comprehend the pain his mistakes caused. He was upset that small countries like Iran were giving him a hard time, confounded that the rest of the world wouldn't always cooperate with his plans. When it came right down to it, he wasn't afraid to push to get his way. The flag took on a bit of the character of Ronald Reagan.

The fact that most of my comedy career was during the Reagan administration made for easy pickings. A headline in the *S.F. Chronicle* declared: "Reagan Says God Backs Budget." The article went on to say, "Beginning a campaign to sell his new budget proposal, President Reagan asserted yesterday that the Lord and the scriptures are on his side in his struggle with Congress to continue the US defense buildup. Reagan also said he was receiving divine guidance and help in the budget battle."

The next day, a transcript in the *New York Times* of a press conference held by President Reagan illuminated the issue further. Reporter's question: "Mr. President. Theologians recently criticized you for saying in defending your military budget that the scriptures are on our side. I wonder, do you think it is appropriate to use the Bible in defending a political argument?" Answer: "Well, I was actually speaking to some clergymen, I checked that with a few theologians if it was appropriate. Well, what I meant about appropriate, was I interpreting it correctly? Was it a warning that you should be prepared and otherwise ask for peace because you are outnumbered and well we would say outgunned by the other side?" Reporter: "But to follow up: You don't have any problem with using the Bible in the political context?" Reagan: "Well, I don't think I've ever used the Bible to further political ends or not."

In the 1990s, after the announcement of Reagan's mental problems with Alzheimer's disease, he draws sympathy; but in those days, it seemed almost pathetic to have such a bumbling president. The headline following a brain surgery drew laughs at the president: "Reagan Brain Surgery; Nothing Found."

A popular section of the show involved reading the newspaper, holding the clippings in my hand. I developed files and files of newspaper clippings sent to me from all over the world that illuminated the comedy of everyday life. "Help Wanted: Person to work on nuclear fissionable isotope radioactive materials. No experience necessary."

I wrote a letter to the Secretary of Agriculture:

Dear Mr. Secretary,

My brother in Idaho just received a one-thousand dollar check from the government for not raising hogs. So I have decided that I want to go into the not-raising-hogs business. Many of my friends in San Francisco also want to go into this lucrative business. What I want to know is what kind of hogs would you like me not to raise? Would you be willing to pay me not to grow the corn I would be feeding the hogs I am not raising?

Then this got me to thinking, and so I wrote to the Secretary of Defense:

Dear Mr. Secretary,

My brother in Idaho has made me aware of a program run by your fellow department in the Cabinet, the Department of

Agriculture, which pays people not to raise hogs. I am writing to suggest that your department, the Department of Defense, begin a program to pay people not to build nuclear weapons. I have been not building nuclear weapons for as long as I can remember, and thus would bring a lot of experience into the field. As my enclosed feasibility study indicates, I would be able to not build the launchers for the cruise missiles for between $1.2 and $1.4 million. Is this a saving you can afford to pass up?

Meanwhile, my explorations with the nuclear study group had begun to show me the comic possibilities tied up in the nuclear threat. After I had done some research into the government's plans for civilian defense, I called up the regional office of the Federal Emergency Management Agency.

"I have just a few questions after reading your literature," I said. "How can you get radiation out of the air that's coming into your fallout shelter?"

"We don't know," came the reply. "The Congress cut that research out of the budget."

"Well, what about the soil? After a nuclear war, won't the soil be so radioactive that the food produced on it would be hazardous to eat?"

"That's another area the government hasn't funded. Sorry." It seemed that the government hasn't exactly thought out their nuclear war.

I discovered the sheer power of laughing in the face of the bomb at our nuclear study group's weekend retreat. The next day, I got together with Charlie, who was not in the study group, and proposed the idea of developing a show focused on all the absurdities involved in nuclear weapons, nuclear war, and nuclear power. The laughter of the previous evening had left me with an enormous amount of energy and focus. "We've got to start doing nuclear comedy." I could see that comedy would be needed to help fight the sadness, fear, and despair that people would have to face as they grappled with the nuclear threat. If they were able to handle their paralyzing feelings, they might be able to unleash their creativity and energy to work against the proliferation and use of these terrible weapons. Laughing together with other people at something that had previously been hidden away in each person's mind would be a powerful and empowering experience, I hoped. Maybe, holding up the absurdity of the situation, without belittling the problems posed by the bomb, would be a healing process. Charlie was a little surprised at my idea, but had been thinking and writing in a similar comedy vein. So we made an intuitive leap and started calling ourselves "nuclear comedians."

My Dad used to tell us that during the Depression, some people became more decent, generous, and honest. Others became more suspicious, greedy, and hateful. He said he hoped that, if we faced that kind of stressful situation, we would act decently.

How can we find ways to be decent in the face of nuclear terror? When I am terrified, I tend to lose clarity, take rash or self-serving action, or do nothing at all. But what happens when a whole population gets scared? When an entire society is filled with the fear of a war, or worse yet, a nuclear war? All that fear, all the crazy things that occur to people in a slow-rolling panic, all the grasping for control and the egotistical efforts to be heroic — these responses made me scared for my country. Looking back, I wonder if some of the motivation for the greed of the 1980s was in part driven by these fears.

During the Black Plague in Europe, another period of terror, the social order dissolved into ugliness and terror. In our own time, Peoples Temple minister Jim Jones repeatedly used the fear of nuclear holocaust to manipulate his followers. When I first learned about the atomic bomb as a young girl, I came home and asked my parents why we didn't build a bomb shelter. My father, who was often farsighted, said, "We could build one, but what would we do about all our relatives and neighbors who didn't have one? How would we feel sitting in safety when the Magels (our nearest neighbors) came and asked if they could come in? And then Uncle Frank and Aunt Rosemary and their kids, and of course we couldn't leave out the grandparents. How big a shelter would we have to build to have room for all the people we could not leave behind?"

As a climate of crisis and fear builds, we lose confidence in each other and ourselves. We have trouble thinking flexibly, and moving calmly and rationally toward solutions to our massive collective problems.

I thought nuclear comedy could provide one small part of the antidote to that social insanity. Seeing the absurdity of the nuclear situation might help people release some of their fear and gain a little perspective. It might free some of the creativity and energy bound up in the fear. And, if done in a friendly social setting, nuclear comedy might build people's sense of confidence and connectedness. Bonding together is an essential aspect of working together. Laughing together challenges one's sense of isolation. "I'm not the only one who thinks this situation is absurd. Look at all these people who agree with me at least on the craziness."

One of the first nuclear comedy sketches we developed was called "What about the Russians?" Charlie played an on-the-street radio interviewer who accosts passerby Patricia May Nicholson with the question: "What should we do about the Russians?" Patricia May responds: "Oh, you'll have to ask my husband that question." The more insistent the interviewer becomes, trying to whip her into an anti-Soviet frenzy, the kinder and more genteel Patricia May becomes. Finally, when asked to imagine what she'd do if the Russians landed in her hometown, she says: "Have they had dinner? If they like American food, we could have them up to the church for supper. After all, they've come all this way. I've never met a Russian and I've wanted to."

Another early routine was an interview with a hopelessly inept minor-league baseball pitcher named Dusty Molloy. Dusty has been in a slump for a while; his record is three wins and sixteen losses. Dusty, however, is unperturbed by his own mediocrity — he has a casual "win some, lose some" attitude. But there is a problem with the team's front office. They make unrealistic promises to the fans — promises of shutout games, no-hit games, pennant seasons. Meanwhile, Dusty is out on the mound trying his level best just to find home plate.

It turns out that in the off-season, Dusty has another job: he works at a local nuclear power plant. "Nuclear power is just like baseball," Dusty remarks. "You have a front office making all kinds of ridiculous promises to the fans: no leaks, no spills, no plant shut-downs. They're promising the fans perfection." But, as Dusty casually explains, "perfection just isn't human nature." When asked if he has any concerns about the effect of radiation on his health, Dusty explains that he has no worries in that regard. "Of course, when we get close to the core of the nuclear power plant, we put our hands over our private parts just to be extra safe."

Charlie and I owed our friendship to the Diablo Canyon Nuclear Power Plant near San Luis Obispo, California, where we both participated in a civil disobedience action in 1978. As the plant's design troubles worsened in 1981, we found ourselves laughing more and more about nuclear power.

Pacific Gas and Electric had decided to build the Diablo Canyon plant in the late 1960s, when nuclear power plants were in vogue. Then, they found that an earthquake fault ran within a few miles of the plant — and they tried to hide this information. That was the beginning of a comedy of errors on their part. The Nuclear Regulatory Commission ordered PG&E to install safety brackets to protect against earthquakes, but the brackets were installed backwards. Every time the plant was about to be licensed, another flaw or cover-up would be revealed. Some friends and I remembered Dusty's words about perfection and human nature, and we created a "corporate sympathy" greeting card for PG&E.

We also anonymously began issuing press releases on PG&E stationary. We sent them out to the local press. First, we announced that PG&E would be moving the Diablo Canyon Nuclear Power Plant from its present location in San Louis Obispo to Moss Beach (100 miles north), using the new, powerful Thompson sky hook. Another time, we used the schematic drawing of Candlestick Park to portray a new device PG&E had just purchased called the "Evacumobile."

One of the real weaknesses in this nuclear power plant was the lack of a community evacuation plan. Evacuation was almost impossible out of San Luis Obispo, with the ocean on one side, steep mountains on the other, and only one road going north and one road south. On the drawing of the Evacumobile, we labeled areas for toilets, clinics, entertainment center, and antinuclear campaign center.

The public relations spokesperson for PG&E looked pathetic denying these fanciful press releases. Occasionally, a radio station would play the press release without looking at it carefully. Then, PG&E would have to call and make a correction. We figured it was positive that people were laughing at PG&E. These press releases were often used by radio stations as they were released, until someone called attention to the absurdity of the content. Occasionally, a piece would be printed by newspapers as comedy material. Finally, we issued a release saying that to counter the people who were issuing the fake press releases, from now on the media should know that PG&E would put their real releases on a special color of paper. "All other releases should be considered to be pranks." This voluntarily ended our career as alternative media consultants to PG&E.

One day, Charlie arrived for rehearsal just as Alex, a realtor friend of mine, was leaving. Charlie and I tried to interest Alex in the nuclear issue. He didn't seem responsive, so we began to tell him what nuclear war would do to the real estate market. Thus, our "Realtors for Social Responsibility" sketch was born. I Played RSR founder Hermione Pledge; Charlie was again the earnest interviewer.

"Mrs. Pledge, what is the basic concern of your group?"

"We are very concerned about the effects of nuclear war on property values. You know, it is very difficult to sell a large hole. Nuclear war would take property off the market. A nuclear explosion sucks up pieces of real estate into a mushroom cloud. That's what a mushroom cloud is! It's pieces of property that have been sucked up and made radioactive; then, they fall down on other pieces of property — what you might call "hot property." And that's not to mention that in the same mushroom cloud, neighborhoods would mix!"

We had a lot of fun inventing sketches. Some nights, the material came rolling off our hearts like an avalanche. We screamed with delight at each new idea. After rehearsal, we would go out for ice cream with our friend Myra, who had become producer and censor of our comedy show. We'd get our ice cream, sit in the car, and perform the evening's new material for Myra. Occasionally, she would shake her head and say, "Well, I don't know," and we would know that we had gone past the bounds of good taste and common decency.

To be a comedian, one has to suspend certain limits on sensibility that normal society uses to keep itself civilized. For example, we worked out a piece about groups of photographers planning their strategy to capture nuclear wars on film for posterity. One section concluded that the reason the Japanese always carry cameras now is that few of them actually photographed the explosions at Hiroshima and Nagasaki. Myra objected to the stereotype and said we'd gone over the edge. Regrettably, we agreed with her. Myra played the discretionary role for us and saved us from our most disgusting selves.

Our friend Jim suggested that we develop a full show and perform it at a friend's house. So we invited all our friends to a Sunday night show, and they laughed enough to encourage us, but not so much as to delude us into thinking we were very good comedians yet. Charlie had some dramatic training in college, but I had taken only one drama class in high school and one at summer camp when I was twelve years old. For me, acting wasn't fun. Communicating was. The transaction with the audience — watching them listen and reflect — was the thrill. And applause was a real torture for me. We performed together for four years before I could enjoy the applause.

We continued performing in San Francisco, trying out our sketches for audiences at nuclear freeze petition parties. And then, we set out on two tours in February of 1982: one to the East Coast and one to Colorado. Everywhere we went, there were small but enthusiastic audiences. After the shows, people often came up to thank us for helping them laugh at the nuclear threat. We balanced our comedy shows with a few minutes of serious talking from the stage, and with workshops on the toll of the arms race.

During the day, we would lead workshops concentrated on what people already knew about the arms race and nuclear power, and how fears about nuclear war affected their lives. We also held strategy sessions about what each community could do politically to activate people at the grassroots to express their concerns about the nuclear issue to political leaders. We heard the terror that people lived with, and how nuclear fears had influenced their decisions, their dreams, and their hopes for their children. Then, in the evening, we would do a comedy show, giving them a chance to laugh at their fears. We called our program "Living and Laughing in the Nuclear Age."

Our Colorado organizer, Carol Rothman, showed us a piece of "indigenous nuclear comedy": a government booklet entitled "Crisis Relocation: Guidance for Residents of the Denver Metropolitan Area." This was not about what I initially imagined. I thought this booklet was about a government office that, if I developed a crisis in my home, like a plumbing crisis or trouble with the children, would relocate that crisis to someone who could afford it. Instead, the booklet was about leaving the "risk area" and relocating to an outlying "host area" in the event of a threatened nuclear attack. At one show at a nightclub in Denver, we tried out some of the "material" that had been written by the government:

"Before you leave home, close all curtains and drapes and turn all home heating and appliance thermostats to the lowest setting... Be advised that your pet may be placed in a temporary pet shelter [do they really think we believe they have things so carefully taken care of?]... You are NOT encouraged to take firearms to the Host Area... What to take with you. Prepare to take those things that you would take on a two-week vacation trip, plus..." There is a checklist of what to bring that includes such items as work gloves, work clothes, shovels, axes, picks — it's going to be a hell of a vacation! — as well as deeds, insurance policies, stocks, and bonds.

And then — the government is so thoughtful — the booklet suggests bringing "extra underclothing." I guess they figured we'd see the nuclear explosion and just shit in our pants.

The government also suggested that we bring income tax information. As if we were going to pay money to a government that had gotten us in such a mess as a nuclear war.

The Denver audience was howling at all this, but they absolutely exploded when I read: "What to expect on the road: Traffic will probably be heavy..." Wherever we went, we found that people enjoyed that pamphlet. It was one of our funniest sketches. Other communities had similar pamphlets. One in Australia suggested that if "you are in your car and see a nuclear explosion, pull your car over to the side of the road, roll up the windows." In New Zealand, a pamphlet suggested a really exotic menu to bring to shelters. In fact, as we examined menus suggested in other countries, New Zealand seemed to be the one with the best food. Their pamphlet also suggested that people bring an air gun, because "air is readily available." The comedy written by governments is some of the best around. We can't write material as good as that.

Another show on that tour that I'll never forget was at the University of Colorado at Boulder. Looking out at a packed auditorium, I saw several people laughing with their hands clasped around their heads. It was as if little comedy bombs were going off inside, and they were trying to hold their heads together.

I often felt comedy bombs going off inside me when we generated material. One afternoon, Charlie and I were working on our sketch about Colonel Curtis Catapult, a twenty-one-year veteran of the US Airborne who was recently traded to the Soviet Army. We had already established his fondness for Russian vodka and his professionalism — being traded didn't affect his love for "the game." But the sketch hadn't taken off. Then it happened. Colonel Catapult started spinning out a plan to retrofit Soviet nuclear missiles with motorcycle seats, handlebars, and maps with little arrows, so his Airborners could ride them down. Why sit on the sidelines in a nuclear war? Naturally, the boys in the Soviet Airborne had never seen the United States, and they wanted to, and a nuclear war might be their only chance. So Colonel Catapult decided to circle some tourist spots on the maps, like the Empire State Building and the Golden Gate Bridge, so the boys could enjoy some sightseeing before continuing on to their targets. Sometimes, I feel as though there are two realities, separated by a curtain. One reality is our daily lives; we see people scurrying around, doing their work, living their lives, acting as if everything is fine. But every now and then, we peek out from behind the curtain, and see a second reality: the world as a whole, poised on the brink of several disasters at once, our planet befouled, ethnic warfare, fifty thousand nuclear weapons, people starving, the rich amassing wealth way beyond any possible need, while the poor find it increasingly difficult to afford even necessities. "Hey, there is a world out there, and the situation is really crazy! Oh my heavens, is this us? How embarrassing!" The two realities collide for a moment; I feel like a hostage on a planet of fundamentally deranged creatures, and I suspect I may be one of them.

I recoil for a while at the insanity of it all, and close the curtain. A wave of sadness, anger, or fear passes through me. Then, something starts to go off inside me again. I peek through the curtain once more, and through the terror and absurdity, a roar from deep inside comes up and out. It is a cosmic roar, a roar of survival, and a burst of true energy that relieves just enough of my suffering to unleash the fury to heal and work even harder.

Our show usually ended with the "Wrath of God" sketch. Gabriel brings God the news that the human beings down on the planet Earth have just started a global thermonuclear war. Millions have been killed. At first, God can't believe it; then he turns angry. "If I told them once, I told them a million times: 'Don't leave it all up to me!' They said, 'God won't let a nuclear war happen.' Those infantile jerks! They probably thought nuclear war would bring on Armageddon, and they'd get a free ride up to heaven. Well, they've got something else coming. Close the gates, Gabriel! No one else gets in! Anyone who would let this happen — let them stay down there on earth and rot!"

We performed "The Wrath of God" as part of a lecture we gave to a religion class at a college in northwestern Iowa. After the sketch, a thoughtful young woman asked us if we didn't think God was a forgiving god. Wouldn't He forgive us if we had a nuclear war?

I've thought a lot about that question since then. Finally, we added an ending to deal with the young woman's question. I portray myself arriving in heaven, waiting in a long line with all the other creatures, and finally getting to God, the Judge. He looks at me.

"Were you party to this mess, Frances Peavey?"

"Y-Y-Yes, sir."

"What do you have to say for yourself?"

"Well, God, I guess it kind of got away from us. Before we knew it, we had a big stockpile and a lot of industrial and psychological investment in continuing the effort. Stopping production would have cost a lot of jobs. And, well, we didn't seem to know how to turn around, once we had come so far. That's the truth. We didn't destroy the world exactly on purpose."

God just sits there, overwhelmed by sadness, thinking of all the lilies of the field and the sparrows destroyed in the holocaust. All of the humans whom He loved.

"And what part did you play?" He asks me.

"Well, God, I paid taxes for the weapons, and I thought the bombs weren't so bad in my early years."

"And what else?"

"Well, I was just a small part of the whole thing."

The sketch ended with a sorrowful God and me in an embrace. I was too ashamed to ask for forgiveness. God was too sad to think of offering it. "I'm so sorry, God" I say.

"I'm sorry, too," God says.

The sketch ended with Benny Goodman's lone clarinet playing "Send in the Clowns" and the lights fading to black.

Traveling with our comedy show, talking with people all over, we learned a lot about the price we pay for nuclear weapons and for the defense policy. In 1984, I visited the Soviet Union and was shocked to see the poverty there. They didn't even have construction concrete really mastered, yet they were pouring so much money into defense. That they were competing with the United States seemed a crime. That the US pours money into nuclear weapons when its schools and mental health treatment are so neglected is also a crime. Rather than build nuclear weapons, that money could be better put to creating a better life for the people in all countries.

In the spring of 1983, we toured up and down Great Britain, performing in alternative "fringe" theaters. The parliamentary election campaign was in full swing. Nuclear policy was a key issue, with the Labor Party challenging the conservative Thatcher government's position, and arguing for unilateral British nuclear disarmament.

We were surprised and pleased that our British audiences liked nuclear comedy so much. The American flag sketch was a real hit, especially the flag's extemporaneous answering of questions from the audience.

The country whose empire once dominated the world now seems to them to be occupied by the United States. Britain, a country no bigger than California, houses more than one hundred US military bases, and the US nuclear weapons stationed there are under American control. Activists complained that the American planes flew low over the countryside to intimidate the citizens. "I'm having some troubles with Great Britain," the flag complained. "We just can't figure out which of us is the empire and which is the colony."

We took our show to Greenham Common, the US air base where cruise missiles were to be (and have since been) installed, and the site of some of the most determined work against deployment — including a permanent women's peace camp. There were grandmothers; professional working women who had left jobs to be at the camp; housewives who had left home to stop the arms race on their land, and whose kids visited them on weekends; an infant who had been born at the peace camp; and very "punk" women who wore safety pins poked through skin flaps in the bridge of noses, ears, and between their fingers. They must have been wearing twenty safety pins in places I could see, and I wondered about the places I couldn't. Looking at them made my teeth vibrate and hurt, so I had a lot of trouble looking for very long. Later, the other women told me stories about them, which allowed me to see that there was more to them than the safety pins.

We had somehow forgotten to bring our props with us to the peace camp, and several women set about finding some hats that might be appropriate for our characters. We cut out a red star for Colonel Catapult's hat, and someone stuck it on a plastic police officer's hat with Marmite, a particularly viscous food spread, which the British seem to put on everything they eat. They suggested that we perform as close to the main gate as possible, because the American guards get bored and might appreciate a comedy break.

Word went out that a comedy team from America was doing a show at the main gate. Military men came to stand on one side of the fence, and women from several parts of the peace camp gathered in front of the fence, squatting against it so the military could see our routine. I felt a little like Bob Hope, entertaining the warriors, giving them a break from their wearying tasks. I was especially glad to have something both "sides" could participate in. I am happy to report that laughter emerged from both sides of the fence.

Several days later, at the US Air Force base at Upper Heyford, we performed for some of the peace activists who were blockading the base. Our "stage" was a one-foot-wide strip between two white lines on the motorway pavement. Behind us, a row of British police officers and passing cars; in front of us, a bulging crowd of protesters, more police, and several military men peering out from behind the fence. As we did our "Colonel Catapult" sketch, the enthusiastic crowd grew larger, overflowing onto the road. The police officers got so involved in the show that they let the crowd grow until there was a traffic jam.

Another tour took us to the West — Nevada, Utah, Colorado, Wyoming, Montana, and my home state of Idaho. An hour out of

Las Vegas, our rented car broke down and a stranger came to our aid. He was a retired marine, who told us he had transported nuclear weapons around the country. An appropriate start to our tour, we thought. While we waited for our replacement car, we chatted a while.

Bob told us that his brother, who had served in the army, had been exposed to radiation during an aboveground weapon test at the Nevada test site in the fifties, and later died of cancer. As for nuclear war, Bob said, "Dead's dead." Still, he expected that a nuclear war would be Armageddon, and counted himself among the faithful who'd be saved. He was so tedious on this point that later Charlie referred to him as "Bobgeddon."

A few days later, we found ourselves standing where Bob's brother had stood some thirty years before. People from all over had come to a peace vigil regularly held at the Nevada test site. Busloads of workers drove past us. Some workers waved. I kept wondering how they felt about their work, and what its impact was on their health and the quality of their lives. And what were the long-term effects on the desert, the plants, ground water, and animals.

And I remembered the atomic veterans I'd met in other parts of the country who had been exposed to radiation during weapons tests. They had been told to place their hands over their eyes when the bomb exploded, but the light and radiation from the blast was so intense that they had seen the bones in their hands, even with their eyes closed. One ex-soldier remembered having the strong conviction, upon seeing the bomb go off, that there was no God. He reasoned that God would not bestow such a horrible power on such foolish humans.

I had done a research experiment in my college zoology class, where I put a queen bee beside a dog having an X-ray. This was a very low-level X-ray, but still it incapacitated her from laying viable larvae in her hive. The hive died out, because the workers could not tell that the larvae were not able to develop, so they did not develop a new queen. I also remembered the X-ray machine at the Buster Brown shoe store in Twin Falls. It was like a toy. I would run down the street ahead of my mother, put my foot in the machine, and look at the skeleton of my toes as I wiggled them. And then, I remembered once seeing a flash and mushroom cloud, when I was driving across the Nevada desert, going from Twin Falls to San Francisco. Nuclear reality had played a part in my own life, and I had hardly noticed.

In southwest Utah, in an area downwind of the test site, the jump in the cancer rate has been linked to the radiation released by atmospheric tests during the fifties. Though aboveground testing has been banned, accidental leaks from underground tests are not infrequent — one occurred a few days before we arrived to do our show.

People we met in St. George, Utah, were angry and felt betrayed by their government — which had told them the fallout they saw on their land and in the air was safe. Now, they felt their loyalty and patriotism had been used against them. They had clear evidence of the rottenness issuing forth from the nuclear madness; they were painfully reminded of it every day. Too many people in their community suffered from cancer, birth defects in their children, and other unusual illnesses. An older man named Ike had lost his wife to cancer and carried his bitterness heavily. He told us he hadn't laughed since his wife died, and didn't think he could. But when he saw some of our sketches, he laughed in spite of himself.

We returned to Boulder, Colorado, one of the great nuclear comedy towns in the country, to participate in the Conference on World Affairs. There we met Mira Petrovskaya, a woman who works with the Soviet bureau that studies the United States and Canada. She got to see some of our sketches, including "Colonel Catapult" and "What should we do about the Russians?" She enjoyed the idea of nuclear comedy and told us she didn't know of any nuclear comedians in the Soviet Union. We became concerned that the Soviets had fallen behind in the nuclear comedy race.

Some years later, I had a chance to perform in Moscow. At the institute where Mira worked, they enjoyed the comedy, but at a show for the general public, which was televised, no one laughed. I was very disappointed. Later, backstage, many people came and laughed very hard. One even fell against the wall with laughter. I asked, with some irritation, why they had not laughed during the show. It was clear that when they were being televised, they knew better than to laugh at anything political.

I shudder every time I see another strand of the nuclear web we human beings are weaving. Denial became increasingly difficult as we traveled the "nuclear circuit," meeting atomic veterans, downwind victims, and uranium miners. Listening to young people share their feelings and knowledge is shocking. During the 1980s, everywhere we traveled, even in small towns like Sheridan, Wyoming, and Storm Lake, Iowa, we met people working with determination to prevent nuclear war and reclaim the future. My own hometown, Twin Falls, had an activist peace group. Other signs of hope emerged when town after town and city after city declared themselves nuclear-free zones. People worked, and finally political leaders got the message. When Ronald Reagan started working for an end to building nuclear weapons, and some were even dismantled, we all held our breath. Every corner of the country has a part to play in the changes in nuclear policy.

Outside Madison, Wisconsin (itself a nuclear-free zone), Charlie and I toured the American Breeders Service plant, the world's largest producer, or rather collector, of bull semen. Through scientific breeding and artificial insemination, dairy cattle in the United States now produce more milk per capita than they used to. And, we found out, the Soviet Union that year purchased millions of dollars of bull semen from ABS to improve Soviet dairy cattle. This means that there are now hundreds of thousands of Soviet-American cows running around Russia and the ex-republics. Would we have the heart to bomb cattle that are part of our family?

After eight years of partnership, Charlie and I amiably decided to dissolve our comedy partnership. I continued to perform as the Atomic Comic for some years, enjoying some fine tours in Australia and New Zealand. There, the nuclear struggle was different, especially in New Zealand. US ships carrying nuclear warheads were entering New Zealand ports, and the public carried on an intense struggle to have them blocked from entering New Zealand waters. They wanted nothing to do with nuclear weapons. They were intensely proud of having said "NO!" to the US I also took strength from knowing that someone had been able to do that.

Possibly, others of us will be able to say "NO!" to all kinds of nukes. Now, we see the unviability of nuclear power plants and the struggle over storage of nuclear waste. There is hope everywhere. But, one cannot help wondering how many bombs are being built now. We hear about some destruction of weapons, but somehow I wonder if we are really counting down, or just updating.

It was the Gulf War that finally convinced me to move from comedy to being a performance artist with a good sense of humor. Laughing at that carnage was just not appropriate. I decided to work more laughter and story telling into my lectures, rather than have the only criterion for inclusion of material be "is it funny?"

I've performed in nightclubs with other comedians and find much of their material off-putting. I think there is comedy that laughs at situations, creating the illusion that the person laughing is superior to those being laughed at. It doesn't feel good to me to laugh in that way. For myself, I prefer to laugh at myself in the situation that is the object of the humor. "We're all in this pickle together, and isn't it crazy?" This does not put me or my group down or up. I call this compassionate comedy. I continue to experiment with it in a variety of ways in talks and performances. And I still laugh often while reading the newspaper. Life is really crazy.

One moment that I was deeply grateful that I understood laughter was in 1993, when I was working in the former Yugoslavia. I was handing out bundles in a hospital for raped women close to the Hungarian border. I squeezed one package as I gave it to an older woman and said, "I hope this one has socks." (Older women often asked for socks.) The fifty or sixty women standing around laughed. I asked the translator, "Why are they laughing?"

"They think you said 'sex'!" For a moment, I wondered how to handle the awkward situation. Then, I remembered how healing laughter can be, and that I am a trained comedian. I played it for every laugh I could think of. I pretended to be embarrassed. They would laugh. I would say 'socks'; they would say 'sex'; and then we would all laugh. Helplessly I said, "You don't think I'd joke about sex in a place like this, do you?" They roared. It was that kind of precious laughter that feels healing and empowering. It is as if we were roaring back at "the one who has hurt us. He does not have the power to keep us cowering in the corner!" When we left, someone said, "We laughed more tonight than we have all year." What a joy to have been able to bring a little laughter to that place.

Every day, I am barraged with grim news about people violating life on this planet: wars, murders, suicides, rapes, ecological disasters. And, in my brief snatch of time on this beautiful planet, I have to contemplate the possibility that a nuclear explosion could obliterate all this beauty, or turn our society against the differences within itself.

Yes, the danger is real, and we may have to walk through major disaster in our time. But instead of cowering in the face of doom, I choose to face the disaster and roar with laughter. That laughter slices into any silence and penetrates my own numbness. And I keep walking, trying to bring humanity and deep laughter to any dark corner. And I try to keep myself laughing — and crying, too.

Chapter 9

American Willing to Listen: A Silly Idea Bears Fruit, 1979–83

INTERNATIONAL TOURISM has never appealed to me. I just can't picture myself staying in a luxury hotel in Rome or Tokyo or Cairo, visiting museums and monuments, and scouring gift shops for souvenirs. I don't relish shopping, am shy, and find approaching strangers difficult. The message I got from the parable of the Good Samaritan was that if you went out into the world, strangers would fall upon you and beat and rob you. So for many years, I traveled abroad very little.

But the more I studied the nuclear threat, the more I became consumed with a desire to learn what was happening on this endangered planet, to talk with people around the world, and find out how they felt about the future in general, and the nuclear situation in particular. I wanted to enlarge the context of my work to prevent nuclear war. Although theoretically I was fighting for the survival of every human being on the planet, I didn't actually know many people outside the United States. And since I was getting a glimmer of how important it was for me to be connected to the people I was fighting for, my goal became finding people around the world to know and love. I really loved people only in California and Idaho. I needed a bigger heart. I needed a global heart.

So I sold my house, paid my debts, and bought one of those around-the-world airplane tickets. They are really not that expensive. Actually, the ticket limited me to the Northern Hemisphere, but that was enough for a start. Later, I would find ways to visit Southern Hemisphere countries. At my request, friends sent me names of people to talk to and stay with. I planned to go only to cities and towns where I had four or more contacts. After interviewing these contact people, I would ask them to suggest others. But I also wanted to interview people at random. So I came up with the idea of sitting in a park or other public place, with a cloth sign that said "American Willing to Listen." Maybe people would come and talk to me. I didn't dare tell my friends about the cloth sign for fear that their disapproval, or even enthusiasm, might crush this fragile, tentative idea.

Before leaving the United States, I drove down to Santa Barbara to test my plan. I interviewed a few contact people there and asked them to refer me to others. I tried sitting on a park bench with a sign — "Willing to Listen." I felt shy, exposed, and embarrassed. But it seemed better to get a start on those feelings close to home. People did stop to talk, and some of the conversations had depth. This encouraged me.

But on the plane to Japan, my doubts and fears resurfaced. What if my interviewing project failed? Perhaps it was a big mistake to try. I had never traveled alone in the world. What if I got sick? What if thieves fell on me? And at the same time, I felt excited; I was doing something no one in my family had ever done.

The project began in Kyoto, Japan. First, I met my contact people: a Buddhist priest, several environmental activists, and a women's studies class at Kyoto University. It took a few days before I made my "American Willing to Listen" sign, and a few more before I got up the nerve to use it. Waiting for a train in Osaka, I said to myself, "If I'm ever going to do this, I should do it here, where nobody I know will see me." Unfolding my two-by-three-foot cloth sign, I laid it on the floor in front of me and sat down on a bench. Time passed. People came over, sized me up, and walked away. I tried to smile pleasantly. If I busied myself with reading or writing, I was sure that people would not talk to me for fear of interrupting. So I just sat and smiled, all the while thinking, "This is a bad idea. I've spent a lot of money on my plane ticket, and the plan isn't working. I'm making a fool of myself. How will I ever get to talk with ordinary people? Maybe they don't speak English."

It was thirty or forty minutes before someone finally stopped to talk — a man in his forties who worked at a shoe factory. He wanted to know what I was doing. I tried to explain, but he didn't understand, and I began to fear that I didn't understand either. I was so busy answering his questions that I never managed to ask him any of mine.

After another few minutes, a man of about thirty stopped to chat. He discussed some of his concerns: the border war between North and South Korea over control of rubber trees; consumerism in Japan, and the level of consumption in developed countries in general; the investment of massive amounts of Japanese capital in China (he felt a China-Japan alliance might be destabilizing in the region). Closer to home, he was thinking about relations between the sexes. His wife was part of a women's consciousness-raising group, and he and the other husbands had felt jealous of it. They'd tried to start their own group, but it hadn't worked. He was disappointed, and the issue seemed to be unresolved for him. He couldn't figure out why the group failed to bond and chose not to continue meeting.

Boarding the train in Kyoto, I felt happy and relieved. The second man I'd talked with had understood what I was doing and thought it was a great idea. And he had shared a little of his life with me. My confidence grew as the process of meeting people gained momentum. I met people by arrangement and at random, in their homes, schools, and workplaces, as well as in cafes, train stations, universities, and parks. I refined my interviewing technique, asking open-ended questions that would serve as springboards for opinions and stories — questions like "What are the biggest problems you see affecting your country or region?" and "How would you like things to be different in your life?" Being limited to English put me at a disadvantage, but people often volunteered to translate for me.

Early interviews showed me how little I knew about the world. There were vast fields of information that I had never heard about. For instance, nearly everyone I talked with in Japan mentioned Kim Dae Jung, a South Korean opposition leader who had escaped to Japan and then had been sent back to Korea. Relations between Japan and South Korea were not a part of my world picture. In my world history classes, this part of the world had been absent. In the United States, these issues had seemed unimportant and had received only minimal coverage in the news media. Now, I was meeting people to whom they were very important. I began to see glimmers of the many ways in which non-Americans saw the world. In 1997, Kim Dae Jung became leader of South Korea, and this little piece of history I had learned as part of my American Willing to Listen project fit into a much larger context and was relevant to world events.

It was exhilarating, but exhausting. The rapid succession of new issues nearly overwhelmed me — the homogenization of Japanese culture, women's gossip in an Indian village, the flight of capital from Australia to the Philippines and Korea, the aspiration to know God, the near-meltdown of a Japanese nuclear power plant, rural Indian mothers' fears that their children weren't getting enough protein, doubts about the tradition of arranged marriage, regional conflicts over resource and capital allocation, and the frustration of people everywhere who sensed that their destiny was controlled by the superpowers, and how undemocratic that was. It occurred to me that I might have to go on interviewing full-time for the rest of my life to get any sense of what was going on in the world. I continue to want to know what is happening in my time, what winds of philosophy and ideas are blowing in the complex interwoven fabric of life while I live.

Seventeen years and hundreds of interviews later, I no longer feel quite so confounded. I have continued the practice, though I don't usually use the sign. I just walk up to people and ask them if they would mind talking with me. I'm beginning to get a sense of social and historical currents around the world. On my first world trip, I listened to people in Japan, Thailand, India, England, and Scotland. Subsequent trips have taken me to East and West Berlin (when they were separated), Israel, Palestine, Sweden, Vietnam, Russia, China, Brazil, South Africa, Australia, New Zealand, Austria, and the former Yugoslavia (Croatia and Serbia, where I also met with Bosnians in both those countries). While traveling, I've also met people from other countries in Asia, Africa, Latin America, and the South Pacific. My listening project has become a continuing practice, both in the United States and abroad.

On the Punjab Mail, a train from Bombay to Hoshangabad, I interviewed the woman who shared my compartment. The wife of a retired railroad worker, she appeared to be in her mid-sixties, and she was traveling with a well-made wooden box that contained a cake for her nephew's wedding. As we rode along, she spoke of her worries about her son, a drug addict who was now in Saudi Arabia. The woman's English was quite good, but she had trouble with my name. Peavey is not a common Indian name. So I gave her my business card, which identified me as a technological forecaster. "What's a technological forecaster?" she asked. I tried to explain that I had studied technological forecasting in college, and that in technological forecasting we try to anticipate what technological inventions will be available in the future, and roughly when these innovations will be available for people designing systems or structures to be built far in the future. Her face lit up. "Oh, you mean a fortune-teller?" Preoccupied with getting ready for bed, I wasn't paying much attention. "Sort of," I replied. She started asking me about her son. Was he still on drugs? Would he return to India? Or might he marry someone in Saudi Arabia and lose his religion? I said something mildly encouraging about parents and children.

Then, she left the compartment. Twenty minutes later, she returned, reporting that she had gone through the train announcing that a blue-eyed fortune-teller was on board. A group of people had gathered and was waiting to hear their fortunes. She would be happy to translate.

Discovering a line of twenty or thirty people outside our compartment, I tried in vain to convince them of my lack of talent or training in fortune-telling. But they replied, "You gave her a good fortune — you must give us one, too." I was up most of the night giving friendly advice and encouragement.

A middle-aged farmer wanted to know about his cow. The cow had been sick, and her milk yield was poor. Would she get better? I asked a few questions and eventually suggested he consult an animal specialist and get some help. He seemed grateful for my listening to him and for the advice.

A couple came in and asked, "Will we find a husband for our daughter, and will she be happy in her marriage?" I said, "Yes, if they work hard at their marriage, I think they will be happy." They looked at each other with relief. "Will we be able to find her a husband close to our village? We want to have our daughter close to us." As they asked more questions, my translator explained to me about Hindu marriage arrangements. The bride lives with the husband's family, and difficulties can arise if the bride and the mother-in-law don't get along. I suggested to the couple that they interview only potential husbands close to their home if that was their goal, and to interview prospective mothers-in-law to find a cheerful one for their daughter.

Another couple was traveling to visit their grandchild for her first birthday ceremony. Would the granddaughter grow up to be happy, healthy, and prosperous? I tried to get some hints. Was she a healthy baby? I said something mildly encouraging. They said: "In your country, you beat children and treat them badly. That's because you don't believe in reincarnation." The woman explained that her beloved mother, who had died a year or two before, had been reincarnated as the baby. So, of course, this baby was very special to them.

After my stint as the blue-eyed fortune-teller of the Punjab Mail, I felt more at home in India. I'd begun to empathize with some of the problems Indians had in their lives. They were worried about their children, just as I had worried about my younger sister's marriage. They were concerned about the health of their parents; I had been through that, too. It seems silly that we have to be reminded of the common bonds we have with people all over the world, but it is continually important.

Listening to people, I began to learn how each individual was puzzling out large issues from her own vantage point. In Varanasi, India, a woman told me that when the Brahmans were thrown out of power in southern India, her husband could no longer find a satisfactory job there. So they moved north to Varanasi. She currently had no job, she said, because Varanasi was a place that didn't respect women working. Now, she feared that the lower castes would revolt in the north, as they had in the south. "Already", she said, "Brahmans are unable to provide strong leadership, because they feel so insecure." She expected people to become "more and more selfish, only thinking of themselves, no one thinking of society. And corruption has been getting worse and worse. Corrupt politicians are responsible for the misery in every sphere of life."

In Edinburgh, Scotland, a man who worked with the Scottish nationalist party told me that his country was a colony of England, and England would never grant them independence, because the English wanted their offshore oil. The Scots, for their part, can't mount an effective independence movement, he said, because they are so fiercely individualistic that they can't work together.

In Darjeeling, India, I met a thirteen-year-old from Bhutan who wanted to become a freedom fighter, to help his region gain independence from China. He earnestly told me about his desire to study hard, to become a strong man, to help his people. I was surprised to see such determination in a person his age.

Two Kyoto women in their twenties were thinking about why Japanese young people were so uninvolved in world affairs. The explanation they had developed was historical: Japanese people had been told that they would win the war against the materialist United States, because Japanese spiritual values were superior. So Japan's defeat in World War II was considered a victory for materialism — which the Japanese now embraced fully. Materialistic, hedonistic values had taken over, they told me, and parents had neglected to give their kids the love and sense of security that would allow them to be involved in larger concerns.

I visited the Rasulia Center near Hoshangabad, India, where about thirty people — most from the untouchable caste — live, farm, build biogas plants for energy, and work toward self-sufficiency. The leader of the community told me that India's culture used to be one of the greatest in the world — in the forefront in mathematics, art, and religion. India was no longer a leader, he said, because colonialism had squashed the Indian's initiative and destroyed the legitimate traditional leadership structure and ways. As petroleum becomes more expensive, he projected, societies that are not so dependent on oil (especially less-developed countries) can become a stronger force in the world. He was researching planting crops in a way that barely disturbed the soil. Tractors were not needed. He didn't expect that trend to take hold for another hundred years or so, but he was very hopeful about the future and was preparing for it.

The entire village was exhilarated by the selection of a man from the untouchable caste to head the dairy farm. In the past, the position had been filled by a college-educated man. The real work had been done by lower-caste men; recently, the director of the village had noticed that one worker knew a great deal about the running of the dairy, and had often been consulted by the educated man. The selection of the long-time worker to take the place of the educated man when he left was very exciting to the entire village. This was seen as opening up possibilities for everyone. "Someday, maybe an untouchable will be the president. Why, maybe a woman will be able to head the dairy, too," a village woman said to me. In 1997, a man was elected president of India who had been born to the untouchable caste.

A conversation I had with a nuclear engineer in New Delhi lasted six hours. We started out at the YMCA, where I was staying; then, he drove me to a fancy club he belonged to, and we ate dinner on the verandah there. We talked at length about nuclear power and his doubts about quality control in India's nuclear power industry. He also helped me understand the fear generated by the state of emergency declared by Indira Gandhi in 1975. Opponents of Mrs. Gandhi's regime were thrown in jail; so when she called an election, people were afraid to admit to one another that they were planning to vote against her. "When I went into the voting booth," the engineer told me, "I hadn't asked my wife whom she was voting for, and she hadn't asked me. Nobody knew how anyone else was going to vote. Privately, we were all afraid that if Mrs. Gandhi won, she would declare another state of emergency and refuse to hold elections in the future. Then, we'd never be able to get rid of her." I could see how much he enjoyed being listened to, and how important it was for him to talk about things he said he hadn't been able to discuss with anyone else. I was very interested in the state of nuclear power in India and appreciated his perspective on that.

In all of my conversations, I would look directly at the person I was interviewing, and at the same time observe the context we were in — the sounds around us, the birds, the wind, the way people nearby responded to our presence. I would listen to the person as openly as I could, trying to get a glimpse of the world through his eyes. Usually, when the conversations lasted long enough, I would start to feel the soft stirrings of a connection — some uncovering of our common root system.

"Are things getting better or worse in your life? For your family? In the community you live in? In the world? These questions always got people talking. In Hoshangabad, I began to notice that men tended to think things were getting better, while the women were generally more pessimistic. A woman to whom I mentioned this observation responded: "That's because the men don't do the shopping."

When I asked about the future, many people went directly to the possibility of nuclear war. Near Kyoto, I spoke with a seventy-two-year-old farmer whose family had lived on the same land since the twelfth century. He feared that the population explosion had made nuclear war more likely. And nuclear war would make it impossible to grow healthy food. "We in Japan are downwind from everyone," he told me. He had a world map in the room in which I interviewed him. He said it was an old map. Japan was colored bright red and was in the middle. Looking at it, Japan looked almost as large as the United States. If I had been raised seeing that map, I might think that attacking the US was feasible.

A Tibetan businessman I met in an antique store offered to take me to "the wisest man in Darjeeling." I followed the businessman through an alley, up a dark staircase, and into a little room. There we met a Tibetan monk, a stout man who sat surrounded by his scrolls. On one side stood an intricately arranged altar; on the other, a large window overlooked the Himalayas. The businessman translated as we chatted.

At one point, the monk abruptly changed the subject. "What I really want to talk to you about is nuclear war." He reached in among his scrolls, brought out a world atlas, and asked me to show him where Hawaii was. A friend from Hawaii had told him about nuclear war. Since then, he had spent a lot of time thinking about it, and had come to believe that the root of the nuclear threat was anger. Did I get angry often? he wanted to know. Did people often get angry with me? He advised me that this was an important area to work on. He looked out the window at the majestic Himalayas and mournfully observed, "Nuclear war would ruin these mountains."

A scientist in Varanasi was more sanguine. Nuclear war might solve the population problem, he suggested.

In London, a political activist I met in a bookstore was concerned that the United States would provoke a war in Europe. "You think you can protect your own country by keeping the wars on our continent. That's why you want to put your weapons on our land. We are your front line. Don't you care about us at all?"

I often encountered hostility toward the United States. A young doctor at the Rasulia center said, "You Americans have so much, and we have so little. Your aid comes with strings attached. You can't give a clean gift; you can't help without getting something out of it, even if it's only a slightly less guilty conscience." Foreign businesses come to India in search of cheap labor, he said. For every dollar they invest in India, they take out three dollars' worth of goods. "That is how you get things cheaply in your country." By now he was yelling. "We don't want your help, your charity, your money! Get your ships out of the Indian Ocean, and get out of our lives!"

Listening to him, I felt personally attacked. I wanted to tell him that I wasn't one of those industrialists. Yet, I wasn't wholly divorced from the situation either — I ate cashews from India, and I'd never felt good about food being exported from a hungry country to the United States. So I kept listening, and noticing my own defenses.

A woman in New Delhi said her daughter wanted to know why American protesters did not continue to care about the Vietnamese people after the US troops had gone home. How could we cut the connection so easily? The question stung. As she spoke, feeble excuses ran through my mind. Once our troops had left Vietnam, we no longer had much information about what was happening there. Anyway, hadn't we done our part by forcing our government to withdraw the troops? It seemed such a natural thing to go on to other issues. Even as these defenses arose, I could see I was struggling to convince myself of my own righteousness. But finally, I inwardly admitted that there was no justification for my own fickle attention to the plight of the Vietnamese people. Self-righteousness is a delusion, and as such, a dangerous position to defend.

One day, I stumbled into the Nonaligned Nations Conference in New Delhi. I stepped into the Oberoi Hotel to make a phone call, and then sat down at an unattended desk to write some notes. A woman wearing a brightly colored dress came up to ask directions to the toilet. I saw from her nametag that she was from Tonga. I gave her directions and asked if she would come back to answer some questions. I asked her to tell me what world issues most concerned her. She expressed outrage about the expansion of the US military base on Diego Garcia, an island in the Indian Ocean, where the US government is building a large military base. Other delegates I talked with at the conference shared that concern. They were sure that the base would be used for surveillance of southern Asia, northern Africa, and the South Pacific, and would potentially be used as a springboard for military intervention. The woman from Tonga was alarmed that I had no knowledge of any of this. She wanted to know whether my ignorance was typical of the American people. How could I consider myself well-informed and yet know nothing of this important global issue that involved my government?

She offered to bring other people from the conference to talk with me if I would come back in the next few days. I asked her if she weren't worried that I was from the CIA. No, she said, if you were from the CIA, you would surely have known where Tonga was.

So every afternoon, I sat down at "my desk" at the Nonaligned Nations Conference. Delegates and others at the conference came to talk with me. The hotel staff began to recognize me and bring me stationery and water. These conversations gave me a sense of how powerful a force the United States is in the lives of people in many places all over the globe. They envy the comforts we take for granted, and long for a fair share of their own resources and the fruits of their labor. They are afraid of being devastated in a nuclear war they never agreed to take part in. They are bewildered that the American people don't seem to know or care about what our government is doing in the rest of the world and what is happening internationally.

I developed two rules for listening to people talk about my country. First, I do not explain or defend the United States. My goal is to see how we look to others, and to let that understanding inform my being. Although I continue to feel defensive when my country is criticized, I try to keep listening. Second, I do not divorce myself from criticisms of America and Americans. I do not say or imply, "Yes, some Americans or some parts of our country are that way, but I'm not." I try to take the criticisms seriously.

But it's not only criticisms I encountered. I've also heard out-and-out adoration of the United States. In a park in East Berlin, I met a young couple out for a Sunday stroll. Right away, I noticed the American flag pin on the man's shirt. The woman was noticeably pregnant, and both of them had high hopes for the future. They had already applied once for permission to emigrate to the United States, but their application had been denied. They had heard all about America from the man's sister, who lives in California, and they longed for the freedom she had told them about. They wanted to work hard, advance in their careers, and be free to buy all sorts of things.

In Varanasi, two women students — one from Iran, the other from Bahrain — told me they knew all about the United States from watching "Dallas" on television. They especially admired the kitchens in "Dallas," and all the electrical appliances and space. I told them that not everyone in my country had such a high standard of living — that some people didn't even have electricity. Some people are so poor they don't have homes. I could see they were struggling to believe what I said.

Throughout my travels, I met people who had studied in the United States, including many of the delegates at the Nonaligned Nations Conference. Many people spoke of the inequality of the cultural exchange. A woman in Tokyo who had studied at the University of Chicago put it forcefully: "We send our smartest people to your universities to learn from you. But you don't send your students to learn from us. When you come to our country, you stay in fancy hotels, go on shopping trips, and travel around in your buses. There's a lot you miss. Yours is a young society, and you have a lot to learn from us."

I have found people to be grateful, surprised, and excited that an American has come to learn from them. In Tokyo, Bangkok, Varanasi, and New Delhi, people lined up and sometimes waited for hours to talk with me. Around midnight on the night before I left Varanasi, I was busy packing my bag when I heard a knock on the door. It was a Bangladeshi man whom I'd met briefly at the university. He had heard that I was about to leave and he wanted to be interviewed. An engineering student, he was also very interested in international cooperation and wanted to make sure that Bangladesh was represented in my listening project.

I often asked people: "What have you learned in your life?" Some had learned about time's constant movement. Others spoke of sorrow and suffering. A revolutionary in Bangkok had learned that "you have to be very careful." He had helped start a people's credit union, but government agents had infiltrated it, shut it down, and confiscated all the money.

In New Delhi, a woman spoke of discouragement in her profession. Once a doctor, she had given up practicing medicine.

"What good does it do? I get them well, but they get sick the next day. They don't have enough food. If I use my medical training, it only means that they are going to suffer longer." Now, she makes decorative plaques. I felt saddened by her depression and sense of futility.

One of the best known people I interviewed at the Nonaligned Nations Conference was Fidel Castro, who was the chairperson of the conference. He was very busy and somewhat distracted. Finally, I asked him what was the most important thing he had learned in his life. He looked far away and said, "It's worth it. It's worth the hard work and struggling." He then stood up and left in a very gracious way.

On my second day in Bangkok, I took a taxi driver's recommendation of a place to eat breakfast. The restaurant was a large room with about thirty tables, all but two empty. The only people in the place were two European men at a booth in front, and six or seven Thai women, who were sitting or standing around another table nearby. They all looked up as I walked in. I sat in the booth behind the women, and soon I began to sense that the men were either the owners of the restaurant or of a brothel in which the women worked.

From a nearby table, a woman looked at me and mouthed the words, "I love you." I was so confused I felt like a block of wood. I had come for breakfast! She gestured to ask if she could join me; I shrugged my shoulders noncommittally and nodded my head. Another woman came up behind me and started rubbing my shoulders. She said softly, "You want a massage? You want to come up to my room for a massage?" I said, "No, thank you." The first woman scooted around and sat next to me. I tried to carry on as meaningless a conversation as possible. What's your name? Where do you live? I ordered eggs and toast for breakfast. It was about seven o'clock, so I said to the woman next to me, "You're here early this morning." She said she'd been here last night, too, until 1:00 a.m. She was a short woman, not over thirty years old. She touched my arm with a cold hand — she must have been as scared as I was. Rubbing my arm suggestively, she asked if I'd like to come up to her room. "I can make you very happy." I could no longer escape the conclusion that she was a prostitute who thought I'd come for her services.

Putting my hand on hers to stop her from rubbing my arm, I remembered my interview book! I whipped it out and told her I was traveling to learn what was happening in the world. Would she be willing to talk with me? Yes, she would. She told me her job was to sleep with men and let them touch her. She had to work hard to feed her two children. It cost too much to send them to school, so they stayed with her mother during the day. The woman's husband had been killed recently, when the truck he was driving turned over.

By this time, my eggs had arrived, bathed in grease. I couldn't bring myself to eat them. The other women started coming over to my table, trying to get me to go upstairs with them. I realized what a mystery I must seem: I hadn't eaten my food; I'd just been talking with this woman; perhaps there was something else I wanted that they could give me. Soon, all the women were sitting with us, talking about husbands and children and work and life in Thailand. They spoke of their envy and fear of the American and Japanese business and military men who used their services. Americans are friendly and have a lot of money, one woman told me, but sometimes when you get them upstairs, they're awful.

The women had mixed feelings about the Thai government. A big problem was that houses were being torn down and people were being thrown out of their neighborhoods. The threat of eviction was terrifying. But they did have electric power and lights — that was an improvement over past years.

We talked about children. The women all wished they could send their kids to school, but they couldn't afford the tuition. When I spoke of schooling provided for free by the government, they all started talking at once. What a great idea! I mentioned the school I'd visited the day before in Bangkok, where poor people could send their children for one baht (about five cents) a day. They hadn't heard of it.

Before leaving, I offered the woman who'd first sat with me some money for her time and her teaching. Maybe she could use it for some days of school for her children at the One Baht School. She looked at the European men at the next table. Obviously, the money would have to go to them. I said "OK." I wouldn't give her any money. Then, as I slid out of the booth, I surreptitiously slipped it into her hand, which she had extended under the table.

Still feeling the effects of jet lag, I returned to my hotel room and tried to sleep. But I was too excited. I kept thinking about the Thai women I had just met, about how much fun it had been to chat with them, how lively our discussion had been. I thought of what I'd learned about the impact of widowhood. Several of the women I'd talked with had turned to prostitution because they had children to take care of and no husband or other source of support. I could understand their decision, but I fervently wished they had other options. I remembered how an idea that was familiar to me — free public education — had seemed thrilling to them. And I wondered why I had been so afraid in the first moments in the restaurant. What had been so threatening? I had never been propositioned by prostitutes before. What does a decent person do in that kind of situation? I felt irritated at the taxi man taking me there, rather than to a place that specialized in edible food. I had been unprepared for the visceral pleasure and interest I'd felt. And yet, even in the midst of the fear, I had known I was in no real danger. I had to laugh at my fright, and myself.

The next day, I returned to the One Baht School to talk more with its founder, Prateep Ungsongtham. A tall, graceful woman in her late twenties, she had founded the school at age fifteen. At the time, she had been a child care worker, and she began to be concerned about the children who brought their younger siblings to her, but couldn't afford to attend school themselves. So although she had little schooling herself, Prateep began teaching the older children to read. In exchange, they paid her one baht each and helped with child care. Now, the school had grown; there were two buildings and a basketball court. Prateep had finished college, and some of her former students who now had college degrees had returned to teach.

The One Baht School is in the middle of Klong Toey, a community of forty thousand squatters. Built on stilts over a canal, their dwellings are made mostly out of found wood and are generally very clean inside. I found myself wondering: In such terrible situations, where do people get the ideas, the will, and the drive to make things better, not only for themselves but for others? The land is owned by the Port Authority, which at the time was taking steps to evict six thousand slum dwellers in order to build a container port. The school had been a focal point for the efforts against eviction. Prateep said, "To feel secure, we need to know that we can stay here for thirty or forty years."

When Prateep found out that I'd had some experience fighting eviction, she called in the other teachers. It was a Saturday, so there were no classes. Ten of us sat together, and I talked about the International Hotel, the American Indian struggles against uranium mining, and other land struggles. Every now and then, our discussion would have to stop because someone would come in with a problem: an old man was dying, or a woman's electric bill was forty times what it should be. The teachers were also community workers, and with each interruption, one of them would leave to help resolve the problem.

I dredged up everything I had learned at the I-Hotel about fighting eviction — resistance tactics and techniques from England, China, Japan, the Philippines, and all over the United States. We talked about nonviolent political tactics, organizing ideas, and so much more. Each idea seemed to suggest others to them, and they would take off in their own language, talking excitedly. They had dreamed of defying the eviction order to gain a political advantage, but had thought of their struggle as an isolated one. Hearing that others around the world had the same dream was exhilarating to them. I had never shared information with a more eager and intensely interested bunch.

During my time in Japan, it slowly dawned on me that I had not seen any slums or poor people there. I began asking the people I interviewed where the poor people were. "We don't have poor people in Japan," I was told again and again. "We are all middle class." Or occasionally, "Oh yes, we have some, but I don't know where. Maybe in Tokyo." These answers seemed implausible, so I continued my inquiry. The poverty illiteracy in such a society is shocking. Many people do not know about the situation of poor people. I have known people in my home city who have as little knowledge about the poor in their community. They do not know how to "read" the signs of the poor they see on the street, nor how to care about what they see.

Finally, I heard about a district in Osaka called Kamagasaki, where day laborers and poor people lived. Church people from Osaka and Kyoto had organized a night patrol in the area, so that people who fell asleep on the street would not freeze, and those who were injured could be cared for. Each night of the week, a different group was responsible for the watch.

One night, I tagged along with a visiting group from Friends World College. We arrived at a small church in a bleak part of Osaka about 9:00 p.m. Our first job was to check the log books for news of the previous night's shift. Then, the eight of us doing the watch that night gathered our supplies — gloves, first-aid kits, lanterns, and click counters — loaded them into two pull-carts piled high with quilts, and walked to a nearby building. I was amazed at what I saw there. More than a hundred people were sleeping on cotton mattresses covered with colorful quilts. It was an open-air sleeping center, a 25-by-75-foot area sheltered by the overhang of the building.

We picked up two containers of warm rice balls, put them in our carts, and set out in search of other people who needed a place to sleep. We divided into two teams of four and headed in different directions. As we walked, we found men sleeping in little hidden places. We kept track of how many we came across and where they were sleeping. My Japanese partner approached each sleeping person and checked. "Good evening. How are you? Are you warm enough? Would you like some rice?" If he was cold, we would give him some directions to the sleeping center. If he couldn't walk there, we would put him in our pull-cart and take him there.

A toothless old man came up to greet us. His dog followed. The man reminded me of some of my Sixth Street Park friends. To make a place to sleep, he had leaned sheets of plywood against two ramen-noodle carts. He accepted a warm rice ball and chatted with us for a while.

Who are the twenty thousand people who live in Kamagasaki? Most are Koreans (the target of much discrimination in Japan). Others are poor Japanese. Many are men who have left their families. In Japan, when you apply for a job, the company looks up your family name in the books of family history. If you do not come from "a good family," or are Korean, you have a very hard time getting a job. There are few training programs to help these men. Many are alcoholics. If a man can afford it, he rents a tiny room for about 250 yen (one dollar in the early 1980s) a night. At the time of my visit, the landlords had recently doubled their profit by splitting the rooms in half. They would build an additional floor to divide each room horizontally, yielding two cubicles just big enough to crawl into.

Why is it that men are the gender that is on the streets? Are they pushed out of families or housing, or do they feel themselves tough enough to take the streets, whereas women are more aware of their vulnerability and make the compromises that at least keep a roof over their heads? All over the world, I see poor men sleeping on the streets, and only occasionally women. It seems that society's treatment of poor men is different from that of poor women. Whatever gender is outside, exposed to the elements with no place to call home, it is sad and a condemnation of the society.

At midnight, we returned to the sleeping center, where by now about 180 men were sleeping. Another crew arrived shortly after we did, carrying a man in their cart. They checked his eyes with a flashlight. Each time a new man arrived, a member of the day laborers' union would carry a mattress and quilt to a spot on the ground and make up a bed for him. The worker would tuck the man in, make sure he was warm, and say goodnight. The physical contact and the personal care moved me. Workers stay there all night, standing guard so that no one can rob or take advantage of the sleeping men, and covering them up if their quilts slip off. I thought again of the people on Sixth Street in San Francisco, wishing the same kind of tenderness were available to them.

We went back to the church and slept until 5:00 a.m., when we returned to the day labor hall. By that time, all the bedding had been put away, and a nearby alley was full of minibuses with signs in their windows advertising for workers — ditch diggers, dirt carriers, and so on. But there were not enough jobs, and two-thirds of the men were left milling around.

At breakfast, I interviewed one of the regular watch volunteers. He told me that Koreans have always been badly treated in Japan. They were once slaves, and they still do the lowliest work. Counting the street people is important, he said, because the society doesn't want to acknowledge its poor.

On the train back to Kyoto, I thought about poor people and tried to envision better ways to get the world's menial work done. If we had a society where everyone was treated well, who would dig the ditches, pick the crops, and clean the buildings? If the United States didn't have a constant stream of immigrants to do that sort of work, who would do it? Are there ways to distribute menial work more evenly, and to value that work? How can individuals and groups create a heart connection to the poor, so that together they can think about how to make changes that will benefit the poor?

Everywhere I traveled, there were aspects of the society that I found disturbing. I tried to notice these, and to see whether my discomfort changed over time. For instance, in Varanasi, one of the predominant smells is that of burning cow dung. At first, I really disliked it. I lost my appetite and wished I could turn off my nose. To put myself at ease with the smell, I studied the cow-dung cycle. I watched people gather the dung with their hands, mix it with a little dry grass, and slap it onto a nearby wall. There is hardly a vertical surface that isn't adorned with dung patties, clearly imprinted with the hand of the patty-maker. The dung is left to dry, and later plucked off and either burned or sold. This is the fuel most poor people use to cook and keep warm. Some patty-makers have a design sense and cover the walls in an artistic fashion; others seem to slap it up without thought or plan. As I became better acquainted with the process, the people, and the city, the smell bothered me less and less, until the discomfort finally left entirely. Now, when I return to Varanasi, as I do regularly, the smell of burning cow dung signals to me that I am "home," as I have come to feel this ancient city to be one of my homes on this planet.

When I returned from my world trip, I also returned to my job at Sixth Street Park. In a staff meeting, some of the guys asked me to tell them what I had learned, especially about poor people and what they were doing to help themselves. I said I had been struck by the poverty in Japan, Thailand, and India. I told them I had seen people in Bombay living like animals in their own excrement, and people with severe disabilities out foraging for food on their hands and knees. Bird, who was sitting directly across the table from me, looked at me squarely, with a tear in the corner of his eye. He said, "It broke your heart, didn't it?" I could tell that even through he was very poor by the standards of the society around him, he had seen poverty much worse — maybe in the service or the merchant marine — and it had moved him. The park staff talked of their relative good fortune, and of the idea of starting an international union of down-and-out people that could go on strike for better treatment. Bird asked if I had figured out anything that people in the park could do to help the poor people I had met. I had to admit I had not, but the question was a good one.

A few years later, I was invited to work in South Africa for a month or so. My job was to determine whether black Africans wanted to be integrated into Afrikaans universities. This meant that I would be interviewing black leaders and students. In the airplane traveling to Johannesburg, I tried to envision how I could both achieve this and continue my American Willing to Listen project. I was interested in seeing how the world looked to the police who were in the difficult position of enforcing oppressive rules. I wondered if I could find a way to talk with them, but I also thought it unlikely that I would get up the courage to do that job.

The World Council of Churches gave me a guide and bodyguard, Mobutu, so I could get to my meetings in the townships. It was in Capetown that the opportunity to interview police came to me, through a most unexpected route. A township in those days — the mid-1980s — was a walled community designed to keep people in and visitors out. One needed a police pass to get in, and no passes were issued to international white people. But to do my work, I had to enter townships, so Mobutu took me in the "back way."

One day, we were driving away after a meeting, in our inconspicuous red rental car, when the police stopped us. They frisked us and went through all the papers in the car, finding some papers authored by Bishop Tutu. That was enough evidence of rebellion for them to take us to the police station. I was angry and afraid. In such moments, I try to find a comedy thought to help me through the moment. As we were going to the police station, whenever I would feel really afraid I would think, "I don't have to worry, the marines will come get me." Then, I would laugh inside because of the extreme unlikelihood of such a rescue, and how pathetic it was for me, who was always out protesting whenever the marines would invade somewhere.

But then I remembered my desire to interview police. This trip to the station was an ideal opportunity. Mobutu was put in the yellow police truck, and I was to follow driving the rental car, with a mulatto policeman accompanying me. I asked him how he felt about what was going on in "the emergency," which had only been in effect for a couple of months at that time. He replied tactfully, "I may not like where I have to live, but I have a job to do and I must do it." We talked further about his anger about the violence of blacks against blacks, about how gangs ran townships, and how quickly street demonstrations turned into violent eruptions. We talked about his family of three girls, about their school situation, and how he wished they could get a better education.

Finally, we reached the station and went inside. Unbelievable though it may seem, as we walked in the song playing on the radio was "To dream the impossible dream." The interior was really plain, with no drawings or family pictures, nothing personal that would humanize the place. We were held there for about eight hours, questioned by several officers. Although they did not touch us, through the wall I heard them beating a woman. I decided to ask them questions, too.

They did the traditional "good cop/bad cop" routine. The "good cop" I called "Cowboy," because he wore cowboy boots with a holster affair on the boots, with a hand gun in each boot. He said, "Where is the list of people you are talking with?" "In my vest pocket," I replied. "Give it to me," he insisted several times. "I know you can take it from me. You have all the power on your side. But I will not give it to you voluntarily." (I never carry all my lists anyway.) I was very glad in that moment that I had been in jail enough not to be too intimidated by him and his threats. Meanwhile, someone went to my hotel room and went through it, looking for my contact list.

Finally, they let us both go without getting my contact list. Mobutu said he would not sleep at home for a month or so. I finished my work in this place that continues, with its philosophy of social change, to inspire me.

It used to be that when I thought of India, I'd imagine the outline of the country on a map. I'd think of hungry people, women in saris, wild animals, mysticism, gurus — just floating impressions. Now, I know what India looks like, smells like, feels like. I know some Indian people and have seen how their lives work in their own environment. I have a sense of some of the unresolved issues in the lives of individual people there. The same is true of South Africa, Vietnam, and New Zealand. I also have a sense of what the American government, multinational corporations, and the World Bank are doing to the lives of real people very far from me.

This perceptual shift reminds me of going on field trips with my college zoology professor, Dr. Stanford. He would take us to an open field that didn't look special or interesting to us. Then "Doc" Stanford would say, "Let's take a look at just this one square meter." We'd explore its ecology in detail — the grasshoppers and beetles, the lichens and grasses, the parasites growing on the stalks of plants. Three or four inches below the surface, we'd find worms, and a new set of bacteria; further down, fungi were growing on the roots of plants. We'd measure the acidity of the soil and note the kinds of plants it supported. We'd study the wind patterns, the geology, how water percolated down through the soil. We could take hours studying a square meter.

And that's the way I feel about the world now. I used to picture the world as a globe, with continents and oceans and countries painted orange, yellow, and pink. Then, when I saw photographs of the earth taken from space, I saw a living whole. Now, I see life on that spinning blue ball: specific places, faces, rivers, concerns, real lives.

I'm continually thinking of the people I've met around the world: the couple on the Punjab Mail; is their granddaughter growing up healthy and strong? How are the street people in Kamagasaki doing? Have the squatters near the One Baht School successfully resisted eviction, or have they been resettled in a better place? In August, I think about the monsoons in India. I can see the waters of the Ganges rising.

My listening project is a kind of tuning-up of my heart to the affairs of the world. I continue it almost as a spiritual discipline as I travel now. I no longer use the sign. I just walk up to people and ask if they speak English, and would they be willing to talk. Or I start a conversation with a question, and then build on that. This practice helps me move from the limitations of my own social context and the boundaries of my heart. I hear the news in a very different way now, and I act with a larger context in mind. Conspicuous consumption has become unappealing to me, now that I have met poor people around the world. I hold myself accountable to the people whose lives I have encountered.

I carry with me the pain of some of my partners in the world, but it does not weigh me down. Pain may be too easy a word. I have known torture, anguish, fear, and depression, resulting from thinking about what I am experiencing with the world. Much of my life and environment have been designed to isolate me from this pain, but I have come to see it as a kind of holy nectar. The more I drink, the more I can taste what is happening on this planet. I cannot do much to help my partners in life in our time, but I can do something. And that I do.

Chapter 10

Would You Do This to Your Mother? Cleaning the Ganges in India, 1982–present

Y AMERICAN Willing to Listen project took me to Varanasi, India, where I met the Ganges River, known as Ganga by everyone who knows her well. Three hundred million people live along the banks of Ganga in India and Bangladesh. Ganga is worshipped by the Hindus as mother and goddess. They call the river "Ganga Ma" — Mother Ganga — and they see her as the source of everything they have. While generally a south-flowing river, Ganga turns and flows north just before Varanasi. Could this explain the magical essence most people attribute to Ganga? Possibly, but there is so much more that goes into the power of the relationship.

In some small way, I could understand this veneration. I grew up loving Idaho's mighty Snake River. Its size and power never let us delude ourselves into thinking we human beings were anything but totally dependent upon water. My father used to say, "Everything we have comes from the Snake." All the wealth in Idaho's Magic Valley came from farming, and all the farms were dependent on the river's water for irrigation. Even if you sold shoes, or insurance, your livelihood depended on the water from the Snake.

We drew our electricity from dams along the river: one at Shoshone Falls and one at Twin Falls. Because of the electric power plant, my generation never saw one of the twin falls. I used to wonder if the Snake River was resentful that one of the falls had been cut off by human needs. But the nature of rivers is to keep moving; I don't think they harbor resentment. Thinking in river time, everything will be worn away — it is only a matter of time.

Ganga plays an even greater role in people's lives than does the Snake. The most devout Hindus bathe in Ganga every day — not just to wash, but to worship in a religious sense and to express devotion. Hindus regularly take small brass or copper pots to the river, fill them with water, and place them on the altars in their homes. High stone steps, called ghats, line the western bank to provide fast foot traffic from the city to and from the river, and to protect the city from floods during the monsoon season.

Ganga is a beautiful, wide, slow-moving river, with light gray porpoises playing in its waters. But the river's blemishes are also immediately apparent. Although Hindus consider it holy, and although the Indian people are very conscious of personal hygiene (they even have a special implement for cleaning the tongue), they have allowed Ganga to become badly polluted. I was viscerally disgusted to see many people sweep their hands along the top of the river, removing the feces floating there in order to clear a place to bathe or drink. I would occasionally see the corpse of a buffalo or a person floating down the river. The Indian sense of *collective* hygiene is very low and seems out of control to the ordinary, personal-cleanliness-conscious Indian. Many individuals dearly wish the common spaces in their community were clean, but they seem not to know how to achieve this goal using voluntary efforts, public relations, or government.

It was in Varanasi, also known as Banaras, that I met not only the river, but also Dr. Veer Bhadra Mishra. He lives on the bank of the river and bathes in it every day. A humble, graceful, tall man with black wavy hair (now, eighteen years later, it is almost entirely gray), Dr. Mishra is professor of civil engineering at Banaras Hindu University (BHU). He is also the *Mahant* (hereditary priest) of one of Varanasi's most honorable temples. He is respectfully addressed as "Mahantji." The "ji" is added as a way of showing respect and love. Since adolescence, he has practiced one of the strictest forms of orthodox Hinduism. He works long hours steadily; his only hobby is his love of music — he takes great joy in his twice-weekly singing lessons.

When I first met Mahantji in 1981, he told me how he loved the river and wished something could be done to heal it. "People, ordinary citizens, are cleaning up rivers, lakes, and ocean water all over the world now," I told him. "They pressure the government to make laws, to build sewage treatment plants, and they force the government to stop industries from putting their waste into the water. You could do that here."

Looking back now, I think it was quite uppity of me to suggest that he begin a campaign to clean the river. Though I told him about some of the ecological campaigns I knew of in the United States and other parts of the world, he felt that action to clean the river, other than praying, was hopeless.

My comment may not have changed Mahantji, but I think it changed me. The day I left Varanasi, I went for a last walk along the riverbank. I felt as I often had at the end of a visit with my aging grandmother — who knew what she would suffer before I saw her again? I could not know the sorrow this awesome river would endure and carry to the ocean. I did not know how powerfully Ganga had entered my heart.

That summer, Mahantji left India for the first time. He came to New York and talked with Pete Seeger and other activists in the Hudson River Clearwater project. He was inspired by their achievements. Many times, Mahantji quoted Pete, who had said, "You in India have a great advantage over us in the United States. Your people already love and revere the river. We have to first awaken that love in our people, because they have forgotten their rivers."

Mahantji then came to San Francisco. We met in my office. He said he wanted to talk seriously about Ganga.

"OK, Peaveyji, I am ready to begin the campaign to clean the river, if you will agree to help me. I will need so much help and advice in this mighty work. I know how to move water, but you can help us move our society to a clean river. Will you help me and Ganga?"

What could I say? A girl raised in Idaho doesn't think she will be called upon to do such a task. But here it was. Mahantji is not the kind of person one says no to.

After more discussion, I made a pledge to him that I would come to India once a year for five years, and do whatever I could to help plan and carry out strategy. He said his newly established foundation would be responsible for my expenses for in-country travel, food, and housing. I would raise the funds for my airfare.

Mahantji reported that he had already gathered a group of trusted friends and prestigious people of the city, and asked them to be on a board of directors of a new foundation destined to carry on the work of cleaning the river. The foundation would be named for Mahantji's temple, the Sankat Mochan Temple. Sankat Mochan means "removal of suffering." It seemed like an appropriate name.

"You will need a name for your campaign," I offered. Mahantji thought for a few minutes. "Swatcha Ganga. That has a fine sound. It means 'clean Ganga.' I will have to discuss it with my colleagues, but it is sounding good to my ear." We called a meeting at my house for all friends interested in this campaign, and on the spot formed an organization, Friends of the Ganges (FOG), that would work in the US to support what would be needed in India.

One of the oldest living cities on earth, Varanasi is considered by many to be India's holiest. For thousands of years, it has been a center of Hindu philosophical discourse. According to Hindu mythology, the god Shiva selected Varanasi as his home on earth; saints have seen the city as a column of light. Pilgrims from all over India come on pilgrimage to Varanasi, as the city itself is seen as a temple. Just as people there walk in a clockwise circle around a temple, they travel around Varanasi on a well-known circular path, always going in a clockwise direction.

The lifelong desire of many religious Hindus is to have at least one holy dip in the sacred river before they die. Many Hindus come to Varanasi to await their death. In this city of 1.4 million people, forty thousand deaths occur each year. It is considered particularly auspicious to die in Varanasi and have one's ashes placed in Ganga; many people believe it ensures that the soul will not have to be reborn in human form again, but will be able to achieve salvation. I don't know exactly what "salvation" means in this context, but that question rests in my enormous file, "continuing mysteries and things unknown about India."

People's relationship to Ganga is born of habit. For thousands of years, parents have been taking their children to the river, teaching them their religious devotions and other daily routines. In earlier days, Ganga may have been able to carry the load of people toileting, and sewers emptying, directly into the river. With the present population explosion, however, the river can no longer take care of that raw sewage.

The BHU campus and the neighboring area, at the upstream end of Varanasi, houses over fifty thousand people. When our campaign began, the Assi River carried the untreated sewage from the university vicinity directly into Ganga. A bend in the river held the sewage against the city-side bank of the river. One hundred yards downstream of the Assi, a pump drew up the city's supply of drinking water; its intake pipe drew water from the edge of the river, where the concentration of sewage was highest. Early city planners never dreamed the city would develop so far south as to affect the drinking water intake.

In 1982, as Ganga flowed beside Varanasi, many open ditches discharged raw sewage into the river along the same bank where people bathed and washed their clothes, dishes, and animals. Most homes do not have indoor plumbing, so people are accustomed to leaving the house to do this private act. On an upper level of the ghats, men defecated, and their feces were swept by ghat caretakers into the river. No sewage treatment facilities existed for treating city sewage. One rarely went to the river without being confronted with human or animal corpses floating in view.

Although about 90 percent of the pollution problems are caused by human sewage, there were industrial waste problems as well. A diesel locomotive factory, also upstream from Varanasi's water intake, discharged mercury, chromium, and corrosive acids directly into the river. And a paper factory further upstream injected its noxious chemicals into the river. The dyeing of silk and cotton fabrics also damaged the river. Water samples from Ganga have turned up arsenic, mercury, lead, and other heavy metals. The Indian government was planning to build a large "industrial colony" five miles south (upstream) of Varanasi. Fancy houses and hotels were being built south of the city without sewers planned or built. And a nuclear power plant was under construction in Narora, a small town much further upstream. The situation when we began was indeed quite grim. No wonder everyone thought cleaning up the Ganga was impossible. If it was impossible, we thought we should get started right away.

In the initial group of people that Mahantji gathered around him were his closest friends, Dr. S. N. Upadhyay and S. K. Mishra. Both men were, and still are, professors at the university with Mahantji. Many teachers at the university come home for dinner with their families and then go to their "club," where they talk about sports or play cards. These three men came to the foundation office instead of going to a club.

S.K., as I have come to call him, is a cheery, open, and friendly man in his late forties, who teaches hydraulic engineering. He lives in a neighborhood close to Mahantji's house and to the office. Upadhyayji teaches chemistry at the university, is studious and conscientious, and tends to be quieter in the meetings. He teaches us how every new turn in the technology works. Both men are close to their children, and through the years I have noticed that they spend a great deal of time trying to find husbands for their girl children and wives for their boys. All foundation decisions are made collaboratively by the men. This has its strengths and its weaknesses. If one of the three is away or busy with other business, it is very difficult to get much done.

For years, most evenings, the three men could be found talking and working together simultaneously. What that means is that they talk and write, design a brochure, or proofread some material simultaneously. Very often, as they are discussing a situation, S. K. takes a divergent point of view, which drives Mahantji crazy. He shuts his eyes and rolls his head back to indicate that now that this other point has been brought up, the discussion will have to go even longer. From my point of view, this diversion is often valuable and balances the group dynamic. If one of them has any disagreement, the decision is postponed until consensus can be found. All three men have finely honed senses of humor and love to laugh. They frequently tell funny stories and laugh together.

These men love to eat and to talk about food. If we're going to have a meeting that involves food, the menu will be the most discussed item of the planning meeting. They were not politically active in their university days, and took care initially to talk about how this was not a political campaign, but a campaign based on spiritual concerns for the river as well as for the people.

Meetings are held in a combination of English and Hindi. Higher education in India often involves instruction in English, so the foundation members are skilled at understanding and speaking my language. I'm grateful to them for the effort it takes to discuss things in English. I have learned some Hindi and can understand it better than I can speak it. Often in meetings, I will sit listening during many minutes of discussion in Hindi, which to my ears is a very interesting and beautiful language. You can learn a lot about a culture simply by studying its language. For instance, the word *kal* means both yesterday and tomorrow. This is today, and then there are all other days, past and future.

To announce the beginning of the campaign, people from Swatcha Ganga went through the city streets broadcasting their goals on portable sound systems mounted on bicycles. We did not know what we were going to do to clean the river or how to proceed. When I arrived in Varanasi for the first time on official river-cleaning business, in 1981, I was aware that people expected me to be some kind of foreign expert on cleaning rivers. Not only was I not that kind of expert, but I find that strategies developed in a place are more powerful than imported ones. Mahantji had formed the Sankat Mochan Foundation, and this group had begun the Swatcha Ganga campaign.

I made appointments with each of the men on the board of directors to hear their thoughts on what should be done. I asked what ideas they thought would be effective in creating the social, political, and technical changes that would result in cleaning the river. I also tried to figure out their "change view" — how they understood changes that had occurred in their society. How they explained the cause and sequence of change in Varanasi and India was important in deciding what to do.

Several people I interviewed said that ordinary people "do not see the sewage floating on the river." Initially, I found this puzzling. I knew it could not literally be true. Finally, I came to think of these as statements of social distance between the speaker and those he was talking about. It is like people in one social or economic class in the US saying, "Those people (in another class) don't care." Of course they do care, and of course they do see the sewage on the river; but because the person being judged does not share those sentiments publicly, such assumptions are made.

Finally, I asked questions that related directly to the project: What stories can you tell me about Ganga? How has Ganga changed in your lifetime? What have your parents and grandparents told you about how Ganga used to be? Why is it important to you to clean the river? What do you want to do to clean the river? What can ordinary people do to protect Ganga? How do you explain Ganga's situation to your children?

From my interviews, I found that there was a tremendous disparity in factual information among people working to clean the river. For instance, someone told me that the water department never treated the water taken from the river for drinking. Others said that the department put two or three tablets in the water each week. Another person told me, "When the government can afford it, they put in chlorine tablets. If the tea tastes bad, you know they're treating the water. Our tea rarely tastes bad." Others indicated that cleaning Ganga was of the same magnitude of change and consequences as their liberation from British rule. Maybe this is the Ganga liberation movement!

After each interview, I'd ask, "Whom else should I interview about Ganga?" They sent me to a pathologist who studies illnesses resulting from water pollution, a priest who sings religious songs about the river, a boatman, an insurance salesman, a surgeon at the university, and the Maharaja. Initially, I interviewed more than twenty people. More than a few of them said that cleaning Ganga was such an impossible task that I should give up and return to my home.

Early on, I learned that I must take care not to insult this river that the people worship. It would be a major error to insinuate that the river was not perfect. To say "the river is polluted" would be to suggest that pollution was a characteristic of the river. This would make the river seem central to the polluted condition. It would be more respectful to say "the humans are not taking care of the river." Humans are central to the pollution of the river. I learned that there is a way of looking at the river as being holy, the water itself being pure, but carrying (as if between the molecules of water) the pollution. One day, someone in the campaign said, "The river is holy, but it is not pure." Statements like this helped guide me in my exchanges with people. How we talk about a problem tells a lot about how to structure the campaign and the literature.

To uncover some strategies for the campaign, I tried to discover focal points for concern about Ganga. "What is it that pains you most about the river?" I would ask. "How do people feel when they see corpses floating in the river? What do you feel about the lack of sewage treatment? The use of soap for bathing and washing clothes?" Interestingly, one thing everyone mentioned as disturbing was people spitting into the river. There was consensus on that issue — it should not be done. In ancient Hindu religious taboos, spitting is mentioned. Another common concern was the effect of the water on children's health.

When we began this work, we had no idea how far we would have to walk before the river was clean, but it was obvious that the first steps had to involve our own hopelessness that anything could be done by a citizens' group. Many people in the initial interviews mentioned the uselessness of even trying to clean Ganga. They discussed the corruption of the government bureaucracy, the poverty of the area, the massiveness of the problem. I began to think that this campaign was going to take longer than I had anticipated. So, to my list of questions I added: "How are you preparing your children to clean the river?" Cleaning the river will take a long time; people who are now school age will have to carry it on.

One day, when we had gone to Lucknow to visit the governor and check out an innovative toilet design, someone interrupted my afternoon shower. "Peavey, Peavey, come quick, we have had a great idea!" They would have a poster contest for the children of Varanasi, asking them to depict the situation with the river. Then, the foundation would hang the winning posters at a popular folk music festival, so that the adults could see what the children see.

That year, we took a slide show about Ganga to a dozen schools; after seeing it, hundreds of children drew pictures of the river for the contest. In most subsequent years, a poster contest has been held, and environmental education has been one of the main legs of the campaign.

As my interviews continued, new questions arose. For example, it struck me as odd that all the key people in the Swatcha Ganga movement were men, so I began asking, "Where are the women who care about Ganga?" When I asked this of a woman whose husband was a board member, she volunteered to bring a woman friend over to discuss it. We had tea, talked, and decided to call a larger meeting. This time there were twenty women, and they decided to organize a women's conference about Ganga. Two months later, more than four hundred women came to a *shamiyana* (a brightly colored tent), erected on the banks of Ganga, to hear about the pollution of the river. There was lots of singing, poetry, and speeches.

In the course of organizing the conference, I learned an important lesson from Leela Sharma, the convenor. Before each meeting, I noticed that Leela was in her seat at exactly the time the meeting was announced to start. All over the world, people find beginning meetings punctually a problem, and this seems to be true in India, also. One day I asked, "Leela, why are you always in your seat and completely ready when the meeting is announced to begin, when you know many people will not arrive until later, and the meeting will not really begin for another twenty minutes or so?" "Well, Peavey, I worked with Gandhi when we were fighting the British. Gandhi said, 'When you say you are going to meet at two o'clock and you begin at two o'clock, then you can *believe yourselves* when you say you are going to throw the British out of your country.' I want us to believe ourselves when we say we are going to clean Ganga. This is my way of building confidence in ourselves that we will clean our river." YES!

Our work began with a public information campaign. For the first five years, the work of the foundation was primarily sponsoring dance/drama competitions for school children, folk music/poetry festivals for adults, poster making and debate competitions for young people. Thousands of people sat late into the night listening to music and poetry. One song created for the festival by one of the poets was particularly moving for the audience: "The mother is alone in her suffering. Even though she is ill, her only thought is: If the mother is sick, how can the children be strong?"

When members of the foundation began talking about the need to clean up the river, people laughed and made fun of them. Indira Gandhi came to Varanasi and wished the foundation well in its efforts, but said that cleaning Ganga could not be a national priority. Very privately, though, she asked her advisors to begin to study what would need to be done to clean the river. Mrs. Gandhi is surely the mother of the Ganga Action Plan.

After Mrs. Gandhi was assassinated, Rajiv Gandhi, her son and an environmentalist, became prime minister. In his first message to the nation, Rajiv Gandhi announced that cleaning Ganga would be a high priority of his government. He announced the formation of the Ganga Action Plan. We rejoiced. Major changes seemed close at hand. Money was allocated, and we had no doubt things would be moving now. We had no idea of the government's capacity for error and boondoggling, but foundation members were cautious.

Occasionally, we would have a speak-out, where people came and openly discussed the campaign with members of the foundation as well as civic leaders. Several hundred people would gather under a shamiyana to share their specific concerns. "How can we stop people from going to the toilet in the most convenient place, along the river?" The answer was education and more education, until we held a children's drama festival. The commissioner (an official more powerful than a city mayor) attended an event where hundreds of school children performed stories about Ganga's arrival on earth, and about her suffering at the thoughtlessness of the humans. The commissioner was so moved by the vision of the children that he announced the formation of a "home guard," a para-police unit that would patrol the river front and remind people of their duty to keep the river clean; if necessary, they would use a stick to enforce the rules. This idea was very effective until another commissioner was appointed; he had other priorities.

Varanasi slopes gently toward the river. The two main sewers run under the roads that run north and south parallel to the river, but many people live between the first sewer and the river. In 1972, large pumps were installed with World Bank money to pump the sewage from the densely packed buildings between the sewer and the river. These pumps were designed to send the sewage up to the sewer under the road, where it could join the trunk sewer.

The pumps were housed in round, pink concrete structures. For seven years, these pumps did not work. Every day, men went to work at the five pumping stations, played cards, drank a little tea, and came home from "a hard day at the office." The pumps stood idle. It wasn't hard to tell that they weren't working. Pumps make considerable noise. These pink monsters rested mute, while the World Bank collected interest on the money given to build the pumps. No infrastructure of accountability was in place to make sure the pumps were working.

We wondered why these pumps were not alleviating the over sixty outfalls of sewage into the river. The head of Jal Nigam (the

sewage department) visited Mahantji several times to persuade him
to stop talking about the pumps. The official insisted that the pumps
simply couldn't be made to work and offered technical information
to support this position. Bribes were offered if the foundation
would keep silent. But that was not our way of doing business.

After Rajiv Gandhi created the Ganga Action Plan (GAP) and
appointed the Ganga Project Directorate (GPD), the government's
decision-making group for implementing the GAP, the engineer
who had been convinced that the pumps could not be made to
work was replaced by R.K. Sharma, who promised to get the
pumps working. Toward the end of my visit in January 1985, I started hearing people say, "The river looks cleaner." Foundation members speculated that maybe the pumps were working. I wanted to
know for sure. So with my friend Todd, I hopped on a rickshaw and
went off to visit two pumping stations. I heard the whirring of the
motors, my feet felt the vibrations of the pumps, and I saw the
sewage surging through. They were really working! No longer
would much of the city's sewage be contaminating its drinking
water supply; people would be ingesting fewer vitality sapping
intestinal parasites. I danced down the stairs of the pumping station.

The foundation asks me to do all kinds of tasks when I am there.
But surely, one of the most novel tasks was a tour I took of the
sewage system conducted by R. K. Sharma, the man who got the
pumps working. He was so flattered that I had included him in
some of my writing that he made a surprise visit to my house one
day with several subordinate engineers. He asked if I would like to
go on a tour of the entire sewage system at 6 a.m. the next day. I
eagerly accepted. I knew pitifully little about sewage, so when I
talked with the foundation members that evening, they told me
things to look for and questions to ask. Mahantji prays for several
hours in the early morning, so he could not come on the tour, and
the other members decided it would be better if I went alone.

The sewage system is most active in the early morning. I guess
you can figure out why. Mr. Sharma picked me up in a white
Ambassador car, followed by five other white Ambassador cars filled
with engineers, who were brought along to answer any questions I
might have. A video crew had been hired for the event, so they
could record the questions and explanations for future use for people interested in GAP's activities.

We drove the full length of the sewage system. Every now and
then the cars would stop, and we would all get out and look down

a manhole, or at a pump. I would peer down the manhole, or at the large tank at the bottom of a pumping station, and they would explain with pride what I was seeing. They said that until a year before, they had not had a map of the sewage system. The British had taken the maps with them when they left India decades before. So when Mr. Sharma took over, they had to map the entire system. They used an ingenious method: someone dropped a Ping-Pong ball into one manhole, while men were posted at all the nearby manholes, watching until the ball appeared.

The television camera was filming. All the pumping stations, including the new one, were working. It was quite difficult to think of what to ask or say. The smells were overpowering at times, but we kept going.

Finally, we visited the "sewage farm," where they were doing research on using sewage for trees and plants. It was a beautiful farm and an interesting research project. About 150 people were there for my visit, along with a priest who had been brought in for a ceremony welcoming me to the farm.

A comedian is not to be trusted with serious ceremonies that are very long, and this ceremony pushed me to the outer limit of my capacity for sustained seriousness. There, in front of the crowd and the television camera, the priest and I were seated on the ground. The priest asked me to throw rice over my shoulder, tie a string around my wrist, and do all kinds of ceremonial acts meaningful for them, but mysterious and a little funny for me. I planted a mango tree as part of the ceremony. I have since seen the mango tree, which is now about twelve feet high, composed of strong, twin vertical trunks.

After the ceremony was over, I was led to a large table, maybe fifteen feet long, laden with all kinds of food piled high on large platters. As he led me to the table, Mr. Sharma proudly announced, "Look! All this food was grown from sewage!" I felt helpless in front of all the people and the camera. Just then, I was not so interested in the food. But for the sake of goodwill, I bravely filled my plate with food, trying to forget the smells of the morning. I was able to eat some of the fruits and other food. It tasted fine.

Clearly, GAP Phase 1 had some achievements. With GAP money, the two existing pumps were updated and another pump, at the end of the sewers, was constructed. Getting the pumps running — even if only when electricity was on — was a victory. Except when the electricity was out, one did not see coherent pieces of feces floating on top of the river. In the non-monsoon months, when electricity was available, there was less sewage flowing into Ganga than previously. But around the time of the heavy rains, the pumps were shut down for five months, because silt would flow into the pumps and damage them. Too much water would overwhelm the pumps. The Sankat Mochan Foundation started to lose faith in the system, and adopted the slogan "a seven-month solution to pollution is no solution."

Through the years, the problems with these pumps have become more and more obvious. Almost every day, the electricity goes off for some period of time. When the pumps are off, raw sewage flows into the river. After all the energy they had put into getting the pumps working, it was difficult for the foundation to make the decision that the electric pumping system was not the best system. We needed another way of transporting the sewage that did not depend on electricity.

When foundation members heard from a *Boston Globe* reporter that the Massachusetts Municipal Water Resources Authority was using gravity to move its sewage, they were excited. "Why must we be dependent upon electricity to move our sewage? The river flows north. Why can't the sewers use that same gravity to move the sewage to the new sewage treatment plant north of the city?" So we decided to hold an international conference in Varanasi, where experts on sewage transport would consider how we could free our sewer system from the problems of erratic electricity.

Nineteen ninety-two was an especially powerful year for connecting human resources from Europe. The US Friends of the Ganges (known as FOG in English-speaking countries, and Ganga Vener in Sweden) managed to convince sewage transport experts from the Boston Harbor project, the Thames Authority in England, and Sweden to attend a conference to study alternative methods of moving sewage through the city.

It was my job to find the key experts from the US in tunneling, sewer design and public administration as well as funding, and to get them to come to the conference, although we had no money to pay them. I put on a suit and visited each of these engineers. Many of these men regularly charged thousands of dollars a day in consultation fees. "We need your help to clean this holy river," I would say. To a person, they responded to the challenge, "Sure, I'll do my part. You just get me there. I am honored to help." It is my experience that more often than not, when you ask people to help with a job that really benefits the earth, they will agree. I continue to be inspired by this willingness — no, eagerness — to do "their part."

The conference set in motion relationships that continue to this day. As of this writing in 1999, we are well on our way to getting the government to build the gravity interceptor.

An industrial treatment plant at the Diesel Locomotive Works, a small sewage treatment plant at the university, and a very large (and expensive) sewage plant north of the city of Dinapur were all accomplished with money from GAP Phase 1. One day, I decided I simply had to see the new sewage treatment plant in Dinapur. I do not know why foundation members rarely like to go and see for themselves, but I suspect it has to do with their academic training. I went on my own and was very impressed with the size of the project. The head engineer took me on a tour, and told me that this plant was designed to generate more electricity than the entire system (including the pumps) would need. It sounded wonderful to me. When I came back and reported what I had seen, Upadhyay was very dubious, skeptical but hopeful. S. K. spoke more directly: "We don't know how they can build a treatment plant without studying the quantity and quality of the sewage first." Mahantji just smiled. "We will just have to watch." With all this going on, the foundation decided its job would be to hold the government accountable. We would keep watching to see that all the things built were kept running, but foundation members were skeptical.

When finally sewage treatment plants were built, we thought we could rest and simply be a government watchdog. We no longer saw excrement on top of the river, so it was a safe assumption that it was cleaner. From the beginning, I found it hard to believe that there were no laboratory tests on the quality of the water. Mahantji published an early study that showed that the biological oxygen demand (BOD) of the river recovered between cities. Oxygen is dissolved in the water, and the more oxygen there is, the healthier the river is. Because the water in Ganga falls from such a height in the Himalayas, it carries a lot of oxygen from all that bouncing as it falls. The more organic matter there is in the water, the more oxygen is consumed in breaking down the waste.

There are several important variables in the health of a river: BOD and fecal coliform counts are two. Fecal coliforms are those little bacteria parasites from the intestines of warm-blooded animals that accidentally get into the water. It is fecal coliforms that enter the bodies of humans and cause many diseases in babies and weak adults. Those parasites often result in diarrhea and death. Mahantji often says, "It isn't that these fecal coliforms are evil, it is just that they are in the wrong place. The parasites are meant to live in the intestines of cows and are always trying to get back there. Pollution is simply things out of place. We human beings have moved things around, and that has caused many problems. Our goal should be to put everything back where it belongs. Then we will have no pollution."

I used to be very judgmental about the man at the post office in Varanasi for being so slow in calculating the postage for five letters going inside India. That was until I had seven different parasites one year when I came home. I must have gotten a little careless about my drinking water. My contact with these seven buggers was a beneficial experience for me in some ways. On a physical level, I was able to know why the river needs to be clean. With these parasites in my system, I lacked energy and found it difficult to think, especially to think creatively. I experienced my mind as a very dull instrument, happier sleeping than holding itself awake. It was clear to me that parasitic diseases can devastate the vitality and intellect of a people. I developed empathy and compassion for the post office worker. If we want a cure for cancer or AIDS or any other problem disturbing us, we should clean up the water of the world, so that many more minds are freed from parasites and able to do intellectually challenging tasks for the world.

Gastrointestinal diseases are the biggest killers of children under the age of five in Varanasi. In the US, it is auto accidents. Some people refer to the exploding population in India, cynically implying that high infant mortality is beneficial. But the UN has found that if infant mortality goes down, it takes only two generations for the birth rate to drop significantly. So, cleaning the river not only makes sense for the sake of the river (reason enough to do our work), but also eliminates much suffering in the long- as well as short-term.

I had once asked Mr. Kamal Nath, the minister of environment, if he would release the results of the government's water testing. He refused. I asked why. He replied without missing a beat, "I am afraid that the people would riot if they knew the figures."

We wanted to know what the load of fecal coliform was. So, in the early 1980s, I got a group in the US, called Water Test, to donate a couple of free water tests. In order to produce valid results, the samples would have to reach the East Coast laboratory within thirty hours after the sample was taken from the river. My travel agent carefully planned my itinerary and found that it could be accomplished if I flew via Europe, stopped in New York, and sent the water by overnight express to the lab.

The foundation met for hours, planning how to minimize the

time in Varanasi. Watches were synchronized, and someone was sent ahead to the airport to check me in and ask the airport manager to hold the plane until I could arrive with the water. I waited at a specific place until a motor scooter and a rickshaw arrived with the samples from upstream and downstream. Then, we raced to the airport. In New York, a runner met me, took the samples and rushed them off to Federal Express. But, that night a storm closed many roads, and Fed Ex was not moving. So, we only got results of the heavy metals in the water and not the fecal coliform. There was excessive magnesium in the water; we figured that this was from the Diesel Locomotive Works factory in the city.

When the pumps were working, the water was visibly cleaner, and we hoped that this meant that things were substantially better for the river. But without tests, we could not be sure.

I had begun bringing friends from outside India who thought they could help with the campaign in some way. In 1992, Sue and Col Lennox, teachers in Australia who specialized in teaching about water, visited India. Sue and Col brought two blue plastic suitcases filled with water-testing equipment. The night they presented these gifts to the foundation was one none of us will ever forget.

We were all exhausted from a seminar on sewage-transport technologies that had just ended. The meeting was to be short. Sue and Col made their presentation. Mahantji wearily asked, "What can we test with this kit?"

"Oh, BOD, temperature, how clear the water is, and fecal coliform," they responded matter-of-factly.

"FECAL COLIFORM?!!" all the foundation members said in unison.

"Yes," Sue and Col responded, not knowing how exciting this was to us. We looked at each other as if we had just been granted access to a magical power we had long dreamed of. I still get goose bumps writing this. It was a moment that cast our campaign forever in a new direction.

The first test indicated that there were millions of fecal coliforms. A safe reading is between 200 and 500. We were shocked. But the cool scientists knew that the tests had to be done over and over. Before we could make any announcement, we had to check everything, and have hundreds of tests with the same results.

For a year, the kits were our source of information. Then, a group of teachers from Sweden who were working with the foundation managed to get a grant to build a first-rate water-testing laboratory. Located right on the bank of the river, the laboratory has

three rooms, including a sterile room. We have a computer, an incu-
bator, and all the equipment to reliably test the water. Staff were
hired from this grant, and they work daily. The strategic implica-
tions of this development cannot be overestimated. Water testing
has become a cornerstone of the foundation's strategy.

When final test results were available, they were staggering. I felt
as if it were my grandmother, whom I had always known was not
well. She had not looked healthy and had been complaining for
years. Now, we had the "blood tests," and knew beyond a doubt that
the things being done to get her healthy were not working. New,
stronger, and more effective measures had to be employed.

One evening, the head of the GPD, a man named Aggerwall, came
to visit us. The sun had set, and coincidentally the electricity was
out. Not finding any of the foundation people in their usual places,
he looked around the area. He came upon the laboratory, which
had just been established. A newly painted sign over the door was
barely visible in the fading light of dusk: "Water quality testing laboratory: Sankat Mochan Foundation."

Agerwal peered into the open door to find Vipul, Mahantji's son,
and a friend doing their water tests by candlelight. "What are you
doing?" Aggerwall asked. The two young men did not recognize
him. "We're testing the water." "What are you finding?" he asked.
With an openness characteristic of the foundation's work, the students showed him the record book. Looking at the results, Aggerwall
became quite agitated. The students later reported that he was so
upset that he was shaking. He took one of the candles over to the
desk and drafted a "show cause" letter to the people in Jal Nigam, the
government corporation responsible for sewage processing and transport. As a policy planner, Aggerwall was upset by the corporation's
handling of the sewage treatment plant. Also, he knew that when the
results of our testing were made public, his administration would be
held responsible and some people would be fired, jailed, or demoted.

Somehow, the story of Aggerwall's visit did not reach Mahantji
immediately. He did not know that Aggerwall had visited the laboratory until the two men met on the road on their way to a musical
event the following evening. Aggerwall called to Mahantji and related the story of his visit. Mahantji told me the story that evening:

"I could see that Aggerwall was upset. He was so upset that I
didn't want to tell him about the BOD count at Khirki Nala (the
most downstream point) of 505!" (Mahantji is not one of those
stick-it-to-them-and-turn-the-knife social change people.) "But I

did tell him, 'We don't want anyone to lose their jobs, we don't want any more seminars, we don't want any more concerts. Please. We want the river cleaned!' Aggerwall himself brought up the BOD count of 505 at Khirki Nala. He said he was very concerned about this figure and what it meant to the life of the river."

Months later, when Vipul read in the newspaper that the GPD was claiming great achievements in cleaning the river, he called a press conference. To their credit, the GPD did not include Varanasi as one of their successes. One might suspect that Varanasi was left off the list because a certain citizens' group knew the truth, whereas citizens do not monitor the other cities. Soon, our young scientist/activist Vipul appeared on the front pages of the nation's most prestigious papers, challenging the GPD with his facts. The next generation is getting ready to take over the campaign.

It is not only what we are doing, but how we work that will clean the river. I shall never forget the trip I took with the foundation members to initiate the DO meter. One Sunday, we took a boat from upstream (before any effluent from the city flows into Ganga) to a spot in the middle of the city. The scientists, Dr. V.B. Mishra (Mahantji), Dr. S.N. Upadhyay, S.K. Mishra, and Ashok Pandey (administrative assistant to the foundation), measured the water and gave the results to Sara Ahmed, a South Indian Muslim doctoral student. She had come to study the river-cleaning project for her advanced degree at Oxford University.

Sara wrote down the results. Hari Ram, a poet and radio announcer, composed and sang poetry whenever the spirit moved him. I looked around as the boat slipped through this beautiful arrangement of liquid. The sun was warm, as were the feelings about our work and each other. We laughed, worked, and talked together, while testing the water. I thought this was the perfect social change work for me: Muslims and Hindus; scientists, poets, and political people; women and men; the sun and the river; Indians and an American — all doing their work for the earth, her waters, and her people. For that moment, in that place, the work seemed nearly perfect.

Thirteen years into our work, Vipul, who by now was doing his residence as a medical doctor, asked me to help him organize a short-term clinic for water-borne diseases. Thus, I had an opportunity to learn about another part of the sewage story. By now, three sewage plants were working, but we knew there were real problems with their effectiveness, due to inappropriate design, bad management, and leaking sewers.

Two years earlier, in 1993, the Dinapur sewage treatment plant had begun treating the sewage of Varanasi, with the promise that raw sewage would no longer flow into the holy river. But from tests carried out in our laboratory, we knew that the sewage leaving the treatment plant was almost as poisonous as when it entered. The burden of the Dinapur Sewage Treatment Plant (STP) — the largest of the new plants — was falling onto a few small villages outside the town. The effluent had gotten into the groundwater and had poisoned the wells in Kamauli, making the people sick. But we did not know the exact degree of infection.

Early on a sunny Sunday morning, four of us from the foundation took off to investigate the possibility of a clinic in Kamauli. Dust flying, our jeep bounced through the streets and over the back roads. Bump, bump, bump.

In the jeep were Shukla, the driver; Dukhi Tewari, who had recently been fired from his position with Jal Nigam, the company running the sewage plant; Vipul Mishra, a resident medical intern; and myself, a social change worker. We anticipated that it would be a tough day. For an hour and a half, Shukla drove us around broken-down trucks; between rickshaws, bicycles, and cows; until finally, we stopped at a concrete channel filled with a brackish liquid speeding from the sewage treatment plant into Ganga. We walked along the channel, looked, smelled, but did not touch. It smelled foul.

Several years earlier, we had had such high hopes for this sewage treatment plant, and had felt that our job of cleaning this most holy and beautiful river was done, now that such a large and "advanced" treatment plant was in place. But slowly, we discovered that sewage was backing up into homes, that where the effluent joined Ganga the water was very high in fecal coliform and BOD. Then, we heard about the sad plight of the people of Kamauli, located on the effluent channel, and we knew that this plant was a massive exercise in misdesign, mismanagement, and slavish following of Western pump machine technology.

Kamauli, a village of about 3,000 people, is one of the poorest I have seen in India: mostly small grass huts, with only a pile of straw to sleep on covered by a quilt. Nobody had shoes on, even though it was winter and cold. But there was no poverty of spirit in this place. Lovely art — drawings of flowers, people, and symbols — adorned the mud exteriors of the few solid buildings.

Close to the houses, smelly sewage water stood in the barrow pits created by the channel construction. Here, the land was low enough to allow seepage from the channel carrying the "treated" effluent from Dinapur STP.

As we got out of the jeep, Vipul and Dukhi softly introduced themselves to the few men who approached us. Through a short series of exchanges, a spokesperson, Jalandhar Prasad, stepped forward. Vipul asserted repeatedly that we were not from the government, but from a private organization concerned about the condition of their water.

We were taken on a tour of the village's four wells. "This used to be some of the best water in the region," one man told us. "When this area was first settled, hundreds of years ago, this was the first well, and people used to travel here for good water. Now, we feel ourselves prisoners, with no way to return our groundwater to its former state." Above ground, the wells are round brick structures with wooden pulleys overhead. At each well, a bucket was brought up for us.

Vipul touched the water, scooped up a handful, jiggled the water slowly in his hand. Like a doctor feeling the belly of a patient, he moved the water gently, watching, listening with an inner water ear. Polluted water does not have the intricate vibrations of clean water; clean water has many patterns on its surface and almost dances when it is jiggled. This water looked clear, but the wave action was sluggish, as if it had been drugged. Vipul brought the water to his nose. Inhaled. Dropped the water to the ground. Pulled a handkerchief out of his pocket to wipe the poison away.

Neighbors gathered at each well, eager to tell their stories. They showed us their infected scabies, their babies with sores and rashes. I am sorry to have to say that about 70 percent of the villagers in Kamauli had horrid sores. There are those who would say that these sores resulted from poor hygiene, but if you don't have clean water, how can you keep yourself clean? The villagers pointed to their stomachs and talked about the invisible wounds, about babies dead from diarrhea, about the children made orphans by deaths in the village.

"Until four years ago, we did not have these problems. Then the Dinapur Sewage Treatment Plant was built and we noticed changes. First, the water level in our wells rose. Previously, we needed a rope over thirty feet long to reach the water level. Now, we only need a rope about sixteen feet long to bring up the water. Also, we have noticed other changes. Sores, stomach pain, hepatitis, a general decrease in health. And our farms suffer. No one will buy our potatoes, they are so hard and tasteless." Another man stepped forward and said that he depended upon a mango tree for his income, but now the tree is dead. What can he do?

The social costs in Kamauli are also great. "Now, word has spread of our misery, and no one will marry our sons and daughters. What will become of us, our families, our village?"

Hearing of this suffering, we must ask ourselves many questions. For instance, scabies is not a waterborne disease; it is caused by unhygienic conditions. Doctors say they can treat the infected scabies in two months, but the sores will reappear. "The real medicine is clean water," Vipul asserted.

Within days, Vipul went to the district health officer to get permission for a clinic. He found some medical students to help, got some drugs donated, and found a couple of people to do research on the exact nature and quantity of the suffering at Kamauli. These data will help in our overall campaign to force the government to build an adequate sewage system and resettle the villagers.

The clinic was held outdoors, on the banks of the sewage channel. Vipul had chosen a place equidistant from the housing of both castes in the village, "owned" by no particular group. The symbolic value of having the clinic within ten feet of the cause of many of their illnesses was not lost on the villagers. They went into the sewage plant's pump house and took out a chair for Vipul, and a small table for him to write on.

The other two doctors who were scheduled to come to the clinic that day had to cancel at the last minute. One was suffering from diarrhea; it's not only the poor and uneducated who suffer from waterborne diseases in this area. So Vipul ran the clinic alone. There was a representative from the foundation to add legitimacy, an education worker/economist, and the ever-present water-testing technician. The education worker went around to the villagers' homes asking questions about the water and about diseases. The lab man walked from well to well gathering water samples in sterilized bottles. We would later learn that, except in the deepest well, the water had a dangerously high fecal coliform count. More significantly, there was lots of nitrate in the Dinapur effluent, which can cause blue baby syndrome and infant death, as well as cancer in adults. Over time, farm animals drinking this water will also be damaged.

Then, there was me, an almost useless appendage. Not speaking Hindi very well, I could not talk with villagers; not being a medical worker, I could not help on the medical side. But when I noticed Vipul struggling to tear open the pill packets and divide them into appropriate dosages, I offered to help. I squatted next to Vipul, and he oriented me to the variety of medications he had brought in two cardboard boxes.

I became the nurse, counting out pills, finding the medicines Vipul called for, taking care of the paper work. I witnessed illness and pain in a way I had never known I was capable of. I usually find it difficult to look at sores, injuries, and infections. Physical suffering makes me feel creepy inside. But there on the banks of the sewage channel, I found in myself a fresh response to suffering. I had a role to play, a way to participate in the healing process. And to participate, one must look. One must attend to the suffering if one is to help.

So, that was our team and our task. To research, to diagnose, to treat, to educate. For about four hours, we did all those things with care. A crowd gathered around Vipul's little table. He would call out the name of the next person to be seen, who would come forward. He listened as the patients described their complaints; he touched their stomachs, looked at sores. Soon, many women appeared as patients; Vipul concluded that the villagers were coming to trust the clinic.

One patient, a man looking to be in his sixties, dressed in white clothes and white cap, came with a complaint. Anoop, our sociologist/educational worker, asked me to take a photo of Vipul touching the patient. Later, Anoop told me he could tell by the man's dress that he was Muslim. "I am so proud of how Vipul touched this man. This is my India. A Hindu Brahmin was caring with respect for a Muslim. This picture tells more than anything what kind of a clinic we are and what kind of a foundation we are."

A very young limp child was carried by his parents. Vipul diagnosed the boy as having polio; after discussing with the parents how essential it was that they attend to this matter in a hurry, he gave them a referral to the city hospital. Another thin baby was brought to Vipul. The parents were told how to boil water and given oral rehydration therapy powder. This should help the child overcome the diarrhea that had resulted in severe malnutrition and dehydration, all caused by parasites in the water. If given the medicine in time, she might not die.

There were many problems in the village; Vipul attended to each one, giving some of them the medicine we brought, telling others to go to district clinics or the hospital. That day, we saw about eighty patients.

The villagers' suffering was a direct result of inappropriate and mismanaged technology. "It is as if those people live underneath the toilets of Varanasi," Mahantji said later. "This suffering is intolerable. If we had been less trusting of the government engineers, we would not have allowed this plant to be built without a more careful study. We couldn't believe in our wildest imagination that such blunders would be committed by engineers. Now, this village is at the end of the toilets of Varanasi, and the wells are full of stinking water." He is proud of his profession as a civil engineer, and the government and Jal Nigam's betrayal of engineers' moral principles was a blow to him.

But now, the village is economically dependent on the Sewage Treatment Plant. Several villagers said, "Please don't close down the channel. It brings us more water to irrigate our crops. Yes, it is true that the potatoes are small and hard. It is true that some trees have died. But other crops are more abundant. If you close the channel, how will we make a living?" It's the old jobs-versus-environment, short-term vs. long-term story all over again. Those who have died of waterborne diseases don't have a voice in the discussion.

And it is not even that simple. Some of the suffering is borne not of water, but of poverty and lack of educational and health services. The interest on World Bank loans for the sewage technology has drained away government resources that could have been used for more direct services.

For twenty-five days in October 1994, sewage stood waste deep in Urmila Dwiedi's lane in a neighborhood of Varanasi. She described the scene: "We could not move. Our children could not go from home to school. Shopkeepers could not open their shops. Their livelihood was threatened. It was terrible. It was dangerous to our families' health. The sewage was not only in the lane," Urmila said, pointing to a stain on her living room wall; "our entire ground floor was inundated with sewage. We had to move upstairs. We are accustomed to the floods. Every year they come. But sewage! That is too much. A rickshaw driver's feet would be in sewage, if he allowed them to follow the pedals of his bicycle around the lower end of the pedaling cycle. Stinking sewage. Dangerous sewage. Children walk in it. Men and women try hard, but fail in their efforts to avoid walking in it. Finally, some of my women friends and colleagues and I decided that we had to do something." The women decided they would stop the traffic on one of the main roads of the city. "What else could we do?"

Two hundred women occupied a major intersection in the city for two days. Traffic was tied up. The women talked and sang songs. They gave speeches to each other and to anyone else who would listen. Finally, they went to the office of Mr. Hammad, the head of the sewage treatment department. With the force of their numbers and moral authority, they "invited" him to accompany them to their neighborhood. For two hours, they forced him to stand waist deep in the sewage in their lane.

Mr. Hammad, a tight-lipped, proper man, was humiliated. He had been so proud of his important position with U.P. Jal Nigam. As general manger of the Ganga Pollution Control Unit, as well as the supervising engineer of U.P. Jal Nigam, no doubt he was the source of much pride for his parents. He was deep not only in sewage, but also in denial of the impact of the engineering decisions he and his unit had made. It is not known whether he knew of the effect of his treatment plant and pumping station on the lives of the people of Varanasi. If he didn't, he should have.

One thing is known. Before the GAP came into effect in 1994, the women in Urmila's neighborhood did not have such problems. There were also other neighborhoods in Varanasi where sewage now regularly backed up in toilets, especially when it rained. Whatever the GAP "fixed," it created a brokenness, evidenced by the sewage standing in Urmila's lane.

To say that the sewers of Varanasi are old would be something of an understatement. They are ancient, like so much of this city. During the Moghul period, open ditches were built to carry storm water. Increasingly throughout history, these storm drains have also been used to carry sewage. In the early part of this century, under the British, the two main sewers running parallel to the river and lateral branches were constructed. These sewers are rectangular, rather than round, and are constructed of brick.

Sewers are designed to have an air space at the top, so that sewage can flow freely. If there is no air at the crown, pressure can build and break through. Sewers that are adequate for day-to-day sewage may become overfull when rains come.

In most cities of the world, when it rains, storm water is collected into the sewers, where it mixes with sewage and proceeds to overwhelm the capacity of the sewage treatment plant. In most situations, including my home, San Francisco, a decision is regularly made to simply bypass treatment and send all the untreated wastewater into the river or ocean that regularly receives the treated effluent. The alternative to this is very expensive, involving construction of parallel storm sewers that carry only storm water.

Not only are the ancient sewers of Varanasi inadequate to carry the huge load of storm water, but when the sewers become too full, the pressure causes the sewers to collapse, and streets to cave in. Houses, cars, and people become involved in a real mess; indeed, several houses collapsed due to sewer cave-ins during 1994. Now, the World Bank has funded an expansion of the water system in the city, but it is ludicrous to almost double the water flowing into the sewage system without also enlarging the sewer system.

To understand more about the mystery of the problems caused by the GAP, we must know a little more about sewers themselves. I know this may not be high on your wanting-to-know priority list, but please be patient. It is actually surprisingly interesting.

At this point we need to talk a bit about sewers. A sewer is a tube through which wastewater and specifically sewage flows. In case you are wondering, sewage is household waste; wastewater is a more general term including industrial waste, and storm water is rainwater with debris (leaves, oil, pesticides, dust) gathered by the rainwater as it moves toward the sewer.

A sewer is usually round, with the bottom known as the "invert" and the top known as the "crown." It should have sufficient capacity at the crown for air. A full sewer is a sewer that is going to back up — either at the manholes or in the homes and toilets of the city. The sewage has to go somewhere, so it will go to the lowest point. If allowed to flow freely, it will move through; otherwise, it will back up. At the end of the line, it is very important to have a free fall of sewage into a large tank. If the tank is too small for the free fall of sewage, the water in the tank acts as a dam and blocks more waste-water from coming in. Again, that dam causes a back-up, or in sewage talk, "heading up" of sewage at — you guessed it — the lowest spot where it can escape. In the case of Varanasi, that is the neighborhood in which Urmila lives.

All sewage comes to the Konia pumping station. Initially, it falls into a holding tank, and from there to another tank, which has three enormous screws resting at an angle in the tank. These screws, turned by electricity, raise the sewage up so it can fall through screens, which remove solids like plastic bags, rocks, and sticks. Then, sewage is pumped through gradually sloped pipes (called "rising mains") toward the Dinapur STP. The sewage often moves so slowly through the main sewer that it cannot relieve the pressure from sewage behind it. Then, it falls into a tank. It is the depth of this tank, and the tank at the base of the giant screw pumps, that causes many of the problems.

Engineers who worked at the construction site said that the tanks were designed to be much deeper; however, during construction, the underground water was struck. It costs a great deal more to build a tank at such a water-infested place, rather than on dry land. No one had the foresight to think of the possibility that water would be so close to the surface where the tank was to be built. The cost for underwater construction for a sufficiently deep tank was not budgeted. So the decision was made — we are not sure by whom — to simply build the floor of the tank right to where the water was and then stop.

It probably seemed like quite an innocuous decision, surely not one with life-and-death significance. Indeed, it must have felt almost necessary. "We only have this amount of money, and we have to complete the job." But its impact has been murderous. People — especially children — are dying from that decision.

Because of the overpacking of the sewer itself and lack of air space at the top, because of the lack of appropriate slope in the pipe from the special manhole, combined with the absence of free fall of sewage due to lack of depth in the receiving chamber at the Konia pumping station, sewage backs up into many neighborhoods of Varanasi.

When people must walk through parasite-infested sewage, they can become ill. If they are not strong, they may die. When they bathe in the river where sewage has been dumped, it is equally dangerous to their health. Ganga herself is holy, yes — but just now she is carrying too much of a dangerous load. The humans are not caring for Ganga. Those pointing out these problems about sewage flowing into Ganga and into the streets of Varanasi are in no way disrespecting Ganga. Indeed, it is those in Jal Nigam, in the Ganga Action Plan (now known as the National Rivers Conservation Directorate, NRCD), and the engineers responsible for keeping sewage from flowing into either Ganga or the lanes and homes of Varanasi, who are guilty of disrespect and malfeasance.

Another effort of the government in GAP Phase 1 was to rid the river of human corpses and dead bodies of animals. Bodies of dead people on stretchers covered by red and gold fabric are carried through the streets by the men in the deceased's family, sometimes accompanied by a band or drum. Occasionally, these bodies are dumped directly into the river, but mostly they are cremated at a burning ghat on the riverbank. The ashes don't pose much of a pollution problem, but many people cannot afford enough of the expensive wood for a thorough cremation. Cremation at the burning ghat costs three months of an average worker's salary. So they buy as much wood as they can, then dump the partially burned corpse into the river. When people who have no relatives die in the local hospital, orderlies are given a little money for wood and told to take the bodies to the burning ghat. But all too often, the orderlies dump the bodies off the bridge at the end of town and pocket the money. These bodies float down the river, pushed by the current toward the populated bank, as the river makes a gentle curve going though the city. Dead buffaloes, cows, and other animals are also dumped into the river when they die, to float until they are eaten by dogs and vultures. More respectful citizens drag dead animals across the river to the sand bar.

With money from GAP Phase 1, an electric crematorium was built. We know that people will use such innovations if they are working and religiously appropriate; in the electric crematorium, all religious rituals can be done with one exception — the cracking of the skull to let the soul escape into the atmosphere. Most middle- and lower-class people accepted the electric crematorium. There was always a line out the door of people waiting to get the bodies of family members burnt.

Shortly after the crematorium was opened, it was noticed that the bodies were not lying in the correct north-south direction, so the inside had to be redone. The crematorium was opened, but neighbors complained about the smells, so it had to be closed again and a higher chimney put in. But then, the expensive heating element wore out. So it's been an on-again, off-again affair with the electric crematorium.

One very difficult thing about the way the government makes capital investments in the infrastructure is that the central government builds the item, in this case the electric crematorium, and then turns it over to the state or local government to run. State and local governments are able to collect very few taxes, so they have little money to pay for repairs or salaries for workers.

At the point that our water-testing results consistently showed very high fecal coliform counts in the river and in groundwater, the foundation made a key strategic shift, one many NGOs do not make. They decided to change from being a consciousness-raising organization, criticizing the government, to researching the alternatives that would be better suited to Varanasi's needs. Becoming a positive advocate carried some danger: "Our greatest problem is that we might be successful and have some responsibility," Mahantji said.

We moved from criticism to research and advocacy, and the shift was painful and difficult for many members of the foundation. Two brothers, Rana and Dukhi Tawari, who had started hanging around the foundation, encouraged the change in the strategy. These cheerful and determined fourth-class sewage workers at Dinapur had been our spies in Jal Nigam, and had brought us many valuable pieces of information. The stories they told about the mistakes made in construction and the constant failures at Dinapur were troublesome to us. They both lost their jobs for their association with the foundation; they became community organizers with the foundation and are integral to all its functions.

Dinapur is an example of a sewage technology very popular in the West called "activated sludge plants" (ASP). These types of sewage treatment plants use lots of concrete and pipes and electricity. They are not designed to treat fecal coliform, and in United States when the treatment of fecal coliform is necessary, chlorine is added to the sewage at the end of treatment. In India, they can barely afford to have chlorine for the treatment of drinking water. Also, chlorine is not good for the environment, so it seemed foolish to suggest it as a solution to fecal coliform.

Another problem came to light when we studied the functioning, or rather malfunctioning, of the Dinapur STP. In the West, there are more meat-eating people making deposits to the sewage systems, whereas in India there are more vegetarians. Varanasi has too low a BOD to run electric generators, so the investment of that element was wasted. Had adequate studies been made of the character of the sewage, it might have been discovered that an ASP plant, while possibly useful in the West, was inappropriate to Varanasi.

In our search for a more appropriate technology, a FOG member in Berkeley found one that is a modern adaptation of an oxidation pond using algae to clean the water. This technology is known as an advanced integrated wastewater pond system (AIWPS), invented in Berkeley by Dr. Bill Oswald. On one of his trips to the United States, Mahantji visited this type of sewage treatment plant and was impressed by a number of its features, but most of all by the fact that it treated fecal coliforms, needed very low energy, and did not smell. The foundation began to advocate this technology.

One day, Mahantji said to the Tawari brothers that the only problem with the AIWPS technology was that it requires quite a lot of land for the ponds. The Tawari brothers, who zoomed around on motorcycles, immediately suggested building the sewage treatment ponds on a sand bar upstream called Sota. The government already owned it, so land would not have to be acquired. This would save a huge amount of money and make the AIWPS economically superior.

Bill Oswald and his associate, Bailey Green, visited Varanasi and the Sota site the foundation was proposing for the new sewage treatment plant. The villagers around Sota were very enthusiastic about the proposed treatment near their city. They greeted the Oswald/Green team with so many malas (flower necklaces) that they could not see in front of them. Bill Oswald said that the Sota site would be ideal for the treatment plant. We all rejoiced. Now, the foundation had a full plan for sewage treatment and transport: an AIWPS treatment plant at Sota using gravity rather than pumps to collect and move the sewage along the river.

Members of the city council (called Nagar Nigam) came to the foundation and asked why the sewers were being selected and constructed by the national/state body Jal Nigam (the engineering body of the state government). "We have been unwilling to take over Dinapur because it is so expensive and inefficient. Jal Nigam will use the wrong criteria for the treatment plant, and then will want to turn expensive systems over for us to run. Let us decide what technology should be employed, and then let us build it with the money from GAP Phase II. When things go wrong, we are the ones the people come to with complaints."

The council had taken a lot of heat about the backflowing sewage in the streets. They studied and accepted the foundation plan for gravity sewers and AIWPS.

The foundation, in addition to fighting for its technology, now finds itself fighting for local control of sewage works. An addition to the constitution, Article 75, authorizes local governments to control key elements of the infrastructure, like water and sewage treatment. Local bodies are also allowed to collect the taxes necessary to maintain these facilities. This has brought a new wave of democracy sweeping through India. In the foundation's struggle to get control of these decisions, and to convince everyone that the technology we have selected is the best, one victory that is substantial for all of India is almost overlooked: the NRCD (formerly the GAP) has concluded that it will only approve of technology that treats fecal coliform. This will benefit the entire country.

Possibly you have noticed that my commitment to this project has extended long beyond the original five years I had envisioned. The fifth year, I arrived for my regular visit. Foundation members would start each period of conversation with complaints about this being my last year. In fact, that was mostly what they talked about. As a professional, I had taught them to do the kind of questioning I do to help them with long- and short-term planning. I call this "strategic questioning" (see *By Life's Grace*).

"Yes, we know how to do your work — to ask questions and decide what to do. But we must do our work. We are engineers. We need you to continue with your work." Finally, I realized that this cleaning of Ganga was going to have to be a continuing part of my life. I noticed that some of my finest friends were associated with this work, that I deeply loved the river, and that I was constantly learning from the work I was doing. Even though my professional training had taught me never to have a client dependent upon my skills — to work toward independence — this principle had never met this river and the heart of these people. The members of the Sankat Mochan Foundation are no longer clients; they are friends.

When I first started working in India, I thought of myself as *"helping them with their river."* Over the years, I have come to question both parts of that concept. I no longer believe that I am helping them. We work together on a concern that we share. I hate being "helped" by someone who considers her position somehow superior to mine. And I notice how the dynamic of helping keeps us locked in roles of dependency and hierarchy. In some significant ways, this keeps the helped from challenging the relationship.

After some time, I came to love the river and started to feel that this was my river too, even though the concept of ownership of rivers is not accurate. That sense lasted for a couple of years, until I noticed my perception of the relationship change again. I now feel that the ownership issue is turned around. *I belong to the river.* I am her social change worker. I belong to Ganga. When I die, I have put in my will that half of my ashes will be put into the Snake River in Idaho, and half into Ganga. I figure I am large enough to have two portions of ashes.

What I have learned from Ganga, from my friends in India, and from the Indian sense of strategy has turned around my thinking about control, about the usefulness of excitement, and about the ego's relation to work As I struggle to understand how global economics works, I see the world through the eyes of sewage. We work together — Indian friends in the foundation, public officials, Friends of the Ganges, and Ganga herself — for our health, for Ganga's health, and for the health of all of India and the earth. I hope that one day in my lifetime Ganga will be clean enough for me to take a holy dip in the river.

When we started our campaign in 1982, most of the population would have insisted that Ganga was clean; now, the great majority knows the water is seriously ill — she is still holy, but not pure. There used to be dead bodies floating in the river; now, the electric crematorium is used by so many people that those in charge of traditional cremation are fighting to close it down. Sometimes the people from the crematorium win, and sometimes the people from the electric crematorium win.

When we started working, there were no sewage treatment plants operating, and now there are three. Each of the new treatment plants is fraught with problems, and we are working to solve them at the proposed Sota plant. Sewers still leak, and not all the sewage is treated. We are planning for improved technology, and continuing the education and cultural campaigns.

We sometimes despair, realizing how few people are working actively on the campaign. The quote from Margaret Mead: "Never doubt that a few people can make a difference; indeed, it is the only thing that ever has," still sustains us.

Eighteen years after its birth, the foundation is composed of very few people. The three main directors are still there, and a fourth director joined the group a few years ago — Dr. Sundd, who has been made executive director. Dr. Sundd was formerly with the water department; he came to meetings secretly before he retired and could openly align himself with the foundation. Easygoing and conscientious, he does a lot of the lobbying in Delhi, as he understands bureaucracies.

There are surely others who have contributed significantly, from city officials to staff members. But still the task rests on precious few shoulders. What is it that makes someone take on an impossible job? None of us know. We only know it's our task, and we must be faithful to it.

In 1997, Pete Seeger and his grandson gave a concert in Varanasi to an overflow crowd. When talking about the enormous task the foundation has taken on, Pete said, "Miracles will happen." A few months later, as we walked out of a meeting with a major funder of our work, Dr. Sundd said, "Pete Seeger said miracles will happen. I guess this is all part of that miracle." We had been working night and day for weeks, preparing a proposal for consideration by the government of the foundation's plan for sewage treatment and transport. Everyone wondered why miracles take so much work, but a jubilant spirit was present among us.

There was and still is an active debate about whether we are cleaning up the river for the life of the river, or for the life of the human beings who live on the banks of the river. Is this campaign river-centered or human-centered? This is a god we are working with and for, and that makes a big difference.

On social and political levels, many other changes will need to be made if the river is to be healthy: transparency of decision-making with citizen input; taxation closer to the source of the problem, rather than having all money and authority come from the central government; enforcement of decisions made by legislative and judicial bodies. Fortunately, in Indian traditions there are prescriptions about respectful behavior regarding Ganga. No spitting, no defecating close to the river. We can look to traditions for strategy, rather than having people think we are proposing new policies. If we were to appeal only to science, we might create resistance; engaging with both science and tradition, we work with the current of the river, rather than against the current.

I have no doubt the river will be clean. A second generation of workers is coming up. Ganga will one day be restored to her natural state of cleanliness and purity. "To clean a holy river is a mighty task, but it will be done," Mahantji says. Anyone who doubts that statement simply hasn't met the river and the people who have set their lives to her restoration.

Chapter 11
The Earth:
Everyone Has a Job To Do

I N THE SUMMER of 1980, I heard a speech that changed my
thinking. American Indian Movement cofounder Russell
Means described capitalism and socialism as more alike than different. Both systems sprang from European civilization; both, he
said, are wedded to the European "despiritualization" of the universe. Capitalist and socialist countries are industrial societies, out of
touch with the forces of nature; both have decimated indigenous
peoples. Both economic systems have not been able to resist
destroying the environment.

He traced environmental problems to the European view of land,
which is in terms of its utility to the industrial economy. "The mountain becomes gravel, and the lake becomes coolant for a factory."

In the European system of "development," individuals and companies can own more land than they can responsibly care for. Means
sketched out an alternative: a land-based political philosophy that
would give decision-making power regarding the land to those who
live on it, care for it, and have a direct stake in its long-term well-being.

The talk Means gave was part of a week-long "Survival Gathering"
of American Indians, ranchers, and environmentalists in the Black
Hills of South Dakota. The land-based idea struck a chord with
many of us there. The concepts were exhilarating; hundreds of people sat up discussing them long into the night.

Clearly, executives sitting in Bank of America headquarters in
San Francisco shouldn't make decisions about pesticide use on
farms they own hundreds of miles away! They have no direct relationship to the full range of costs. If their families aren't breathing
air thick with pesticide spray or drinking water poisoned by chemical residues, they are likely to base their decisions about pesticides
on abstract economic considerations. Those who farm the land, on

the other hand, need to be aware of the pesticides' effects on their health; so public health studies are important, as is the dissemination, by publicly funded agricultural extension agents, of research findings by scientists and statisticians. I began to wonder: How can we evolve industrial forms that are more connected to those who pay the human and environmental costs of development?

This started me thinking about land and rivers having legal rights parallel to the rights of citizens. Possibly, someone could sue in court on behalf of a river — The Snake River v. the People of the United States. The judge and jury would go out and walk along the riverbank, listen to the river, the birds; open their hearts to the pain of the river. Testimony on behalf of the river would be heard, as well as that of the people who live alongside the river, and the business interests that need the services of the river. River liberation, land rights. Earth's freedom from slavery to humans. Ownership of land is not the ultimate right; the rights of the land have to be considered before trees are cut, development decisions made.

Means had talked primarily about the Indians and their need to control the Black Hills land they'd been given by treaty, but I could see urban applications of his idea as well. The International Hotel struggle and the establishment of Sixth Street Park were essentially land-based campaigns. Both were not so much about who owned the land as about who controlled the land, and the things possible on that land. If someone else has control over your home and wants to turn it into a parking lot, you cannot shape your own destiny.

The land-based idea became part of an emerging frame of reference for me. It has helped me understand the relationship between human beings and our natural environment: in my own experiences of environmental degradation, in the story of a pioneering antipollution battle in Japan, and in my work with a campaign in India to clean up the Ganges River.

I grew up loving the land in Idaho. As I watched seeds planted in the dark, rich, volcanic soil grow into food and flowers, how could I help standing in awe of this planet? I loved the trees; the sagebrush that smelled so fragrant after the rain; the powerful Snake River with its splendid canyon; even the dark, unbroken lava rock, fifty miles north of Twin Falls, that looked like the surface of the moon. I loved swimming and rowing around Pettit Lake in the summer; the water was so clean that we brought it in buckets from the pier for drinking. I loved floating for hours on inner tubes down the Salmon River among the glorious Sawtooth Mountains.

But I also remember the dredged rivers I saw when I was young. On vacations, our family used to enjoy exploring Idaho ghost towns. We walked down streets where miners and settlers had walked, saw the old hotels and mines collapsed where they had stood. We wondered about the indigenous people, and how these mines and settlements must have seemed like invasions to them. As we explored the dumps for bottles and cans, we found treasures. Often we found obsidian arrowheads. We imagined the fights that must have taken place between the Indians and the residents of the town to have resulted in those arrowheads laying on the land.

Several times, we came upon rivers whose banks were piled high with rocks and sand. Although the rivers were still flowing, nothing grew alongside them. They looked ugly and vandalized. My father told us that miners had left this mess after they dredged for gold. They had come with big machines that had chewed up the river and spit out the gravel along the banks — and they hadn't even tried to restore it. Everyone in the family was outraged. We were seething as we drove along those rivers. Eventually, my father stopped taking us along that route, because what we saw upset us so.

Another continuing theme about the land was the Fish and Game Department's efforts to get trout into Pettit Lake. We already had plenty of good fish in the lake. We had redfish — a rare, landlocked salmon that is fun, but difficult, to catch, and delicious to eat. We had suckers and whitefish, known as trash fish because they were not good to eat. Isn't that arrogant! But the Fish and Game men wanted trout, and they decided the reason there were no trout was that they didn't have places to live in the lake. So they cut down some trees, wired them together, tied some rocks to the trees, and then sank the trees to the bottom of the lake to provide homes for the homeless trout.

That didn't work.

Years later, the Fish and Game men came up with a new idea. They waited until fall, when all the redfish theoretically had left the lake, and planted depth charges to explode the suckers and whitefish — which they figured were eating the trout. Hundreds — maybe thousands — of dead fish floated to the top of the lake and down the outlet.

Still, there were no trout. And there were no more redfish. The suckers and whitefish were gone, too.

No one who loved the lake would have sunk trees in it, or planted depth charges. The people who made those decisions didn't live near the lake, didn't know it; they weren't constantly reminded of the consequences of their actions.

In the mid-seventies, I started a bee farm with some friends in Watsonville, California. We thought Watsonville would be a perfect place to keep bees, because there were apple orchards all around: the bees could collect nectar from the apple blossoms. But strangely, our bees began to die. The pile of dead bees grew outside the hives; soon, they were all dead.

At the county agricultural extension office, we told an agent what had happened. He said that the orchard owners had been spraying chlordane, an insecticide, to protect their apples from bugs. Our bees must have been in the apple orchards during the spraying, and the chlordane had poisoned them. (The reason the growers spray chlordane, I later found out, is that the Agriculture Department grades apples based on the lack of insects. They take random apples, and if they find insect damage, they downgrade the apples. Apple growers have to make sure their fruit is insect-free to get a grade A rating. So they overspray; better to put too much than not enough.)

I was furious; there seemed to be nothing we could do. We had gone to great lengths to make our farm organic; we'd even gotten untreated seeds for our vegetable garden. We didn't feed our chickens anything except garbage and day-old bread from the health food bakery. And our bees were dying from our neighbors' chlordane. What was that pesticide doing to *us*?

When the Three Mile Island accident happened in 1979, I had already been protesting nuclear power and had no illusions about nuclear safety. From the research I had done in college on the effects of radiation on the reproduction of bees, I knew that even very low doses of X-rays rendered the queen's eggs incapable of developing normally. I was concerned: instead of trying to protect us, the utility company and the Nuclear Regulatory Commission were trying to reassure us. And I was scared, because I knew that if the ground water gets irradiated, then well water becomes unsafe, and springs for hundreds of miles around become contaminated. There wasn't much discussion of that danger.

I still shudder at the thought of what a meltdown would do to the ground water. Some information is available about the effects of the Idaho National Energy Laboratory on the Idaho aquifer. It isn't positive. I am filled with repulsion and shame to think that our overconfident attitude toward technology could allow us to ruin land and water for generations to come.

I remember hearing about the radiation damage among the Dine', a Navaho people. At the Survival Gathering, I attended a workshop led by a Dine' woman in her forties. "I want you to look at this," she said, holding out a sheaf of papers an inch and a half thick.

Dine' men had been working as uranium miners, and she had suspected that their exposure to radiation was causing health problems. Although she had no training as a researcher, she had taken it upon herself to investigate. She went from house to house on her reservation, interviewing the women about stillbirths, miscarriages, birth defects, incidents of cancer, and other health problems. "There's hardly a family that hasn't suffered from these health problems," she said. "This is what's happening to my people." I'll never forget that woman's determination to see that this suffering be acknowledged and stopped.

Somehow, human economic systems, both socialist and free-market, have allowed environmental consequences of economic development to be ignored. Corporations decide to mine uranium without considering the suffering of the miners; the nuclear power industry fails to think through the care of waste and leakage problems inherent in the technology. Using water to cool nuclear power plants warms the water, and putting warm water into the rivers or oceans affects the entire system.

How is it that people who are otherwise intelligent fail to act intelligently on behalf of the common good? Some wires must have come loose in their thinking system. Something must disconnect when people get together to make decisions and have no individual responsibility for the effects of the group; and group pressure acts to keep people from discussing their doubts and concerns about new ideas.

The logic that is built into capitalism, into bottom-line priorities and maximization of profit at any cost, creates systemic problems. The flexibility of democracy has done a better job than socialism of forcing industries and cities to respond to pressures from constituencies, but it still isn't up to the needs for a healthy earth. I don't know of any economic system that deals adequately with long-term consequences. Russell Means makes me wonder: How can we develop social forms that *do* promote social responsibility?

And what relationship do I have to the degradation of the environment? When I lived in Los Angeles, this question was laid out in all its complexity. At first, the smog shocked me: I looked toward the mountains and saw beige air. When I left the city for a few days — long enough to get used to air that didn't smell foul — coming back to Los Angeles was particularly jarring. Some days, there were smog alerts on the radio; the air was so bad that kids weren't allowed to play in the schoolyard, because they would breathe too much of the polluted air while running around.

I knew I was contributing to the problem by driving my car, but what could I do? Years before, General Motors had bought up Los Angeles' public transit system and dismantled it — now there was virtually no way to get around that sprawling city except by automobile. I tried to live near my work and to drive as little as possible. Eventually, I moved back to San Francisco, where the daily effects of my car exhaust were less visible, less disturbing, but no less damaging to the environment.

If we are serious about being environmentally responsible, it will take collective as well as individual changes. We will need to radically alter both our personal habits and some of our society's arrangements.

I get a magazine from time to time that promotes a paving moratorium and reports on campaigns to tear up roads. Neighbors in Bernal Heights, in San Francisco in the 1980s, were interested in pulling up the asphalt on one block of Andover Street. This street was at the top of a hill, and on either side there were other streets carrying the very light traffic up the hill. They reasoned that their street was not needed, and that they would be happier without the road. All the neighbors were in agreement, so they went to the city with their proposal. Pulling up the road was such a radical idea that the issue would have to be referred to the Planning Commission, the Roads Department, and so many other agencies that the idea got lost. The neighbors kept pushing, but the city's stall tactics wore on their patience.

After several years, one older neighbor decided that they had all waited long enough; one morning he went out with a pick and shovel and tore out the street in front of his house. Others saw what he had done. By night, the street was gone. Paths for walking were laid out, flowers planted. No one from the city government noticed, until one day a police officer asked one of the neighbors working in the newly established garden, "Didn't there used to be a street here?" "Yes, I think so, but it's hard to remember it." The streetlessness of the third block of Andover continues to this day.

At fifty-one, I relearned to ride a bicycle. While working in Australia, I lived in Byron Bay, which is flat, with the entire town within an easy bike ride. I felt so liberated to be able to do my business under my own steam. When I returned to the San Francisco Bay Area, I bought a used bike, named her "Hortence, the hurricane hurler," and made little forays into the traffic-filled surroundings. The area where I live is not laid out for walking or bicycling.

I can go to the movies, a bookstore, and a few other places. It is not my favorite bookstore, and there are other problems. I cannot buy groceries close enough to walk or use my bike. But I can bike to a lake when I need a break from sitting and writing. I look across the lake to the steady stream of cars on the freeway. It can't be good for the lake, having those fumes falling into it.

Every time I hear about another toxic dump, I wonder what products I use whose manufacture required those chemical wastes. When I reach for a piece of beautiful, bug-free fruit, am I voting for the continued use of a pesticide that is harmful to the farmworkers, to the living environment around the apple tree, and ultimately to my world?

Several months after the Survival Gathering, my American Willing to Listen project took me to Japan. A friend there introduced me to Aileen Smith, a wonderfully engaging woman with sparkling eyes. When our interview began, I had no inkling that her life had been dramatically changed because of a major environmental battle.

Aileen's father was American and her mother Japanese; she had lived alternately in Japan and the United States. Now, she was on Christmas vacation from New York University, where she was studying environmental health. She told me that although she felt emotionally connected to the Japanese people, they ostracized her because of her mixed heritage.

After we had talked for some time, Aileen casually mentioned a book called *Minamata,* which she had written with her late husband, American photojournalist W. Eugene Smith. I was intrigued. The book documented a citizens' struggle to overcome the effects of industrial pollution in Minamata, a fishing and farming town on the southern Japanese island of Kyushu.

In the early 1950s, Aileen told me, residents began to suspect that something was wrong. They noticed fish floating on the sea; then shellfish, birds, cats, and other animals showed strange symptoms. Soon, townspeople began to fall ill: limbs and lips tingled and became numb; speech slurred; motor functions went out of control. After wrestling with these symptoms for some time, some people died. Children were born disabled. In 1959, mercury poisoning was identified as the cause. The mercury was reaching the population through fish, which had been contaminated by chemical wastes discharged into Minamata Bay by the Chisso Corporation.

Aileen and Eugene Smith lived in Minamata for three years in the 1970s, documenting the lives of victims and their families, and the multifaceted struggle for financial compensation and social responsibility. Victims repeatedly told the Chisso Company: "The question is not whether you can or cannot pay; you are responsible for paying. You *must* take care of what you have done, to the end."

Eventually, the Kumamoto District Court ordered Chisso to make indemnity payments to a group of "verified victims." The 1973 verdict stated: "In the final analysis ... no plant can be permitted to infringe on and run at the sacrifice of the lives and health of the regional residents... The defendant cannot escape from the liability of negligence."

A year earlier, during a peaceful demonstration outside Chisso's corporate headquarters, men hired by Chisso to do strong-arm duty beat up several Minamata disease victims and smashed Eugene against the pavement, crushing several vertebrae. He died several years later as a result of those injuries. Talking with Aileen, I got a sense of the magnitude of the costs of environmental destruction, and how furiously business will fight to avoid changing. Not only had the people of Minamata suffered from the poisoning, but also their campaign had taken a heavy toll. For Aileen, the price had included her husband's life.

Hearing this story, I realized I was listening to someone who had helped win a victory for the whole planet. She and the people she worked with in Minamata had shown how ordinary people could turn a terrible situation around and force a company to take responsibility, to deal with the consequences of its actions. I asked Aileen, "Have you ever told your professors at NYU that you helped document one of the first recognized cases of health damage from industrial pollution?"

"They never ask what the students have done," she told me.

The suffering that arises from environmental pollution is borne by individuals. But for change to occur, that suffering must be made visible, so the community can say, "This is ours." In Minamata, the first step in the townspeople's campaign was to acknowledge to each other what was happening. In the fifties, when the first human effects of the poisoning were cropping up, no one knew the cause. Minamata disease was believed to be contagious; one shopkeeper would take money from victims only with chopsticks. Many people tried to hide their ailments, or pretend they were healthy. Divisions arose between the healthy and the sick.

But as long as they hid their suffering, they were powerless. For many people, "going public" was the most difficult step; they had to give up the pretense that nothing was wrong, that their families were all right. Only then was it possible to determine the patterns of the problem.

At the Earth Summit in Rio de Janeiro in 1992, there were some forty-five thousand people working actively on issues involving the environment. In one locale, government people concerned with negotiating agreements and taking testimony were meeting. At a large, colorful park, across the city from the place where governmental meetings were being held, the nongovernmental organizations were working. There were lectures, workshops, demonstrations, concerts, and displays — located in tents erected for this weeklong meeting.

Walking along the pathways, I heard many different languages, saw many intriguing arrays of dress. There were community activists, scientists, journalists and writers, lawyers and legislators, women and men, young and old, from every continent and country in the world. It was very reassuring to know that so many people were concerned about the environment and working to make the changes necessary.

Each person I talked with was working on a specific goal; for example, forest preservation or replanting, clean water or clean air campaigns. People from Southern Hemisphere countries were working to keep the Northern Hemisphere's toxic waste from being dumped in their countries.

Where you were on the economic scale, as an individual and as a country, seemed to determine the degree of danger of the environmental issues you were dealing with. Poor people in the overdeveloped world bear the brunt of the burden of toxic dumps and toxic-spewing industries in their communities. The poorer countries are more likely to be the sites for industries no longer tolerated in the overdeveloped democracies, where the people cannot be forced to put up with the environmental damage. Everywhere, it is the poor people who work in environments with dangerous levels of chemicals and radiation. Listening to the reports of activists around the world, I found that environmental injustice was very evident.

There was also much confusion. When people spoke from their own experience, it was clear that they had evidence of the problems in their locale. The barely spoken questions had to do with the evidence of the cumulative effect of interrelationships between various environmental problems. No one could say how much time the human family had to make these changes before a chain reaction of breakdown would escalate into disaster. One young woman from Peru said to me privately, "Sometimes I think I must be crazy.

Everyone walks around as if they don't know that we are all in a mess and have to make big changes very soon. No one says much about it, and I don't see the planning for those changes."

Industries deliberately create confusion, because they have a lot to lose economically if the part their corporation is playing in the deterioration of the environment is brought to light. Some scientists are paid well to conduct studies "proving" that nuclear power is environmentally friendly, that additives are not dangerous.

The Food Quality Protection Act of 1996 was one example of governmental complicity with dangerous industries. The Delaney Clause of 1958 had imposed a strong ban on carcinogens in processed food. This clause was especially odious to the food and chemical industries, and they worked consistently to get it removed. In the name of protecting children, Clinton administration EPA director Carol Browner determined to gut Delaney, calling the law "unenforceable and an unnecessary burden on the marketplace." Now, under the so-called Food Quality Protection Act, instead of eliminating carcinogens from food, the standard for determining the allowable chemicals in food will be a "cost-benefit analysis" and "risk assessments." In the Food Quality Protection Act, scientists employed by the food and chemical industry will provide "significant" information for the determination of what foods are safe.

The combination of corporate economics, the funding of elections, and industry representatives working in regulatory agencies serves to create a dispirited public will, and to enable negative changes. Increasingly, international trade organizations make decisions secretly regarding the pollutants and pesticides that can be used in food. On top of all this, seeds are being genetically engineered to kill bugs, or to not produce seeds. Do they honestly expect that we will willingly eat food made from genetically damaged industrial wizardry?

I frequently ask students for their own direct evidence — not gathered from the media — of trouble in the environment. They report forests they grew up among being cut and houses built in their place, the rise of skin cancer as well as other diseases, new viruses, changes in how the sun feels on their body. "The sun used to feel warm and comforting, now it feels sharp and stinging." They talk about extinct species. They report an increase in hostility between people, as evidenced by church, synagogue, and mosque burnings, and the rise of the white supremacist militia. Others report that they observe nature rebounding in health. "The foxes are coming back in my neighborhood!"

It is difficult to stay present to the condition of the earth. I sometimes wonder if all the distractions of the overdeveloped world function to keep us from paying attention to what is happening, and doing what we can to help life thrive in the place where we live and in the body we live in. All of life bends toward survival — including human life. But the continuation of life will not be automatic — it will take our attention and intention to be on the side of life.

The great interrelationship of all parts of life means that a collapse of many systems at once is possible, but it also means that any place we work for health affects other places we cannot perceive. I have heard of a mother being able to lift a car when it was on her child, and other people seem able to dip into some deep resource when survival is at stake. I know we all have that capacity, and I must trust we will find the individual and collective will and strength to make the changes. Meanwhile, I recycle what I can, buy food with less packaging, and try to watch my consumption and driving habits. Mostly, I try to ask the questions as I face a new decision or an old habit: what is the best thing for the earth and for the spirit of all life? Not, what do I want to do? I've gotta be ready for the changes. The criterion for each decision, no matter how large or small, is the effect this decision will have on life — human, animal, and plant. It is important that as I heal my own behaviours, we all will need to heal the systems. I can only be as healthy as the world is healthy.

I occasionally teach a class on social change. One day, a student came into class after the lunch break complaining that the deli in the supermarket across the street used too much plastic and Styrofoam in wrapping the food it sold. After a few minutes, another student entered the room with the same lament. We started speculating about what it would take to get the store to change this practice. After some discussion, the students decided to take this on as a project.

Several students offered to get to know the deli manager. They went over and found that he himself had wanted to use butcher paper, but had no confidence that he could get the store management to make the change. The store was part of a very large chain of markets, with all decisions made close to the top. He was a useful resource for the research on alternatives. He said, "I've been wanting to talk to them about wrapping the sandwiches in butcher paper, but I don't think they would listen to me, and I need this job. Maybe they will listen to you."

One student took on the task of researching alternatives, another did market research on how many students were in our school. A letter was drafted to the CEO and also to the division manager, suggesting that butcher paper would be less expensive and more environmentally friendly, as well as appreciated by their clientele. Another person agreed to coordinate all the work and keep people informed of the progress. Within a couple of weeks, the management had agreed to stop using plastic, not only in the store across the street from our school, but in all 130 stores in the region! The students organized themselves to watch to see that this promise was kept, and that this effort was publicized in the school paper, so that people would expect this practice to be continued.

Each small act helps. Each act of faithfulness and attention to what is happening around us is part of the way out for our species and for the earth. I don't know our prognosis as a species, but whatever happens, that we remain caring and alert people is important. Whatever we face, we face as families, as neighborhoods, and as communities. One key is building communities strong enough to make the changes that will allow life to continue. Secretly, I deeply believe that our species, which is so dangerous, will turn around. We will come to know a better and happier, more fulfilled life. I know gloom is popular, but I'm betting on survival and health.

Because I have observed the power of people working well in community, I am confident that groups can make very large changes by paying attention to what is happening to the earth. I interpret alienation and apathy as fear of caring too much. So my question is, how do we build communities that are not afraid of telling each other the truths they observe, sharing dreams, and strategizing together?

If our ship is going down, let us go singing and dancing, loving and taking care of all parts of our extended family in a responsible manner. This is the source of power to find solutions that will sustain life — community. Of course, there will be those among us who get scared, mindless, and greedy. Even, occasionally, *we* may fall into these most human faults. Our choice is whether to respond in a greedy and fearful way, or to do our best to change what is killing us — our self-centeredness, short-sightedness, and lack of attention to what is happening around us. If we can do the latter, maybe we will find a way to keep the ship afloat.

It is my faith that we will find a way — and I am looking for those ways every day. I see others around me in my community doing that, too. Because I travel often in my work, I know that all over the world, people are concerned and looking for a better way to live. I believe we will find ways to keep life going and reach for a better life for all of us. It may require new economic arrangements, new forms of making decisions, new educational and child-raising practices — indeed, everything may have to change to some degree if we are to survive.

Chapter 12

The Human Family at its Worst: Holocaust and Genocide, 1980s

The first time I heard there was to be an international conference on holocaust and genocide, I knew I had to go. The conference was billed as the first one where holocaust/genocide specialists would apply what they had come to know to the issue of nuclear holocaust. As I worked to prevent nuclear war in the early 1980s, the conference brochure reminded me that millions of people had already faced holocaust. What could those who had survived such horror teach us about facing the threat of global annihilation?

I flew to Israel in June 1982, shortly after the Israeli invasion of Lebanon. The weeklong conference was held at the Tel Aviv Hilton, on the Mediterranean shore. Most of the several hundred participants were Jewish survivors of Nazi concentration camps, and many were now Israeli citizens. There were also people who had protected Jews during the war, as well as some who had been hidden, children of survivors, and scholars of holocaust and genocide. And people from other genocides had come to share their experience, and to learn from others.

Members of the Armenian community talked about the genocide against their people by the Turks between 1915 and 1922. A man from Tibet said that the Chinese had killed hundreds of thousands of his people since the 1960s, and that the destruction of the culture, religion, and traditions of the Tibetans continues to the present day. Accounts were given of the holocaust and other genocides against Roma (often called Gypsies), Cambodians, Australian Aborigines, and indigenous peoples throughout the Americas.

Some Jews argued that the word "holocaust" should be reserved for the genocide perpetrated by the Nazis as it was so massive. Although the participants disagreed about what constituted a holocaust, there was consensus that this century was unique in the magnitude of suffering inflicted by human beings on other human beings. More than most periods of time, our century has involved massive killings of people for no reason other than their identity. What had caused some members of the human family to deliberately turn such horrible brutality against others? It is as if the human immune system has been turning against itself and attacking parts of its own body.

No one knows why these genocides have occurred on such an enormous scale in our time, but it seems clear that a key prerequisite is dehumanization. Victims must be portrayed as less than human (as when, during the Vietnam War, the Vietnamese were called "gooks," or when General Westmoreland said Asians didn't value life as highly as we did). Perpetrators of genocide are also dehumanized in this process; they must subjugate their innate connection with other human beings to the principle of "saving the Aryan race" or "protecting national interests" or "the American way of life." Systematic dehumanization seems to be at the root of what makes possible the massacre of groups of people different from one's own.

Could our closeness to technology create distance from our own humanity? There are those who speculate that the dehumanization characteristic of our age may be rooted in our attachment to technology, which makes it possible to kill many people without coming close to the victims. Possibly the tendency of individuals to identify with machines plays a role in the lack of empathy with others.

The tyrannical trivialization of human experience may also be a factor. The limitations of language to communicate pain, and to distinguish massive pain from small pain, are substantial. It is difficult enough to communicate about pain sufficiently for one person to perceive how it is for another. When a person hurts, it is all consuming and undeniable. But listening to a person talk about the pain he is enduring gives rise to many questions: "Is the person telling me the truth?" "What should I do about this information?" The more massive and "unbelievable" the communication, the more questions arise.

It is extremely difficult to communicate horror on the scale of a genocide. Language has a flatness that does not adequately allow the bredth of scale of pain to be shared. For instance, linguistically to say "let's kill one person" does not convey the enormity of the difference from "let's kill the whole — group." Possibly for this reason, it has taken forty years for survivors of Hitler's regime to begin talking openly about what happened. At first, it had been too horrible to talk about, as the survivors tried to heal and create normal lives for themselves.

Researchers at the conference warned that traditional safeguards, such as laws and social institutions, have not proven adequate. Every society that has committed genocide has done so in violation of its own laws. The researchers suggested that empathy mitigates against genocide. I learned that people at the United Nations Human Rights Commission are looking for ways to measure cultural empathy in order to develop an early warning system to prevent genocide. They have developed a scale to examine art and literature as well as print media for compassionate portrayals of the other in a country. The more a target group is seen in complex, nonstereotyped presentations, the less likely that society is to move toward genocide.

But what about a nuclear genocide? How does our dehumanization and lack of empathy, our isolation from others, permit people to contemplate destruction on such a large scale as would be involved in a nuclear war?

One of the first meetings I went to was "Long-Term Effects of Survival." At this meeting, a group of about thirty people, most in their fifties and sixties, were nearly all survivors of Nazi concentration camps. As this information sank in, my mind began to race. What right did I have to be there? I had not shared their suffering. Was I merely a spectator, satisfying my curiosity? Would the survivors identify me with those who had perpetrated the holocaust? Would they turn their anger against me? And what about my own feelings about my background? The United States government had been complicit in many subtle, and many not so subtle, ways: for instance, not allowing vulnerable people like Jews to immigrate, not bombing railway lines so that concentration camp–bound trains would be interrupted. How would I feel about being confronted by those acts committed by people with whom I shared a national or religious identity?

Defensively, my mind began churning out evidence to show that I'd had nothing to do with the holocaust. I hadn't been there. I was born in 1941 in the United States. Even though my features might appear Aryan, I was not German. Anyway, *I* wouldn't do anything like that.

On the other hand, I found myself wondering what I would have done as a gentile in Nazi Germany. Would I have been immune to the denial, passivity, anti-Semitism, and disengagement that allowed so many to collaborate in or acquiesce to genocide?

Would I have found the courage to object to the brutality all around me? Would I have worked against the very context surrounding me? The fear of being part of something fundamentally awful swept over me. I hate the feeling of shame.

The issue of individual guilt versus collective guilt was at the bottom of these questions. To what degree is a whole people responsible for a crime, or is each person individually accountable? As one person said, "Does each tree rest on its own trunk, or do we look to the ground for answers as to why genocide happens?"

On the second day of the conference, I presented a paper on how to talk with children about nuclear war. To my alarm, most of the twenty people attending my talk walked out in the middle. What had I done wrong? Had I somehow offended the holocaust survivors? I was crushed not only personally, but also because I so desperately needed the advice and wisdom of those who had faced holocaust before.

Several days later, a man from Los Angeles addressed a group of seventy-five people, most of them survivors. "When we saw the Nazis gaining power," he asked, "why didn't we do anything? We knew it was coming. Why didn't we fight?" This is a question that plagues many survivors, and they began to discuss it.

I listened eagerly, for this was, above all, what I had come for. My assumption was that those who had survived, who knew the costs of denial and passivity, must have thought deeply about what they might have done. Surely, the ideas they had developed would be crucial to preventing nuclear holocaust. But as I listened, I heard few ideas and no answers.

The more they talked, the more I felt the urge to ask my question directly. Finally, I stood up, shaking, and spoke from the back row: "I know some of what you were feeling back in the thirties. I see a potential nuclear holocaust coming. You say you didn't know where to go, where to hide. The same is true for me. You say it was overwhelming and you didn't believe what you saw. I feel that way now. I may be standing where you were standing in 1939 or 1940." People around me started to cry. "I don't know what to do," I continued. "I've come here to ask you for guidance about how to live in this period and how to prevent a holocaust. How do we activate ourselves at a deep enough level to take seriously this threat and work against it. We all see the warnings." When I sat down, the room was absolutely quiet.

Many survivors came up afterward to talk about powerlessness and to empathize with me. Some felt as I did, that a global nuclear holocaust was increasingly likely. And I came to understand why some survivors had walked out during my presentation a few days earlier: they feared they didn't have the strength to face the warnings of another holocaust.

While we inside the Hilton were talking about past and future wars, the sound of helicopters overhead reminded us that a war was going on less than a hundred miles away. Israeli troops were occupying southern Lebanon.

To try to better understand the conflicts behind this war, after the conference I resumed my American Willing to Listen project. I wanted to find out how people on all sides were thinking about this war.

In Ramallah, on the West Bank, I sat on the steps of a building at Birzit University and talked with three Palestinian college women. We exchanged jail experiences. They had all been in jail a few times. Once, Israeli soldiers had rounded them up because they were standing near a wall on which an anti-Israeli slogan had been painted. But they didn't have much to say to me about the war in Lebanon.

Then, I met a very friendly Palestinian professor of thirty-five or forty. "What is it like for you, knowing what's going on in Lebanon?" I asked. "I have to keep that wall closed," he replied. The war was too painful for him to talk about. But he was eager to discuss the refugee camps in which thousands of Palestinians were being housed in very poor conditions, as well as the human rights abuses suffered by the Palestinians at the hands of the Israelis. When asked why the Palestinian Liberation Organization wouldn't recognize Israel, he said that after much discussion in the PLO meetings he'd attended, a consensus was emerging that it was time to do so.

In Tel Aviv, I asked a restaurant owner how the war was affecting him. He was upset because he couldn't serve moussaka, the house specialty, anymore. His moussaka cook had gone off to the war, and all his customers were complaining.

I talked with a twenty-five-year-old woman in the Israeli army. Her regiment had been sent to break up an Israeli peace demonstration in the West Bank. They went in swinging clubs, and the demonstrators fled. Some Israeli Jews had hidden under the counter in a fabric shop run by Palestinians. The soldier said the war was driving a wedge between Israeli Jews. She had never had a Palestinian friend and thought of Palestinians in very stereotypical terms. It was inconceivable for her to have a relationship with a Palestinian.

I also followed the war through the local news media, reading the *Jerusalem Post* cover to cover every day and going regularly to the Palestinian News Service to pick up press releases. A woman at the News Service suggested that I go see the war firsthand. She told me I could get press credentials and go into Lebanon in an Israeli Defense Force press car.

I dismissed the idea out of hand. But soon a French journalist asked me to go with him into Lebanon and take photos to accompany his article. It seemed as though opportunity was knocking a second time, urging me to take in this information. Though still strongly resistant to the idea, I began to wonder: How credible is a peace activist who is unwilling to see what she is working against? Why not look directly at the pain, rather than working only in the moral abstract?

For years, I had been confused by the complexities of the Middle East conflict. Now that I was there, the situation seemed even harder to comprehend. Listening to Israeli Jews and Palestinian Arabs, I had learned a lot. But deep down, I still failed to understand why members of these two groups were hurting each other. They both wanted to own the same piece of land, but how that difference could give rise to such hatred and killing did not necessarily seem to follow.

Illogical as it was, I could only conclude that both sides were absolutely right in their needs — and absolutely wrong in their extreme actions. Both sides needed a place for their people to live and to have rights to self-determination. I feared that seeing the war would deepen my confusion. And I suspected my own motives. Would I be a voyeur? Was it drama I was seeking? And what if I got caught in the crossfire? I could be killed! Wars are unpredictable events.

I was afraid, too, that I would see something that would so outrage me that I would try to stop it. I imagined a soldier stopped in a jeep ahead of me shooting helpless people. I might start shouting and try in some way to interfere. I was also afraid I might stand by helplessly, and forever have to live with that shame and memory. More than anything, I didn't want my life ruined — just like everyone else in the situation. But I had the luxury of choice. The night before we left, I lay awake all night, my head swirling in self-examination and criticism. But in the morning, I went to Lebannon to work.

At the border, we signed a release agreeing not to hold the Israeli government responsible if we happened to get killed. That was the first absurdity. The noise of helicopters and gunfire in the distance was ominous. I had to keep reminding myself that this was not a war movie. We climbed aboard an Israeli Defense Force jeep flying a white flag, and drove into Lebanon. Our driver was an IDF press attaché; my fellow passengers were the French journalist and a reporter for a European news service. There was no roof on the jeep, and I thought, what will I do if a hand grenade comes flying in? I'll throw it out. If someone starts shooting at us, I guess I can hide on the floor by the door.

It was the first day of the first cease-fire (though shooting was still going on), and Israeli troops had advanced to within ten miles of Beirut. We drove through the towns of Tyre and Sidon, which had been devastated. Buildings had gaping holes, streets were filled with rubble, and walls were riddled with gunshot grooves.

In some villages, we saw no people at all. Had they been killed, were they hiding, or had they taken flight? In other towns, we saw people standing or squatting despondently, talking to each other, shaking their heads, often smoking. Some gestured wildly. A few times, people shouted at us in English, demanding that we press people share with the world what had been done to them. One woman yelled: "You tell them that they bomb schools!"

I felt for the people whose homes and businesses had been shot up and destroyed. Now, instead of improving their homes, they would have to rebuild from scratch. The work of whole generations of builders was squandered.

I was surprised to see soldiers resting, eating little crackers. I had never pictured a war zone as a place where soldiers could have cracker breaks.

As we drove along, our guide would point to a destroyed building and explain, "We found rifles here," or "This was a PLO headquarters." We came upon a school for mentally retarded children that had been badly bombed. Children walked around aimlessly, confusion on their faces. Many had been seriously hurt and were bandaged. A boy about twelve years old wailed unceasingly as he clung to a tree, his body rocking back and forth. Our guide said that he didn't know anything about this bombing. In the press jeep, we were outraged, and grew silent as we took in the scene.

We stopped at a civilian hospital, where I saw people of all ages, some horribly hurt and others with minor wounds needing stitches. A woman came up to talk to me, speaking rapidly in Arabic, with her face uncomfortably close to mine. As our guide translated, I learned that her home had been bombed, one of her children had been killed, and another had been injured. She was hysterical.

Helpless to do anything, I felt sorrow in every muscle of my body. I put my hand on her shoulder and said, "I'm sorry, I'm so very sorry."

Once, as our little group stood on a little rise, a shell exploded about fifty yards away — where we had just driven. Could they be shooting at us? I started to tremble and felt wetness trickling down my legs. Our guide hurried us off. In that moment, as we rushed into the jeep and bounced away, I knew I never wanted war to happen to me again. I knew I never wanted war to happen to my friends and family, and I never wanted it to happen to people who were not yet my friends.

Back in Israel, I kept thinking about what I'd seen, rerunning it in my mind — the rubble, the blank faces, the people screaming in the hospital. One day of seeing the terror had filled me with sadness, confusion, and fear. How do people survive the experience of war, day after day? For several nights I could not sleep, and for months the images returned in my waking and sleeping moments. Although I had seen only one day of a relatively small conventional war, it was several months before I stopped waking up at night sweating with fear, before the memories stopped playing like a continuous movie in the back of my mind, before I could return to the security of being an American woman who isn't supposed to have to think about such things.

I got angrier and angrier. I was angry that somebody had ordered this misery to happen, had deliberately decided on it. I was angry that the women, the mentally retarded children, and the old people were suffering so. I was angry with the Israelis for starting the war, with the PLO for storing the weapons that had served as the Israelis' pretext for invasion. I was angry about the injury to the men and women whose eyes looked through the sights of the guns and pressed the trigger. How will they ever feel good about themselves in a universal sense again? I was angry that this had been going on for thirty years. I was angry because neither side had just stopped and started negotiating!

I made a return visit to Birzit University in Ramallah. There are a lot of rocks in Israel/Palestine. I picked one up to carry home in my pocket. A friend asked me if this was my disarmament campaign. I felt surprisingly at home as I chatted with Palestinian students and their professors. I was impressed with the informality between them — they talked and joked as friends. Then we heard that Israeli troops had surrounded the campus and were not letting anyone come or go. This had happened before; it was a form of harassment the students and faculty had learned to endure. They began to prepare for a pro-tracted stay, rationing food from the cafeteria and holding meetings.

Students and faculty met in a large auditorium to discuss what to do. Several women were eager to translate for me. One said, "We never really know where each speaker is coming from, as they may belong to hidden groups with their own agenda. There are many secrets alive in this room." They considered resisting the troops with various strategies in honor of their "fallen allies in Lebanon," but decided instead to take a wait-and-see posture.

While we waited, one professor made me an interesting offer: "Why don't you come here and live with us? We will find you work and housing. You will really learn our struggle from the inside. Work with us." My life at home pulled me; I said that it was not possible for me to live in Palestine just now, but I would work with-in the United States. I was able to leave the university in a reporter's car late in the afternoon. I read in the newspaper that the siege ended later that evening.

I went to Tel Aviv the next day to see Shlomo, a man I had met while attending the holocaust conference. He was in the electronics business and, like many other middle-aged Israeli men, was also a reserve officer in the army. As we walked along the Mediterranean, I poured out my anger and deep confusion about the war. Shlomo was a caring, intelligent person; he listened and shared his own ambiva-lent feelings. Though he felt drawn to fellow Israelis who were protesting the war, he was still ready to serve if called up by the mil-itary. Shlomo also told me about the sufferings of Israeli people at the hands of the Palestinians — the people killed in bombings of school buses, airports, kibbutzim (collective farms). Isn't it interesting how people use the crimes of the other to rationalize their own crimes.

The attraction between the two of us offered some physical consolation, but further confused my mixed emotions. At the end of our time together, I felt only more confused. I was sure of just one thing: there was too much suffering in that region. Shaken, I left Israel the next day.

On the plane, images from my trip came to mind: holocaust sur-vivors, war victims, students and teachers at Birzit, my friend Shlomo. The farther I got from the Middle East, the more clearly I could see that both sides in the conflict were absolutely right, cor-rect in every detail. Both had causes, and each had been wronged by the other. Each side blamed the other for starting it, and no one seemed to know how it could end. Both sides were absolutely right

— except that they were killing each other. The situation for the two populations was not equal. With considerable aid from the US and control of the land that had been in Palestinian hands, the power was disproportionately Israeli. What is the difference in the justification for the use of violence when power is so unbalanced? What does a decent person do in such a situation?

Upon my return home, friends asked me to tell them about my trip. Usually, I love to tell stories, share my experience, as a way of learning more from the dialogue. This experience of touching the war was something I did not want to share. And it has not gotten much easier with time.

I don't want to tell you, dear reader, about the faces of the people I saw in Lebanon. I don't even want to remember. The pain that I glimpsed — pain that was deliberately caused by policy and design — is so obscene that my civilized mind censors it for you. Perhaps that censorship angers you. It angers me, too. I am furious that some people can create pain so horrible that it violates the human spirit to remember.

What angers me most about war is what it does to our confidence in our fellow beings, and in the possibilities of our history together. I do not attach much meaning to anger. In social change work, it is often a sign of self-absorption and is not useful to organize behind. But it is a signal that something is wrong, and each of us must do whatever we can to stop it. War is the ultimate succumbing, the final failure of resolve to make things work out well for the common good. It is with calm and determination that my best work against war comes forth.

As I feared, seeing war has shaken my optimism and customary happiness. I've begun to wonder why we in the United States seem so happy and optimistic. One explanation could be that our happiness is a function of our fear and state of denial and attachment to the delusion that everything is OK. Could part of the reason be that there have been no wars on our land in the last century? Wars that have been fought by our country have quickly fallen or been pushed into a forgotten place in our collective and family memory. We seem able to have parades, but are less willing to hear what those who fought went through. Or is it that our experience of war is so sanitized by movies that we deny its impact on the inner lives of those who fought, killed, and saw friends killed. We have riots or uprisings, which is as close as we have come to wars. We do not carry memories of major disruption in the flow of human affairs, so we can obsess about the latest fashions, the top-ranked football teams, and other frivolities. I do not wonder that people from the Middle East cling so tenaciously to life.

It was the Nazi holocaust that first convinced me that human beings, former sweet babies, innocent schoolchildren, loving parents, people who worked hard for a decent future, can perpetrate horrors against other human beings, also former sweet babies, innocent schoolchildren, loving family members. Part of me wants to say, "We would never do anything like that. Americans aren't like that." But no society is free of shame. We Americans have our Ku Klux Klan; Thomas Jefferson was one of the largest slaveholders; we have carried out the slaughter of our native peoples, the Dresden firebombing, the atomic bombings of Hiroshima and Nagasaki, the Vietnam War, the My Lai massacre; and we surely are the leader in preparations for all-out nuclear war. The weapons used by the Israeli forces were probably funded by American taxpayers and made in American factories. We are not immune from contemplating, planning, and carrying out unspeakable horrors. But it was the Gulf War and its continuing devastation that really taught me about my country's ability to lie, to bomb wholesale without any concern for the earth, and perpetuate terror on the ordinary people who were caught by those bombs.

In August 1990, the threat of war in the Gulf became a public reality. I was out of the country, so the seriousness did not hit me until I returned in October. Coming back to the United States was like stepping into mud. I felt sucked into a reality with no clear resolve, no energy for resistance, and lots of guilt and doubt. Like so many of my friends, I started asking myself, "Could it really be that war is coming? Are the indications that war is a possibility strong enough for me to set aside other things and work against the war? What should I do?"

It seemed inconceivable in this time of dreams of a peace dividend, when we had so much other pressing global business, that a war would be seen as useful. Most of the generals from the Pentagon were recommending against a war in the Gulf. But this was not a military war so much as an economic one. What hold did Kuwait have on the US that we could be called to fight their war? The emir of Kuwait threatened to dump major stock holdings in the United States, which would have plummeted our economy faster than it was already falling.

A war in the Gulf was the nonissue in the November election. It was not even part of the debate in that election. But representatives of the Bush administration were out promising to forgive large debts of countries that would support the war effort in the United Nations. It was like a bad dream, where it was difficult to figure out how to get a handle on what was happening.

Then, in late December, I went off to work in New Zealand, and found that some people in that lovely island country took the threat of war seriously and were actively working against it. When a friend handed me an article about a grandmother who had gone to a peace camp on the border of Iraq and Saudi Arabia, I knew immediately that I would go. An international organization had organized the Gulf Peace Team, which had attracted people from all over the world to the desert to nonviolently protest the war. People from fourteen countries were assembling there to stand nonviolently between those two armed forces to demand peace. I didn't feel particularly afraid, nor particularly brave. It just seemed like the most creative and powerful antiwar action I could take.

I could not help but wonder why this peace camp had not come to the attention of peace activists in the US, why my friends and I in the US peace movement didn't know about this action. I was furious that I had not heard of it sooner. I was thus given a preview of the media lockout of alternative viewpoints and actions concerning the war.

It took some time to finish my work in New Zealand, get my supplies organized, and get accepted as a member of the Gulf Peace Team. Because I was not in my home country, it took the team's administrators a little longer to figure out that I would be a stable presence in the camp, and that I was not with the CIA. Finally, at 11 p.m. the night before I was to leave, I got a call from someone who had just returned from the camp. He warned me of infighting there, that travel to the camp would be difficult out of Baghdad, and that I would have to sleep on cold asphalt. He gave me the contact names and addresses and other essential information, and encouraged me to keep copies in several places in case I was searched. He also said that my visa would be waiting for me in Delhi, and that they were looking forward to a comedian joining the camp. I took a few props as essential tools.

Friends at home were not happy with my decision, as they still had not heard anything about this peace camp. I was clear about going. For me, it was not exactly a decision to go as much as a decision to do whatever I could to stop a war. I felt timid, but a much stronger feeling was that I was in a state of grace. I felt focused, calm inside, and blessed with work that I had confidence in. Ultimately, dear ones concluded that they supported my decision, whatever it was.

It was very difficult to make such a decision so far away from home, but the many friends I had made through years of touring in New Zealand stood in magnificently. The New Zealanders helped me get myself physically and spiritually ready. They helped me pack and took me to the airport. But as I walked through the gate at the Auckland airport, leaving the support of my Kiwi friends, I felt simultaneously alert and very alone, very much on my own. On the plane, I wrote this letter to the world:

Dear World,

Here we are again
just you and me
    alone again.

I can see on your face
    in your screaming newspapers
    you are scared of this war.
    Me too.
Two of your children
    prepare to fight to the death
each bragging bullyish boy
    trying to out-bluff, out-shout
    out-macho the other.
Neither of these men is a particularly nice guy
    one had attacked and killed thousands of Panamanians
    and the other has killed thousands of Kurds and Iranians.
"Oh, please don't," I beg, "please
For all of us — stop."

Could we turn to our old enemy —
    Mother Russia — now a new friend — for help?
    When we were your enemy
    you stopped us.
    Would you do any less for a friend?
    Now that we are your friend
    can you stop us before we kill again?
Are we so friendless in the world
    that no one will stop us?

The Iraqi and Jordanian visas were supposed to be ready for me in Delhi. I was to pick them up and then wait for the twice-weekly flight to Amman. As the January 15 deadline approached, I spent three days in and out of the Iraqi embassy in Delhi, getting to know the workers and the ambassador. Each day passed without a telex from Baghdad giving permission for issuance of a visa. I'm sure the Iraqis had more pressing things on their telex than my visa.

On a map, India is just inches from Iraq. Since I was on the same continent as the proposed war, I started to wonder if I would feel the beginning of the tragedy in my body. Would the ground shake when the bombs started falling upon the earth? Would I feel the roar of the jets thousands of miles away? Could I sense the change in consciousness on the earth when the deliberate harm people do to each other increased?

I suppose everyone remembers what they were doing, where they were, and how they felt when they heard that the war had broken out. For me, the war in the Gulf began when my plane to Amman was canceled due to the war. I stood there on the sidewalk outside the airline office looking at a large electric News Bulletin sign, and a cold chill went through me. "War"— there was that word and all that it means. Not a maybe war, but a real one. A complex combination of emotions surged through me. I was glad I was not at the peace camp underneath the bombers, sorry that I had not been able to do what I had decided to do, embarrassed that I had not gone sooner so I could have achieved my goal. As it turned out, the people at the peace camp were not bombed and returned safely home.

I had thought that a period of negotiation and initiatives would follow after January 15. I had misjudged George Bush's determination to push the war ahead on schedule. I went immediately to the Iraqi embassy to express my sorrow at the turn of events. The embassy workers were as cordial as always, offering me coffee and limp handshakes. I still wanted the visa, since I thought I might need it later. The telex had not come, but the ambassador gave me a visa on his own authority. I asked him why he had not done that earlier so I could have been on my way. He replied that he was concerned for my safety. I have an Iraqi visa in my US passport dated January 15.

I wanted to be home with my friends in the US When the world is in crisis, one wants to be with family, so I rushed home. The planes were only half full; people weren't flying. I asked the flight attendant, and she explained that the low numbers were due to fear of terrorism.

Immediately upon reaching home, I called a group of friends and their friends together one Sunday night to talk about the war: how we saw it, what we could do about it, and how it affected our lives. We decided to continue meeting at five o'clock every week-night. Anyone who wanted to think about and plan our responses to the war was welcome.

We didn't all know each other before we began meeting togeth-er. We met in my living room every evening after work, because we needed to be there. An interesting group, composed of Christians, Jews, Muslims, Buddhists, and feminists. We regularly had in our midst Hans, John, Michael, Peter, Rita, Spence, Susan, Teri, and Tova. Vocationally we were a computer repairperson, a program-mer, a nurse, several administrators of nonprofit groups, a social worker, an artist, a carpenter, and a house painter.

Unlike George Bush, we had never supported Saddam Hussein. In fact, the more we got to know of him, the more critical we were of Hussein. But this did not mean we thought he and the people in his nation should be crushed. Slowly, we noticed that we were becoming a group — that we were coming to care about each other. We learned a whole lot about ourselves and our world look-ing through the lens of the war. Some of what we learned disgust-ed us, some was merely interesting. While we were preponderantly opposed to the war, there were those among us who felt that "good things may come out of it." Perhaps the Palestinians' and Kurds' issues would finally be addressed by the world. Maybe Israel would finally be more secure in the region.

Each night we began with a check-in — how our lives were going, how we were feeling about the war, and what we were doing. We watched the war shatter some of our dreams, force us out of denial about the nature of the society we live in. Our denial asserted itself over and over again. "This can't be happening." We saw the censorship and manipulation of the truth in the media. It was as if we were beckoned by a deep sleep, urging us to return to unconsciousness. The deep ache of an earth suffocating from fumes from burning oil wells, and suffering from bombs slamming into the earth and burning human and animal flesh, was too much.

We never heard about war dead, only "collateral damage," the term euphemistically used by military spokespeople. We struggled to keep remembering that even though the newspapers were full of emptiness about the true impacts of the war, it was still exacting a terrible toll. We talked about our dreams, our energy, and our efforts to run away from reality through too much work, getting sick, and other mechanisms the body uses to deal with nasty realities.

Some people felt that the coming of this war invalidated all the work for peace and social justice they had done in their lives. We went in and out of depression. In the face of the war's horror; the gloating, lying, and bragging in the media; and the gullibility of the public, we questioned the value of the work we had done for the nonviolent creation of change.

But maybe war cannot invalidate the work we have done before. If my house is burning, that does not make meaningless all the vacuuming I did for the years before — it only means that when the firefighters leave, a big clean-up job remains in order to continue living there. We have to live in the present, fighting the fire in all the ways we can. Our work goes on, and we continue doing our duty to the life force that is ours, building in each moment the future we want for our ourselves and descendants.

As we met together and witnessed our shared pain, each of us found our own way to work against the war. This work was important, no matter how much we felt we were swimming against the popular tide. Acknowledging our grief and shame allowed us to keep going. We admitted our suffering and let it flow through us like a river. We did not struggle to resist our suffering, nor did we build a temple to it. We just recognized it and kept moving.

We explored the land of suffering, for in that land are the seeds of new growth: compassion for those with opposing views (in this case, those supporting the war); and new ways of being — the new institutions and new ways of thinking necessary for life to continue. And the creative opportunities of the moment — even amid the suffering — were tremendous. No longer could we deny that war and death were among us, inside of us, sleeping in bed with us. They were, and are, here. Through our citizenship, we participate in the death of others, and we will die. In some almost incomprehensible way, these two phenomena are linked, though it is difficult to penetrate that reality with the mind.

In our meetings, we turned our collective attention to the war. Each night, we brought in clippings, notes from traditional and alternative media, as well as stories we picked up at peace actions we attended. We also had access, through family and friends in other countries as well as e-mail, to information from abroad. We taught each other the facts, tried to discern the lies, and worked to think together about what was happening in the Gulf, in our country, in other countries, and inside ourselves. Occasionally, we invited someone from outside the group to share views on a particular topic. But basically, we taught ourselves. Over and over we asked, "What can we do about this war?"

What did we do? What did I do?

Some days I lay in my bed, heartsick. Not a very noble thing to confess. Of course, there were other days when I went to meetings, with other people who felt confused and outmaneuvered by the promilitary forces in the country. I wrote thousands of words about and against the war. I joined other women outside military recruiting stations and military bases, washing flags, and crying tears of grief and betrayal. I did whatever I could think of in the face of such raw power. I called the president every few days to get on his poll of how his acts were being perceived by the public. I demonstrated in underreported demonstrations. I wrote letters. I did what I could.

One day, I went with a friend to the army recruitment center in downtown Oakland and talked with several recruiters and one young African American man who was enlisting. He said that he felt the army would be safer for him than the streets of Oakland. He could not get a job, and he wanted to do something worthwhile. I could not argue with his perception of his options. I know there are more options — but they were not real for him. Damn! The young man was a fine human being. I could see that. He wanted respect. He wanted to be a part of his country. We talked for about fifteen minutes. The recruiters were trying to get rid of me, but I held my ground long enough to plant some questions about the morality of military actions and US policy. I have come to believe that the only sacrifice greater than losing one's own life is being forced to take another's life. Killing another is a life-defining event that forever leaves the soldier with a profound internal wound.

It is very tempting for the people not doing the fighting to retreat into judgment and self-righteousness, as if they themselves have no responsibility for the war — or the holocaust or genocide. "I am not doing the killing; those people out there are doing it." But it's really all of us together doing it. There are those who would say that it's cleaner to be there doing the act, as well and as cleanly as you can. I would say, however, that some things are not worth doing, and they are especially not worth doing well.

Women cannot claim any high ground. Was it not Margaret Thatcher who said, in her usual commanding voice, when discussing what the US should do, "Don't be a wimp, George"? When women arrogantly put men down for fighting in a war, let us remember how few refuse to pay the taxes that pay for the war, how few decide to earn so small a salary that taxes will not be due. Women have equal responsibility for creating the atmosphere of war. When our heroes are the men who have the wisdom and courage to resist war, there will be peace.

My former brother-in-law was among the US troops that invaded Grenada. He told me how impossible it would be for him to refuse to do what he was ordered to do: "It's the entire United States against me, Fran. I have been taught to respect my leaders in this country. I'll do my best not to kill, really I will. I know that killing is not right." And yet in the moment, when faced with all the urgency of war and someone else shooting at you (or perceived as willing to shoot at you), it is hard to swim upstream and say no. It always sounds a little crazy to talk about "innocent victims," as if somehow the people in the military are not themselves victims. While one side of the mind claims they are victims, the other side screams, "Criminal! Murderer!"

Forgiving oneself and others for the horrible things that are done in war is a difficult but important task. It took me a long time to work my way to forgiving the vets who came back from Vietnam. I have not yet forgiven my society for asking them to do those horrendous acts. I continue to long for women and men strong enough to resist orders to kill, and mature enough to work only for life. During the Gulf War, I met one woman and many men who refused to go when ordered to the Gulf. They were put under terrific pressure, but their characters strengthened and stayed the course of resisting.

As it turns out, the war was over for the Americans almost as soon as it started. If it had been a boxing match rather than a war, it would have been stopped in the first round, so unbalanced were the forces and so brutal was the beating. The opponent fought back very little — he hunkered down in the sand and waited for it to be over. As thousands of Iraqi troops hid in their trenches, US troops bulldozed sand on top of them. Other Iraqi troops were killed in retreat — shot, burned to death. How do the killers now forget what they did, how do they come back to civilization with those memories? And what will they say when their children ask, "What did you do in the war?"

What did I do? I watched. I tried to stay awake as the television lulled me to sleep with talk of "smart bombs," collateral damage, more hype and propaganda. Reporters rooted for the home team, showing glee on camera at the news of great bombing victories. In live press conferences, they sat mute, refusing to ask the probing questions that might get them removed from the pool of elite reporters who were "allowed" press credentials. If they questioned the war itself, they might lose their jobs. What could be worse?

The war I saw on my television set seemed more like an advertisement for our smart technology than news. The news broadcasters constantly told us of the victories of the aircraft, the "patriot" missiles, and those powerful tanks that rolled over the desert cover, crushing the topsoil and plants. What of the fragile life of the fighters, of the birds, of the desert itself, and the citizens? Oh, I ached for them all — the Iraqis, the Americans, the Israelis — cowering night after night as the sky lit up with death.

What did I do? I wept. My heart ached for everyone living in fear all over the world, but especially in the Middle East. I feel a little silly, maybe self-critical, about admitting that. But it is one of my main memories of the war. I often thought of my ancestors in past wars, the women who wept at home for the suffering caused to and by the men they loved.

I realized that I was focused on the damage the war was causing human beings and human institutions, but one day my new kitten, Pebbles, climbed up onto my computer. At that time, Pebbles and I wrote the following piece, and I learned an important lesson about war: it affects all life.

How can I 7==887 write about war and suffering when a precious little black and gray kitten, tentatively named "Pebbles," is running her new wondrous life all over my desk, climbing up my arm, curling up on my shoulder, licking my chin, and generally displaying her need for affection and her adventure with life? This is her first day with us, everything is new. And this little fluff ball is into checking everything out. 122tyf266ygv777fvyyyy 222n yyg77ggvyh yyuf7666666644677777777777

Freely translated, that is a message from the kitten world about the joy of life, and how wonderful it is to be a distraction for a writer who is probing a very painful and thorny reality. The urgency of the war gone, I find I now write from a colder, more thinking place. I read and think, but words do not come easily. What was this war about? Why did it happen? How is going to continue into our lives? I think not just about this war, but about the "big" wars and the "little wars," too. Horrible caves of questions haunt my computer, haunt my mind. Who are we who have done this? Is megadeath the necessary consequence of our life now? Why should anyone focus on the darkness of life, the miserable realities, when there are kittens to play with, friends to love, gardens to grow, and birds to watch?

Tippy-toed, Pebbles goes to the back of the computer, then comes back, puts her baby paws out to touch and distract my fingers flying over the keys. Her marbled gray and black head held at such a dignified angle, her big steady eyes looking so squarely into mine. Licking her paws and tail, she tries to clean herself up. Wipes her face and whiskers. Then, she sits down under the warm light, pulls her feet underneath her body, and watches. A representative of a nonhuman species, holding me accountable for writing the truth. The animals are watching us now. Possibly, Pebbles might be here representing the kittens and cats — maybe the dogs, goldfish, and other precious species of Israel and Iraq. What must the war be like for them? Pebbles asks me to remember those creatures in this book. It must have been frightening for the cats of Iraq and Israel.

How many cats died? The military doesn't release those figures either. The terror in their uncomprehending eyes as they heard explosions, watched their homes collapsing, trapped in the madness. Surely, they looked one way, then another, hunkered down in fear. The hair on their backs standing straight up. No words to explain, no concepts like "I am an Iraqi cat, those are US bombs; for some reason, those people thousands of miles away want to kill me." Eyes alert, breathing in terror, breathing out fear. How many hungry cats are on the streets of Baghdad or Basra, families dead, homes no longer recognizable, food now hard to find.

What about the wild animals? Where do they get clear, clean water to drink now? How did they understand what was falling from the sky? Did they smell the fear in the wind? What did they see, what did they know? They are watching us now — all the animals. How they must wonder about us. How do they understand evolution, and "civilization?" How to explain massacres of thousands, tens of thousands, of people and animals to an animal that primarily kills what it needs in order to live.

I wonder what Pebbles can know about these massacres. How could she understand anything except the folly? It matters little to her that she is an American cat. She is so little, so young. I hope she doesn't know. I hope she doesn't care. If she does know, it is sweet of her to pretend not to care. She leaves me to care, to find words for the wordless reality I know only fragments of and wish I understood — either less or more.

Pebbles sleeps now, her little black and gray body a contrast to all the papers on the desk. A furry balloon expanding and contracting with each breath. She is experiencing peace now. She and I are safe for this moment. The contrast between my personal reality of love and things getting better and better in my own life, with the social reality I see around me in my city, my country, and the world, makes me a little crazy. Life is so warm. So good.

Wars are always very bleak times for people who are awake, alert, and sensitive to suffering. This time had been shattering in other ways: the failures of savings and loans institutions, which illuminated the folly and pervasiveness of greed; education falling apart in many parts of the country; environmental disasters in every region.

In many ways, our group perceived brokenness in the public sphere of our lives, yet for many of us our personal sphere was filled with joy and accomplishment. The contrast was confusing and crazy-making. It does not seem surprising that many citizens have withdrawn from public participation, but it is a concern. When people leave the common tasks of taking care of the community to the most aggressive and to those who have the most to gain, this bifurcation of the population is socially dangerous.

Many of us were deeply concerned about what else happened while our attention was so riveted on the Middle East — the funding of more weapons to El Salvador; the domestic turmoil, instability, hunger, and repression in the Soviet Union and the Baltic States; and the Balkans heading for war. And, of course, global economic and environmental troubles are growing more serious by the year. I saw bumper stickers that said, "Saddam Hussein still has his job — do you?"

One could not help but wonder what international event would be used next to rationalize our enormous defense budget and distract domestic rage over the troubles of our land. The economic dysfunction had ravaged the farmers, driving some off their land and the land into large corporate hands. In some ways, the greatest tragedy has been the drastic cuts in the arts. When we can no longer afford to experience beauty and explore truth, as well as give them expression through the arts, something is very wrong. Our culture will suffer in significant ways. And education. In Michigan, in the year of the Gulf War, children were sent home because the schools had no money for a full school year. Something is broken in our spirit and with our decision-making process. Our public life is rotting, and the stink is driving us into our houses.

To make the issue of war even more confounding to the antiwar activist, we now have places in the world where some segments of the country are begging for the US to come in and stop the fighting in their area. Our friends in Dubrovnik, Croatia, were bitterly disappointed when George Bush didn't send the navy to stop the shelling of their city that lasted more than a year. It was election time, and Bush felt he could not undertake such an act. I, who have worked for years to keep the American military home, was in an awkward position when colleagues would say, "It is only the US that can stop the war in the former Yugoslavia." The machine of war is very difficult to stop. What is the responsibility of the superpower now in the world?

It makes me ache to remember the hope that preceded the war in the Persian Gulf. Nelson Mandela was out of jail and on speaking tours, the Berlin Wall was down, the cold war was no longer, Eastern Europe was in the process of freeing itself, and a playwright was in power in Czechoslovakia. In the US, we were hoping a peace dividend could be liberated from the budget to address some of our chronic homelessness, AIDS, poverty, arts and education troubles.

Oh, we had dreams of a new day, when the world could work together to clean up the rivers and the air and restore the earth to a livable place. Could it be that the longing for democracy seen around the world could also find hearts in the United States that would question the two-party monopoly of power, as well as take seriously the role multinational corporations and moneyed interests play in buying elections and politicians? Having been colonized through years of advertising and authoritarian education, are we capable of overthrowing the very system that we have been taught is the American way for greater democratic participation of the people in their government?

It helps to remember that we do not have to go through war or other repressive times alone. Even in the bleakest times, it is important to keep dreaming our social dreams. For each of us not only has our individual dreams for our family and ourselves. We also have social dreams of how we might live together, participating for the common good. There are six billion other seekers who are looking for tender ways to live together, in this world of expanding access to information and communication that knits us into a more and more interconnected whole. The hatchet has fallen: we have seen the horrors humans are capable of in genocide, holocaust, and war; at one level we are scared, and at another level excited and awakened. Is there a role being recast for the military, in which it flexes its muscle but does not kill? The role the UN troops played on the Macedonian border during the Bosnian war, which kept the war from expanding, did not involve violence. The threat of force is still violent, but it is a big step away from the use of killing to stop killing. New dreams are being born now. And we remember the old dreams of peace, too.

Chapter 13

The Worst Again: Yugoslavia and the Bosnian War, 1993–Present

Dear Friend,
You are invited to send a small packet of connection and support to a woman in the former Yugoslavia.

THAT'S THE WAY the story began in 1993. I wanted to go to the former Yugoslavia, find out what was happening there, and consider what people in other countries could do. Historically, the Balkans have been a distant warning area for issues that would come to affect the entire Western world.

In the papers and on television, I saw stories of war, of women being raped in order to drive them from their homes and to drive their families from the land they had lived on for generations. A *Nightline* special on the use of rape as a war strategy touched my heart. I learned of women repeatedly raped, often in front of their neighbors, so that the humiliation would motivate them to leave their land. I learned of women impregnated and forced to stay in "rape camps" until abortions were out of the question, so that they would have to bear the children from this unholy union.

Rape has always been a disgusting part of war. But this was different. Instead of being a side effect of having too many "fighting men" congregated together away from their families, this rape was a premeditated strategy, commanded by officers, carried out by men under orders to reach into the savage part of themselves and dominate in the most brutal and mutually debasing way.

I was aghast. I called organizations in the US that I would expect to be working on this issue. No one had any programs in the area. I started asking the spirit of life inside myself, "What can I do to help?" I waited patiently and impatiently for an answer. I asked people around me. A common feeling seemed to be, "We said we would never again allow genocide like this to happen in Europe, and now that it's happening, we don't know how to respond." It seemed that the whole world was in the same position. Our passion about the Nazi holocaust seemed to interfere with our ability to think clearly.

Finally, I decided not to wait for the perfect idea to come to me while sitting in the US I would go and ask refugees, antiwar workers (there are always people working against war in every country), and ordinary people in the former Yugoslavia what we in the US could do to participate with them in stopping the war and healing those who were so terribly wounded.

When a friend offered me a two-week job in Rumania, I jumped at the chance to get an airplane ticket to that part of the world. Wanting to visit Yugoslavia, but not wanting to go empty-handed, I envisioned a simple idea: carry little bundles from my friends to the women refugees. These wouldn't be parcels to save lives; no blankets or food, no grand gestures. Others were doing that. Our small bundles would simply be women's things, like a nice scarf, an embroidered handkerchief, shampoo, soaps, hand lotion, lipstick, makeup, and other things that would express our support and connection. Bringing items that could help a woman feel good about being a woman might be a sensitive way to show our caring.

I checked the idea out with friends and people who knew the region. Several Yugoslavian women visiting the US on a speaking tour were very encouraging. Their faces brightened, their eyes glistened. "What a lovely thought!" I asked what kinds of things would be especially appreciated. One replied, "Use your imagination! The women are in refugee camps. They have very little, especially they have little to remind them of the joy involved in being women. Just think of what would be special to you."

They told me that women in each region had created centers to help women from all sides of the war. At these centers, Muslim, Catholic, and Orthodox women from Bosnia, Croatia, and Serbia could get counseling along with some financial help and personal support. I planned to bring our bundles to these centers and talk with the women. I was told that, while some centers focused on women from a particular ethnic group, most were "nonnationalistic" — ready to help any woman who requested help. In this way, they defied the logic of the war, which tried to separate people ethnically.

I knew we could also participate in defying nationalism by visiting Serbia as well as Croatia. Most of the US media at the time favored the Croatian point of view, but I was interested in connecting with antiwar workers in Serbia and Bosnia. I hadn't heard about them in the media, but I knew they would exist.

Carol Perry, a friend from Australia, was visiting. She thought the idea was interesting and agreed to mail twenty copies of my letter to Australian friends. I sent sixty-seven letters to US friends, and invited them to send copies to their friends. With a 5 to 10 percent response, I estimated that there would be two hundred to three hundred bundles, which I could pack in four large suitcases and carry by hand to women on all sides of the terrible conflict in Bosnia, Croatia, and Serbia. I specified the exact size for the bundles: length plus width plus height should add up to a maximum of 17 inches or 43 cm. A friend, Gail, agreed to have the packages sent to her office, as it would be open all day to receive shipments.

I decided to do this project on a small scale. I am sending this letter to my own network and encouraging you to copy this letter and share it with whomever you think appropriate. I am interested in how this networking organizing can work, so please think about who — anywhere in the world — would like to participate in this small caring act, and send a copy of the letter on to them.

Several people evidently put the announcement on Internet bulletin boards. I had no idea what an outpouring this little idea would create. Over six thousand bundles in the US and two thousand in Australia! The trip had to be postponed so that we could ship eighty large boxes by boat and then by truck to Vienna; from there we carried them to refugee camps and women's centers in Croatia and Serbia.

The initial letter had gone out under my letterhead to my personal mailing list. I hoped to convince a friend, Tova Green, to accompany me, but she was hesitant. Several days before I was to leave for work in New Zealand, a friend who had received the letter called and said she wanted to deliver four hundred bundles. This was my first warning of the tidal wave heading our way. Tova agreed to watch out for the project while I was away. She called me in New Zealand to report that the closet at Gail's office was full. Sensing that I did not yet grasp the problem, Tova said, "The closet is as big as our bathroom and it is completely full."

"Even the bathtub is full?" I asked incredulously.

"Yes, and up to the ceiling!" Tova was beginning to understand that I was going to need help. She was also moved by the faxes and phone calls that were pouring in. The spirit of human struggle in the former Yugoslavia was compelling. Graciously, Tova stepped in as a full partner in the project and came on the trip.

Carol Perry lives on a farm in Australia. Her post office is in a country store in a very small town, the Channon. Every day, the clerk at the store called Carol to come down. "There are so many packages here, we don't have room for them." Carol would return home with a carload of little bundles. Soon her house, garage, and verandah were taken over by bundles. Carol decided to join us on the trip and to hand out the Australian bundles herself.

My support group agreed to repack the bundles into larger boxes and get them ready for shipping, as I would be away working in Australia. Another friend, Barbara, knew how to ship things, as she had shipped an art exhibit to Russia. Others came forward with connections. One person who knew about Yugoslavia led to three others. Faxes began to arrive from organizations in the former Yugoslavia saying they would welcome our bundles and us. One fax from a women's center in Belgrade said: "We have received your letter and your plan was good news to us. We are happy that you have decided to help the women who now live in difficult circumstances... Waiting for your visit, we are thankful and send you our hearts' regards."

Groups in both Lismore, Australia, and San Francisco gathered on the same Sunday at the end of July to take each bundle from its outer wrapper, remove the self-addressed envelope provided to send our report after the trip, and read the list of contents for each bundle so that we could make a larger list for customs. Then, the bundles were snugly packed in a large carton, and the carton was taped closed.

One could not help being moved by those bundles. They came wrapped in scarves, in zippered bags and decorated boxes, in beautiful wrapping paper, and in manila envelopes. Thoughtfulness and love were evident in the items that were sent, the way they were wrapped, the letters enclosed. Companies like Hewlett-Packard, Rodale Press, Microsoft, and Ingris sent large boxes of bundles from employees, who got together on lunch breaks and prepared beautiful things for women far away. A group in the Federal Aviation Agency sent a box of bundles. Starr King Unitarian Seminary, Tassajara Mountain Zen Center, and many churches, synagogues, and Buddhist groups responded to the call and did what they could. School children and senior citizens' groups sent boxes and letters of hope and prayers. One man, who had felt unable to enter his wife's room since her death a year earlier, had gone in to get scarves and jewelry to send, because "she would have wanted it." We received letters and calls from men who wanted to contribute, because "this rape is really hurting in me."

Many people enclosed letters to me:

Dear Fran,

We are grateful for this opportunity to extend a small amount of love, healing, and caring to our sisters, mothers, and children across the globe... Thank you for being our messenger. It was so nice to sit with this group of friends and talk and sew. It felt like we were in a quilting bee — such a nice way for women to get together.

Twelve women from Eugene, Oregon

Dear Fran,

Thanks so much for sharing this great idea about sending love via care pkgs. to women in Yugoslavia. I received your instructions through a colleague's husband's computer network and shared them liberally. Couldn't do just one. A friend contributed some nice scarves; my 80-year-old mother added a lovely old handkerchief for each box!

Dear Ms. Peavey,

This was presented by the staff of the law firm where I work. Everyone was very interested.

Dear Ms. Peavey,

Thank you for the opportunity to make amends if only in a small way to those women who are trapped and abused by the cruelties of men at war.

Sincerely, David

Some people sent pictures of their group, others just a note of thanks for being included. It was a truly amazing outpouring of love.

Now, we had new problems. We had not expected to face thousands of dollars in shipping expenses, with even more money needed to rent a truck to take the bundles to their destinations. It was suggested that we leave some of the bundles in the US, since we had not bargained for such a big job. But these bundles seemed like a sacred trust. Even though we could have taken the same money and bought new items in Vienna to distribute, it was not merely shampoo, lotion, scarves, and makeup that were being delivered. We were custodians of connectedness and caring. It was an agonizing decision, but we had to postpone the trip several months in order to raise the necessary money to ship the boxes.

Had we had made a mistake in not asking each person who sent a bundle to send a little bit of money? I was involved in an exercise of self-criticism when John Seed, of the Rain Forest Information Center in Australia, piped up with this wisdom: "You made the right mistake. Your heart was clear about its intent. This was not a moneymaking idea. You just didn't realize the idea's power." I sent out another letter asking for help with the increased expenses. By the time we left for Europe, not all the necessary money had been raised, but we felt confident that it would come. It did. I love the idea of making the "right mistakes."

There was, in fact, no way I could have prepared myself for the experience that awaited me in the former Yugoslavia. Our European base was in Vienna. Our friend Joanna suggested that we stay with her friend Peter; a phone call resulted in an invitation. The first task, not a simple one, was to get the boxes freed from customs. The governments of the warring countries and those nearby were very concerned that humanitarian aid not fall into the black market. After much effort, we found a registered humanitarian group to sign the customs papers. But then we could not find a rental company that would rent and insure a truck to go into a war zone. We finally realized we would have to travel by train to Zagreb, Croatia, rent a truck there, drive back to Vienna, pick up the packages, and drive back to Zagreb to distribute the packages.

When this idea was conceived, I knew very little about the history or geography of the Balkans. Miraculously, the path opened before us. Mentioning to friends what we were doing brought many connections. Once feet are set on a path, ways open. Connection builds connection. Everywhere we found people willing to share their thinking and experience with us. Friends at home had given us plenty of material with which to educate ourselves about the historical context of this war. So we were able to frame more intelligent questions about the war and what people outside could do to help.

We estimate that we personally handed out over four thousand bundles to refugee women staying in Croatia and Serbia; many were Bosnian Muslims, but there were also Croatians and Serb women from Bosnia. We left the distribution of the remaining bundles to groups we met and trusted. We did not want to work with large groups, governmental or otherwise, like the Red Cross or UNHCR. Mostly, we worked with women refugees who had organized self-help groups, or with local women in grassroots organizations that had taken on the task of helping refugees or working against the war.

When we found a group we trusted, we went with them to refugee camps or to the support groups they had organized. Refugees were housed in hotels, resorts, retired railway cars, and old army barracks. We also visited with refugees in homes and at group meetings. One woman who ran an NGO estimated that only 5 percent of the refugees were in formal camps; the rest were on their own or living with relatives.

Many refugees came to live with relatives thinking that they would have to stay only a month or two. Years later, they still need a home. Shortage of money and space made the situation increasingly difficult for all parties. In Croatia, a country of four million people, there were 750,000 refugees. At this writing, two years after the Dayton Accord supposedly sent refugees home, hundreds of refugees are still living in camps. The NATO troops have not facilitated returning home, either to the house or even to the land where they lived. Ethnic cleansing has been continued through this policy.

Giving out the packets was more complex than we had imagined. We had a letter translated into both Croatian and Serbian that we distributed with the bundles. Prior to the war, there had been one language, but now certain words were not to be used in one region or another because those words were "of the other." So our letter, which had originally been translated into Serbo-Croatian in the US, had to be retranslated when we went to a new region. Usually someone read the letter aloud to the women before we handed out the bundles.

> *We will be communicating with the people who participated in this project, and we will act as a clearinghouse for other projects and other groups to help in the Balkan region. We will work in two directions:*
>
> *1. We will urge our countries to take actions to end the war. As we are pacifists, we will not urge more killing to stop the killing.*
>
> *But we believe earnestly that there are policies that will allow all of the peoples involved to live in harmony in this region, and it is important for all people on the globe to encourage such policies.*
>
> *2. We will work to find ways to assist the people caught up in*

this terrible conflict. We will work with the organizations we get to know on our trip to keep us informed about what is needed. We have a small but concerned network.

Because the gifts were varied in size and shape, we found it important to convey the spirit of caring with which the bundles were sent, rather than focus on the exact contents. The letter went on to say:

> *There is a wide variety in the size and quality of the bundles. We apologize if you did not get one that pleased you. We only hope that something in the bundle was useful to you and communicated the care that we feel for your situation.*
>
> *Please receive our best wishes for your life, for your family, and for your people. Please know our sorrow about the turn of events in your country and our hope that peace will again come to your land, that you may know the fulfillment of your life's dreams. Please know that with these bundles comes our respect for your dignity as women, and the preciousness of your life to us. We send our prayers and love with these packets.*

The women would gather at the back of a truck or around a table in the dining room. Then we would begin handing out the bundles. Someone from the camp would read out the list of women and they would step forward, hands outstretched. Solemn faces, beautiful faces, older women's faces, young mothers carrying children, adolescent faces — all unsure of their future. Eyes that looked another woman straight in the eye with respect, unspoken questions. Young girls wondered if they were old enough for a "woman's bundle." "Yes," we answered, "if you are old enough to ask, you are old enough to have a bundle." Their beaming faces were a joy to behold. *"Hwalla"* (thank you in Serbo-Croatian), they would say. Often they would say more. "Thank you. Please tell the women of the United States and Australia that we hope this never happens to them. And thank them for caring."

The transaction was sometimes difficult. Occasionally someone would want a package other than the one we had handed her; sometimes someone would try to get two packages. More often it was wonderful. Our task was to help the women not to focus so much on the bundle, but on the caring that someone had sent with the bundle. Just hearing the letter expressing connection was important for some women. Tears would flow. The women would take the bundles and vanish into their rooms to open them. Then, they would return to the public space smiling, wearing the lipstick or a new scarf. These women liked to look good, they enjoyed cosmetics — Croatian, Bosnian, and Serbian women alike. I will never forget the sight of one older woman dressed in black, walking across the grass to the barracks in a camp close to the Hungarian border, her package held in front of her like a great treasure. She was smiling. I could almost see her many years earlier, as a child who had been given a special gift.

It was obvious that most of the younger women had been accustomed to dressing stylishly. Their new circumstances were especially hard on their sense of themselves. Over and over we heard, "We do not come from a third-world country. We are modern European women accustomed to washing machines and nice things." The older women appreciated socks, scarves, or items they could give to their daughters or grandchildren.

It was important to many of them to give something back to us. Some gave coffee or food, some a warm hug or a little item they had knitted or crocheted. We had not been prepared to receive gifts in return. Now, we recognized more clearly that these were mature people who wanted to relate to us as peers, not just as recipients of help.

Most refugees were women. Men either were staying in the family home to protect it from looters and squatters, or were in the army, or were in torture camps or dead. We heard that more civilians were being killed and wounded in this war than soldiers. Many refugees were older village women, dressed in black to honor the loss of loved ones, with faces that spoke of years of hard work in the outdoors. Having seen two wars, many wanted to talk about what they knew. We heard of several suicides of older women who could not face another war.

Over and over again we heard, "The militarism of war affects all relationships." Weapons were readily available to families and neighborhoods. Domestic violence skyrocketed. Street violence increased. As in all wars, when soldiers returned home, broken either by what had been done to them or by their guilt for what they had done, they brought violence with them.

We met some women who had been made refugees by Croatians and Serbs, others who had been abused by Bosnian fighters, either Muslim troops or the multiethnic national army of Bosnia. We met refugees who had been caught in the cross fire between two competing armies, or gangs of Serbs or Muslims. We struggled to find words for what we were learning, and to communicate our understanding that, while all sides had engaged in hor-rific acts, the disproportionate responsibility for evil, especially eth-nic cleansing, rested with the Serbs — no, the Serbian *nationalists.* We met many Serbs who were strongly opposed to the war. Not all Serbs bear responsibility for this barbarism.

A strikingly tall and strong young woman told us that she had become a fighter when her town of Vukovar had been attacked by Serbs. She told of rape and pillaging beyond imagination. Now that her town had been destroyed, she was a refugee living in a small hotel room in Zagreb with two others. We did not ask for descrip-tions of rape or torture, but we did not have to. These stories came pouring out of the refugees and antiwar workers. They seemed grateful to have fresh ears willing to listen.

It is a common misconception that any region in the former Yugoslavia can be divided cleanly along ethnic lines. In fact, in these communities there were many mixed marriages and many activities in which diverse populations participated. Many women told us of their parents' mixed heritage and/or their own marriage to a man of a different ethnicity.

International media and negotiators perpetuate misunderstand-ings when they speak of Serb, Croatian, and Muslim regions. This isn't even a matter of apples and oranges; it's more like confusing peaches and pizza. It would make some sense to speak of Eastern Orthodox, Catholics, and Muslims, or of Serbs, Croatians, and Bosnians. But even that is too simple, because within each state are people of all religions and all ethnicities.

Western negotiators drew borders based on this misunderstanding, either because they did not perceive the mixed nature of all the nations, they subscribed to their own version of ethnic purity, or they were unable to resist the pull of separatist thinking in the region. Women often shared their anguish about being forced by the war to define themselves in terms they personally found offensive or meaningless.

What were people really fighting about in this war? What moved so many to resist the forces of ethnic cleansing? What were the people in Sarajevo dying about, for month upon month of shelling? One formulation I came to was that they wanted to live in a diverse neighborhood. Since I could not bring myself to ask anyone about his or her rape or torture, I do not have any statisti-cal information to report. Many women and a few men offered their stories, and I listened respectfully. I hope that telling the story helps in the healing. Can life ever forgive violent, meaningless death? As people searched for meaning in their sorrow, I felt there was a useful role in listening, witnessing the suffering, honoring the person who walked the rugged path.

The causes of the war were complex. It was a time of transformation in the Communist world, and the coming of the free market inspired greed in many people, both inside and outside of Yugoslavia. Nationalism — thinking only for the benefit of one's own people — is a dread disease, and it was spread by the media in a consciously drawn campaign orchestrated by the nationalist leaders.

In difficult times, some leaders slid into a kind of brutal nationalism to enhance their power. No one was looking out for the common good. Both the Croatian and Serbian governments' tactic was to disenfranchise and scapegoat minorities. Both governments took jobs from minority people in their regions and gave them to members of their own ethnic groups. So, members of those groups began preparing to protect themselves. This was a war from the top down; individual leaders saw nationalism as the path to power, and they chose that path. As richer regions like Croatia and Slovenia performed their dance of desire for self-determination, they paid no attention to others in the region — especially to the question of how their goals could be met without destroying the chances for Bosnia to get out of the struggle intact.

In the name of privatization, some branches of the media were taken over, and other branches were simply manipulated with blatant lies. Nationalism was the gun. The trigger was pulled primarily by Milosevic in Serbia, and secondarily by Tudjman in Croatia. The economics of restructuring by the International Monetary Fund and the world depression in the mid-1980s contributed to destabilization. It was the countryside that contributed most of the soldiers and most of the enthusiasm for the war, and that suffered the heaviest losses.

Once the war was begun, there were other forces keeping it going. Those who benefited from trading in war supplies — the guns, overcoats and boots, ammunition and airplanes — as well as those who profited from the sale of goods looted from conquered homes didn't want to stop. Shiny big cars moved through the streets of Bosnia, Croatia, and Serbia. Friends pointed to them, made a face, and said "War profiteers." Bosnian friends who visited me recently in the US said upon seeing limousines in the streets of San Francisco, "War profiteers." I agreed.

Other European countries and the US missed nearly every opportunity to act responsibly. The authors I have read on the war, Susan Woodward in *Balkan Tragedy* (Brookings Institute, 1995) being the most prominent, have brought forth increasingly deep and complex analyses. I suppose we will be looking for the causes of the unusual violence and greed in this war for a long time.

Lepa Mladjenovic, a feminist writer and activist from Belgrade, sees the roots of the war in male habits of aggression and conquest, the drive to put a name on what one has conquered and extract benefit from it. As a woman, I am interested in the role women play in the move toward war. Aggression is surely at the root of the problem, but the seeds of aggression must be present in all genders. Mrs. Milosevic, the wife of the brutal president, was a virulent nationalist.

Intuitively, I feel that humiliation is at the root of much individual violence; Dr. James Gilligan, noted prison psychiatrist and Harvard professor, says this is true of men who are homicidal. Women have a role in the humiliation of men who will not do the nasty acts of protecting us; women belittle the feelings of men and boys who deal openly with their vulnerability. How does aggression rise in a people at a particular time? I look to the work and commitment women put into supporting men who refused to serve in the Vietnamese war as a guide for how to stop war from the women's side. What can people of each gender do to safeguard the humanity of men and reduce the violence in the world?

As we left the former Yugoslavia, winter was coming upon the land. I knew winter would not be easy, for many of the rooms I had visited did not have heat. One of the hardships of working all over the world is that just as often as one says hello, one must say good-bye for now. It is never easy, but that first trip to the Balkans was especially hard. We asked ourselves what else we could do.

We returned to the US with many suggestions from the people we had met. We prepared a two-page list of all the ideas refugees and antiwar workers had given us of ways to help. For example, some multiethnic groups would appreciate art supplies, and camps would appreciate volunteers. We distributed the list to newsletters, and with our report to all the people who had sent bundles. Little did we know that these small acts were building connections that would continue long into the future. For years, the phone rang almost every day, bringing questions from someone who wanted to work in the Balkans. Connection in action was our job: giving information, organizing, connecting those who wanted to participate with those who needed the available energy and resources.

In planning our next trip, we did not want to bring bundles again. Tova had the idea of bringing some friends who are professional performers and could share their arts in refugee camps and with antiwar organizations. Later, they could also speak with US audiences about what they had learned. So after a trip to the region to organize the tour, we went back with a group of ten performers, artists, and organizers. We wanted the experience to be as language-free as possible, so we selected mostly improvisational performers — Barbara Borden (drummer), Rhiannon (jazz singer), Ruth Zaporah (improvisational dancer), and Naomi Newman (writer/performer). Actor Vanessa Redgrave, when speaking to *New York Magazine*, said: "Doctors mend bodies; artists mend people's spirits."

One day, someone asked me to meet a visitor from Malaysia who was creating paintings about Bosnia. Zuriah Aljefri was a Muslim woman who had never been to Yugoslavia but ached about what was happening there. I liked her right away. She sparkled with life and questioning. I suggested that she go to the region and learn firsthand what was happening. Instantly, it occurred to both of us that she should join our group. Zuriah arranged to bring her friend Norma Nordin, a Malaysian theater producer. In Croatia, Zuriah and another artist, Franceska Shifrin, guided children in painting with art supplies they had brought. Franceska had gone to Sarajevo to paint a year earlier. A very brave young woman, she had painted in the shell of the destroyed National Library, just around the corner from where a sniper had been picking off people. She brought slides of her paintings about the war. Zuriah also brought some of her paintings, which we displayed. Penny Rossenwasser, a radio producer and skilled theater organizer, decided to join us. We were a multiethnic group that included Jews, Protestants, Catholics, and Muslims. The group called itself the Doves and adopted a logo (designed by a friend, Barbara Hazard) of a dove that was obviously pissed off.

Together we shared a vision of jazz, improvisation, drumming, interactive events with refugees, art with children, and exhibits of art about this war. There would be workshops during the days and performances in the evenings. We decided to call our tour "Honoring Loss/Celebrating Life."

I don't believe much in helping people. Sometimes, when I've been in a group that was "being helped," especially by professional people, I've felt like a farm that was "being farmed." The farmer (professional helper) gets all the goods, and the farm only gets to continue to be farmed. The helpers get a sense of superiority and often income. The dynamic is frequently insulting to the ones being helped. The Doves did not want to help, but to enter into a mutual experience from which all participants, including the Doves, would benefit. And that's the way it turned out. The experiences on the tour illuminated and benefited all of us.

In a refugee camp outside Belgrade, the refugees joined us in a large room with chairs around the outer perimeter. The children went off with Franceska to another room to draw and paint. (The Malaysian members of our group had been prohibited by their government from traveling to Belgrade, so Zuriah and Norma were not there.) Over a hundred women and a few men came into the room. Some of the older women were crying. Their life is sad, and in refugee camps there are some women who cry most days.

It was my job to start things out. With a translator, we would all introduce ourselves. Then I would say: "Even though your heart is filled with a lake of tears, it is important to laugh every day. So let us start with our laughing exercises." Wary eyes met mine, but the participants stood up. I directed them to let little chuckles roll around in the tummy. Pretty soon, members of the group started to laugh. One of the saddest women broke out in laughter. I reached for her hand. "Let's do the laughing dance." Of course, as a comedian I exaggerated each step. I looked into her beautiful crinkley eyes. She looked into mine. We laughed. Everyone laughed. I thanked her, and we all sat down for a couple of performance pieces.

Barbara drummed on the wall, on the floor, on a stool. She had not been able to find drums of a quality she felt confident in, so she used whatever she could find. The stool moved as she kicked it, and she could never quite control it. But she kept drumming. The audience loved it. Surely they knew how it is to do without what you need, to be out of control, and still to try to make life function normally. Ruth came out with a harmonica and played to lots of appreciation. Naomi recited a poem she had learned in Serbo-Croatian — *Pouratak Staglu Vremena* ("A Return to the Tree of Time") by the famous poet Vesna Parun. The audience was surprised and pleased to hear their own language.

Our translator asked if there was anything people wanted us to tell Americans back home. When an old woman started to speak, others tried to stop her. They thought it was important to be polite to guests and not embarrass us. I stepped forward, took her hand, and looked squarely into her eyes. "Please speak to us. We need to know." Each misstep of the Bush and Clinton administrations was enumerated bravely. They felt that the economy would be in ruins, that moneyed people from outside were planning to buy up the region after the war, and were happy to let the Yugoslavs kill each other. They let their bitter and angry thoughts come out.

"Why don't you stand by us? Why doesn't your government help us or let us help ourselves? We looked to America, and you have betrayed us. We've lost everything, including our children's future." Serbians are told by their propaganda that the world, especially America, hates them. We explained that this was not true. It was a complex transaction through translators, but the fact that we were there spoke more than any words.

An old man told us about his cow. Later, I wrote a poem about him:

MEMORY'S BURDEN
Upon returning from the former Yugoslavia, 1994
It's hard to come back to my home
   my mind returns to the refugees' faces
   in a moment memory takes over with the stories of their difficult lives
     with their dignity in the face of loss
       with their deep questions about trust and human nature.
        What hunger does this war feed?
Back in America, a country fascinated with sordid details of murder and sex
   The questions posed by Eastern Europe pull at me.
   What institutions can stop the fighting?
     Driving down the road I do not see bombed-out houses
      Troops at checkpoints
       village people walking along with slumped shoulders.
Home sadness — that's what I saw
   that's what touched me.
   Forced to leave their homes each fragile human had moved to the horizon,
     many reported that when they looked back they saw only a pile of stones
       where their homes, their farms, their lives had been.
        Where their ancestors had tilled the soil for generations.
   "I remember my cow," one old man says.
   "I remember. " He speaks looking out through the walls of the refugee camp
     out past the city, which now holds his body
     he looks beyond the fertile hills of the land around him
       remembering his own fertile hills in Bosnia.

   His memory penetrates the still wet national borders
     painted with the blood of families and of the young who went to fight
       because someone said it was the thing to do.
The not-really-the-enemy army prevents him from returning to find his cow.
     "There is no home there for me now. As I left I saw it burning."
So the man steps to the center of the circle and sings of his cow
   tears dropping from his hollow sun-withered cheeks.

He knows that nothing else is left standing.
The old man remembers his cow
  his eyes scream such piercing questions
    "How did this happen to us?"
      Brokenhearted, he is a refugee.
      Brokenhearted, I remember him. When it gets cold
        I will remember there is no heat in his room.

Rhiannon came out and sang scat with full audience participation. Then all the Doves sang a song they had learned in Serbo-Croatian. Only at that point did we learn it was a New Year's song. Tears of recognition and maybe homesickness came to many eyes. Since we were there in June, it was silly, but some people said it helped them feel cooler. Then Rada, from the antiwar organizing group called Women in Black, leapt out of her chair and started singing a Bosnian song. The young Bosnians sang with her, and then we sang an American song.

A young man with a badly wounded eye and other injuries told us of his torture by Bosnian soldiers. He had been a Bosnian Serb soldier and had been captured. As we listened to his pain, I also wondered what he had done to others. People spoke about how they have been victimized, but not about the shame they bear for participating in the crimes of war. One of the Doves put her arm around him and comforted him. It was a complex, twisted, emotional time. It was important to know that the Serbs were also tortured.

After the formal part of our time together was over, the Doves talked with residents, and some drifted off to residents' rooms for coffee and visiting. The connection was made. Some time later, we had to get back on the bus to return to Belgrade. Good-byes are always difficult. I will always remember that group of refugees gathered around waving as our bus pulled out. "Hwalla," we said with sincerity.

One can never fully know the results of any work in social change, but there are some results I have seen. Penny, on returning to the Bay Area, produced several radio shows, including interviews with refugees and antiwar workers in the former Yugoslavia. In many subsequent performances, each of the performers included something about ethnic violence. We sent a report to our mailing list of over twelve hundred people, telling them what we had learned. We distributed embroidery thread to women's groups in Croatia and Serbia, and they used that thread to make items that brought money to the refugees. Although Zuriah reported being very depressed when she returned home, she has continued to create art and to speak about what she learned.

Several stories appeared in the press about our trip and work. One article featured Ruth's experience and reflections on Yugoslavia. Barbara wrote a piece in a drumming magazine that doesn't usually have political articles. Presentations and slide shows still continue. The Doves' lives were changed. The scapegoating of immigrants we saw in the 1994 California election frightened us, and we spoke out with added knowledge of the dangers of targeting specific weak populations as a way to gain power. The common good becomes all the more precious to one who has experienced the tearing of the fabric of wholeness in a population.

When we returned to the Balkans nearly a year later to evaluate the tour, we got positive feedback and interest in having the Doves visit again. Radmila Manojlovic-Zarkovic (Rada), in a book published by Women in Black in Belgrade, wrote of the refugees:

I wanted to find the obstinacy in them again, to find life in them again, to awaken hope in them again. And they ... being betrayed a hundred times, abandoned by all people, they felt only pain. *And immense loneliness.* The loneliness ruined them from the inside. Isolated from any background, in foreign places, eager to have a minute of privacy in over-crowded rooms, so lonesome in their souls... When women artists from America ... sang a song in Serbo-Croatian, a woman from Slovonia stood up and said: "I do not like American leaders, they did us a lot of harm, but I would like to embrace you." Embraces, laughter, tears. Melancholy songs came from a corner... No, they don't have more food today; they are even more cold, and more often there is no water. Their camps are still surrounded by lack of compre-hension, and neither politicians nor those who are in power need them. But there is a new strength in them. They are not lonely anymore.

International support work is important for a number of reasons. For refugees and antiwar workers, having their suffering witnessed and honored is part of putting themselves back together. There is nothing worse than thinking no one sees or cares about your suffer-ing. At this moment in history, when governments and multination-al corporations are pursuing their interests and interfering with life all over the globe, it is important for common people to have direct access to how other common people view the situation. Having built a network through the bundles project, I feel it is my duty to inform that network about what I learned and think as I work in the Balkans. There is no substitute for direct communication between people at the grassroots level who can feel their common bonds.

In this particular conflict, peace workers on all sides were unable to communicate with each other; phone lines were cut between the two countries, no mail was allowed through. There was no way to say, "I feel awful about what is happening. Can I help with some small part of your burden?" or "I am protesting the war and think of you often." Foreign peace workers like us were able to make connections and to carry messages back and forth. We carried verbal greetings and news, letters and gifts. Jany, a friend in Dubrovnik, Croatia, was angry at the Doves the night before we left for Belgrade, because Serbians and Montenegrins had besieged Dubrovnik for fourteen months. "It is not time to go to the enemy. If you are our friends, how can you go for a friendly visit with our enemy?" It is important that international friends stand outside the hatred of war, bridging the gulfs between people, offering ways to build new connections.

Knowing that there are people working against this war — and all war — helps me with my own discouragement when I hear horrible news about the acts of governments and armies. Brutality reaches the bright light of the news; nonviolence endures in the quiet silence. Decency abounds in awful situations — this is beyond doubt. One of the most rewarding aspects of working for social change internationally is getting a personal glimpse of what is happening in the world. Events in the world are connected, and often international events help me see trends at home more clearly.

I become intellectually and spiritually stimulated in ways that would not be possible grappling with the issues from a distance — reading newspapers, following the media. I wonder about good and evil, about what causes people seeking power to order other people to kill. I wonder about the battle between men and women in these times. Is there a way to change this relationship, so that men can no longer be manipulated into doing horrid things that their families and communities have taught them never to do? I continue to wonder what I can do about the ethnic and other conflicts developing in my own society. So many questions. I often wish I could make a more powerful offering to peace in this region. In my dreams, I would go to Milosevic, to the US embassy, and to Tudjman and demand that they do what they can to stop the fighting.

I continue to visit the region. Now, I visit friends without working out in advance what we will do to participate in the healing of the pain of this terrible war. Often I carry vitamins, medicines, or embroidery thread to people on all sides. The board of Crabgrass, the small NGO I formed to carry out my social change work, insists that I take a colleague with me, so Crabgrass has had to grow. We bring back products made by the refugees and sell them to friends or at craft fairs. A month or so before our trip, we send a postcard to our mailing list: "If you would like to send money to the groups in the region, now would be a good time to send it." Money comes and we distribute it gladly to groups with whom we have an enduring relationship of trust.

Occasionally, friends or organizations ask us to bring something special or to give a workshop that will be useful. Moving from place to place, I find work to do. We sell small wristbands made by refugees and displaced women in Dubrovnik, Croatia, slippers and potholders made by refugees in Belgrade, Serbia.

In May 1995, I found a lovely book of refugee women's writings, *I Remember*, which I brought back and arranged to have published in the United States (Aunt Lute Press, 1997). Responding to requests from Kosovo, we brought a manual typewriter for a girls' school, as well as some vitamins and diaphragms for a clinic for women and children. In Belgrade, we led a workshop called "Living with Differences: Becoming Allies." Then, we raised funds to bring four students from that workshop to the US for further diversity training.

On the 1995 trip, we became concerned about the situation in Kosovo, a semiautonomous region of Yugoslavia that was included in Serbia when the country split up. About 90 percent of the population are Albanians, an ethnic group that speaks a different language, but is not physically distinguishable from Serbs. This region is known as Kosova by the ethnic Albanians, as Kosovo by the Serbs. As a gesture toward fairness to all, the word will subsequently be spelled Kosova/o.

The area has tremendous symbolic significance to the Serbs. A famous battle with the Turks was fought there many years ago. Although they lost the battle and tens of thousands of Serbs were killed, the anniversary of that battle is one of the most celebrated Serbian holidays.

The Bosnian war began in Kosova/o. Before the war, the Albanians ran the region, but when the war began, it became heavily occupied by Serb forces. Huge infusions of Serbian military were sent there, as it was symbolically and strategically important for

Serbia to control Kosova/o. The Serbians also quickly moved Serb refugees from Croatia into Kosova/o, both to build up the Serb population and to resettle Serb refugees from Bosnia and Croatia. They evicted Albanians, built more apartments and houses for Serbs, and generally made life miserable for the Albanians, hoping to intimidate them so they would leave the area.

In general in this region, people's ethnic identity is revealed not by their appearance, but by their names. This is true not only of the Slavic peoples (Serbs, Bosnians, Croatians, and Macedonians), but also of Albanians and Hungarians; the Roma, a darker-skinned people, are subject to discrimination by all groups. Many, though not all, of the Albanians are Muslim. But Mother Teresa, famous for her work in India, was also an Albanian.

The complexity and ambiguity of work in Kosova/o are sometimes difficult for me to cope with. The daily brutality of the Serb police toward Albanian citizens was without recourse; they took money, cameras, and valuable goods from citizens. The violation of human rights and the constant harassment were repulsive. When Albanians ran the area before the war, however, there were criminal abuses of power against the Serbs.

The fight for domination involved Albanians not only in Kosova/o (presently a legal part of Serbia), but also in Macedonia and Montenegro. From conversations spanning several years, it seems to me that the Albanians in these regions would like to be together in a country, but not the country of Albania. In the long run, some leaders of each group do not envision living in a diverse environment where both have rights and respect each other. Some Albanians have told us they have had enough of living with the Serbs; they cannot conceive of living in a peaceful multiethnic environment.

As if this were not complex enough ethnically, strategically, and philosophically, add the commitment to violence on the part of the Serbs and the commitment to nonviolence on the part of the Albanians between 1991 and 1997. Remaining nonpartisan in this environment has been quite difficult, given our commitment to nonviolence and diversity.

Human rights were a major concern throughout this period. All Albanian professional people (medical workers, university staff, and teachers) as well as most skilled workers were dismissed from their jobs. Elementary schools were segregated and terribly crowded for Albanian children. If they wanted to study in their language after eighth grade, they had to attend makeshift schools in basements, garages, and apartments. Atrocities and human rights violations steadily increased. When we first visited Kosova/o in May 1995, it was illegal for more than three people to gather together. For a time, this meant they could not have concerts or cultural events. Some Albanian women likened their situation to that of apartheid in South Africa; others compared it to that of Palestinians in the occupied territories; still others saw their situation as similar to that of a Jewish ghetto in Nazi-occupied Poland.

Adem Demaci, known as the "Albanian Mandela," was chair of the Council of Defense for Human Rights and Freedoms. He led a non-violent struggle for the Albanian people. We met Adem and found him to be a reasonable, open, and careful man, able to listen to women without fidgeting. Every day people lined up at his council office to have their pictures taken and to tell stories of physical abuses inflicted by the police in overnight arrests and evictions. Adem showed us thick books with photos and stories of torture and killing. We wanted to shut the books and spare ourselves from seeing; instead we cried.

We were embraced by Albanian women in Pristina who had formed a network of women's organizations. They met clandes-tinely in cafes. They struggled for three years to open a women's health center and were almost ready to open it when we first visit-ed. In a subsequent visit, we saw the clinic bustling with clients and volunteer workers. They proudly showed us the space, with pedi-atric and gynecological examining rooms, a counseling room, an office, empty bookshelves. These women are proud of their culture, their art, music, and poetry. We spent a wonderful evening with about thirty women in a cafe, where they read their own poems and played flute and violin.

Returning to Belgrade, we told our friends of our concerns that something awful — a war or major genocide — was brewing there. Although the Albanian story was also part of the Bosnian war, it was seldom discussed in the media. But we anticipated that the day might come when the Serbian nationalists, having "finished" with Bosnia, would turn their bloodthirsty attention to Kosova/o in order to sustain their expansionist visions and ethnic cleansing poli-cies. Kosova/o was also the biggest region in Serbia with large num-bers of Muslims.

We softly suggested that our friends begin to build bridges to peaceful people in Kosova/o. None of the people we met with knew any Albanian Kosovars. Many had never been to the region. For two consecutive years, we gave them a small grant to cover bus fares. Over time, a network of women developed.

It isn't possible to know where this connection to the people and land of Yugoslavia will take me. I have learned a lot about leaders who whip up ethnic issues for their own power or enrichment, and this has helped me work in my home city to protect the rights of potential target populations like immigrants and people of color. When I hear Pat Robertson talk about a cultural war against Jews and gays, I take it more seriously than before. But mostly, I remember the fine people I have met in the Balkan region and consider them sisters and brothers in the human struggle to learn how to resist war.

I especially remember the women. I remember one woman who knitted a rug out of yarn from donated sweaters. I remember Alicia, the 20-year-old Bosnian Muslim woman who told me, "I know the enemy. My skin has felt him." For Alicia, the enemy was Serb. Later she told me, "I do not hate the Serbs. Sometimes I have hateful thoughts. Then I think — he did bad, but sometime in the future he will know his wrong and be sorry."

Sometimes people in my memory reach out and touch me more directly. On my birthday in 1995, I was writing in my castle (actually more like a shed, but to me it is a castle). As a writer, I am often grumpy when the phone interrupts my concentration. But the afternoon of my birthday was not a time to be grumpy. I picked up the phone. A woman with a heavy accent apologized for her English. She was slow and hesitant with each word. Surprisingly, I found the grace to turn the computer off. "Take your time, I am listening."

"I am calling from Massachusetts. Two years ago, a woman came to Zagreb where I was living. I had been forced to leave my home in Bosnia. It was such a hard time. A terrible time for me and my family. A woman came and brought me a present. Last night, I dreamed about that woman and told my new friends in the factory about my dream. They said I must call the phone number I had on a card, even though I do not have such good English. They said I should find that woman. She brought me a present and gave me hope."

"Was the woman curly brown-haired, or straight gray-brown-haired with a round face, or short and curly gray-haired?" I asked, roughly describing the three of us who had brought the little bundles.

"Round face, straight brown-gray hair," she replied.

"That was me!"

"You gave me a card with this number on it. I hope you don't mind that I called. Now I live here in the United States, and I have a baby who is a citizen of the United States. It is a miracle. You encouraged me so much, and the present meant so much to me.

Now we live in Massachusetts, my husband has a job, and I do, too. Our baby was born here. She is a citizen. It is so much better. We miss our home, but we are happy here."

"Were you the woman whose husband was a metallurgical engineer?" I asked.

"You remember me! How amazing! All those presents to give out and you remember me."

"I think of you often."

"I think of you often, too. And I want to thank you. I dream of so many things now, but sometimes I dream of you standing there, smiling with the present, and with hope. I want to send you a picture of our family in our new home. And our new baby, who is a US citizen. Did I tell you that? Born in this country."

"Yes, you did mention it. I am so glad you are here. Welcome. I hope you are happy here. Please send me the picture and your address. Maybe I can see you sometime when I come East."

"Wonderful!"

That day, the television kept showing pictures of Bosnian buildings being burned, of Serb and Muslim refugees treading the roads tired and hungry, of fearful Albanians in Kosova/o, of announcers predicting an expansion of the war. In many large-scale ways, the day was a hard one for my heart. But one family who had received a present three years earlier now dreamed and had hope. I got a great birthday present.

Some days later, a letter came from New Bedford, Massachusetts:

Dear my friend!

I can't forget your heart. I met you in Zagreb when I had especially difficult time in my life. My wounded soul was bleeding and crying.

When I met you, in my heart I returned [to] believing in other people. Energy went in my body. I started believe to better tomorrow. What happened after? I now live in New Bedford together with my family. I now have new life and a baby. My baby's name is Amina who was born in New Bedford, June 12, 1994. I am happy when I meet nice friends. I will be very happy if I meet you. I am waiting for you to come. I believe that I will meet you. Excuse me for my Englesh, because I now learn Englesh.

I remember all the older women still looking for a home and a way to understand the powerful and devastating events in their lives.

They wear black scarves, black sweaters and skirts, indicating grieving. I remember their round peasant faces worn with care. As I handed out bundles, one or two would often stand very close to me, gently squeezing my arm. I don't know why they did it, but it happened over and over wherever we went. I remember one special "squeezer" who stood next to me at the Raped Women's Hospital. I was surprised that about 40 percent of the residents were in their sixties and seventies. So vulnerable. When I sat down, she sat next to me. Speaking in Croatian, she told her story. I do not understand Croatian, but I understood this woman. The way she used her hands against her body, her eyes and face told me a story that my own body heard. Her tears brought tears to my eyes. Her story was so sad. She made gestures indicating that terrible things had happened, and now she was very sick. I held her in my arms and cursed the war and the people who had harmed her.

A young girl interrupted to present me with a gift from her father. It was a macramé plant holder that he had been making. It wasn't finished, but it was all he had to thank us for giving his wife something that made her happy.

The young women, the old women, the children, the war. The accumulated mass of suffering. When I participate with people in deep change and healing, I also am changed. As we were about to leave the Raped Women's Hospital in Croatia, my friend, the older woman who had told me her story, came up for another hug. "What will make them stop?" she whispered in my ear, looking at the floor. I wish someone knew the answer to her question. For it is my question, too.

Chapter 14

A Wish To Be Proven Wrong: Kosova/Kosovo, 1995–Present

FOUR YEARS before the war in Kosova/o began, we saw the troubles coming. When the issue of Kosova/o was not dealt with in the Dayton Peace Accord of 1995, it was not difficult to predict that disaster was imminent in the region. Milosevic had shown himself to be capable of great crimes against Muslims in Bosnia, but we did not foresee the barbarousness of NATO.

To prepare ourselves, we had asked our Albanian friends in Kosova/o whom we should work with in Albania and Macedonia in the event that we could not contact them directly. When we talked about what we had learned with our network at home, many people volunteered to help. So we organized a Kosova/o Ready Response Team, which met once a month for a year in 1995–96. We learned a few words in Albanian, a few words in Serbian, became familiar with the map, and started to think about what it might be possible to do in the event of increased conflict between the Serbs and the Albanians over the land known as Kosova/o. I visited Macedonia, and other team members visited Albania, to develop the relationships with groups our friends in Kosova/o trusted. In the event of conflict in Kosova/o, we would work with them to support our Kosovar friends. Twenty people said they wanted to be contacted to give funds in the event of an escalation of troubles.

I desperately needed a sabbatical and so applied for and received the Bunting Peace Fellowship at Radcliffe/Harvard College. I hoped that the situation in Kosova/o would not blow up, as that was the only reason I would give up the fellowship and go back to work. Human rights continued to disintegrate, but there was no large-scale flare-up of violence during my sabbatical. I read and thought about the situation and used the opportunity of living on the East Coast to contact people interested in the Balkans. But I found the situation similar to that on the West Coast — almost no one knew or seemed to care about what was happening in Kosova/o. Bosnia was still of concern. Kosova/o might as well have been on the moon — but then, people might have heard of it. As one of the transition points between the familiar (Europe) and the Moslem world, Kosova/o did not register with people.

In October 1997, a very large nonviolent student movement evolved; but it was brutally crushed by police over and over again, and the violence began to escalate. Years earlier, Albanian faculty had been dismissed from the university, and only Serbian-language instruction was permitted. Even though an agreement had been signed by Milosevic and Rugova (leader of the Albanians), allowing Albanians to return to the University at Pristina, Milosevic did nothing to make this agreement a reality. Another example of his broken agreements.

For eight years, the Albanians had organized a parallel high school and college system in basements of homes and garages. But the students wanted to go back to the university, and they began demonstrating in October, when they were accustomed to beginning their school year.

I arrived in Pristina just after the first big demonstration. Everyone was jubilant. Parents said, "We thought our children were going to be willing to live in an impossibly repressive situation, but now we see that they will fight for their freedom. We're proud of them."

The students at the underground university in Pristina were elated with the experience of power. Twenty-five thousand students had nonviolently assembled in the streets demonstrating their determination to go back to the university, which had been closed to instruction in the Albanian language since 1991. Speaking of the first demonstration, one student said, "Our lives will never be the same! It was the greatest day of my life," and others nodded in agreement. The demonstrations continued, even though the violence of Serbian military and police escalated.

When the world did not pay attention to these nonviolent demonstrations, when the Serbian authorities did not grant the Albanian students' requests to share the university with the Serbian-speaking students, many frustrated and disappointed activists began to train for armed conflict. Even though the numbers in the UCK (known as the Kosovo Liberation Army or KLA outside the Balkans) were very small, the world media began to pay attention to them.

The KLA began attacking police stations and killing Serbian police. On the pretext of crushing the "terrorists," the Serbs began more intense fighting, killing family members in the Drenica area and driving people from their homes.

In February 1998, an envoy from the US government indicated that he agreed with the rationale of killing people in Drenica, since they were "terrorists." When you assign people a name that is hated, like terrorist or murderer, then almost any action is justified in the international mind-set. The Drenica massacre included women and children as well as men. Low intensity warfare was conducted all over Kosova with the armed Albanians resisting actively with violence of their own.

Young people had formed an organization beautifully named the "Postpessimists," composed of both Albanian and Serbian youth. Westerners loved this group, because that was the way we thought they should live, together in dialogue. Increasingly, however, the Albanian members were pressured to stop seeing their Serbian friends. It became dangerous for our Albanian women friends to be seen with Serbian friends in Pristina. KLA forces began to threaten the nonviolent student groups and anyone who was not behind the KLA. This dynamic of escalating violence, and media attention to the violent forces, further encouraged violent elements within the Kosovar Albanian society.

In March 1999, the dance of violence built into a wild tempest, further encouraged by the NATO bombing. The bombing was the signal for increased intensification of the killing, torture, and expulsion of the Albanians from Kosova/o. Not only Albanians were expelled, but Roma, Turks, foreign journalists, international observers, and NGO activists as well. Over and over, we heard stories of military coming into villages and family compounds, separating the men out, killing them, and forcing the women and children to leave their homes.

I had promised some of my friends in Kosova/o that when the trouble began I would be with them, or at least as close as I could be, working in their interest. How could I not be with them? In 1996 Tova and I travelled to Skopje and Tetova to make contacts in the event of trouble in Kosova. So in April 1999, after the NATO bombing began and Serbian military action against non-Serbian ethnic groups further intensified, Jan Hartsough, of the Ready Response Team, and I set out for Macedonia.

Intuitively, I knew that I should go to Macedonia, that I would find work there needing to be done. As we prepared to leave, many of my friends asked incredulously, "What will you do there?" I didn't have a crystal clear picture, but I knew enough about refugee situations to know that some large organizations would be very busy doing the big jobs, and that many smaller, more individualized needs would get left out in the crush of a crisis. We would look for the small jobs. But I must admit that the constant questioning about what I would do created some apprehension. What if I couldn't find anything to do, and it was a waste of money, time, and the confidence Crabgrass had in me?

And so it came about that Jan and I traveled to Macedonia as Crabgrass. When we reached Macedonia, we applied for a UNHCR (United Nations High Commissioner for Refugees) card authorizing us to go into the refugee camps. When we looked closely at the card, it listed our organization as "Grabass."

The very first day we were there, as we came out of the United States embassy, whom should we bump into but the doctor from the Center for the Protection of Women and Children in Pristina! We went to tea with Vjosa and her sister, Pranvera. Vjosa was to leave soon to go to the US and Europe, to speak to the media and raise funds. They invited us to a meeting the next day, and gave us the phone number of a mutual friend, who had also been "deported," as they like to say.

Vjosa and others I met there reject the term "refugees," as most of them were not given a choice about leaving Kosova/o. A Serbian police or military person had knocked on their door; kicked the door in, or in some other way grabbed them; commanded them into a bus, train, or car; and forcibly moved them to the border. We asked about other friends, and it seemed that everyone was accounted for except Sevdije, who despite everyone's begging her to leave Pristina, would not leave. She, her husband, and one son were "still inside." I couldn't help feeling anxious about her.

Over tea, our friend Vjosa told us her "coming-out-of-Kosova/o" story. She was forced to stay in an automobile with several other people, including two children less than two years old, for over twenty-four hours. None of them were allowed to leave the car or even to open the window. Finally, they were allowed to leave the car to join with thousands of other people who were held in "no-man's land" — the area between the Yugoslavian and Macedonian borders, where up to thirty thousand refugees were held for hour upon hour before being allowed into Macedonia. Because of Macedonia's fears of being flooded by Albanian refugees, from time to time they would close their borders, and any refugees who came would simply have to stand, often in the rain, and wait. Some people told us of going back home and then coming again weeks later.

Vjosa told of going about her business as a doctor, doing what she could to relieve the physical suffering of the people in no-man's land. Someone brought a very ill seventeen-day-old baby to her. She went to plead with the Macedonian authorities to send the child by ambulance to a hospital. They refused. The child died in her arms. "In that moment I lost my professional manner," she told us shakily. "I yelled at the top of my lungs, 'You fucking assholes!' I lost all control and broke down."

Vjosa invited us to a meeting in Tetova, a large Albanian town in western Macedonia, where the staff from the center in Pristina would gather for the first time since their expulsion. After the meeting she caught a late night flight. But we noticed, in the conversation with Vjosa and Pranvera, that in this moment it was very difficult to talk about the future. They were still in shock, and needed to spend most of their time talking about the horrible experience they had just been through.

Jan and I slept in a youth hostel in Skopje and, on many days, traveled by bus to Tetova, an hour's ride away, to meet with the center staff. We also attended meetings with UNHCR and other refugee service providers, which were held in Skopje.

We found an Internet café in Skopje, where we could send daily reports to our friends and colleagues in the US, who were no doubt wondering how we were and if we had found anything to do. I will include a few of these e-mails for you to see how it was in the moment.

Monday, April 12, 1999. Subject: The Great Escape: A Tsunami of Sorrow
I must be in shock. I can't think. I don't feel present. Yesterday, I met a wave of sadness — 15,000–16,000 teary-eyed refugees at the Stankovic refugee camp just outside Skopje, Macedonia.

In a lovely valley surrounded by snowy mountains, spring was evident all around. Lilacs spilled out their sweetness, tulips and daffodils were everywhere shouting the glory of spring. A friend from Pristina who is now living in Struga mentioned that her mother-in-law had been separated from them when they came across the border and is now in the large refugee camp known as Stankovic, which is close to Skopje. She was worried about her mother-in-law, a woman whom I have met and who has cooked many fine meals for me in her home. In the night, I woke up thinking about this situation. The next day was Easter in the Eastern Orthodox religion. I knew that Easter is a very big holiday and that little work would be done. I thought about what I had heard the day before, listening to Vjosa talk about how international people were able to come into no-man's land. They had been able to simply walk into the area, find people they knew, and bring them out, as the Macedonian authorities were reluctant to mess with internationals. I wondered if it would be possible for us to go into a refugee camp and just bring out this woman and reunite her with her family.

In the morning, we went to a prestigious hotel to talk to reporters to find out if we could get into a camp to get our friend's mother-in-law out. Everyone we talked with said we would not be allowed into the camp without proper credentials, that it was impossible to take anyone out at this point, and that we were pretty foolish to even think about such a thing. I figured we had nothing to lose, as we would learn as much in the search as we would in the finding, so we decided to persist. We called Pranvera, and she said we should go and offered to be our translator.

As our taxi pulled up to the first set of guards, I whipped out my business card as if it were the card of a very important person, and with a few words from the taxi driver and from our translator, we passed the first set of guards. The second set of guards also put up little resistance to my Crabgrass business card routine. Over 16,000 people now live in this camp — all in tents. The camp is about 200 yards deep and 500–700 yards wide, with square beige tents and round white tents arranged in long rows, with numbers and letters spray-painted on the side. Occasionally, an artist had added a flourish, and even more regularly a family name was on the tent.

Upon entering the camp, one is immediately confronted by a very long line, mostly of men, standing for hours and hours waiting to register. There are also lines for food and for going to the toilets. In midday, many people sit in tents talking, smoking, crying, and smoking more. "It's the only pleasure in my life now," one woman said. Children run around kicking and chasing balls. This camp is known as a "transit camp." All these people are to be sent to other countries, near and far away.

We are looking for one older woman, Mrs. Vula, who has become separated from her family. She was unable to walk across the border, so had been taken by ambulance. This is how she had become separated from her family. First, we go to a tent to see a list of older people who are alone. She is not on that list. Then, we go to one of the three hospital tents in this camp. The Israeli government runs the full surgery and bed unit. Old and ill people lie on the ground on mats covered by clean, fluffy, brightly colored quilts. Staff members wearing latex gloves look on the list. No, she is not here.

Whenever we stop, a crowd gathers around us, waving small strips of paper. They gently request the use of our cell phone, visibly hanging from a pocket. "Just one minute," they ask. "My husband does not know where I am, or if I am alive." How could anyone say no to such a request, but saying yes would mean an avalanche of requests. Phones will be installed in the camp in a few days, we are told. We walk somewhat at random, looking for a group of white tents, where someone who has seen Mrs. Vula says she lives. It is like looking for a needle in a haystack.

The camp is located on a landing strip with very uneven land, tent ropes and wires all over. On the perimeter, holes have been dug and canvas walls erected, to keep the toilets from being seen. The stench from the toilets is strong. There are no handicapped-available toilets, and as we walk we notice both physically and mentally disabled people. What must a war be like to a blind person, or one who is in a wheelchair? People walk from the food line carrying cardboard boxes with canned tomatoes, crackers, oranges, bottled water, canned meats. Many tent families have arranged small cooking areas just outside their front door. From time to time, we see people bent over between tents, as one person pours water on another to wash the other's hair. A child fusses as his mother insists on washing his upper body and hair. Some litter can be seen, but not much. Most people look clean and sportily dressed. It is only when I look deep into their eyes that the sorrow is evident. It is as if those eyes could speak, moaning, "Oh, what I have seen."

From time to time we stop as Pranvera, an electrical engineer who worked at a power plant in Pristina, sees a friend and must stop to talk. People tell her stories of their ordeals, either hiding in Pristina or traveling to the border. We get snatches:

- "We were not even allowed to go to the bathroom. You can imagine how the children cried."

- Six days hiding in the basement without food, without water, without news of what was happening — then suddenly being forced into the street by military or paramilitary forces carrying automatic weapons.

- Women walking in the middle of the street, their clothes torn off.

- Going two weeks without a shower.

- Watching neighbors or family members harmed, tortured, or killed.

- Being held hostage by Macedonian authorities Albanians said: "The devil was behind us, and now another devil was not even allowing us into a temporary new home. We expected a welcome." While Macedonian authorities were not welcoming, private Albanian Macedonian citizens have opened their homes and hearts to as many as twenty-five members from one extended family.

- Being helped by Serbian neighbors or friends who warned them that they must leave. "My Serbian neighbor was in the military; he could not protect me, but he did escort me and my family safely to the border."

I start calling out, "Mrs. Vula." I envisioned Mrs. Vula sitting in her tent, and when she heard her name, coming out to see us. I frankly felt a little silly in that moment. Finally, Pranvera shouts, "She is here!" We all come running.

She sees me, the only one from our team she has met previously. Quickly, we move toward each other. Someone shouts that she has not spoken for eight days. She has been silently sitting in the tent of a family not her own. We hold each other, and now she opens the gate, sobbing, talking, and sobbing. Finally, after nearly an eternity, she pulls her head back to look at me. Through my tears, I can see her tears streaming down her radiant face. Someone brings a blanket and we sit in the middle of the path between the tents. She talks so fast that the translator cannot translate. I don't need to hear her words; my heart understands her completely. She has been through a very, very painful experience. Ever the hostess, she takes a break from talking to go into the tent, and brings out cookies and apples to share with us.

Now, the team has a difference of opinion: Shall we try to get her out, or would she be unable to bear the disappointment if she is not allowed to go? While we are discussing this matter, she settles the question by beginning to pack her suitcase. She is ready to go. We decide to take her to the medical tent and try to get a medical pass out of the camp. Various neighbors are standing around watching the spectacle. As we begin to walk away from the tent, one young man says, "If you put your hat on her, the guards will think she is a foreigner."

On our way to the medical tents, the front gate distracts us. What if there was some way to just walk out of that gate, past those guards, down the long road past the other set of guards, and into the taxi? Jan and Mrs. Vula hold back while the translator and I look for a way out. An unshaven man comes up and in a friendly tone asks, "Do you want to smuggle her out?" We know it is not possible legally to get her out, so we say "YES." A few cars with humanitarian licenses are discreetly approached. "No, we can't do it," they say. "Other NGOs have been arrested trying to smuggle people out in their cars." Someone approaches a kindly looking British female army officer. She nods to three men over by a truck. "I can't tell you just now," she says. "Ask them." They give us the regular line that no one can leave now. This is a transit camp, and these people will all be shipped out to another country.

The Macedonian government does not want refugees wandering around their country. They think they already have enough Albanians, and any more will tip the very delicate balance of power in their country. They are determined to send most ethnic Albanians either to Albania or elsewhere. In fact, a few days prior to this event, people from selected tents had been rounded up and, without their permission, without being united with their families, they were put into buses, which took them to airplanes, and eventually on to Turkey. Other people were being sent to Germany and other European destinations. That this old woman could be separated from her family any longer seemed a crime.

At this moment, our smuggling consultant says, "What's happening?" There is a lot of movement of troops, cars, and a motorcade with a siren and lights flashing — press people are everywhere. We know that the Turkish ambassador is coming today and assume that this activity is related to his arrival. "If you're going, go now. Now is the time," he says.

I walk back to Jan and Mrs. Vula. "Walk through the gate with her. Just keep walking, don't stop," I tell Jan. Remembering the advice of the young man back at the tent, I take my hat off and put it on the old woman's head. She does look more like a foreigner now. (Foreigners come and go as they wish here.) The woman and Jan move through the gate as if invisible. The Macedonian guard asks Jan for her pass, and they just keep moving. She says she doesn't have one. Two of us move off, diverting the attention of the British guards. I move quickly to a high point, and watch as Jan and the lovely woman in the hat move slowly down the road. It's a long walk. "The woman was shaking so hard," Jan told us later, "I wasn't sure she could make it to the waiting taxi." As we move through the gate, we nod to people from the tent area where we found Mrs. Vula. They are watching her walk down the road, seeing her to off to safety, possibly hoping that one day they will move down that road also.

"We all want to go back to our Kosova/o homes when it is a free country," they have told us over and over again. "Please don't betray us again," they plead. "You Americans betrayed us in Dayton, and then in October. Now is our last moment. We have lost so much." Their sad eyes wander over to the mountains where every night they see missiles passing over their heads, going towards Kosova/o. Their homes are there; many friends are still hiding there. What a tsunami of sorrow is in that camp. May it carry them home one day.

Thursday, April 15, 1999
Today's work was particularly rewarding and instructive for future work. For two days, we had been hearing from Vera that there was no food in El Hilal, the primary distribution NGO (non-governmental organization) in Tetova, where there are at least 35,000 refugees, mostly staying in private homes. El Hilal is also primarily responsible for supplying people in the no-man's land between Kosova/o and Macedonia. Today, we decided to go to Tetova, to meet with that group to see what the problem is. We have been going to meetings with UNHCR, so we know a little about food availability and have some phone numbers.

All day, we were on the phone calling UNHCR, Catholic Relief Services (CRS), Mercy Corps and NATO, trying to get food released. We are happy to report that 500 kilos of macaroni, three tons of oil, one ton of canned beef, five tons of flour, three tons of beans, one ton of toilet soap, two tons of canned goulash, one box each of new and used clothing, and hopefully some fresh fruit and vegetables will arrive tomorrow around 10 a.m. We plan to be there to welcome the three trucks with all these goodies, and see that they are moved into the empty warehouse.

One of the calls was particularly funny. Somebody from CRS recognized my name and asked, "Aren't you a writer? In fact, aren't you the American willing to listen?" I said, "Yes, usually I am the American willing to listen, but today I am the American willing to find food!" He's going to help El Hilal. We will meet with him and his executive director on Monday to draw up an agreement that will provide food on an ongoing basis. What the problem is, we cannot yet say. Why they have not been getting food until now we do not know, but we suspect that one reason may be that the Macedonian Red Cross is more a part of the government than a nongovernmental organization.

In the meantime, our glorious memory is of the truckload of 400 loaves of bread that arrived just before we left Tetova. Now, at least they will have something to distribute at the border tonight. We made arrangements for milk to come tonight as well. Tomorrow, the big load will come.

Now, you might ask, how did we achieve all this? We worked in partnership with the Albanian NGO and our translator/friend, Pranvera (Vjosa's sister). We put our international skills to the service of people who couldn't figure out why no food was available for them. We are leaving El Hilal with all the phone numbers and contacts, so that they can take over this job themselves.

When they asked what Crabgrass was, we replied that "it is a very small organization." "Not to us," they replied. "To us you are a big organization, because you have been the first organization to come to us and not just make promises. All the other organizations asked us what we needed, made lists and left. You're the first one that came and sat with us and found the food. Then, when the food came, you helped us unload it. To us, you are a big organization."

For lunch, we went to the new women's center and met with some of the staff there, including the woman whose husband we found last Sunday at Stenkovec, with his eighty-four-year-old mother. We are preparing for our training in trauma counseling starting next Monday, where we will focus on listening skills, not getting swamped by memories, and a few other things too complicated to explain here. We will leave it to the professional trauma counselors who are coming from Croatia and/or others to complete this work, but we are giving the staff a chance to share their memories with each other now, as they begin to build a new center. That's it for today. To quote the singer/songwriter Betsy Rose, "This is just our work, we're doing what we were given to do, hope we can do it our whole life through."

Friday, April 16, 1999

Today, we went to Tetova at the crack of dawn, and saw the milk that had arrived after we left last night. We also noticed that yesterday's bread had been distributed. Two large UNHCR trucks came at noon. A friendly Danish man drove the lead car. A whole team of young and old volunteers formed a human chain to unload all the food into a former car showroom. At four in the afternoon, the twenty-six distribution centers of El Hilal were coming to pick up their share and get food out to refugees living with host families in and around Tetova. Also, food will go out to no-man's land tonight, because they have heard that 2,000 people are arriving during the dark of night. "If only we could get food to the people in the hills," they said from time to time. We heard that bad abuse of deportees is occurring again, and the flow of people coming out is increasing steadily. Then, we returned for the NGO/UNHCR briefing.

Each meeting begins with a go-around of names and what organization you're from. So and so from UNICEF, so and so from UNHCR, so and so from World Health Organization, and so and so from NATO. Then, they come to us and we say, "Fran Peavey and Jan Hartsough from Crabgrass." We try to repress a chuckle, as it would blow our cover. At every meeting, there is a NATO briefing, and we are impressed with how attuned those guys are with public relations. As we walk to the meeting room, we pass a colored display of photos and statistics, and their press center. But don't worry — we are not being deluded by their bullshit. We know they are killing people, and there is no way to gloss over that.

Today, we heard about the bombing of a fertilizer factory in Pancevo. I think this is the town outside Belgrade where one of the houses with Serbian refugees we have been working with for over three years is located. I am worried about the Lastavica (the name of the house means "swallow") women, with all those chemicals in the atmosphere. What they must be going through. Sometimes I wonder what we will ever say to them when we see them again. But then I feel guilty thinking of my own discomfort when it is so bad for them. Oh, what a mess!

Wednesday, April 21, 1999
It's Wednesday afternoon, and we've just returned from visiting the two camps closest to Skopje to help friends from Pristina get more family members out. The camps are overflowing, and buses are arriving all the time, full of more refugees. They are trying to fly as many out as they can, and a new camp is not yet open. It might be good to contact US representatives and ask them why the US has not yet accepted any of the refugees.

When we talked with young people recently deported from Pristina, they reported little food there, missiles coming in every night; but they were not afraid because they knew the missiles were going to Serbian military targets. It seemed useless to mention how fallible these missiles are. The people we talk with say that they are certain that Serbs are planting tanks and other weapons very close to apartment buildings in cities. We have not met anyone who feels that the explosions in Pristina are from NATO; either they are Serbian in origin, or they occur because a tank was close to the building. It is inconceivable to them that NATO would be behind the explosions in Pristina in residential areas. Refugees are confident that NATO makes no mistakes. They all support the bombing, even though they know it has made their lives more difficult, and has intensified the violence against them. They seem willing to pay this price, since the price for NATO doing nothing was troublesome for years.

When progressive friends in the US object to the bombing now, we ask them, "Where were you when the violence was going on since 1989, and especially these last two years?" It seems that there were no good choices left by the time NATO took to the skies. We do not support the bombing, but since it has begun, it must not be stopped peremptorily, leaving the Serbian military and paramilitary to their horrid tasks of evicting and killing people. We must move to a negotiated settlement that does not leave the Albanian people of Kosova/o vulnerable again and the Serbs to retaliation. When people say "stop the bombing," more and more I feel that this is a partisan statement supporting the Serbs. I believe it is better to demand a stop to all the military violence in the Balkans! This statement should be addressed to the KLA; the Serbian nationalist military, paramilitary, and police; and the NATO troops — in other words, all the parties that are employing violence to achieve their goals.

Very often we envision our next trip to this region to be a visit in support of our friends in Belgrade, because surely in this moment they must be feeling abandoned by the antimilitarist people of the world.

We are still finding that only bread is going to Tetova, so we are back on the track of sorting out this complex problem. We hope to go to the border tomorrow with a local car. The camps are beyond their capacity now, and the situation is quite volatile with Macedonia. Some street violence has been directed at international NGOs, and problems are beginning to develop in the camps with the pressure of too many people. We are writing early today, because we are going out to dinner with UNHCR people after the briefing to get the inside scoop.

Thursday, April 22, 1999
It's Thursday afternoon. We spent the morning with Roma NGOs seeing what work they are doing to get food out to Roma refugees. We shared all the information we have learned working with Tetova El Hilal, and are trying to pull together a meeting to challenge Macedonian Red Cross' monopoly on food distribution to refugees staying in host families. We keep hearing that no one gets food when

they register at Red Cross. Roma refugees have more difficulty registering, so we are focusing on this problem today. We don't have time to make a long report, because we are leaving for the border to see for ourselves how people are registered as they enter, and maybe to Red Cross for more research on how they process registrations and distribute food here in Skopje. Bye for now. We are both fine.

Saturday, April 24, 1999
It's Saturday night. We have now visited the Macedonian Red Cross offices in both Skopje and Tetova. Through our questions, we have developed a new openness around sharing food between El Hilal and Red Cross. This is probably one of our most significant contributions, aside from leaving the Center for the Protection of Women and Children in strong shape.

We told the women that Vjosa would be bringing underpants to be distributed. Most women left home with maybe a change of clothes, but rarely a change of underpants. So we had offered to Vjosa that our network could send underpants to her when she was in the US The women shyly asked if they could have some, or were they all for clients of the center? I said, "Is not one of our goals to leave the Center for the Protection of Women and Children strong and able to work? Well then, these underpants must be for you. How can you be strong if you have to wash your underpants every evening?" We all chuckled.

In reflecting on our trauma training, we noticed several things that need to be shared. One is that few stories we heard failed to mention some kindness of Serbian people. The incidence of this is much more than in the Bosnian war, although we don't have a large scientific sample. One woman told of how her Serbian neighbor, whom she had never trusted because he was a Serb, came to her house to say, "I can't keep the police from coming to get you anymore. They are coming today and will force you to leave. All I can do is take you myself, and escort you to see that you get to the border safely." She was so surprised and grateful to him that she cried telling the story.

We have heard about one rape of a young girl in a public space in a neighborhood. Almost all coming-out-of-Kosova/o stories involve at least one story of a robbery by paramilitary or Roma people. People are stopped on the road and told that the wife or child will be killed unless a large amount of German marks is paid. The stories are fascinating tales of human creativity and endurance, and horrible in details of what human beings are capable of.

Which reminds me that one of the two major women behind the center, Sevdije, is still in Pristina. Several people went to her and urged her to stop hiding, but she refused. She is not staying at home. I know she had a cellar full of food and will be good at hiding. I hope she is well. She is a very brave and stubborn woman. Her weekly reports to us about what was happening meant a lot these last months, until the phone lines were cut and reports ceased.

On Thursday afternoon, we went with a young Macedonian woman, Valja, in her car out to the border crossing of Blace, beyond the big Stenkovec transit camp. This is just across from the horrible no-man's land, where so many were trapped some weeks ago. A small tent camp is temporary housing for a day or two, before the refugees are assigned to camps. Pieces of plastic are strewn all around. It is really inexcusable for the Macedonian authorities to leave the refugees out there for so long.

Over 2,000 had crossed that day, and 1,000 had been waiting at the actual border crossing — stuck until buses came to take them to camps. You should know that it is raining and often cold here. We cannot help thinking about what that means if you are standing for hours waiting to cross a border, or to get food. Maybe you have to huddle in a tent for hours.

Today, we went again with Valja to see a pretty pathetic distribution at a Skopje Red Cross site. Then, we went on to see another camp less visited by the press and less reported on. It is a smaller camp, run by the Bulgarian government. It is said that the Bulgarians didn't want refugees coming into their country, so they made a bilateral agreement with the Macedonian government to run this camp. They are doing a great job, with good sanitation, two hot meals served each day (Bulgarians evidently are great cooks), washing facilities, and gravel over the muddy pathways. People can go out of the camp to buy fresh vegetables and cigarettes, etc.; children are going to school in the local Albanian village close by. They have a large playing field right outside the camp, where the children can run and play soccer. While the refugee experience is not a pleasant one, this camp is surely an improvement over the huge camps we have seen nearer to Skopje. It is set at the end of a valley with snowy peaks all around.

We finished our trauma training yesterday at the center, and were generally pleased with the effects on the women of the center. Their morale is high, and they are focused on finding housing. We really like these women personally, individually, and as a group.

We have had some great conversations with individuals, both Macedonian and Albanian, young and old, and feel we are learning from them about the complexities of this time in Macedonia. Last night, we came upon a large Serbian-led demonstration with pictures of Milosevic, flags, and signs. People are afraid here that the war will expand into Macedonia, and that Macedonia will cease to exist. It is a very small country anyway, but if the Albanian western corridor (primarily populated by ethnic Albanians) joins with Kosova/o and Albania, there will be nothing left for the "rump" Macedonia. Maybe Greece will gobble up that part. They are also afraid that Serbia will expand the war to Macedonia, and they will be caught in a trap. Several people in camps have said that they fear Milosevic will figure out that a good way, given his logic, to get rid of a lot of Albanians would be to bomb the refugee camps. A wild look came into the eyes of the people telling of this concern. What is it to know that someone (or a whole army of someones) wants to rid the world of you and your people?

Life here is a very delicate balance. Probably, all life is a delicate balance, but here that perception is inescapable daily. You can see it on the faces of the people in the streets, you can hear it from the taxi drivers, you can see the struggle to maintain hope in the midst of a deteriorating political, military, and economic situation.

Every day, there is an almost perceptible shadow to the northwest across the hills where missiles explode the lives and society of Serbia. We are already wondering what we should be preparing to do when we are able to go to Belgrade and visit our friends there. What support will they need from us? They are with us, sitting on our shoulders, wishing for an end to this military demonstration of prowess. We are more and more thinking that Rambouillet (negotiations prior to the bombing leading to an agreement which the Kosovars signed but the Serbs did not) was a setup to create the pretext for NATO to launch the war and to create a powerful presence in this region that will last into the future. As usual, people are simply pawns in a power/land grab. The Albanians are remarkably cheerful in the face of this insanity, because they feel that something they have longed for is now within reach. Maybe we are cynical, but we expect NATO to sell them out once again. But we dare not say that here   they have such hope.

Monday, April 26, 1999

Sunday was going to be our day off, as we were tired and the heaviness of the situation had begun to weigh on us. But our cell phone rang in the morning to tell us of an important meeting scheduled for the evening with a special envoy from the United Nations asking for suggestions from NGOs about how things are going with the refugees, and how they could be improved. Since we had a few issues we were eager to bring up, we went enthusiastically, after a lovely dinner at a big hotel with a fancy dessert for each of us (shame, shame!). It was a very small meeting around a large table, and was for the most part not defensive, but genuinely open. We are learning a lot about the inside workings of UNHCR, UNICEF, the World Health Organization (WHO), and the World Food Programme (WFP), as well as the refugee "support industry" of international NGOs.

Today, we began to wind up our activities here. We changed our tickets, so we will arrive in the Bay Area this Thursday. We feel complete and proud of our work here. We went to Tetova to visit our favorite women's center. We were happy to be able to provide a down payment on the first month's rent for their new building. Peeking in to the new facilities, we saw that all the new walls were up, even painted, and lights were being installed. It is going to be a beautiful space with stone tile floors, lots of light, and a lovely meeting room in the back on a patio. It will have a kitchen and a large storage space for supplies, as well as examining rooms for the medical work. They are planning to begin work sometime this week, although Meli has already begun holding trauma classes with young women at the nearby refugee camp. The girls, she reports, are enthusiastic, and looking for something to do. We talked to her about an economic project that might bring some money in for young and old, and result in some products for our handicraft sales campaign to bring income into women's hands. We are going to need more distributors for Balkan products, and hope we can count on our friends all over the country to help support a self-help project here.

Feelings were so warm, and we genuinely feel we leave them much stronger than when we arrived. We are still working to get them some sleeping bags from El Hilal, and housing for one family, but many of our goals with them, finding food and teaching them how to gain access to food and other services, have been accomplished.

Then, we went to visit the refugee camp called Neprosteno, close to Tetova, where Pranvera is working fifteen hours a day. One thing that is probably underreported is how hard competent translators and organizers are working, while being refugees themselves. However, today our taxi driver reminded us not to call them refugees: "We think of them as guests." He has ten guests in his household. The refugee camp is mid-sized now (6,000), but the flow of refugees continues every night, so this, as all camps, may have to grow. All facilities are bursting at the seams. At this camp, they are organized by rows and sectors, and they are planning to have cooking tents for every ten tents. Soon they will be able to have hot meals, which makes a big difference in camp life. The tents in this camp — big, military-type tents — have wooden platforms, and actual bed frames. Many have stoves to warm them. They are dark green/brown and dreary now, and will be terribly hot in the summer. Everyone is worried about the possibility of epidemics this summer, when it will be hot in the crowded conditions.

We went to lunch with the women from the center, and then to El Hilal. We met with the distribution manager, whom we have liked working with very much. He is open, honest, and cheerful. In the middle of the meeting, everything had to be stopped, because the truck was about to go out to no-man's land to take bread, milk, and canned meat to new arrivals. It seems there are a large number of them at the nearby border crossing, but we did not hear a specific number. We were glad they had these supplies for those hungry people, and felt a little joyfully responsible for that. They have learned how and where to get food from the system. We again put in a request for some sleeping bags, which is our continual struggle. However, the main man we needed to speak with was not there, so we must go back one more time on Wednesday.

These next few days, one of our main jobs is to give away all the money we brought. We have figured out how to get money out of the ATMs here, so people have been able to donate in the US, and we are able to get it right to the grassroots organizations here. I have felt the presence of my community blowing like wind at my back, supporting and encouraging me. I know that when I say "*We* care about what is happening here," I speak for many friends and supporters of Crabgrass.

We zoomed back by taxi, paid for by El Hilal, to attend the UNHCR NGO coordination meeting. It seems that some NGOs are fighting with each other over turf, more refugees are pouring in at every border, and education is beginning to happen at most camps. Even the immunization program, which we have been hearing about at every meeting, is beginning. We met afterwards with the logistics man to find out exactly how items can be sent into this country.

Several times we have heard UNHCR staff people comment quietly that so much more food and other supplies are being given to the Kosovars than to the refugees they have worked with in Africa. They seem bitter about this obvious reflection of racism.

Tuesday, April 27, 1999

What an exciting day for our next-to-last day. It started with a food meeting at the WFP offices, where we were able to put names and faces together with the people we have been talking with on the phone, as well as meet the Macedonian Red Cross lady of Skopje. She was slightly defensive about criticisms others had made about the Red Cross. We didn't need to be critical, but supported ideas put forward by others to broaden the food distribution instead of having a Red Cross monopoly. Several NGOs are beginning to get food out into the host communities.

Then, we went to visit the Roma Center of Skopje, a small NGO that is doing a fantastic job. We had seen them distributing food last week and had decided to give them some of our money.

When people ask us "What is Crabgrass?" we say it is a small NGO working in the cracks between the big organizations. We specialize in small, impossible jobs. We've come to a new slogan for Crabgrass: "Crabgrass: thriving in the cracks." People mention that we have been the first ones in, and we are grateful to be able to move so quickly and be in that position. Now, we see other small organizations coming to pick up the slack.

We gave the Roma Center the money, and then asked, "Is there anything else we can do for you?" They said, "One other problem is that we have a Roma family living in a cardboard shack in the garbage dump of Skopje. It leaks when it rains (it rained a lot when we were there). Could you help us find a tent for them?" Quickly we called our friend "Dan," whom we have never met but talked to on the phone a lot. "Yes, we have a tent — for how many people?" Our friend Azbija said there were at least twelve in the family. "Sure, do you want to pick it up now?" So off we went to find the UNHCR warehouse to pick up a tent (from Russia), which ultimately turned out to be big enough for thirty people.

We took it out to the Roma encampment, where the people were living in very poor conditions and had dangerous water. A number of young men carried the heavy tent through the community, and we saw the temporary cardboard house the family was living in. The entire neighborhood was so poor that it broke our hearts. Before our eyes, two babies threw up. They told us that their children were dying. They thought it was due to the water. The community was surrounded by garbage. Few children looked healthy to our eyes. The men set about figuring out how to put up the tent. One man finally decided to come back with us to UNHCR to get some instructions. We were so happy to leave them that tent, and know that the next time it rains they will be dry. (The sun is shining today, finally.)

Tonight, our women's center friends from Tetova are joining us for the weekly UN community service meeting, so they can meet the key people they will be working with when we are gone. It is quite controversial to bring local NGO people to these international NGO meetings, but one of the main reasons we know what to do is because we go to these meetings, find out who is doing what, and what resources are available. For example, when Azbija went in to get the tent, she met the dispatch person, who said, "If you would like to, you could come back and get some clothing tomorrow."

One of our tasks has been to connect local people with resources. Now that we are leaving, we have spent the last few days saying good-bye, distributing money, and making sure they know how to do what we have done. It's not a miracle; it's nonviolently working with people who are suffering the consequences of war. We're short on theory, longer on practice. We wish we could stop the war. That not being possible just now, we can alleviate a few of the war's horrible effects. We will continue to work to stop the war when we get home.

Tomorrow, we will go back to Tetova for a final meeting with El Hilal and its director, with a stop-off at the women's center, in hopes that Vjosa is back. While we have missed Vjosa, we have very much enjoyed the opportunity to work with the entire staff, getting to know them more as individuals with families and lives. We have also been able to help them solve a few of their problems. Then, we will come back to Skopje for one more meeting with the Roma guy, Elvis, working with Soros, and then the UNHCR NGO meeting. We have made some real friends there, to whom we will be sorry to say good-bye. We have come to have a great deal of respect for the emergency committee that has formed around this war.

Finally, we will catch the 9:30 p.m. shuttle van to Thessaloníki, Greece, and a 4 a.m. plane to Frankfurt, on our way back to all of you. Thank you so much for enabling us to be here and do this work. We've had a lot of fun and heartache, but we wouldn't have missed it for anything. No matter what is happening in any war, there is always plenty of good work to do. And there are always people working to stop the war and heal the suffering it causes. Signing off now — Fran and Jan.

Can anyone imagine the joy of being able to find food for people who are hungry, bring people out of refugee camps, or find a tent for a family enduring cold and rainy days in a poorly put together cardboard house? I have learned a few important lessons for life from this period of work. One is to pay attention to the level of decision-making you exert your control over. We had about $5,000, which we had collected to share with organizations that needed the money at this time. Supporters of Crabgrass donated the money in San Francisco, and we were able to withdraw it from an ATM in Skopje. We felt that it was important to give the money to groups that we trusted, and we gave the money openly, always with more than one person from the organization present, so no one would be tempted to put the money in a personal pocket. And we did not tell them what to use the money for. We told them that we trusted their sense of priorities to determine whether it was more important to buy baby food or gasoline for the truck.

We were not able to establish trust with all groups we met. This does not mean they were not trustworthy, but rather that we were not able to establish the level of trust necessary for us to know some of the consequences of our gift. Trust is such an intuitive process, and one can never fully know the consequences of any act in life. No doubt we made mistakes, but I am confident that the money was, for the most part, used wisely by the grassroots groups we met. Groups we did not find ourselves able to trust we did not give money to. Speaking of trust, I am reminded that the primary anti-war radio station in Belgrade, B92, has as its motto: "Trust no one — not even us." Trust is a very precious commodity these days.

We learned how important it is to have attention put on the small tasks in the midst of large organizations taking on the big tasks. In the early days of organizing for this disaster, all kinds of tasks emerged, such as teaching local Albanian and Roma refugee organizations how to get food and other resources from the international organizations. It was not at all difficult to find tasks that were genuinely useful.

As always, we learned to pay attention to what people told us. Vera only briefly mentioned in passing that El Hilal had no food. Again, listening well and finding ways we could participate in the interests and at the request of local leaders was essential.

Vjosa told us to go to the meetings. I protested, saying I hated meetings. She pressed ahead: "Did you come to do only the work that pleases you, or did you come to do the work that was needed?" If we hadn't gone to the meetings, we would have been much less effective.

Probably the greatest learning for me was that I should not let people's fears or doubts cause me to give up dreams. We never would have gotten Mrs. Vula out had we listened to the doubts of others. But we held the dream very lightly, so that it could flex with changing conditions. That day, we achieved more than we had originally intended, because the dream grew like a snowball. Dreams have a way of doing that.

To all those friends who advised me not to go so close to the war zone and into such a chaotic situation, or doubted I would find work that needed doing, I can say that there is really no substitute for good will in a desperate situation. No thinking person can stand by while atrocities happen in our world. Everyone can do something, even if it is just to encourage the work of others. We made a point to compliment people we saw doing fine work, or people we especially enjoyed working with. If we are to feel good about ourselves as citizens and as human beings, we must do something. We must reach out of our little bubble and touch in a human way people who are suffering. When, in my early morning meditations, I ask myself, "What can I do to help life on earth?" many kinds of answers come. Some big and some small. I try to do as many as I can.

It is agony to see a human catastrophe coming to people you care about. Early in our work in the former Yugoslavia, we had set our goal to work with people on all sides of the war, thus refusing to accept the "enemies" dictated by our country, or to chose our own side as the just side. But this is the first time I had known people so deeply on all sides of a brutal conflict. Not only did we know people in Kosova/o and Serbia, we also knew some people in significant leadership positions in those countries. We had a small role in facilitating the Serbian and Albanian women in knowing each other. To make things worse, my own government was bombing both countries.

This was the complete extension of heart politics — I was not only connected to these people, but they were my friends. It put considerable strain on my ability to know how to navigate the oceans of difference in privilege and pain now built into our friendship. What can you write when it's your friends who are being bombed, raped, and driven out of their homes? Simply imagining me standing in front of any group of them to account for my acts brought tears to my eyes. I could do so little.

We had no way to predict the disaster that would befall our antiwar, pro-democracy friends in Serbia. It was the missiles from my own country that devastated their land and society. But we did see the troubles coming to Kosova/o. We wish we had been wrong. When we saw it coming, we prepared ourselves. I wrote to our network of people upon leaving for Macedonia that day early in April 1999: "We will look for needs unfilled and call home so that our network can be polled for people able to fill those needs. The big organizations will save lives with food and shelter. A small, flexible organization can respond to individual needs and to the cracks unfilled by the big organizations. We will look for work for our friends and ourselves. Where a little money will help, we will give that. We will bring a little kindness and tenderness with us."

Just before we left for Macedonia, I wrote to our network, "I guess we are as ready as we can ever be. Frankly, now that we're in the middle of this human catastrophe — and in the middle of NATO violence to citizens (and friends) in Belgrade, Nis, and other parts of Serbia, Montenegro, and Kosova/o — we wish we had been wrong. We can't help wishing that the world's leaders had been able to take this situation seriously, and had moved to resolve the conflict before it became a crisis. That conflict is destroying so many precious lives, as well as harming the earth and the stability of all nations involved."

In the bitter cold of war and destruction, sometimes all I can find to bring to the situation is tenderness. I wish I were the kind of strategic thinker who could reach into some bag of tricks and make the desolation stop. Faced with B-52s, bombs, and barbarousness, one thing I know I can offer is some small measure of kindness from my community and myself. If we start there, maybe we will find nonviolent means to stop the war and violence inside of each culture and each person — including each of us.

Postscript

As you can probably tell, this chapter was written without the benefit of the distance of time available for most chapters. I returned from Macedonia, and the book was due to the publishers very soon thereafter. Since I am still in the midst of this campaign with Serbia, with Montenegro, with Bosnia, with Kosova/o, and Macedonia, I'm sure I will have more reflections about this time period in the future.

It is so very difficult to talk about many aspects of this war. I noticed in the Bosnian war as well as this one that all parties to the conflict have committed atrocities. NATO tries to claim some moral superiority over the Serbs (the declared enemy), yet NATO killed more civilians by the way they conducted the war. They flew their planes so high that they could not tell an apartment house from a warehouse, a bridge occupied by automobiles or by tanks. This was a choice, and those who paid for that choice were citizens, not combatants. Then, when the bombing was over, Albanians began to kill Serbian people and burn their homes. Serbian military and police killed many too, but we don't have any accurate numbers, and I wonder if we ever will. To me it doesn't matter. If dead is dead, then killing is killing. There is no moral equivalency or high ground that any party to this killing spree can claim. This was not a black-and-white war, with anyone able to say they were the good guys.

Several weeks after I returned from Macedonia, my friend Myumi Oda stopped by to borrow something. She had just been to a very large peace conference at The Hague. She was very concerned about the use of depleted uranium in the Balkans. She told of horrible consequences for the earth and for the human beings in that region. As I ponder what she told me, I wonder, "What does a friend do when she finds that her government has created such a mess? As if bombing the region was not bad enough, now Myumi said that the casing of the bombs was made of uranium 238 which, while not very radioactive, has very serious consequences when turned into dust. I wondered about my responsibilities as an American citizen, living in the belly of the beast that had created this disaster in this moment.

I decided that since it was probably easier for me to get confirmation of the scientific information from the government, and learn from the plethora of organizations working on this area of interest exactly what they had done, what the consequences were, and what could be done to minimize the health effects, it was my obligation as a friend to pick up that piece of work. I am not only a friend to specific individuals, I feel myself to be a friend to their society. My Serbian and Albanian friends were in a position to spread the word about whatever I could find to others, through radio or newspapers. It was most important that I send only information that was accurate.

To begin, I must research what is true and confirm all information as best I can, avoiding rumors and speculation, as well as fearmongering. I may be able to find out if there is any way to minimize the damage that has already occurred to the body or the earth. There may be some pills, such as iodine, that would minimize the effects of the radiation, or foods that could strengthen the body. I called together a group of friends to share information and develop the list of questions to be researched. We made a list of people we knew, and assigned tasks. I found out how to get on an e-mail list to ask questions and gather information.

At this writing, August 1, 1999, an American general has confirmed that the United States used depleted uranium in the casings of cluster bombs. This uranium is a waste-product of the civilian nuclear power industry. It is used because it is very hard and can "cut through metal like a hot knife through butter," according to military sources. In its solid state, it is stable, emitting lower-level radiation. It burns upon impact, thus turning the metal into a very fine dust. In the burning, uranium 238 is put into the environment. This dangerous dust can have long-term effects on the human body, and on plants and animals in its vicinity. The depleted uranium emits alpha, beta, and gamma rays, and since they cannot dissolve in water, once it enters the body, it cannot leave. So if it is inhaled, eaten in plants or animals, or drunk in water, it will stay in the body — in the lungs, in bones, or in other tissues, emitting low-level radiation, which over time causes cancers and has other life-threatening effects.

How incredibly stupid. Is anyone in the Pentagon thinking? Other countries such as the U.K. decided not to use depleted uranium, to their eternal credit. It seems that this substance was also used in the Gulf War. This would have to qualify as evil. Evil is not in a person, as in a description. There are not evil people, but evil acts, which prevent us from being able to see life and form relationships. Evil kills without seeing, harms away from view. These depleted uranium bombs — and war in general — are not the result of evil people, but of ordinary people like you and me doing evil things, because of a mindlessness that does not see the face of the victim. I have seen and known evil. I have known people trapped in evil habits, but this depleted uranium takes a prize.

I wonder once someone decides to kill, whether something goes fundamentally haywire in the minds of the military planners who augment that decision. Why should future generations have to pay for Milosevic's and his henchmen's immoral judgments?

I started sending my friends in the Balkans information about what is possible, about the potential risks, and where they can find this information more directly themselves. I felt nauseated in my gut writing suggestions that children not play in the dust of their land, that no one go close to tanks and other bomb sites, and that in windstorms, everyone stay indoors. In my feeling life, I had to confront such a rage at my feelings of helplessness. "We could not stop them," I imagine saying to my friends in Belgrade and Pristina. Once again, I immerse myself in new technical information in the interest of my friends, their lives, and the life of the land on which they live. Many veterans from the Gulf War are convinced that their health problems derive from exposure to depleted uranium. They have been doing a lot of important research on this subject. It constantly amazes me who our allies are.

This research is like slaying dragons. When you cut the tail off, three more dragons emerge. The more I delve into the matter of depleted uranium, the more crazy it all seems. In twenty or thirty years, some president will probably announce that scientists have finally discovered that the complaints of the Gulf War veterans are credible, and that the ones who are still alive should be paid some pittance for all their bother and suffering.

Even now, as I am balancing all that needs to be done in the final work on this book, I am preparing the preliminary work for a campaign about the radioactive casings in which shells and bombs were delivered to the Balkans. I am horrified when I read the evidence of the effects the very tough radioactive metals will have on the land and peoples of the Balkans and of Iraq, the two places that we know for sure these weapons have been used.

I spoke with a legal expert who had been working with the United Nations; it is her opinion that these bombs should be outlawed, for four reasons found in prior treaties that the US has signed as part of UN legal papers and agreements. It is disgusting how arrogant the US is regarding international law and decisions of the World Court. I know we can do better.

This week, I've been thinking a lot of about what a friend should do when she sees her country — the place that she loves and respects — doing something horrible to her friends in another land. I probably would have objected to these radioactive bomb casings before they were used in the Balkans, but not with the same drive and commitment I now feel, knowing that they affect places and people I care deeply about.

I remember a Bosnian war meeting with Bosnian student refugees in Vienna. I had been wondering something, in the selfish part of my mind, so I asked the question: "If we in the US got into a nasty war like this, would you come to help us?" Nearly everyone said, "No, I wouldn't think of it," or "I would be too scared," until a young woman spoke up. "Before, I never would have thought of doing such a thing, because I might not feel connected to those people so far away, but now that I know how important it is for people to come from outside the war, I will come." All the others agreed with her.

As I sit in my office looking out into the dark night, I wish I could see down the road of what's happening in the Balkans as you read did this. I know from other campaigns that they look very different in a year, or five years. I cannot wait, so I will print this, begging for your understanding of how little I knew about this war in August of 1999. How little anyone in the public knows. As the secrets come to light, and as real motivations become clearer, I'm only sure of a few things. One is that terrible things did happen; the killings and torture were not propaganda as some Serbian leaders have alleged. Two, there was terrible demonizing of Serbs in the American media; and three, NATO's motivations were not as noble and humanitarian as they portrayed at the time. Things are rarely as simple as leaders would like us to believe. They had their own expansionistic agenda that was the primary force. There were also, I'm sure, economic agendas. And yet, it is important that Milosevic was stopped in Kosova/o.

For over a year, I have been sharing information about Kosova/o with the staff of my congresswoman, who is on the Foreign Relations Committee in the House of Representatives. Before the vote to bomb, she called for updated information. It was agony for me. If she voted no on bombing, would that mean continuing the path of doing very little? I felt that my Albanian and Serbian friends from Kosova/o were sitting on one shoulder, and my Serbian friends were on the other shoulder. I found that it's tough to think about such hard, fast decisions when I could see the faces of the people who would be affected. The debate had obviously too few options under consideration. Barbara Lee, my congressperson, was the only no vote in the whole Congress.

As a friend of Serbians and Albanians, Bosnian Croatians, Macedonians, Roma, as well as Turks in Macedonia, I still ask, "What does a friend do in these international situations of conflict and horror on all sides?"

The time in Macedonia with the ethnic Albanian refugees, the Roma, and the NGOs has led to lots of further thinking and dialogue among my friends about what a compassionate and caring citizen can do during a war. Returning home, I found the peace movement seriously divided between those whose call was "Stop the Bombing," and those who felt unhappy about the bombing, but felt it was nonetheless necessary, given the Serb military's aggressive movements. In the aftermath of this war, I have only a few contributions to make about the nature of war, and a few suggestions of an alternative way of approaching war for those opposed to militarism.

1. It is not cynical to assume that the United States government and the military that is attached to that government will carry on a war from time to time now. Without another superpower like the Soviet Union balancing the power of the United States, there is no force to adequately challenge the US military and its international partners, composed primarily of European and English-speaking countries. We should assume that we are going to be working against war for the rest of our lives, should build our schedules to have room for such activity, and support organizations that can have continued focus on militarism.

I think it is dangerous for a single country to have as much power in the world as the United States does today. The only alternative is for citizens inside and outside the US to create strategies and alliances to stop the wars. It is up to those of us within the United States to align with progressive forces outside the US to create a movement against the forces that seek American control over the world. Corporations and governments have many ways of building alliances, but citizens do not always have the means, or even the analysis that such contacts will be useful. The diasporas of so many peoples, Chinese, Tibetans, Indians and Middle Eastern people, as well as Jews, Europeans, Africans, and Latin Americans, whether they are refugees or not, are now found all over the world. Usually, they maintain contact with their families and have their own network in their new land. Immigrant people are an important connection to gain perspective and contacts. Progressive, peace-loving people can develop relationships across borders to check misinformation and disinformation. We must work together to prevent military action by some newly formed alliance (as in the Gulf War), or NATO, or the US by itself.

2. In such a punitive and mean-spirited time, we must find ways of preserving and enacting our connectedness to the life force wherever it is found. War is the ultimate act of disconnection, as well as of lack of imagination.

3. During such times of war, those individuals and groups that are opposed to war have two primary responsibilities: to protest war however they can, and to find acts of tenacious tenderness and persistent kindness toward targets of the inhumanity that is war. This means that we should find ways of being tender and kind to the sol-

diers who are committing the acts we despise, who are also victims of war, as well as toward all combatants on all sides of the war. It means caring for the refugees and wounded. We can also anticipate that there will be men and women who resist being put into the position to kill people or to support that killing. They are going to need legal support, as well as emotional support. After the war, they will need financial support, as they will be denied financial assistance for college or for the purchase of a home.

Resisting war has many faces, each a little different depending on the society. In response to the ferocious power of public abuse, we must put that tough side down, and persistently and tenaciously find acts of connection, tenderness, and kindness to exhibit in the world. If this serves only to remind us that the whole world is not occupied by bombs and killing, it will be enough; but if acts of kindness and tenderness are able to also remind others that life is precious, that power is *not* the most powerful force in the world, then it will be a very valuable act indeed.

Tenderness is not weakness; kindness is not soft. They are strong, energetic, committed stands in the world. Doing nothing is weakness. Resorting to violence is weakness. In a time of war, one revolutionary act is to find tenderness and kindness; another is to find the truth about the war; and still another path to revolution is protest and resistance at every node where the war must cross normal life. Working for life-oriented values is a very strong position and in line with the basic nature of life.

I went to Macedonia because I felt strongly that I wanted to be with my friends and see if there was anything I could do to help ameliorate the damage that the military was doing. Now, I feel that there was a certain proactive wisdom to moving closer to the conflict, rather than further away, and also to working in the interests of my friends. At the time, I could not go to Belgrade. I will be going as soon as possible to support the people there in their healing and their antiwar work.

The agony of knowing friends are suffering is a terrible torture. I don't want to make too much of my own suffering, because of my respect for my friends and their suffering. But I write only from inside my own skin, and I know my own shame and almost visceral disgust. For several months, whenever I communicated with others familiar with the region, we asked each other if anyone had heard of Sevdija, one of the leaders of the Center for the Protection of Women and Children in Pristina, and another friend, Albin, who was one of the student leaders during the days of the nonviolent demonstrations, and then later with the KLA. Finally, we heard that Albin had been beaten and thrown in jail. Sevdija and her husband were beaten, and then Sevdija was raped by a Serbian soldier, who thrust his gun into her most vulnerable parts. I heard her speak about this on the radio, as I was driving to a movie. I had to pull over and simply wait until my sorrow for her rolled through my soul like a tornado.

Connectedness is not something that is put away during the war, it only grows deeper and deeper. I know from having carried messages from Bosnia to Croatia to Serbia that each party felt shame, anger, and guilt, and attributed guilt to those on the opposite side who were being uncommunicative. Is there a way that people of peace can stop running away from conflict, but move closer with our tenacious tenderness and persistent kindness? How can we look for every opportunity to shoulder the burdens and bind the wounds of precious lives, whether those wounds are physical, spiritual, or emotional?

I remember, after the war in Bosnia, friends from all sides talking about the wounds in their sense of humanity. "I have healed my physical body; I am in the process of repairing my house. But the most long-lasting troubles I have, the wounds I can't seem to even touch, are the ones about human nature, trust, and friendship. My teacher, who taught me all about democracy, when the war came, went over to the other side. How can I believe teachers again? How can I ever trust neighbors? Now that I know what humanity is capable of, will I ever feel safe and at peace?"

It may be generations before the hatreds from the various Yugoslavian wars recede. Business, trade, intergovernmental relations all require some degree of trust. In such a small region as the Balkans, one wonders how those bridges can be rebuilt, the threads of different peoples knitted into a new fabric, and how neighbors can live together and trade together once more. Those of us who know this region all have a degree of responsibility for reknitting these people back together again. It will probably be a long time before they choose to join together into one country, as nature has cast them in roles on contiguous land. We know many of the anti-militarist players in this generation, and we can imagine that there will be many more antimilitarists in the next generation. Social wounds are the most debilitating; an injured sense of humanity is crushing.

Musings

Chapter 15
Removing Obstacles To Change

C HANGE HAS always fascinated me. Throughout my life I've tried to understand how change happens and what keeps it from happening. I have observed the dynamics of change in many areas. I have watched myself change personally; my work, my values, and my lifestyle have gone through both sudden and gradual shifts. I have explored the learning and teaching processes, trying to understand how people change their ideas. As a counselor and friend, I have watched people struggle to change aspects of their lives, battling to overcome blocks, addictions to substances and delusions, as well as painful experiences from the past. As a professional change agent, I have learned to help organizations get beyond the obstacles that are holding them back. And as a political activist, I have gathered information about how societies change, how policy decisions affect the citizenry, and vice versa. I have worked at the personal, group, and institutional levels; and at the grassroots, community, national, and international levels.

At this point in my life, my primary interest is in social change, rather than individual change. Even though societies change one person at a time, social change requires very different analytic and strategic processes than personal change. The best social change is very slow, almost imperceptible, so as not to alert the opposition to organize resistance. All too often, organizing work serves to create and solidify resistance.

Over the years, I have become dissatisfied with the assumptions upon which much work for change is based. Between nations, within families, and in social change movements, there seems to be an unconscious assumption that effective change comes from imposing one's ideas upon others. But I have found my work to be far more effective when I start from the premise that the change and strategies appropriate to a situation are embedded in the culture, group, or person involved, waiting to be uncovered.

I do not accept that the assumption that people are naturally apathetic, and that the job of the social change worker is to "motivate" them. I assume that each of us has within us the will to make the world a better place, as well as a longing for stability. We live in the tension between these two drives. But we tend to have many more obstacles to acting on the improvement impulse than to resting in inertia. So in my thinking, I've shifted from the question "what makes people change?" to "what keeps people from changing?"

Most social change organizing focuses on "lack of information" as the key obstacle to change. The logic is that, "if people only knew all the facts," the resulting outcry would set the necessary corrective changes in motion. But I view the lack of information as only one among several kinds of obstacles. As we've seen, one's social context is a powerful force that can inhibit change; unquestioned assumptions about the way the world works can keep us from noticing the harmful consequences of the status quo. And, as the following stories show, some obstacles to working for change may be emotionally based.

In the 1980s, a good friend of mine was, from all outward appearances, apathetic about the threat of nuclear war. Although she had been actively involved in civil rights and housing issues, and she recycled cans and bottles, she consistently avoided the nuclear issue. When we invited her to our nuclear comedy show, or when her son wanted her to see a nuclear film, she found reasons why she couldn't go. She had a cold, she'd lost her umbrella, her favorite basketball team was playing, she was too busy with errands. I found it tempting to think of her as not caring. One time, because of my personal relationship with her, she did volunteer to do some promotional work for our comedy show, but found she just couldn't get going on the tasks. This baffled me. I'd worked with her before and had known her to be reliable and conscientious. At this point, I could either assume that she was becoming lazy and irresponsible, or that there was some obstacle in her way.

In talking with her, I suggested that her difficulties might have something to do with her feelings about nuclear war. She froze. She started shaking, and I saw sweat break out on her upper lip. After a few moments, she told me about a childhood experience that had terrified her. During World War II, her city had blackout drills at night — every building turned off all the lights, so that the city would not be visible to potential enemy planes overhead. She was terrified of the dark, but had to endure it. Every time she tried to face the nuclear issue, she was reminded of this terrifying experience. The pain was so intense that she desperately tried to shield herself from the issue. That was the nature of her "apathy."

In the face of terrible forces or bullying leaders, some people understandably, but mistakenly, fall silent. I am sure in some part of their mind they are working on alternative strategies to silence, but this has minimal benefit to society. We all have our intimate lives, as well as our public lives as citizens. There is the small *l* love we have for our family and dear friends; there is also the large *l* love, toward humanity, our country, and the earth. To focus only on the personal to the neglect of our civic responsibilities leaves the public dialogue to those willing to scream hatred on talk radio, those who have something to gain, those making demands, and the cynics who think no one cares anyway. Participation is the key to democracy.

How do we create a nurturing public sphere? How can the large love be activated without manipulation toward nationalism? How can our public lives and dialogue be more engaging and civil?

As the war in the former Yugoslavia began, and savage acts of violence and slaughter began to appear on our television screens, I, like many other activists, found my imagination frozen. "Oh, another genocide in Europe!" It was as if all the Holocaust museums, all the books about how lethargic the world was about the Nazi genocide, kept us from action in this new moment of terror. So many people had said "Never again!" But now, faced with evidence of possible genocide in the Balkans, the social environment produced no ideas for action. It was not possible to find reliable groups that were willing to put aside their already full and funded agendas to take up working on this important issue. As if frozen in the oncoming headlights of a catastrophe, the obstacles to change became clear.

Some apologists for the do-nothing camp in government put forward the analysis that "these people have been fighting for centuries." The truth is that they have fought external enemies more than each other. People were very slow to act; what if the war did not develop, or later stopped as quickly as many people assumed it would? The impulse to do something was strong, but few people had ideas of what was appropriate to do. I felt the same way. I was willing to do whatever I could think of, but I could think of nothing. Horror can overwhelm the ability to think creatively.

The step that helped activate me was deciding to ask the people most involved what people outside the region could do. Although I didn't realize it at the time, my action plan was consistent with my black lessons, and with my American Willing to Listen project. The work in Yugoslavia started from an awareness of my limitations and an openness to ideas from those most involved. While it is surely true that we did not find any magical ideas to stop the war (we didn't really expect to do that), we did find meaningful ways to help, by participating with others in relieving the suffering, supporting antiwar organizations in the region, and informing others about the situation. The obstacle to action for me was thinking that *I* had to have a fully formed idea in order to begin work. Possibly, the work that needed to be done was finding ideas.

During the Vietnam War, I occasionally staffed a literature table in San Francisco for the Downtown Peace Coalition. Our goal was to convince office workers to work against the war. This organization was one of the most effective organizing efforts I have known. From the office, a decision would be made that some leaflet was needed. Bicycle messengers would show up to take the raw material to secretaries, graphic artists, and layout people who had time at their regular work to do a little something for peace that day. A truck would start out at 11 a.m. to distribute tables, chairs, and educational literature to key corners all over downtown. Workers on their lunch break would set up tables, talk to people passing by, and wait until the next shift came to relieve them. At 2 p.m., the truck picked up everything. In the evening, the office was often jammed with people getting off from work, dropping by for meetings, or hanging out and thinking up action plans.

On one occasion, an ordinary-looking guy in a business suit came up to the table I was working that day. He told me that he wouldn't attend our upcoming antiwar rally, because "I get so angry when I hear what they're doing in Vietnam that I'm afraid I'll lose my cool and punch someone."

When we were organizing against nuclear weapons, many friends did nuclear awareness workshops all over the country. These workshops involved going out into neighborhoods and shopping centers to listen to people from all walks of life talk about their feelings about nuclear weapons and the future. Deborah Lubar wrote a moving account of an experience in this exercise. Her task was to find out what people were thinking, rather than trying to convince them of anything. Pad in hand, she introduced herself and asked the following questions: What do you think is the greatest problem facing the world today? What do you consider the chances of nuclear war to be? Do you discuss these concerns with your family, friends, or colleagues? What do you think would make our country safe and strong?

One man, who grudgingly let her into his house, turned hostile when she asked him about nuclear war. He barked, "No, no, no, no! I don't have time for these ridiculous questions." She left, feeling stung by his rudeness. A few minutes later, as she was coming out of another house, there the man stood, with his arms crossed, waiting for her.

"What do you expect me to *do* about it?" he demanded belligerently. "I'm sorry I threw you out of my house, but what in hell do you expect me to do about it? For God's sake, what do you want?" They went for a walk. He pelted her with questions about her survey, and about nuclear war, deterrence, and defense policy. Finally, he shook her hand and walked away.

The next morning, Deborah followed an impulse and went back to the man's house. She felt like a fool — what excuse could she give for returning? After several moments, she went to the door. The man answered, surprised but glad to see her. He told her that he'd had a horrible night, sweating through nightmares about nuclear war. He recounted his dreams in vivid detail. When she leaned over to touch his hand, he started to weep. After a while, his sadness gave way to rage at his sense of helplessness as a human being on a planet headed for disaster. He bashed his fist on the table and shouted, "What a world! It's a misery and a burden to be a human being."

"That moment was agony for me," Deborah said. She wanted to assure him that there was another side, that human beings do have the power to change the situation. "But I knew enough to keep still. Who was I to tell him such a thing? Although what he had said was only *part* of the truth, it was part of the truth. His rage was just; I had no right to argue with its power."

They talked of many things, until the man realized he was late for work. At the door, he took her hands, and they looked each other straight in the eye. "What we learned of one another that morning," wrote Deborah, "was profoundly intimate, and yet it had only to do with our common bond as two human beings groping in the dark to confront and move through the difficult times we live in."

I've had experiences similar to Deborah's, though none as dramatic. Her story helps me see people's anger and pain as expressions of deep caring, rather than of *not* caring. Could it be that some of what looks like apathy is actually the fear of caring too much? The taboo against talking about nuclear war and other painful issues has created chasms between people, and has kept us from sharing some of the deepest parts of our human experience. Isolation from others in the civil society is one of the biggest obstacles to action.

Politics that must avoid those issues has delusion at its core, and is less involving and powerful. Listening openheartedly and asking opening questions can unlock the areas that have been tightly bolted shut by fear and social pressures.

Deborah's story also helps me remember that outbursts of anger that appear to be directed at the person bringing up a painful subject may really reflect anger about the subject itself. (This is true of other strong feelings as well.) Listening to the outburst, not taking it personally, can help the other person move through it.

It was important that when the man kicked her out, Deborah didn't challenge him, didn't push him beyond where he was willing to go. She let him stay in control, she withdrew, but she did not give up on him. Often, we create resistance by pushing people toward our point of view, thus showing a lack of respect for the other person's ability to find her own way. So much of the way politics is usually practiced creates resistance to our goals. Are our opinions so precious to us that we would sacrifice respect for the other person's intelligence? Are we so arrogant as to think that our schools of thought have the future path completely figured out? Our opinions and political positions are important, but not the most important part of us. More important is relationship. The way we carry our politics and identity can be an obstacle to change for another person, and can interfere with communication and the development of community.

It can be difficult to determine when someone is stuck because of an emotional obstacle, but I am learning to recognize signals in others and myself. People may get giddy, focus all their attention on minute details or semantics, get angry, avoid the issue, or seem to go numb — it's as if our emotions have scrambled our brain. We start grasping at straws — repeating something we heard on a talk show, or in school, or at the bridge club. For activists, the flailing in the face of fear often creates ungrounded and unsustainable projects. It's no use trying to convince another person to abandon a position that is held in place by fear, anger, or hopelessness. Fear has been the main horse that political activists have been riding for so long that people are full of fear messages.

A group of environmentalists once asked me to help them with strategy. They had been fighting the damming of California's Stanislaus River for seven or eight years. Most active in the organization were the rafters, who spent summers and weekends on the river. Certain spots were particularly beloved by them. They told me about an old fig tree that had given them shade and juicy figs for years.

The river activists were a passionate bunch. Even after the dam had been constructed, they had lobbied, canvassed, and worked through legal channels to keep it from being put into operation. A friend of mine who worked with the group, Mark Dubois, had chained himself to a boulder in the area that was to be flooded. Journalists were blindfolded so they could not tell anyone how to find Mark and taken to see that, indeed, he was in a position where he would have drowned if the area had been flooded.

In spite of the activists' work, the back-river area was partially flooded. Now, the rafters wanted to prevent the full flooding, but they were finding it impossible to think of strategies. And the more they berated one another for their paralysis, the more hopeless they became.

Talking with the group, I found that none of them had been to the river since the partial flooding had begun. They knew the area that had been flooded. Their old friend, the fig tree, was under water. But even talking about the fig tree was too painful.

I began to understand why they couldn't come up with strategies. By denying their feelings of disappointment in the face of defeat, they had gotten stuck. I sensed that they had to acknowledge and explore their pain in order to go forward. So, following the consultation, some of the rafters went back to the river. They saw the areas that were under water and those that were still intact, and they said good-bye to the fig tree. Gradually, their energy returned; new strategies began to occur to them.

A student of mine in Australia was high up in the local police department, which was undergoing a restructuring. They had done a thorough analysis of what was "wrong with us," and now were ready to redesign their organization. At each meeting, they reviewed what was wrong with them; then, from that position, they tried to envision how they wanted things to change.

Their self-deprecation did not create positive movement. My student reported that when they started the meetings with how they wanted things to change, and what positive alternatives they could envision to create that work environment, the discussion was livelier and more work got done. Then, they asked questions like: How would we like it to be? What will it take to get our work life the way we want it to be? How can we make these changes?

Emotional obstacles contain valuable information for the change agent. Many people are too scared, too angry, too sad to do anything. They get stuck. When we find a way around these obstacles, we gather information for a larger campaign to reach many others and help them around those same obstacles. Through leaflets, speeches, action plans, banners, and signs, we can speak to those obstacles. The language and logic that help one person begin to awaken his creativity and move toward action is useful in creating campaigns, literature, and strategy. Those who seem most hopelessly stuck in emotional obstacles could, upon getting beyond them, make important contributions to the work for change. Who could take a more powerful stand against nuclear terror than someone who has known the deep fear of bombs? Who can speak better against an outrageous war than someone outraged by it?

Painful emotions not only can keep us from working for change, they can also make the work we do less effective. They can keep us from thinking of fresh alternatives that would allow the removal of obstacles. Our best work is inspired by noble and natural feelings, like love for our children; concern for the future of our country, or the health of the environment; love of living in peace; outrage at injustice and suffering. But harping on one's fear of war or screaming one's outrage at injustice will not necessarily be effective in bringing about change. It's important to accept and honor our feelings, but not necessarily by confronting our adversaries. Our goal is to be effective at generating change, not getting our rocks off. Working for social change is not therapy.

In Kosova/o in the former Yugoslavia, conditions were very grim in 1995, when we began working there. Day after day, Serb police entered Albanian homes, tortured and killed people, and stole from Albanians on the street. The Albanians had no legal recourse.

We went to visit Adem Demaci in his office at the Center for Human Rights. After more than twenty years in jail for his political work, Adem had an interesting strategy. Each day, those who had been beaten came to his office to give testimony, and have their wounds photographed for the records of abuse. Notebooks containing photographs and descriptions of the abuse lined his office walls.

He wanted to show us the documentation of the many cases of torture. Page after page showed dead and mutilated bodies, bruises, and wounds — people who had fallen in front of the machine of fascism. For us, feelings at the moment were strong. Of course, tears came to my eyes.

Finally, in 1997, word came that people who went into Demaci's center were being further tortured and harassed for having gone there.

Did this stop the gathering of information? No. Now, though, the reporters went to the people in their homes and hospital beds to get the reports. They were steady in their strategy and systematic in their reporting. They did what they believed would be effective in the long run. I can only imagine the emotional needs of those gathering the information for the books. I hope they got plenty of chance to honor and explore the feelings that must have arisen in the course of their work.

Amnesty International has found that the most powerful way to communicate is with cool language, not hot, inflammatory language, when talking about torture. The mind is already overwhelmed hearing about torture and cannot think of creative ideas of what to do. Hot language only hardens the inability to come up with action responses. When you want action in an overwhelming situation, it is best to do everything you can to communicate in a way that allows people to keep thinking.

Helplessness is one of the hardest emotions for social change workers to cope with. We cannot come in and "save the day," nor can we pretend we have not seen what we have seen. We can do what we can: what our partners on the scene ask us to do, as well as acting on those ideas that come to us. Often, I have seen people who feel terrible about a situation say how they will work to make things better. Promises made in the moment of feelings of helplessness are often exaggerations of what is really possible. It is better to sit with those feelings a few days, do some checking with others, and make an offer; then, simply do the job that needs to be done. It is better to produce more than expected, than to create unrealistic expectations. If you are not in an emergency, allowing the suffering to ripen in your soul is an essential component of appropriate action. Your feet move most determinedly when your head and heart are both engaged.

A sense of urgency can also impair our effectiveness. We feel we must do something, because something must be done, not because we know what is really appropriate to the situation. Working from a sense of urgency for protracted periods of time does not bode well for long-term social change workers. Of course, the drama and sense of significance added to one's little life when working on VERY IMPORTANT ISSUES is a real rush, but long-term, we need to take care of ourselves, our families, and those things that we tend to ignore when working from a sense of urgency. We need to rest, to have time to reflect and dream. Sometimes, things are simply too important to be done in a rush. Sustainable work habits are important.

Of course, action is absolutely necessary when we are confronted by a problem or condition that causes suffering in the moment. We carry a terrible guilt if we have walked away from a job that, had it been done, stood a chance of making a difference in reducing suffering. In that moment, it is better to act.

Stewart Brand was driving by the Marina in San Francisco when the 1989 earthquake occurred. He noticed there were several needs in the emergency: people were buried, fires were raging. Many people were standing around in shock, not knowing what to do. When one person stepped forward (self-commissioned) and started doing what needed to be done, others followed this model of action and took on jobs. When a self-anointed leader started asking people to take on specific tasks, actions began to happen. Brand suggests in *Whole Earth Review* (fall 1990):

> Right after an earthquake (read any disaster, social or physical) nobody's in charge. You self-start or nothing happens… Give people who are trapped all the information you've got, and enlist their help. Treat them not as helpless victims but as an exceptionally motivated part of the rescue team… Join a team or start a team. Divide up the tasks. Encourage leadership to emerge. Most action in a disaster is imitative. Most effective leadership is by example. Bystanders make the convenient assumption that everything is being taken care of by the people already helping. That's seldom accurate. If you want to help, ask! If you want to be helped, ask! Volunteers are always uncertain whether they're doing the right thing. They need encouragement — from professionals, from other volunteers, from passers-by.

People standing by inactive in a situation involving suffering are a monumental obstacle to the occurrence of change. Standing doing nothing becomes the standard of what should be done. When we started our work in the former Yugoslavia, we saw few individuals or groups building bridges from the US, but within a few years we found many Americans working in the region. There are many reasons to take action in major social disasters, but surely one is that by working for justice, you provide a model for others to become activated. But the most significant reason is for your own health and that of the situation.

One of the major obstacles to change is self-interest. Sometimes, a change may be seen as challenging economic interests, or threatening an individual's power or ego. For a change to occur, most often someone's vested interest in the status quo is going to be affected. Over the last twenty years, we have seen the attachment to self-interest, as expressed in commercial interest, grow and become stronger than community interest for the common good. So many aspects of each situation seem tied up in self-interest, everyone invested in her own economic interest. Not only the businesses involved in an issue, but also the staffs of the NGOs working in a situation have an economic interest in the outcome.

When we worked on issues related to clear-cutting of forests, we saw that three groups were adversely affected: the loggers, the owners of logging companies, and all the community services that depended upon the health of the logging economy. In doing a multilevel strategy analysis, we asked, "What would it take for each sector to change?" Our goal was not to shut down the logging industry (we still need wood to build houses), but rather to set it on a path to long-term sustainable logging practices. We had seen the logging company in a neighboring community clear out all the trees in a particular locale, then put the loggers in the unemployment line.

When we explored the creation of job-retraining alternatives, we found that the loggers' obstacles to change were somewhat lessened. The company owners, however, were a different story. They knew that the most efficient short-term practice — clear-cutting — offered the quickest profit. The owners had not lived in the community and had little attachment to the aspects of life threatened by clear-cutting: fewer salmon due to soil coming into the streams; water pollution and soil erosion; as well as the resulting ugliness, which affected the tourism industry.

To work toward a mutually beneficial outcome, we needed to explore tax alternatives, alternative ways of making a profit, and concepts of long-term profit to replace short-term cut-and-run logging practices. "What would it take for your company to stop clear-cutting?" we asked.

Often, the company needs to see that to avoid a loss, either in the form of bad publicity or a boycott, a new way of thinking about profit is needed. Greed is not immutable.

One important use of government is to keep the cost of a social necessity from falling on one sector. What is for the common good should be borne by the common fund. Often, citizens must define the political necessity of pulling community resources and/or government into solving problems. First, though, we must know what is necessary for change to come about; we must co-create the solution with all parties concerned, keeping in mind the need for a win/win resolution where possible.

Another obstacle to effective change is the desire to be right, or at least to be seen as being right by one's friends and community. This is most dangerous, especially for community workers or the people working for NGOs. You can either be right or be effective. You must choose. The immature ego's attachment to being right interferes with relationships on all sides of an issue, and cripples development of a community of mutual respect. This attitude works against co-creation of a plan that meets many needs and incorporates joint–problem solving.

At a fancy dinner one night in Boston, I sat next to a lawyer who had been one of the experts in putting together deals for nuclear power plants. I did not hide my position on nuclear power, and he said reluctantly that he now agreed with my position. I was fascinated. "What caused you to change your position?" I asked. He replied, "Year after year, people explained their position. Finally, the longevity of their work convinced me that they were not working from ulterior motives. I had previously thought that the opposition was funded by oil interests or Communists. But over time, I became convinced that they were genuine Americans who were who they said they were. They were working in the interests of their community. When I finally realized this, I felt a little embarrassed at how I had made a living all that time."

It is rare that a person changes her mind about the viability of a technology or development idea while earning a living from that technology's implementation. Often, it is the *retired* general who is able to articulate the critical voice that had to be silent while in active service. Our organizing should always enable whistle blowers to come to organizers and discuss the ambiguity of what they know. No one knows better than the people working for a nuclear power station or sewage plant how many errors in design or implementation there are. In cleaning the Ganges, there are people working with the government who are secretly leaking documents to us, telling us of the construction errors, mistakes in press releases. At Diablo Canyon Nuclear Power Plant, a major development involved an engineer in the plant coming out with information that brackets had been installed backwards. If we are accessible to people, such connections can be made.

The strongest resistance to change may be aroused when we are faced with new ideas or information. The time between the awareness of an old idea's inadequacy and the finding of a more satisfactory idea is a time of tension. For some people, that tension is unbearable. How could they have been so foolish as to believe something that is not the best answer?

In order to understand social change, it is important to watch the movement of ideas. When the public began to understand that perfection was not really possible in any technology, nuclear power was doomed. Charlie and I noticed the rapid spread of the Hundredth Monkey story, where a few monkeys on separate islands figured out how to remove sand from their food, and "magically" monkeys all over the world had this discovery in their repertoire. Even though the theory has been proven fallacious, it was a global metaphor that built confidence in the antinuclear movement. Another factoid, which serves the same need to have hope, though one's group is in the minority, is that "only 10 percent of the population supported the American Revolution." An important obstacle that needs to be overcome is the idea that change is impossible until you have a large movement.

The analogy of tectonic plates helps me envision the change process in massive populations. Tectonic plates are bodies of earth floating on liquid close to the center of the earth. All the earth's continents were once connected, and over millions of years, these landmasses have slowly moved into their present positions. Many forces continue to act upon these huge tectonic plates — forces of motion and of resistance — often in several directions simultaneously. Nevada, for example, is moving away from California at a very slow pace — about the length of a flashlight battery every nine years.

Social groups, subgroups, cultures, or nations can be seen in a similar way — as large tectonic plates, slowly moving through history in one direction or another. Understanding the forces moving those bodies of shared understanding, language, and culture, as well as the logic they hold, helps us to remove the obstacles to their movement, as well as figure out how to lend energy to the forces pushing them in a particular direction.

The future will be some combination of all the forces not yet visible to us. Sometimes you have to push, sometimes you have to grease the surface in the direction you want to go. And sometimes, it is important to get the obstacles out from in front of the plate, so it can move unimpeded in the direction you wish. And frankly, sometimes you have to sit in the road in front of the moving plate, thus becoming an obstacle to be dealt with. An ancestor of mine invented a logging implement, now called a peavey, used to break up logjams. I often wish there were such an implement we could use to get the tectonic plates moving when they get stuck.

Resistance is an organic part of the change process. When I first heard the idea that the United States should get its troops out of Vietnam, I resisted it. And at first, I refused to believe the reports that our food was contaminated with pesticides. Gradually, as I gathered and reflected on more information, I came to believe both these ideas. Although I have changed my ideas many times, I still have difficulty not resisting new ones.

Living in California in the 1990s, I'm constantly confronted with new ideas: reincarnation, acupuncture, divine light healing, visitations of space people, prosperity training, burning hollow candles in your ears to clean them, or the one where you put food in your bellybutton, and hold your arm out, testing the muscle. (If you can resist someone's pushing your arm down, the food's supposed to be good for you.) Many of these ideas are inconsistent with my scientific training, my Idaho background, and what I have always thought of as my good common sense. Yet, some of these strange practices I engage in, while some are still too great a stretch. I leave it to your imagination to figure out which is which. My mind boggles as the new idea comes in. How could an intelligent person whom I care about be suggesting such silly, outlandish things? A sheepish grin comes over me; I begin to chuckle inside. I know I'm not supposed to laugh out loud, because this dear person is serious, but waves of silliness come over me as my old ideas slip and fall on the banana peel of a new idea.

I've surely carried more than my share of wild ideas into other people's lives: laughing about nuclear war; raising chickens in my backyard in San Francisco; going to the former Yugoslavia to find out what people outside could do to help; shaving my head just for the fun of it every nine years; building a park with street people; working on a campaign to promote the protection of boys, so they do not have to become easy pickings for the military.

I've noticed that some people tend to accept new ideas readily, while others are more cautious. Those who offer some resistance are often likely to work hardest for the implementation of an idea once they accept it; whereas the person who easily changes may be less committed, and may revert to the old position at a later time.

I have come to think that it is important to sit on my own new ideas for a while before putting them out to the slings and arrows of others. Even if others are wildly enthusiastic about the idea, their reaction may skew the idea from its inherent wholeness. The first time I explain an idea is almost always a rough time.

Change theorist Everett Rogers divides people into five categories: innovators, early adapters, early majority, late majority, and laggards. Innovators, a small percentage of any group, are the designers of new ideas.

Haven't you ever wondered why people pushing for a change are a little strange or different from most people? At the old Playland in San Francisco, there used to be a vibrating round plate nearly filled with marbles. Most marbles stayed in the middle, but a few floated around the outer edge. They are the loose marbles, and from their vantagepoint, they can perceive the whole better than those in any other position. They seem to have less holding them to the comfort of the middle, so they roam around looking for something that will offer them some comfort. Those people are already considered different, and have less to lose by taking risks and challenging the norm.

Early adapters are closer to the mainstream of the culture; they act as the conduit carrying the new ideas to others. Those in the early and late majority are progressively more skeptical, tending to value stability over change. The laggards are the most critical of new ideas, and the most resistant to change; I think of them as chronically terrified. But without the late majority and the laggards, we might career into every new idea full tilt. The questions posed by the late majority and the laggards are important to attend to, and to answer respectfully. In an organization, it is sometimes necessary to act without full agreement from later adopter groups. Their resistance is important to the process, and to testing and strengthening the innovation. But to the degree that the laggards are not involved in the process, the organization suffers from disunity.

You can't tell who's in which category by outward appearances, but there tend to be patterns in the ways individuals react to new ideas. One can sometimes predict an individual's response and introduce a new idea accordingly. People do react slightly differently, influenced by factors such as their sense of security, their economic interest, the nature of a new idea, and how it's presented and by whom.

It's interesting to watch people reject ideas. I've come to see resistance as a valuable component of the change process, not merely an obstacle to overcome. It helps me test ideas and see some of their weaknesses.

Sometimes, I can get a sense of the power of an idea based on the force people put into resisting it. When I first met Mahantji and suggested that the Ganga River could be cleaned, his resistance was absolute. I saw no crack in his fatalism, and yet the river, combined with Mahantji's moral courage, found a way for him to pick up the challenge. The deep hopelessness I sensed in him gave me a clue about how powerfully this change might affect the Indian people. To make progress in this seemingly hopeless task would radically expand the boundaries of what they considered possible. When he first approached me to help him, my small sense of myself offered substantial resistance. The degree of my own resistance showed me how powerfully my identity needed to expand to meet the world knocking at the door of my heart.

It is not only my "Idaho optimism" that makes me assume people have an internal drive for improvement that balances their self-interest. I believe that the need for community and common good is in all of our self-interest. Some think of the glass as half-full, and some think of it as half-empty; I ask myself what I can do to get some more clean water in the glass. This stance of action toward the positive direction is practical as well as dynamic. It has served me in many different situations.

One year, I worked as a designated change agent for the San Francisco School District. I was assigned to an innovative school, Everett Middle School, which was implementing a learning center system. Among the teachers the principal asked me to work with were some he considered "major problems." Although I had my own ideas about what these teachers needed to change in order to better serve the learning needs of the children, I put those ideas aside and asked each teacher, "What do you want to improve about your teaching?"

I was surprised that, for the most part, the teachers wanted to improve in the same areas that the principal and I saw as weaknesses. One teacher wanted to keep from venting her anger at the students. Another eventually confided to me that he wanted to stop coming to school drunk. Others wanted new ideas for getting students to work together cooperatively; some wanted help with specific instructional techniques. I had established myself as their ally, which allowed us to work together on their goals. Had I come to them insisting on the changes on my list, it is likely they would have defended themselves against my criticisms. It would have been more difficult for them to change, because of their natural resistance. One of my favorite memories from that time was a teacher asking, "Why do we have to change this year, when we changed last year?"

At Sixth Street Park, we began with the assumption that the street people wanted a park that would work beautifully for everyone involved. Some people feared that if we built a park for street people, they would turn it into a pigsty. Had we operated on that fear, we would have designed the park defensively. We would have put fences around all the trees. We wouldn't have given staff members keys to the toolshed. The park would have been completely paved, to make it less vulnerable to vandalism.

Instead, we created a place that expressed confidence in the park users, a place of beauty and utility. We built benches wide enough for people to sleep on. They themselves asked for trash cans as their first request; it was their highest priority. It's true that some of the trees and the watering system didn't survive. We viewed that as part of the cost of our education. But in general, the park remained well cared for.

In the campaign to clean Ganga, we could assume that the people of Varanasi pollute their river because they fundamentally don't care about it. Based on that assumption, we might try to cajole, shock, or otherwise manipulate them into becoming concerned. Instead, we assume that most people do care, or would care if they were awakened to the real condition of the river; that the plight of the river already causes them pain, either consciously or unconsciously; and that they would like to do something to help improve the situation.

The "whole truth" is that a part of each of us says, "Ganga must be cleaned," and another part has found a way to live with the pollution on a day-to-day basis. So the change agent's task, as an ally of the river, is to acknowledge the latter, while building a campaign based on the former.

Facilitating the change process is like a group sculpting a block of wood. Although we who envision the change may have images of the results we want, we do not have control; there are other carvers, and there is interplay with the wood and its essential nature. Our primary task as change agents is to "raise the grain" of the material we're working with, so that we can work with what is already in the situation, and uncover the ideas and symbols that will contribute to the change strategy. There is a word in Hindi that expresses raising the grain on a collective level: *sunculp*, determination or will, held not individually but collectively.

In this process of raising the grain, or finding sunculp, listening and questioning are key activities. As a listener, it is important to give people an opportunity to explore an issue openly, and to focus on the aspects that are unresolved or painful to them; to find their hopes and visions of how the situation could be different. This allows ideas to emerge that can become the seeds of strategy. Most people have social dreams as well as personal dreams. Social dreams are often very intimate and are rarely shared, because to do so would expose how much we care. Talking together about those social visions as well as how to create them helps develop sunculp.

The quality of the results is directly affected by the nature of the questions. Open-ended, nonjudgmental questions are most likely to open up new avenues. "Where are the women?" for example, is a much more appropriate question than, "Don't you think you should have women in this campaign?" or, "What's the matter with these women that they don't get involved?"

When I began the work in India, since I had little experience cleaning up rivers, I had few strategies to suggest. Albert Einstein had said, "The Atom bomb has changed everything save our way of thinking." I had begun thinking about how to change my way of thinking. How could I think more openly, less defensively, and more creatively, considering many alternatives? How could I find fresh strategies for change, rather than trying to impose old strategies that may have been more appropriate for another moment? So I started thinking about what I have come to call "strategic questioning."

I was looking for the strategies in the culture of that place that would illuminate the various resistances to change, as well as the strategies imbedded in the place. I began by building a series of questions, starting with how the Indians saw the problem themselves. (See chapter 10.) I listened very carefully to how they explained to themselves what they saw. Essentially, I was looking at the logic of their thinking as well as their language. I was looking at their cultural wiring around the river, as well as how they thought about social change. As people articulate their reasoning, they may also discover how much they care. When people are listened to, they also listen to themselves.

I couldn't say, "Oh, I see the river's polluted." In the context of India, it would be a cultural insult, and would only indicate my ignorance; the Indians would stop listening. So I had to find out how they explained the pollution to themselves.

Over and over again, I heard something like, "The river is holy, but she is not pure. We are not taking care of her the way she needs us to." The funny thing is that, after hearing this, I noticed that I started to personally think less in terms of "pollution" and more in terms of "people not taking care of the river."

This shift was an important change of perspective for me. Pollution is an abstraction that avoids addressing the responsibility of the people who are making the mess — by focusing the attention solely on the river. It is almost as if the river is to blame for being polluted! The Indians did not talk with each other at that time about their perceptions of the river, except in the most glorious ways. In such a situation, the symbolic load is so great that to talk about what you really think may seem sacrilegious or crazy to others.

I needed to understand their change view — how they expected change to happen, what kinds of strategies they had confidence in. For the Indians I spoke with over the age of forty, no social change could compare with the liberation of their country from the British, and this affected their views on how change happens. In many ways, they are still in the process of getting rid of ideas and ways of doing things left over from the days of British rule. When I asked how that change had come about, I heard many strategies for change — satyagraha, fasting, direct action, pressuring civic leaders, citizens' assemblies, marches, sacrifice — stories of change that are embedded in that culture. These also became the strategies they were willing to use to clean their holy river. I would then ask, "What would you like to do to clean the river?" They would then think further, applying their change view to this specific situation.

People need to come up with their own answers, appropriate for this moment. Questions and listening can catalyze this process. Don't be disappointed if a great question does not have an answer right way. A very powerful question may not have an answer at the moment it is asked. It may sit rattling in the mind for days or weeks as the mind works on an answer. If the seed is planted, the answer will grow. Questions are alive! They can remove resistance to thinking in fresh new ways. But take care not to ask manipulative questions, as that is simply the old domination game, and will only further disempower the person being questioned.

We have been taught to ask questions where we anticipate the answers that are known. But it seems we need new answers for this time. Because many cultures think in binary ways, we often ask yes-no questions, or questions that concern two alternatives, rather than opening the mind up to many alternatives. When the question is "What would you like to do to help the river?" we assume action and positive action possibilities on the part of the person we are questioning.

Finally, questioning can challenge passivity. In the midst of listening to complaining, a question like "What can we do to change the situation?" has possibilities for action. The way we think is probably the largest obstacle to change. "What can we do?" "What will it take?" Listening carefully — to others and to ourselves — for answers is the key.

In Lismore, Australia, a group of candidates for city councilor used elements of listening as a campaign strategy. Lyn Carson reports in her Ph.D. thesis on strategic questioning: "During the 1991 election campaign, we tried a method of community consultation with which none of us had previous experience: Listening Posts. We selected a busy corner in the Lismore central business district and sat beneath our own sign: Candidate Willing to Listen. We felt quite foolish and anticipated that people would pass us by, sniggering. Certainly that occurred, but many others stopped. They were curious and many wanted to speak. They were angered by Council's activities. They were frustrated by Council's inactivity. They wanted to know what we would do if elected. We tried as much as possible to encourage them to speak and to avoid 'election promises' or allowing our own egos to surface. I realized the difficulty of really listening to others, particularly when they were angry or cynical."

Listening is not the same as silence. It does not imply that as a listener, I lack clear ideas or opinions of my own. In fact, the clearer I am about my own perspective, the less I need constant confirmation of it from others. My opinions and identity come with me, but I can choose not to pay attention to them. I can put them in my pocket for a time, in order to facilitate the exploration of another person's path to change. When my goal is to give the other person an opportunity to explore an issue, inserting my opinions is usually inappropriate. To do so would change the dialogue; the person I'm listening to would react to my views, either by saying things they would expect me to agree with, or those that might provoke me.

When listening, I adopt the attitude of a flashlight: I am trying to shine light into the fascinating cave of the other person, rather than trying to poke holes in her argument, or find brilliant ways of presenting my point of view. When asked for my opinion or ideas, I try to offer them lightly, not to persuade but to encourage further dialogue. In this moment, we are two people looking together for the way out of difficulties. I will hold the flashlight for a while. The unexpected consequence of adopting this attitude is that I see my own ideas shift, and I get new ideas.

Some interesting experiments using these techniques were undertaken by "citizen diplomacy" projects in several countries. One group doing such work in the mid 1980s was the small US-based Mo Tzu Project (named after a Chinese peacemaker of the fifth century B.C.E.). Members traveled to an area of conflict and met one-on-one with members of the parties to the conflict, asking them to explain the situation as they saw it. Taking the stance of impartial but concerned outsiders, they listened patiently and attentively, often enduring passionate speeches about the righteousness of a particular cause. They asked open-ended questions. The goal of such listening was to get beyond the ideology and pat answers into fresh dialogue, where new answers could be synthesized.

To a Palestinian leader in the early 1980s, they posed the question: "Under what circumstances would the PLO recognize Israel?" To an Israeli: "What would enable the Israeli government to agree to a Palestinian homeland?" When the disputants felt that their ideological position was sufficiently understood, they were sometimes able to explore these issues creatively, to acknowledge doubts they had about their own position, and to give voice to new ideas. Intelligent people know ambiguity in their positions, and they long to explore the ambiguities if they are secure enough. Articulating one's own questions and insecurities encourages the creation of new ideas, as well as increasing the will and energy to work.

The interviewers created a relatively neutral social environment — one in which closed questions could be reopened and new possibilities considered. The aim was to discover complementarity in the positions of the conflicting parties. Recognizing this, the parties became less righteous, belligerent, and defensive. Bob Fuller, one of the pioneering Mo Tzu interviewers, wrote: "Our goal is to look together for at least a theoretical solution — one which would leave all parties with their self-respect, and each with a sense that they own a piece of the truth, while glimpsing the possibility of owning a larger truth by incorporating that of the other side." Even after the interviewers had left, the sense of new possibilities remained with the disputants.

I worked with Mo Tzu for a while, and I know that one of the frustrations of such listening work is that the results can never be conclusively ascertained. "We are constantly aware of how small our contribution is relative to the size and seriousness of the problems in which we're immersed," Bob says. "But it's like throwing a stone into a lake: you don't see the water level rise, but you know the stone is sitting at the bottom, so you conclude that the water level must have risen. When we have done well by a situation, we sense that the water level has risen."

I once heard a story about how Tibetan Buddhists handle ghosts, and it is a metaphor for social change for me. If a family or village is having a problem, such as an onslaught of grasshoppers, or illness, or too much bickering, then the local monastery is asked to send a lama to get rid of the ghost who is causing these problems. The lama comes to the village and goes from house to house listening to people talk about everything that has been going on, listening to the most unrelated information, listening beyond the point when an ordinary person would stop listening. And still, he listens more.

When everyone has been heard, the lama goes back to the monastery, thinks about what he has heard, the people and their stories, and weaves a ghost trap out of yarn and sticks. The trap is made of triangles similar to Mexican god's eyes, except they are three-dimensional. He makes one large trap — occasionally as large as six feet — and some smaller traps. At the end of each structural part of the large trap, he attaches a little ball of white cotton. Finally, he makes some little doors out of flat pieces of wood. Now, he is ready to go back to the village and trap the ghost.

The lama finds an appropriate crossroads, makes a mound of mud, and sticks the trap upright into the mound. Around the large trap, he places the small traps and doors in a circle. The theory is that the ghost comes along the road and is a bit distracted by the crossroads. He sees the doors (ghosts evidently love to sneak around closed doors) and, avoiding the little traps, gets stuck in the large one. Meanwhile, the lama has been sitting nearby praying and meditating, and he comes out every now and then to pinch the little cotton balls. When they are wet, he knows that the ghost is trapped. He plucks the trap out of the ground, carries it to a cliff, and flings it over. Now, according to the belief, the ghost has been removed, and life will return to normal.

Since I first heard this story, it has seemed strikingly similar to some of my ideas about how to make social change. What interests me is not the building of the ghost trap, but the transforming nature of the lama's listening.

As a change agent, I can identify with the lama. I begin my work by interviewing everyone involved. I try to look at the problem in its relationship to the entire social environment, paying attention even to those elements that may not seem directly relevant. I let the information I gather occupy me fully. What are the impulses to make change, and what is the nature of the internal resistance? What are the obstacles to change, and how could they be moved? Then I reflect on my understanding of history and innovation theory. I also examine my dreams, idle musings, and common-sense hunches. It is only after this period of examination and contemplation that I "weave" my recommendations for strategy.

I have always wondered what would happen if I didn't return with recommendations for the organization. What would be the effect of the deep listening alone? Might the necessary changes occur as a result of the consultation process alone?

No work has been more fulfilling to me than helping other people remove obstacles in their path to change. From San Francisco schoolteachers to people on the banks of Ganga, to the Earth Summit in Rio, to the streets of the former Yugoslavia, I have seen the human will to improve, to make our lives and our world more congruent with our ideals, and more responsive to the needs of life. I know the pain that comes from not being able to translate this will into reality.

Removing obstacles is an attitude that makes nonviolent social change more possible. I am intrigued by and support the trend toward nonviolence in social change work. Having done much of the nonviolence training on the West Coast during the antiwar days, I agree very much with Hafsat Abiola, a Nigerian activist for democracy and human rights, when she says, "I don't want violent strategies in order to free my people, because that isn't really change. Real change will be the elimination of violence, to my people, to my land."

Chapter 16

The Power of Context

A FTER A MONTH on the job as a teacher at Roosevelt Junior High school, I was given a whistle by the principal. Between classes, I was to leave my classroom and go to a yellow circle painted on the floor in the hall. This was my position. I was expected to stand on the circle, blow my whistle, and yell at the students. In retrospect, I'm embarrassed that I, a mature adult, participated in something so silly. But the activity was part of the generally accepted behavior, and I was among those who accepted it.

Had I stopped to think about it, I might have realized that all my noise and authoritarian behavior not only increased the disorder in the hallway, but was also contrary to my personal values and educational philosophy. Instead, I acted in accordance with the expectation of those in charge of my social context.

Each of us is under constant pressure to conform to social norms; we get signals from people around us about which ideas, activities, and changes are appropriate to consider and which are not. Our social context directs our attention and gives us cues for our thinking, behavior, and beliefs.

Growing up in Idaho, I was struck by the contradiction between the good Christian values of my parents' rancher friends, and the fact that they provided poor housing and salaries for the Mexican fieldworkers tilling their farms. Since then, I have come to understand some of the social dynamics behind this contradiction. The ranchers were accountable to a narrow context, made up of ranchers and other white landowners. Barriers of race, class, culture, and sometimes language kept Mexican fieldworkers from being a powerful force in this social context, and kept the ranchers from changing. The social and economic relationships rested on each creating a political reality that affected everyone.

A conflict remained for the ranchers between their Christian values ("Do unto others as you would have them do unto you") and their perceived self-interest (wanting to increase their own material well-being). But the ranchers' context did not encourage them to resolve the conflict in favor of their best wishes for their workers. Even when profits were high, it was socially acceptable to continue allowing the fieldworkers to live in shacks on low salaries. The work camp had been built many years before, and the issue was considered closed. Organizing the fieldworkers and bringing the campaign into town, into the churches, could have been the way to affect change. But all the social arrangements in our small town were organized to keep that from happening.

Contextual assumptions are our unconscious filtering system, defining the limits of what we consider possible. Bees have a similar perceptual filter, but in their case it is a physical one. Bees' eyes are composed of hundreds of hexagonal facets; they see the world in hexagons. Is it a coincidence that they build each cell of their homes in the shape of a hexagon? For human beings, our contextual and cultural assumptions determine the shape of what we see and what we create. It's difficult to recognize these assumptions, let alone question them. I've come to believe that even those among us who are more independent-minded can only question about one-third of our contextual assumptions.

Moving into a new context, even temporarily, can shift our assumptions and behavior. For example, in my neighborhood grocery store in San Francisco, it was almost natural for my grandmother to hug my black friend, Deputy. After all, I was the one there who cared most about the way she behaved, and she knew I would want her to be friendly. So she adapted herself, at least for that moment, to this new context. My grandmother would have been much less likely to hug him if she had been accompanied by her husband, her daughter, or a friend from her bridge club back home.

The long-term effect of this encounter on my grandmother's feelings about people different from herself was probably minimal. One such experience rarely fundamentally challenges the whole set of attitudes and behaviors that constitute racism. Unlearning racism, or any attitude that assumes superiority and control, requires making strong and continuing connections with people from whom you are different; and, based on those connections, developing a new view of yourself in relation to others, and of those people in the world. This view will, bit by bit, contradict and eventually override the old prejudices.

When you join in actions that benefit the group you see as getting an unfair bite of the apple, you begin to find yourself standing straighter, feeling less shamefaced about how rotten the world is.

The apple is rotten in places, but when you work in the interest of fairness, you feel better about the entire apple — at least you see the possibility of the rotten parts being in a context that challenges the rottenness.

None of us wants some people in our world to experience only the rottenness of this amazing thing called life. And none of us wants to be so naive as to think that the apple does not have rotten, smelly parts. Even if you find yourself located in a life of privilege (and therefore a part of the rottenness of the apple), you can work to eliminate the rottenness — you can unlearn prejudice — and the fact that it falls unequally on some sectors of our community.

If you find yourself stuck in the disadvantage of being given mainly the rotting parts, it helps to see that the apple is spotty, and that some parts can still taste mighty fine.

The moving thing about some black South Africans was that they saw racism as a temporary attitude or illness on the part of the white people. One cannot help wondering whether, if someone sees something as temporary, that in fact makes it less fixed. Solipsism definitely has its limits, but it makes me wonder.

Most of my life, I have been consciously trying to broaden the context in which my heart is accountable. To do this, I have found that I must listen to other points of view with an open mind, knowing that what the other person is saying is part of her worldview, and probably the point of view of many people in her context. I must accept the point of view as legitimate, no matter how it contradicts what I may think. Then, I must care about who the person is and what she sees. We have come a long way in these last forty years, but there is not yet equality of opportunity. For that to happen will require both structural changes and changes in how individuals experience openness and fairness in their context.

An example of working for a structural change, rather than making individual adjustments, occurred in our support group in the San Francisco Bay Area. One of our members came to the group with the observation that new boundaries had been drawn for her son's school; as a result, many of the school's black students would now attend another school, which was poorly funded, overcrowded, and had low reported scores year after year. Each parent in the to-be-transferred-group was figuring out some scheme to get his child to remain in the present school, but my friend wanted to work at the board level, to convince the board members not to draw the line in such a racially biased way. She wanted to change the structure that was enforcing racism in her community.

A most powerful learning about context occurred in my American Willing to Listen project. Metaphorically, I came to see the globe as if representatives of the earth were speaking to me through the variety of people I listened to. I am made mostly of Idaho and California soils; I can hear the earth's story more fully when I bring into my caring center voices from other places on the earth. My context is truer and fuller. My heart is more open, and I am more accurate, complex, and expansive in my thinking. And I find happiness in this connection, even though the sorrow that comes from many places is often hard to hold.

At the 1995 World Conference on Women, in China, forty thousand jubilant women came together from all over the world to work for structural change. An important goal, articulated in many different issues and forms, was an increase in women's voices at all levels. The women wanted rape to be classified as a war crime, with mandated punishment and reparations. We met to talk about many issues, to see how we could work together. To some degree, those brightly colored women are still a felt part of my context. Through that meeting, new possibilities were suggested, as we heard how rarely a girl child is welcomed at birth anywhere in the world. That is slowly changing, and I think many of us grew in our appreciation of what it is to be a woman.

In Sarajevo in 1996, I met two wonderful people. The shelling had been stopped less than six months before. No one was sure that this peace would hold, but relief was palpable. For five hours, riding on a bus from Dubrovnik to Sarajevo, we saw so much destruction. Village after village. The week we were in Sarajevo, we were surrounded by bombed-out buildings everywhere we went. Every exterior wall was pockmarked with bullet holes. Homes had burned roofs, collapsed walls. It was spring, so the contrast between the blooming poppies and irises and the ugly evidence of human hatred was jarring. Still, gardens were being planted, neat rows with vegetables bursting through the brown soil.

In the midst of this suffering, we stayed with Nino and Mina, the parents of a refugee we had known in Vienna. We moved into their apartment building, and into the context of years of intense shelling and fear.

Their friends visited with us; their neighbors stopped by for a chat. We could see how they had made it through the war. They had dignity and powerful friendships in their community. They were Muslims and lived in the Muslim section of the city.

An older, white-haired woman, Miliza, was in and out of their apartment every day. She obviously had a key. Nino told us that she had no one to take care of her during the war, so they invited her to be a part of their family. Their wood would warm her, and Nino could carry water for her from the brewery across the street. Mina could cook what little food they shared.

On the last day of our visit, Miliza asked us if we would like to see the Catholic Church across the street. "Oh Miliza, are you a Catholic?" I asked. "No," she said. "I am Serbian."

The fact that it was Serbs (among others) who were shelling their city for so many months did not change Nino's and Mina's relationship to their friend. The political, demonizing rhetoric had not affected their moral and ethical behavior. It did not change the social contract in that context. The war put terrible strains on their relationships, but these people held together partly out of necessity and partly out of decency and dignity.

Their son, Miki, evacuated early in the war when he was wounded, returned after years of being away. He was afraid that his parents might have done some barbarous acts in the times of starvation. As he walked through the streets, neighbors spoke highly of how his parents had helped them. Miki was relieved.

Many people are afraid they will not be able to withstand the sorrow when they move into environments filled with such apparent suffering. They fear that a context of fear and hatred will influence them, almost as if it were an epidemic. My experience is quite the contrary. Yes, my heart breaks regularly. I needed months of healing after Sarajevo. But the dignity of the people one finds in the midst of suffering fills me with respect and admiration. Memories of human dignity challenge my own arrogance. It is what I remember when I wake up during the night, upset about the world. I know there are caring people everywhere, people working to make things better. I know that within almost all people there is a part that can be tapped for nonviolent solutions to difficult problems. My job is to find those people, or that place in each person I deal with, teetering on the brink of violence, and work as partner with them to support a decent world.

In a larger sense, when I get obsessed with the horror of contemporary life, it seems to me that this is when my own soul has fallen out of balance with issues of life and death. In those moments, I am less connected with the situation, not doing everything I can as one person to help at those despairing moments. It is an affliction of bystanders that they feel guilt for not suffering. If you are doing a one-person-sized job of alleviating suffering, then you can look at suffering squarely in the face. Then, carrying the suffering of any context is not a burden; it is part of your offering toward the healing of the world.

Contextual social change is found everywhere. In the 1980s, the process of creating Sixth Street Park in San Francisco reshaped the context of the street people there. The expectations and values associated with the park were different from ones previously prevailing on Sixth Street. The park context discouraged violence; it supported caring, socially responsible behavior, and encouraged taking pride in one's contributions. These values were present outside the park to some extent; the open discussion of values, and the articulation of them in a group, brought them out more fully, since each person felt the support of the group.

We had membership cards. Anyone could belong to the park and get a card from a staff member. When staff members gave out a card, they were to discuss the rules listed on one side and ask the new member to sign the card. No violence, no drugs, etc. The cards were one way we used to change the context. Quite often, street people responded to those positive cues from their community, rather than to violent, selfish, or self-destructive ones. Of course, not always. One must not expect the impossible. The best we can do in context-changing work is to increase the odds in the direction we are working for. If we are lucky, and effective, it works.

Understanding the power of context helps me facilitate change. It suggests that when people act in ways that seem inconsistent with their basic humanity, it may not mean that they are sociopaths or basically horrible human beings. There are such disturbed people, but it is far more likely that the contextual cues people are responding to are suggested by the social environment around them, rather than coming totally from within them. A person who kills a gay person is likely to be acting out of the environment where he has heard many homophobic remarks on the media or in his church; so he feels his acts are justified, at least to some degree, by his context. Even quite disturbed people in a healthy social environment will tend toward health. But disturbed people are like lightening rods for the hatred of others, especially when suffering from a history of humiliation. People involved in hate crimes take in the hatred of others and put it into action.

Humiliation is one essential element for tipping people, however healthy, into violence. Take the example of a young man who enlists in the army, leaves home, and goes through military training. He is thrust into a setting where the rules of the military are at odds with his previous home and school context, where he was taught that killing people is unacceptable behavior. Now, he is in this new context, which is carefully constructed to destroy the old "do not kill" behaviors and instill the killer potential. Through the humiliation of the command structure, he is taught that he is nothing. He shifts to accommodate the new values and expectations in a war; he kills. We hope that when he returns to society, he is able to change back to his previous set of values. As we see from the difficulties of returning vets, it is not always possible for people to forget what has been drilled into them, and return to society as healthy, nonviolent people.

Contexts can be carefully created to encourage desired behaviors. In Yugoslavia, we heard many stories of how neighbors were turned against neighbors by government officials cleverly changing key factors in the social and political context. In ethnically mixed towns in Croatia, where people had lived peacefully for years, police visited homes long before the war started, telling people that their neighbors might become violent, and giving them guns and ammunition to protect themselves. Such suspicions planted by authority figures are a powerful force in building the conditions for the wildfire of war.

There were also important symbolic as well as very real gestures in the public spheres. When the Croatians, under Franjo Tudjman, began to change the names of the streets that bore famous Serbian or Bosnian names to names of World War II Croatian heroes, it was interpreted by the people from those ethnic groups as a signal that they were unsafe in that place. The flag of the new country used symbols from the World War II period, recalling a time when some Croatian fascists cooperated with Nazis in killing many Jews, Roma, and Serbs. (The truth is also that many Croatians fought against the Nazis.) Beyond symbolic gestures, the removal of Serbs and Moslems from police and government jobs indicated that the government would not protect them.

In Serbia, minorities had severe troubles getting through borders; Albanians' rights were taken from them by decree; and Hungarians living in Vojvodina were photographed if they attended a rally or meeting. When the authority in a context sends signals that it will not protect the rights of an ethnic population, the people rightfully feel justified in organizing.

Individually and collectively, we are always signaling the presence or absence of hostile intent. Most signals are not completely clear initially. When we interviewed Bosnians, Croatians, and Serbs about what first indicated to them that troubles were coming, they mentioned all of the above symbolic and very real threats. They also told of propaganda and direct falsehoods in the media that emphasized crimes committed by members of minority populations, and attributing malevolent motives. The same television footage would be used in Serbia and in Croatia, to indicate how the other side was abusing the home side. This occurred on all fronts of this very complex war.

It is a matter of connecting the dots to figure out how to read the signals. Members of one ethnic group being fired from public jobs, and annual, publicly funded ethnic dance festivals being canceled, street names being changed from one's heroes to those of the "other" group can all mean that strife is coming, unless major corrective action is taken.

But there are many ways of connecting any pattern of dots. When I was a young girl, my best friend showed me a connect-the-dots picture. "Look, if you connect the dots, it makes a giraffe," she said. "Yes, but if you connect them another way, you get an upside down elephant," I showed her. When you are in real life, it is very difficult to read the signals with confidence. There is always a lot of noise in a context.

The equilibrium of a society at peace is a very delicate matter. Words matter, as well as administrative decisions, which send a more concrete message. The rhetoric in Croatia alerted people to potential threat. Jewish citizens reported that Tudjman had said at one point, "I am glad my wife isn't Jewish or Serbian." He followed this with what they judged to be insincere flattering statements. Many were wary, and many left the region.

In the United States, when Christian evangelist and demagogue Pat Robertson declared a "cultural war," anxiety was raised, not only in gay, black, and Jewish communities, but also within those individuals who loved people in those populations. Words from well-known people and political leaders alert the targets, but they also give permission to those unstable people in any population looking for a group to focus their own unhappiness upon.

An unemployed auto worker, hearing that the competition from Japanese auto manufacturers is forcing American workers out of their jobs, may, if he is unstable, blame the Asians he sees on the streets for his condition. If he feels contextual support for his attitudes from national leaders, or from his union or friendship group, he may feel heroic if he beats up the Asian he meets in a dark alley, verbally or physically. Our context creates our concept of what behaviors are heroic or contextually supported. I do not believe that the rise in gay bashing is coincidental in relation to the declarations of certain religious and political leaders.

Inertia in institutions may also be a function of the power of context. Imagine that twelve of us are sitting on the board of directors of a corporation that for decades has been dumping chemical wastes into a river. We have all been presiding over that activity for some time. As individuals in the privacy of our homes, each of us may have doubts about the morality of the dumping. But when we gather in the boardroom, those personal opinions lose significance. The voices in our heads are lost, and other voices from within ourselves enter into the discussion. Here, we answer to the ideology and experience of the context, to the accepted practice of the corporation. We find the mental devices (denial, excuses, fear of being ostracized, fear that one may be thought not to be a team player, etc.) to override our doubts about polluting the river. We dip into hopelessness about our effectiveness in convincing the other directors. "Well, a different method of disposal would affect our profitability. We can't afford it." "This isn't my specialty." "Probably, other people have thought this out." "If we admit these doubts publicly, we may be liable for legal damages; better to keep quiet." In any context, there are many bystander thought patterns. It is clear that if one wishes to find courage to move in a context, support is essential. (See chapter 18.)

Love, while a very powerful emotion, may not be enough to challenge this inertia. My brother, in his position as an engineer for a construction company, was given the job of building a molybdenum mine (molybdenum is used in the manufacture of steel), in one of the White Cloud Mountains in Idaho. We grew up at Pettit Lake loving the White Clouds, which silently but majestically strode across the sky at one end of the Stanley Basin. He and other engineers fought about the plan to take the mountain down to its base. He said that together they convinced the company to take only half the mountain. It was disappointing to hear that they saved the bottom half of the mountain; I was much fonder of the top half. He saved the wrong half of the mountain. But the compromise they worked out with their employers made them feel good.

On a personal level, seeing the power of context has prompted me to examine the context to which I am accountable. Like most people, I am generally more comfortable with those who share my culture and values. Consciously or unconsciously, most of us have been raised to love our families and the people most like us, and to distrust people who are different. With increased integration in schools and the work place, we are broadening our context, and this is important. But as a rule, most people's social context tends to be rather homogeneous, our field of concern relatively narrow. For instance, when immigrants are being persecuted in our country, those of us who are not currently immigrants may not personally know people affected, or feel affected ourselves.

This narrowness makes certain dangerous conclusions appear appropriate. When Carl Reiner interviewed the two-thousand-year-old man, as played by his comedy partner, Mel Brooks, he asked whether in the "rocks and caves days," Brooks had an anthem. "Of course," replied Brooks. "It went like this: 'Let 'em all go to hell, except cave seventy-six!'" This could be the motto of gated communities, and those who drive in smoky-windowed limousines.

There are many ways to consciously widen our social, political, and personal contexts in a significant enough manner so that our voting, consumption, and institutional and community decisions include voices different from our own. Make one criterion — of the spiritual community, school, community activity, family camp, or volunteer activity — be that it is integrated. In many groups, there are committees for building bridges to other groups. I think travel into places where you are the minority, and the "other" has the "home court advantage," is a good idea.

I have tried to broaden the context of my accountability. It is not always easy. It often means that I go to the local grocery store, run by Palestinians, and ask across the counter: "What's happening in Palestine these days? Why is that happening? Does this affect you here?" By reading different voices on Internet conferences, I have access to how events are understood by others. Reading magazines, seeing films made by filmmakers from other countries or with other points of view, I can try to expand my perception.

You can learn only a limited amount about fish by going to an aquarium. You can see what they look like, how they swim, and how they eat in an alien environment. But you don't learn much about the everyday life of an average fish. For example, you don't learn anything about predators. Of course, a trip to the aquarium is safer than going to the fish's environment, because you don't have to worry about drowning or being attacked by sharks — or even getting wet. The aquarium is a good place to start one's aquatic education, but it's important to understand how that context affects what you learn. Ultimately, we are going to have to get in the water and swim with fish.

Going into the black community was an important element of my black lessons. As a teacher, I got some impressions of my black students' lives as I dealt with them in school. But the information I got was skewed, because in the classroom the power was disproportionately mine. The kids were adapting their behavior to the rules of the school context. My fellow teachers gave absurd explanations of the students they felt so distant from. Every day, the teachers got into their cars, and drove into our urban neighborhood. I wondered what came from their prejudice and ignorance, and what could be believed. By going into a situation where the students' culture was dominant, with someone from their culture as my "guide," I was a little closer to seeing the world from their perspective, though I was still far from the understanding I needed to work with them.

I often hear these days that people from black or Latino groups are unwilling to educate people of European background about how it is to "be a minority." They are rightfully tired of doing this, and often feel that they do not see sufficient payoff to make it worth their time. It is a difficult bind for everyone involved. Many workplaces and communities have unlearning racism workshops. Reading or seeing videos of accurate histories (done by historians or spokespeople from the group) that portray the injustices through time may also be a good place to start. Major work needs to be done through reading, and through personal exploration of the relative systematic advantages of people of European backgrounds, before the education will serve any real purpose.

My American Willing to Listen project was also designed to give those I listened to the home court advantage. I can meet Thai people in the United States, but of necessity they have adapted to US society. Going to Thailand, I was the one who had to make the adjustments, who had to forego the security of assuming that my patterns of thinking and understanding, as well as my value system, were shared by those around me. By working on Sixth Street, I experienced the same disadvantage. Naturally, I felt vulnerable and was often uncomfortable. But the paradox is that by making myself more vulnerable, I gradually have come to feel less threatened by differences and more at home in a variety of contexts; I am thereby more secure. I have come to care about the people in those situations far from my own.

It is especially important for Americans of European descent (or any dominant group in a context) to have the opportunity to walk as a minority of one on streets of other cultures. In South Africa, I frequently had the experience of being the only pink person in a room. If you haven't had the experience of being the only person of your racial group in a crowd, it may be difficult to understand the effects of that experience on one's sense of power. Because of Europeans' history of colonialism, white people still carry an assumption of power, even into a situation where they are the minority.

Once, after I had been working in India for about ten years, I had to pick up some essential chemicals from customs in Delhi. I was to carry them back to Varanasi. I had no idea how complex and time-consuming the process could be. I went to the airport customs office and was given a very long and complicated form to fill in. I am not good at forms, especially complex ones. I needed help. The secretary who gave me the forms noticed the confounded look on my face and suggested that I go to a certain room, where there would be many people filling in such forms. I walked into that room, and there must have been fifty men, all wearing brown suits, standing and sitting, talking with each other. I felt very white and very much a woman from a strange world. Those feelings could have swept me away, but by then I felt at home enough in India to set those feelings of alienation aside. I spoke up in a loud voice: "I need help with this customs form, so I can get chemicals necessary for the cleaning of Ganga. Can someone help me?" A young man in an orange-brown suit and a sweet smile stepped forward. "That is my river, my place. I'll help you."

For two hours, the young man and I went from office to office getting one officer after another to sign the form. I asked him if he thought we would be able to get the chemicals before I had to catch my plane in several hours. His reply was steady: "It is impossible, but we must try." This kind of statement constantly challenges me in India. Finally, I had to go, and we had not yet achieved our goal of getting the chemicals. The training for lab workers was to commence at 10 a.m. the next morning. I asked him if there was any way he thought that he could get the chemicals there in time for the training. "It is impossible, but I will try."

I did not see a way. Mine was the last plane out that night. No plane would arrive before 11 a.m. the next morning. An overnight train was possible, but unpredictable. I took out two hundred rupees (about $6 at the time) and gave it to him. Maybe this would help. I missed my plane and so had to stay overnight, catching the first plane out the next morning. When I arrived in Varanasi, the chemicals had already been put to use in the class. No one knew how they got there. Someone had just dropped them off that morning before ten. It is my experience that there are people willing to work for the common good in most contexts, if you can step over your own feelings of strangeness and find a way to reach out to them in a way that they are comfortable with.

Making connections across cultural boundaries (racial, national, class, gender, etc.) makes me feel accountable to people whose lives are very different from my own. Even that sentence is not quite right. It is not only that they are different from me — but I am different from them. We are different from each other. In fact, given the way the world is organized, any of us is different from the global majority. The relationships we create across those cultural membranes are precious.

In Yugoslavia, during the recent Bosnian war, some nationalistic people on all sides worked very hard to make ethnic membranes rigid and impermeable. Anyone with a mixed background, like a woman with a Croatian mother and a Serbian father, was forced to choose a single identity to serve the categorizing demands of nationalistic governments. There were many stories of neighbors killing each other. It is so true that people can erect boundaries in habits, thought, and language that isolate them from each other.

When a culture is open, and relations are mixed, war may be less likely. Cross-cultural connections carry a responsibility. In most wars, there are abundant stories of people working to save lives of others who were of a different racial or ethnic group, because they knew them and cared about them. In the trauma training we did in Kosova/o in 1999, in nearly every story, we heard of a Serb neighbor, colleague, or friend who had helped in some way. Most of those who aided Jews in Europe in World War II were non-Jews who had friends, colleagues, or neighbors who were Jewish. They knew the propaganda dehumanizing Jews to be false.

Of course, it takes moral courage to work in the interests of a threatened people. In the past fifteen years in the US, the support network for immigrants from Central America has emerged. People who have been caught in terrible conditions of war and poverty have come North to a network of people set up to house them, and help them get jobs and education, so their families could thrive. The war that these people were caught up in was funded in major part by US tax dollars, so it is only logical that resistance should develop in the US There are many ways of resisting powerful and threatening cultural norms. Moral courage is not usually an instantly developed talent. It is learned from childhood, but can be practiced anytime, whether you had good childhood models or not.

Ambiguity and complexity are enemies of war, which requires things like identity to be neat and simple. I believe this is why the

US military does not want gays, or members of a religious group involved in witchcraft, among their ranks. The military needs to know that they are 100 percent right and moral in all respects. If the soldier in the next foxhole is a member of a group you consider "wrong," how can you muster up the certainty necessary to kill another human being of another side?

Redwood trees understand context. They are one of the largest living beings in the world, yet these trees are rarely blown over in severe windstorms. One might wonder how they achieve this, since they have a very shallow root system. The way they stay upright is by linking their roots with the roots of the other trees around them. When the wind blows, the trees sway in the wind, but stay planted safely in the ground through the principle of connectedness. The giant redwoods use the support of their context to continue to stand up. When we decide to take a position of resistance in our context, that kind of support is necessary.

Accountability to a relationship may also call forth responses on a larger scale. Real friendship looks for ways to change things in a structural way. It is not enough to make individual accommodations to create equality. It is the common people on the ground who see the effects of policies and systematic decisions that do not live up to our ideals of human rights. When we realize our power to make changes at the grass roots, ordinary people, when they join together, are in the best position to challenge policies.

One of the most difficult parts of broadening the context of my heart has been coming to terms with the pain in the lives of people I have come to care about. After getting to know some of the street people at Sixth Street Park, I experienced the winter differently. Snuggled in my warm bed, I pictured eight or ten men at the park, huddled around a fire to keep warm.

I have come to expect that the first cold, wet days of winter will be sad for me, as I think about the homeless people I know on the streets of my city and world, about the farmworkers who must work in the fields with cold fingers, about the people in unheated refugee camps in the former Yugoslavia.

Many nights during the International Hotel campaign, I would return to my secure small home, where I had four or five times as much personal living space as the hotel tenants, and where I faced no threat of eviction. On the nights I had to teach, I wrestled with the decision to place my personal and family needs above those of the tenants.

When I first learned that the bombs and shells used in Serbia and Kosova/o were covered with uranium — that frighteningly dangerous substance — I felt such shame. How had the military gotten so far from common decency? I asked myself. I went to work to find out the facts, what people could do, and how citizens of the world could stop this insanity. I asked myself over and over, "What does a friend do when she finds out her government has poisoned the land of her friends?" What does a friend do, indeed! Work. Work hard, work smart, work carefully, and work joyously. We carry the lives and concerns of those friends from our expanded contexts into every scene and every movement of our lives.

It has not always been easy for me to care for people who are suffering. It has meant I must somehow acknowledge that I can do very little to substantially change their situation. And yet, there is freedom in doing what I can. I have learned to take the pain of helplessness to the altar of my heart and ask the question, "What can I do with what I know?" And I listen. For I am accountable in this relationship.

I think guilt is a useful emotion. It tells us what we need to do something about. When I look a refugee or homeless person squarely in the eye, I want to know I have done what I could do. How can we have a realistic sense of what one person can do? I do not expect miracles from myself, but sometimes things that seem a little like miracles do occur. I am often surprised. I will do what I can, and sometimes I manage to do what I can't imagine doing.

Helplessness is difficult in any situation. In my dreams, I walk into Milosevic's office and force him to stop the war. In my waking life, I sell handicrafts made by refugee hands, and take the money back to the refugees. This, in turn, makes it easier for me to make connections with these people. I will take some of my life's energy, and work as their partner for a better life for them, their families, and those in my own context who benefit from knowing what is happening to these people.

In the mid-seventies, when the wars in El Salvador, Guatemala, and Nicaragua were so hot, it appeared that Reagan might order US troops to take a role in Central America. Clearly, covert aid was flowing to the forces on the right. People all over America signed a "Pledge of Resistance," which said that if such an invasion occurred, they would participate in civil disobedience. With friends, I demonstrated many times at the Federal Building in San Francisco.

Creating a culture of resistance, one that knows what to do about pepper spray, bail, and provocateurs, for instance, is very important in contextual social change. We change the context from one that accepts whatever evil comes, to one that knows how to struggle with many tools of resistance, and will not stop until the craziness stops.

When, in 1994, a controversial proposition was put forward in California that would deny education and health care to immigrants, I could draw on my experience in the former Yugoslavia. Blaming a specific population for our economic troubles is ludicrous and socially irresponsible. I circulated a letter to friends and our mailing list, sharing my thinking about fair treatment of immigrant people.

Dear Friends,

In October, March, and June of last year, I spent time in the former Yugoslavia. Everywhere we went we asked, "What was the first thing you noticed that indicated a rise in nationalism?" The most frequently mentioned answer to that question was that political leaders began to blame the problems of the society on one group. The process was slow and complex, but circumstances woven together emerged, and we now see the painful results. In Serbia, the scapegoat was the Croatians, who were "the other" — the cause of the problems. In Croatia, it was the Serbs. In Bosnia, it was everyone against the Moslems. Political leaders blamed "the other" for problems — particularly economic problems. Crimes committed by members of that group were highlighted in the press. Lies were also spread. "If only we could get rid of them, we would be better off." This is the logic of ethnic cleansing, and war.

While the exact causes of the war in Yugoslavia are complex, clearly one major factor is that power-hungry politicians started talking hatred of "the other." As economic troubles visited their land, politicians needed someone to blame. When you have an "other" on whom you can blame your troubles, you are creating the conditions for social hysteria. Social hysteria is when a whole society acts in ways that no healthy person would do alone. This sickness is deadly for a society. It is like a wildfire: difficult to stop once it gets going and horribly destructive. We have known serious social hysteria in our own land: lynching conducted by whole communities, the rounding up and imprisoning of Japanese Americans in World War II, ethnic riots. We are not immune to the wildfire. Sometimes as I read the paper I think I can smell the early warning signs. Returning home, I can't help noticing how our leaders are manipulating the insecurity of Californians and focusing on immigrants now.

Now we see some of that same nationalism in our own state of California reflected in Proposition 187. The spirit behind this law says that our budget problems are the fault of the immigrants — especially the illegal immigrants — in our state. They are "the other."

NO on Proposition 187.

When confronted with an issue, sometimes I find myself able to act as a supporter in the moment, but most of the time it takes a little practice. Once in the gas station next door to my house, a white customer was complaining to the Chinese attendant about "those awful black people." I was just standing there, waiting to pay for my gas. As a shy person, I don't like to interfere with what people are doing, but in this moment my friendship with black people was on the line. I never know how to do these things perfectly, but I believe I have to do something anyway. I would be ashamed to be around my black friends in the future if I didn't. "That's not right," I said. "That's prejudice talking. You can't talk about my friends that way."

I try to stay with my own experience and not call names. "You are a racist" — or sexist or whatever category — creates more of a reaction to my statement than helping a person think. I have come to believe that often it is better to act imperfectly than to wait until you know exactly what to do. As Dusty Maloy, one of our comedy characters, used to say, "Perfection is just not human nature." We change our context drop by drop, person by person, moment by moment. In South Africa, I met people who shared the idea that there can be no truly good person in a bad context. We will rise together.

I can also think of many times when, at the crucial moment, the accountability I felt was not powerful enough to overcome my shyness and reluctance to take a risk. Afterwards, I felt I had betrayed my friends and what I knew about human responsibility. I was left wondering what I could have done that would have been more effective and truer to my relationships.

Working with people who have suffered as a result of oppression seems to mean I must prepare myself to be yelled at, or at least distrusted. No matter how hard I try, it seems inevitable that I'll say or do something hurtful to the people I am working with. The unfairness of the situation naturally creates suspicion and envy. Born of this inequality, there is also the inevitability of mistakes, insensitivity, and poor communication. Occasionally, I stumble into these errors in my work or friendships.

"You're just as I expected!" they'll yell. Then some horrible anger, some invective against me, my behavior, my people will fall on my head. "You pigheaded racist. You are just like all white people, who want to control everything. You want me and my people to go back to slavery. Yes sir, yes ma'am." Or "You come here and take our land, our language is stolen from us. And now you want our souls. You and all your thieving relatives."

It seems like an avalanche. I feel as though I may deserve a little shovelful of criticism for my error or insensitivity. Instead, whole mountains, complete with boulders and snow, are dropped on me. Each time, I imagine I won't come out alive. I feel terrible about myself. It doesn't help that there is an element of truth in what they say about my ancestors and about myself. I must be a horrible, arrogant person, as bad as a slave owner or land-thief settler. I, single-handedly, am holding back a whole people. And this person I'm working with, who is important to me, appears to hate me.

I have never gotten into an upset with a person of color without them in some way referring to the difference in our races. So deep is the wound that it is one of the first things mentioned. This does not mean that I must immediately give in to my shame and fear. In fact, that is one of the least useful attitudes. It does mean that I need to take care to be especially respectful in my listening, because this may be new territory for me.

I don't know how many people in my lineage have gotten close enough to learn about the experience of people different from them. Historically, it seems that people of different races have taken their complaints back home, where they will receive support and have safety. But now I am here, able to listen and learn how to live differently. And it is actually a blessing that this person feels confident enough in our relationship to trust me with genuine feelings. I try to remind myself that this anger they are sending my way is a sign of progress, but it is not easy.

I almost always feel defensive in such situations. I have been known to make an ass of myself with my defensiveness. But I have found that defensiveness is almost never the place to begin to learn what I have done, and how it needs to be changed in order to continue a relationship of respect. Teasing, which connotes love and intimacy in my family, may not mean that to someone from a different tradition. I sometimes withdraw for a time, lick my wounds, and think about what has happened. Sometimes, I just have to have a little cry. There is often someone who can help me figure out what happened, and how I can remedy the situation and the relationship.

Gradually, I see my way out from under the avalanche. As the pain of the experience fades, I can usually see some truth in the accusation. Often, I learn more about the accuser's painful relationships with people like me, as well as what I specifically have done to push that button.

My friend Rachel Bagby (an African American lawyer, singer, dancer, and writer) has taught me to stay open in the process of these discussions when I stand accused of racism. She teaches me through her openness and curiosity, when I have done or said something that is racist. "What do you mean by that?" Rachel will ask. Sometimes, I can see the oppressiveness of my act, but often she will patiently tell me how she heard it. That cannot be done without feeling — for which I am thankful. I wouldn't want her to shut off her feelings with me. And so we walk through the minefield of those feelings we both have, and that I have brought up in her. Rachel's and my ancestors may have wanted to find a way to have a relationship of equality, but the power differences between them made that difficult. And it was not perceived by my ancestors to be in their self-interest. Nothing is more important to me in that moment than our relationship. I learn. Maybe she is learning, too. We are friends.

In spite of my highest ideals, I still harbor attitudes that separate me from people who are different from me — or from whom I am different. These attitudes are part of my ancestral and contextual baggage, and cannot be wished away. I sometimes feel discouraged that I am still the holder of racist (and other) oppressive attitudes. I have on some level been working all my life to overcome those bad habits I learned as a child from the society around me. I feel that racism is a dirt that clung to my body from being washed with dirty water for many years. No matter how I try, I cannot feel clean in that area, nor can I avoid making the errors that come from the result of that dirt. I wonder if I will suffer from racism my whole life. I don't know anyone who is clean in this respect. My choice is what kind of a racist to be. I hope I can be the kind of racist who works to crush racism in all its interpersonal and institutional manifestations. I join my friend Lakota Hardin, a Native American, when she says, "I want to end the hatred passed down to me from my ancestors in my lifetime. Let it end with me."

One step toward unlearning such attitudes is to recognize them in oneself. I've found questions like these helpful:

- Do I see aspects of beauty in this person? Am I repelled by the thought of touching this person in a reassuring or friendly way?

- Is my sense of humor unfettered when I'm with them? How do I feel when they are around my other friends? Is there anyone whose friendship I value who I feel should not see me with this person?

- Do I have anything that this person needs? How will I feel if they ask for it? Do they have anything I need? How will I feel if I have to ask them for it?

- How would I feel if this person were flying an airplane that I was in, or drilling my teeth?

- Do I make eye contact with this person, or do I find my eyes wandering away to the furniture all the time?

- Do I secretly feel that I'm better, smarter, or more in control of my life than this person, and therefore will get my way if we have some disagreement? Do I secretly feel inferior, and expect that the other person will get his or her way?

Each of us carries distancing attitudes within us, often unconsciously, and acts on them more or less often. They reflect the fear, suspicion, guilt, and anger that have developed over hundreds of years of bad history, education, and inaccurate media reporting that have served to keep us separate and uncaring. The difference historically and in the present day is access to opportunity; power is key.

My ancestors were taught, and taught their progeny, that people of different races were not human with the ability to reason. They saw it as being in their self-interest to maintain control of society, and to deny shared control to others. Now, children are taught concepts of "civilization" and "development" that have elements of the old superiority thinking. With the diasporas of people, not only Jews but also Asians, Moslems, and people from Central America, Europe, Africa, and Haiti, it is a survival value to learn not only to tolerate, but also to actively engage with people from different backgrounds, and to open up contexts to input from many sectors. There are more Moslems in America than there are Presbyterians or Episcopalians. With the change in immigration policies, racial issues become increasingly complex, with Hispanic and Latino, Korean and Filipino, Vietnamese, Chinese, and Indian faces on many streets in America. Our social context is broadening, which makes some people frightened.

How can I learn not only to tolerate my new neighbors, but to actively seek to understand and engage with them? Tolerance is not enough; we need to employ our curiosity and willingness to learn and participate in these other cultures in meaningful ways. How can we all hold our deepest identities and differences, not in isolation from others but in relationship to each other?

Reaching across centuries of painful experience is never entirely easy. We often have very different perspectives on an event or an action plan. Many people are, understandably, reluctant to speak out about their perspective when they feel they are a minority. Some people have little confidence that such action would be worth the trouble. Facing the pain of the injustice they have endured, especially in the company of someone from a more privileged group, is often more than a person wants to do.

In Belgrade during the war, we were meeting with a group of antiwar activists. They had requested a workshop on how to live with people from different ethnic groups, called "Living with Difference." I was surprised to learn that they have historically looked to the United States as a model for their multiethnic society.

After a day of work together, one woman revealed that she was Croatian. She shared how afraid she was for herself and her family, as they live and work in Serbia. It was her judgment that this revelation would be safe in the group. Immediately, people asked what Serbs could do to help her feel and be more secure. This is the natural response. It was a risk — but it was her risk. No one "told on her," no one encouraged her to take such a risk, which is as it should be. I believe she is safer having built careful bridges from her isolation and fear. If she needs help should ugliness come to her from the police, she will have allies to turn to. They may be able to do very little in a situation, but what they can do may be enough to make a difference. Her context has broadened to include decent Serbian people, some of whom would help.

Her allies are also safer in an interesting way. They have been working against the war and are shamed by what their people have been doing to Croatians and Bosnian Muslims. By knowing the vulnerability of one of their group, they can be looking out for ways to keep mean-spirited forces away from her. There is one person whom they can protect, and in so doing, cast themselves on the side against those who might want to harm someone because of her ethnicity.

Just as there are organizers in the political and social arenas, increasingly there are people who are bridge builders between contexts. Social change workers seeking contextual change are carving out specific ways of working. Several strategies are worth noting here. In the mid-1980s, a group of Europeans researched the names of fifty people in each nuclear-possessing country in the world. Because of the proliferation of opinion leaders in the US in the nuclear industry, they named two hundred-fifty people in this country. These were people who, if they changed their ideas about nuclear weapons, would be able to move the world toward disarmament.

Not only did they have the names of these powerful men (yes, nearly all of them were men), but also information about the context to which they were responsible. They assumed that most of these opinion leaders associated with people who supported nuclear weapons, or at least were not vocal in their criticism. This European group then went to each nuclear-possessing country and found organizations to work with each individual and his context. These local groups were to develop a relationship with the opinion leader, and try to share their thinking openly with him, and listen to his. But they also were to make sure that his context (which included his wife and children) — his golf club, church, civic group, children's school and scout group — had access to disarmament materials, speakers, and items about disarmament in their newsletters.

To help a person change, dissonance in his context may be useful. How much the present shift in opinion has to do with that project can never be demonstrated. But we can see that the ground has shifted, and it is likely that every bit of energy put in the direction of moving it was necessary.

Another example of contextual strategy involved television. In the early 1980s, few people in the US had met a person from the Soviet Union. Soviets did not travel abroad much, and few people from the US took vacations in the Soviet Union. When Ronald Reagan called the USSR an "evil empire," it was difficult from one's own experience to know that this was simple demonizing for political purposes.

A group I was part of started to experiment with the idea of simultaneous conversations, concerts, and events, using television and satellites to link groups. An early demonstration of this idea took place at the US festival in 1983, outside San Bernardino, California. Young people could step in front of a camera in either the US or the USSR and, through a translator, ask a question of someone on the other side of the world. Then, a band in the USSR began jamming

with a band in San Bernardino. The entire audience in both countries could see the group in the other country — the band as well as
specific faces in the Soviet audience — on a large screen in the front.

Bill Graham, the promoter of the event, thought the Moscow
link could not possibly be real. Fearing a KGB set-up, Graham
pulled the electric plug on the satellite link; but for a short period,
it was a real exchange, a sharing of virtual context, a bridge in space
linking people in one moment and one experience.

One of the first full-length demonstrations of this simultaneous
experiencing of a mediated context was at an event organized by an
antiwar group, Beyond War, which wanted to give an award to an
American and a Russian doctor simultaneously. The audience was so
excited and determined to be part of the event that the large theater
was full over an hour before the event was scheduled to begin. The
group had both technical and political advisors in each country.

The technical group was a husband-and-wife team (Kim
Spencer and Evelyn Messinger), who had put the technology
together. Kim was in Moscow, and Evelyn was in charge of the control booth in San Francisco. There were other locations where people could see the event (down-link) but not participate (up-link).
Our audience practiced saying *"dobroe utro,"* "good morning" in
Russian, and the group in Moscow rehearsed a way of greeting us.

Evelyn, in a smashing red dress, stepped to the stage to open the
bridge. She said a few words about the historic nature of the moment,
and then raised her hand, putting her palm out above her head. In
Moscow, Kim touched her hand on the screen and the bridge opened.
There were few dry eyes as the event moved along. We looked up to large
screens and saw Russian people, just like us, sitting, experiencing the same
moment, a shared context in a sense. The place really broke up when a
children's choir in San Francisco sang with children in Moscow. We
shared the same virtual context for a moment, and something changed.

Other simultaneous conversations between women, between
young people, between nuclear scientists, and finally between the
members of the two leading legislative bodies in these two countries were facilitated by the group. I was a part of this group for
years. The congressional conversations were broadcast to millions in
the national audiences in the two countries.

In the Yugoslavian war in Bosnia, the social and political contexts of
people formerly connected were severed. When we first went to the
region, one of the striking complaints of the women in all countries
was how much they missed their friends and colleagues on the

other side. Since the phone lines had been sliced, and mail stopped, each woman could not know how her friends and sisters felt about the war. A woman in Croatia imagined that her feminist allies in Belgrade now hated Croatians, and that specific friends now supported the war. That was what the propaganda she was fed led her to believe. Serbian women said the same about Croatian sisters. One of our jobs was to carry messages, letters, or simply news of antiwar activities from one side to the other. Croatians were shocked and sometimes unbelieving of the news that their friends in Serbia were working strongly against the war.

In 1995, at the Women's NGO Forum in Hairou, China, women attended from all parts of the former Yugoslavia. One day, I saw a sight that really surprised me. Sitting at a table with several Serbian friends was one Croatian friend who had always refused to believe us when we told her about antiwar activities in Serbia. She hated and distrusted Serbs, which was understandable, since for over a year Serbian planes and ships had bombed her city. She had been angry with us for traveling to Serbia after being so supportive of Croatians.

I walked up and greeted each person at the table, especially the people who I knew would be facing difficult feelings sitting there with women "from the other side." "You look so beautiful sitting here together that I don't want to interrupt you for a minute, as I know how important is the work you are doing together. So I'll just sit over there and appreciate the sight. If you need anyone to get drinks or in any way assist the process, just let me know." I was far enough away so I could not hear anything. I rested and had a drink.

Several times, one of the women walked from their table over to my table for support. My Croatian friend said, "I know where you want me to be." "Where is that?" I said, feigning ignorance. "Over with the others. You know it is hard, Fran, I have hated so long. But I am changing, I have to." And off she went. An important contextual task in any war or conflict is reknitting relationships that have come undone. It is a long process sometimes. Bridge builders bring contexts together in ways that promote peace.

I believe that it is an evolutionary imperative that we develop powerful and caring connections with those cultures, the waters, winds, and lands from which we may have been separated. Global business and government are forming powerful connections. We ordinary people from nongovernmental organizations need to make connections. Our ethnocentrism does not serve us well.

In order to prohibit corporations from sending pollution-creating technologies to other lands to make things we no longer permit in the US, in order to stand with other people in their goals of freedom and health, in order to have clean rivers and wind, connections are vital. We need connections that work for the ordinary people on both sides of any barrier. We need to see ourselves as partners.

I see the day when people in India, in order to clean their rivers, will ask the world to boycott fabrics not made with organic dyes; the day when laborers will work together in unions across national boundaries; and the day when we will work across national borders to keep the winds from bringing acid rain into forests. Money knows no boundary now. The lands and oceans are connected. It is only people who have created imaginary boundaries, to keep people apart. How can we construct our identity so that we have the ability to connect with each other across whatever boundaries are created? It is in our mutual self-interest to work with common people for the common good.

I have only begun to understand how to harness the power of contextual work. In my black lessons and American Willing to Listen project, in the work on all sides of the war in the former Yugoslavia, I have deliberately broadened my own context as a means of changing my frame of reference and my behavior. Through our traveling to all areas affected by the Yugoslavian war, we were able to carry messages to groups and individuals who were formerly friends and colleagues, and were now cut off from each other.

Reknitting people and groups that are citizens of enemy nations is important work during and after a war. Conferences, summer camps for children of opposite sides, excursions to visit the "other side," all these are strategies to broaden the context. These connections change attitudes toward policies and laws that are unhealthy for people, other than those in a narrow context. It is becoming more essential every year to work for the common good, rather than for a single interest.

I have a dream that the day will arrive when the peoples of the world will truly come to an understanding of our collective mess, and simultaneously will have such powerful connections with each other that we will decide to come together to work.

Erect and sober people will come from every land, bringing some food, a song, and some comedy with them. They will come from each cultural group in each land. Native people from all lands, and immigrant stock, too, will be at that table. Skins of deep brown, a lighter brown, olive, and pink. Blue eyes, brown eyes, hazel, and green. Round foreheads, flat foreheads, bald foreheads, decorated foreheads, and wrinkled foreheads. All dressed in ways that are comfortable for them, and remind them of the ancestors walking with them and through them.

These will be new people, no longer wanting to dominate others, knowing the compelling need for cooperation. There will be dresses, saris, padded coats, T-shirts, pants. Bright colors, dull colors, flowing clothing, and tailored. Barefoot, with wooden shoes, leather shoes, sandals, and tennis shoes. Women, men, and children, grandmothers and grandfathers, carrying the wisdom from their place.

From every subgroup found around the world, people would come, so that their contribution might have its place at the table. The farmers, the factory workers, teachers, all vocations will bring their food, their music, and their laughter. In the dream, many languages are spoken, but all are comprehended. People with disabilities will be represented. Gay and lesbian people will be at the table, too. Refugees and those exiled from their culture.

When all have come into the room, they will breathe in the awe of the moment. Blessings of all kinds will be offered, and then the peoples of the world will share food. It is the contribution from their place, from their own maturity and insight as a people, offering it to the whole, offering it as a way of putting together the puzzle of how we can all get out of this ecological and wartorn mess we have allowed to develop. We will sing and we will laugh, and then we will get down to the business of saving the world.

Each representative has been looking at the problems and gifts from her own specific place on this globe. Each has a slightly different sense of what needs to happen. Each perspective is essential. This problem cannot be solved piecemeal. We will work slowly, because what we are doing is too important to rush; we might leave a piece out. Those who speak readily will be silent, to wait for the important shy voices to come forward. It will take a long time, but the work is essential.

The end of this gathering is never in the dream; they will work it out. In my dream I have the confidence that they will do the work that is necessary. In my waking moments, I also have that confidence: we will find a way out, because we must. I pray we are able to do it as a whole community of the world.

Chapter 17

Us and Them

TIME WAS when I knew that the racists were the lunch-
counter owners who refused to serve blacks, the warmon-
gers were the generals who planned wars and ordered the
killing of innocent people, and the polluters were the industrialists
whose factories fouled the air, water, and land. I could be a good
person by boycotting, marching, and sitting-in to protest the actions
of the bad guys.

But no matter how much I protest, an honest look at myself and
my relationship with the rest of the world reveals ways that I, too,
am part of the problem. I notice, for instance, that in general I am
more suspicious of blacks or Latinos on initial contact than of white
people. I see that I'm addicted to a standard of living maintained at
the expense of poorer people around the world — a situation that
can only be perpetuated through military force. And the problem
of pollution seems to include my consumption of resources and creation of waste. The line that separates me from the bad guys is
blurred. So much of what is a good idea in one generation proves
to be a problem in the next. Good and bad are movable concepts,
with little purity in real terms.

When I was working to stop the Vietnam War, I'd feel uneasy
seeing people in military uniform. I remember thinking, "How
could that guy be so dumb as to have gotten into that uniform?
How could he be so acquiescent, so credulous as to have fallen for
the government's story on Vietnam?" I'd get furious inside when I
imagined the horrible things he'd probably done in the war.

Several years after the end of the war, a small group of Vietnam
veterans wanted to hold a retreat at our bee farm in Watsonville. I
consented, although I felt ambivalent about hosting them. That
weekend, I had a chance to listen to a dozen men and women who
had served in Vietnam. Having returned home only to face
ostracism for their involvement in the war, they were struggling to
come to terms with their experience.

They spoke of some of the awful things they'd done and seen, as well as some of the memories they were proud of. They told why they had enlisted in the army or cooperated with the draft: their love of the United States, their eagerness to serve, their desire to be brave and heroic. For many of them, the friends they made in such hard circumstances were the best friends they had ever had. Eyes glistened when they recalled what buddies had done for them when they were in danger or frightened. For some of them, the time they had felt closest to anyone had occurred in the war. They mourned the loss of the soldiers they had been. They mourned the soldiers they had not been. There were positive aspects of their service; but on the whole, their return to society left them devastated in their self-esteem and their feelings about the society they returned to.

They felt their noble motives had been betrayed, leaving them with little confidence in their own judgment. Now, some questioned their own sense of manhood or womanhood, and even their basic humanity. They wondered whether they had been a positive force or a negative one overall. What meaning did their buddies' sacrifice have? Their anguish disarmed me, and I could no longer view them as simply perpetrators of evil. The soldier, too, is a victim of the military use, or rather misuse, of human beings.

How had I come to view military people as my enemy? Did vilifying soldiers serve to get me off the hook, and allow me to divorce myself from responsibility for what my country was doing in Vietnam? Did my own anger and self-righteousness keep me from having compassion for the soldiers? From seeing the situation in its full complexity? How had this limited view affected my work against the war?

Dualistic thinking is probably one of the worst aspects of Western thought. It leads us to analyze the world in terms of "us and them." Those different from us are the "other." This creates all kinds of strategic errors in planning campaigns. We may underestimate the ambivalence within our group as well as on the "other side."

After the International Hotel eviction, I interviewed everyone I could who had been involved on any side of the struggle. I found out from the undersheriff that he had lain awake nights worrying about the brutality he expected we would face from his partners in the eviction, the police. We hadn't listened to him closely enough when he had subtly tried to warn us in advance about the violence he foresaw. If we hadn't considered him the enemy, we might have been more alert to what he was saying and prepared more carefully for the police violence that occurred. We never know to what degree there is an ally in the heart of those we find ourselves opposing.

Working in the former Yugoslavia, it was important to see all sides of the conflict. Many Americans went to Croatia, met with Bosnian refugees, and thought they understood the war. On our first trip, I felt as if we were moving behind enemy lines when we boarded the train bound for Belgrade. Even though I philosophically was committed to working on all sides, I had been exposed to an enemy mentality in the media so consistently that it had had its effect.

Things looked very different from the Serbian side. Some people might have expected anti-American sentiment to be rampant and dangerous among Serbians, because the US government was so critical of Milosevic. But we met with hostility only when a counterdemonstration attacked the weekly silent vigil against the war by Women in Black. A man came up to me, tore a sign against the war I was carrying, and said, "Do you know that your president killed twelve children last week?" Breaking the silent aspect of the vigil, I inquired about what he meant. He was speaking about some propaganda he had heard about the effects on the health care system of the embargo of medicines; the consequence, he had become convinced, had been the death of children.

Our experience in the Balkans confirmed my observation that a person interested in finding the truth is usually welcomed on any side of a conflict. Simplistic thinking finds two sides of a conflict. There are usually many other sides that are not publicly acknowledged. They may not even be openly operative at any moment. The world is not two-sided — us and them. It is many-sided, and the dividing line may run within our hearts more than between us. In the process of "othering," we lose an important part of our humanity.

When my youngest sister and her first husband, a young career military man, visited me several years ago, I was again challenged to see the human being within the soldier. I learned that as a farm boy in Utah, he'd been recruited to be a sniper for the army.

One night toward the end of their visit, we got to talking about his work. Though he had also been trained as a medical corpsman, he could still be called on at any time to work as a sniper. He couldn't tell me much about this part of his career — he'd been sworn to secrecy. I'm not sure he would have wanted to tell me even if he could. But he did say that a sniper's work involved going abroad, "bumping off" a leader, and disappearing into a crowd.

When you're given an order, he said, you're not supposed to think about it. You feel alone and helpless. Rather than take on the army and maybe the whole country himself, he chose not to consider the possibility that certain orders shouldn't be carried out.

I could see that feeling isolated can make it seem impossible to follow one's own moral standards and disobey orders, though each war is filled with stories of people who did exactly that. In my work in Yugoslavia, I heard the story of a commander in the Yugoslavian army who shot himself rather than obey an order to bomb the wonderful city of Dubrovnik. We met many young men who refused to fight in that war. Many were hiding, many more had left the country. One town hid all 350 of its young men, rather than send them off to the war. There is almost always resistance.

To have to go to such measures to preserve one's own ethical standards is quite extreme. History does not record those who refuse to kill in wartime, because it is not in the interests of the military to do so. Those people are dishonorably discharged, and their lives are often made miserable by the mark on them. During the Gulf War, I met several young men and women who refused to participate in that war. Years later, they were not able to get financial aid to go to college, and they had difficulty getting jobs. I could not help notice that even though they had questions and some feelings of upset about what they had done, there was an integrity about them that I admired.

Charlie and I performed our nuclear comedy show as a benefit for a peace group in San Diego, a city dominated by a huge naval base. During the intermission, a tall young man with a crew cut grabbed my hand and held it tightly as he asked, "What can we do to prevent nuclear war?" He was in college as part of his navy training; in a few months he'd return to his job on a nuclear submarine. He slept close to the nuclear warheads on his sub. At night, he sometimes thought of the families who were the targets of those bombs. He thought of them sitting down to dinner together, working and loving. They had lives just like his own family. How could he have any role in sending this bomb to bring such unhappiness and suffering to them?

Responding to him, I said something about the importance of not killing people, but my answer seemed inadequate. He did not want to kill, and I believe this is true of all but a very small percentage of the people in the military. His was a common question, but I had never heard it put with more intensity. He was desperate to know what he could do.

How do we learn whom to hate and fear? During my short life-time, the national enemies of the United States have changed several times. Our World War II foes, the Japanese and the Germans, have become our allies. The Soviets were touted as our enemy, but now they are disarming and are on a path to join NATO. Libya, the North Vietnamese, Cubans, North Koreans, Chinese, Serbians, and Iraqis have done stints as our enemy. When Granada and Panama became the focus of our vilification, it seemed almost pathetic.

So many countries seem capable of incurring our national wrath — how do we choose among them? Sometimes, it seems that someone in the Pentagon or White House has decided that American citizens (maybe all people) need an enemy. Their thinking must be that if we don't have an enemy, we will tear ourselves apart; so they randomly pick an Enemy for the Year and proceed to demonize that country. There is, of course, a motive behind this vilification by leaders — greed, the desire to dominate a region, or to control conditions globally. Rarely are we given the real reasons for wars, or for the determination of who our enemy should be.

As individuals, do we choose our enemies based on cues from national leaders? In Yugoslavia, a few leaders at the top saw the opportunity to grab power by pumping up ethnic hatred in unstable times. The International Monetary Fund (IMF) was pressuring the government for repayment of massive loans made when Tito was alive. Economics were tight, so leadership was in a pickle. The people who lived in the villages, where diversity was not a feature of daily life, were able to be manipulated into the kind of hatred that created the worst massacres in Europe since World War II. They learned whom to hate from the lower authority figures, like the police and insecure political leaders who blew with the wind from the top. The media told outright lies over and over every night, until gangs formed out of the sentiments of hatred.

We have seen lies perpetrated by our own government to manipulate us into war: the Gulf of Tonkin, where a US ship was supposedly attacked (a lie); the report that the Iraqi army was taking incubators from Kuwaiti hospitals, thus depriving premature babies of care (later proven to be another lie); the absurd story that the Cuban military "did horrible things with goats" in Granada.

It seems that people can be taught to hate. Must we hate our parents' enemies as part of our family or cultural identity? Does our gang have to hate the other gang in order to have a reason for existing? In Yugoslavia, we saw the effects of people who historically had not been taught to hate, with a government determined to manufacture enough hatred to go to war. Many people said, "My mother is Serbian, my father Croatian; now the government says I have to choose who I am and fight for that side." Most antiwar people we worked with identified themselves as Yugoslavs, meaning neither Bosnian, Croatian, nor Serbian. Yet after only a few years of the media's poison, they had changed identities. But that change was not without agony.

Whose economic and political interests does our enemy mentality serve?

Those of us working for social change tend to view our adversaries as enemies, to consider them unreliable, suspect, and generally of lower moral character. Saul Alinsky, a brilliant community organizer, explained the rationale for polarization this way:

> One acts decisively only in the conviction that all the angels are on one side and all the devils are on the other. A leader may struggle toward a decision and weigh the merits and demerits of a situation which is 52 percent positive and 48 percent negative, but once the decision is reached he must assume that his cause is 100 percent positive and the opposition 100 percent negative...
>
> Many liberals, during our attack on the then-school superintendent [in Chicago], were pointing out that after all he wasn't a 100 percent devil, he was a regular churchgoer, he was a good family man, and he was generous in his contributions to charity. Can you imagine in the arena of conflict charging that so-and-so is a racist bastard and then diluting the impact of the attack with qualifying remarks? This becomes political idiocy.

Promoting an enemy mentality is one of the ways that organizers create resistance to their goals and lose supporters. The rigidity of demonizing removes all complexity and texture, as well as lessening the possibility that you will be able to sit down and work with your opposite in the future. For a future plan to work out, it may be important for our opposite to be part of the cocreation of it. Spreading lies or half-truths about even the most disgusting opponent does not serve nonviolent goals. Far better to find ways of working with all persons in a situation, rather than completely distancing oneself strategically. This self-serving righteousness, presenting one's own cause as 100 percent positive and the opposition as 100 percent negative, is not appealing, and our goals are weakened because people sense the leaders are themselves deluded and one-sided.

Demonizing one's adversaries has great costs. It is a strategy that tacitly accepts and helps perpetuate our dangerous enemy mentality and is an element of dangerous nationalism. Creating the conviction of a real, hateful enemy may be useful for building fanatical, immature energy, but it is not so useful for building long-term focus and strategies.

Instead of focusing on the 52 percent "devil" in my adversary, I choose to look at the other 48 percent, to start from the premise that within each adversary I have an ally. That ally may be silent, faltering, or hidden just now. It may exist only in the person's sense of ambivalence about morally questionable parts of her job. Such doubts rarely have a chance to flower, because of the overwhelming power of the social context to which the person is accountable. My ability to be her ally also suffers from such pressures. This accounts for the swing of a true believer from one side to the other. All thoughtful workers in a campaign know there is ambiguity in the shared context — nothing is 100 percent right, and no one is all devil. We are stronger if this complexity is discussed rather than denied.

In 1970, while the Vietnam War was still going on, a group of us spent the summer in Long Beach, California, organizing against a napalm factory there. It was a small metal-bending factory that had been awarded the government contract to make the canisters into which napalm would be poured; because napalm is made by combining several chemicals together as they are poured into the canister, the company became known as a napalm manufacturer, although it was really only interested in bending the metal.

An accidental explosion a few months before had spewed hunks of napalm gel onto nearby homes and lawns. The incident had, in a real sense, brought the war home. It spurred local residents who opposed the war to recognize their community's connection with one of the war's most despicable aspects. At their request, we worked with and strengthened their local group. Together, we presented a slide show and a tour of the local military-industrial complex for community leaders, and we picketed the napalm factory. We wrote a letter to the president of the large corporation that owned that factory and many other businesses. We were a bit surprised and pleased when he answered our letter requesting to meet with him.

We spent major parts of three weeks preparing for this meeting, studying the company's holdings and financial picture, and investigating whether there were any lawsuits filed against the president or his corporation. We compared the income from military contracts with that from consumer businesses, to see where he might be vulnerable to consumer boycotts. And we found out as much as we could about his personal life: his family, his church, his country club, his hobbies. We studied his photograph, thinking of the people who loved him and the people he loved, trying to get a sense of his worldview and the context to which he was accountable. We wanted to see him as a multidimensional person.

We also talked about how angry we were at him and his company for the part he played in killing and maiming children, women, men, animals, and bacteria in the land necessary to the health of the soil and water. We got a clear, complex picture of the consequences of his manufacturing this deadly substance — all to keep his metal-bending operation making money. Though our anger fueled our determination, we decided that venting it at him would make him defensive and reduce our effectiveness. We found our way to a clear resolve unhampered by anger. Napalm was not needed by humanity.

When three of us met with him, he was not a stranger to us. Surprisingly, he was open, interested in hearing our point of view, and very conversant with the antiwar philosophy we discussed. He offered us smoked almonds, as he was very fond of them. We had a wide-ranging discussion lasting over an hour.

Without blaming him personally, we suggested that his corporation had blood on its hands. We told him we knew where his corporation was vulnerable (it owned a chain of motels and other manufacturing businesses available for boycotting). We asked him either to shut the plant (not our favored idea, as we were concerned about the workers' jobs) or to not bid on the contract when it came up for renewal at the end of that year. We suggested to him that he find something else to do with the plant besides making napalm; some other metal must need to be bent besides war-related products. We offered to work with him to find other ways the workers could be kept employed.

We also discussed the company's other war-related contracts, because changing just a small part of his corporation's functioning was not enough; we wanted to raise the issue of the vulnerability of depending on munitions and war for a healthy business climate for his corporation and for the country. "What if peace breaks out? You don't want the financial health of your corporation reliant upon war, do you?" We correctly foresaw that years later, when the cold war ended, it would be the corporations dependent upon military contracts that suffered the greatest economic dislocation.

We wanted him to see us as real people, not so different from himself. We wanted him to hear our argument not to react to us as a stereotype. At that time, there was a great distance between the antiwar community and the business community. If we had seemed like flaming radicals (even though we were), he would have been more likely to dismiss our concerns. We assumed he was already carrying doubts about making napalm inside himself, and we saw our role as giving voice to those doubts. Our goal was to introduce ourselves and our perspective to him, so he would remember and consider our position when making his decisions.

When the contract came up for renewal several months later, his company did not bid on it.

At the conference on holocaust and genocide, I met someone who showed me that it is not necessary to hate our opponents, even under the most extreme circumstances. While sitting in the hotel lobby after a session on the Nazi Holocaust, I struck up a conversation with a woman named Helen Waterford. When I learned she was a Jewish survivor of the Auschwitz concentration camp, I asked her about her feelings about Nazis. "You know," she said, "I don't hate the Nazis." This took me aback. How could anyone who had lived through a concentration camp not hate the Nazis?

Then I learned that Helen does public speaking engagements with a former leader of the Hitler Youth movement; they talk about how terrible fascism was as viewed from both sides.

Fascinated, I arranged to spend more time with Helen and learn as much as I could from her. After the end of World War II, she had worked taking care of the children of Nazis. Even then, she found no difficulty caring for these vulnerable offspring of the architects of the war and holocaust in which she had found herself. Possibly one reason she was able to stay intact was that she had fought in the underground against the Nazis. She reunited with her daughter, whom she had made sure was out of the line of Nazi fire during the war, and immigrated to the United States after the war.

Then, in 1980, Helen read an intriguing newspaper article, in which a man named Alfons Heck described his experience growing up in Nazi Germany. When he was a young boy in Catholic school, the priest would come in every morning and say, "Heil Hitler," and then "Good morning," and finally "In the name of the Father and the Son and the Holy Spirit …" So, in his mind, Hitler came before God. At ten, Heck voluntarily joined the Hitler Youth, and he loved it. It was in 1944, when he was sixteen, that Heck first learned that the Nazis were systematically killing the Jews. He thought, "This can't be true." But gradually he came to believe that he had served a mass murderer.

Heck's frankness impressed Helen, and she thought, "I want to meet that man." She found him soft-spoken, intelligent, and pleasant. Helen had already been speaking publicly about her own experiences of the Holocaust, and she asked Heck to share a podium with her at an upcoming engagement with a group of four hundred schoolteachers. They used a chronological format, taking turns telling their own stories of the Nazi period. Helen told of leaving Frankfurt in 1934 at age twenty-five. She and her husband, an accountant who had lost his job when the Nazis came to power, escaped to Holland. There, they worked with the underground Resistance, and Helen gave birth to their daughter. In 1940, the Nazis invaded Holland. Helen and her husband went into hiding in 1942. Two years later, they were discovered and sent to Auschwitz; their daughter was hidden by friends in the Resistance. Helen's husband died in the concentration camp.

Heck's and Waterford's first joint presentation went well, and they decided to continue working as a team. Once, at an assembly of eight hundred high school students, Heck was asked, "If you had been ordered to shoot some Jews, maybe Mrs. Waterford, would you have shot them?" The audience gasped. Heck swallowed and said, "Yes, I obeyed orders. I would have." Afterward he apologized to Helen, saying he hadn't wanted to upset her. She told him, "I'm glad you answered the way you did. Otherwise, I would never again believe a word you said."

Heck is often faced with the "once a Nazi, always a Nazi" attitude. "You may give a good speech," people will say, "but I don't believe any of it. Once you have believed something, you don't throw it away." Again and again, he patiently explains that it took years before he could accept the fact that he'd been brought up believing falsehoods. Heck is also harassed by neo-Nazis, who call him in the middle of the night to threaten: "We haven't gotten you yet, but we'll kill you. You are a traitor."

How did Helen feel about the Nazis in Auschwitz? "I disliked them. I cannot say that I wished I could kick them to death — I never did. I guess that I am just not a vengeful person." She is often denounced by Jews for having no hate, for not wanting revenge. "It is impossible that you don't hate," people tell her.

At the conference and in subsequent conversations with Helen, I have tried to understand what has enabled her to remain so objective and compassionate, to avoid blaming individual Germans for the Holocaust, her suffering, and her husband's death. I have only two clues: she has passionately studied history and so has been able to set her story in the largest perspective; she fought the Nazis both in Germany and Holland. Having been active at the time, she may have less internal drive to punish and hate than if she had been passive.

For many people, the only explanation of the Holocaust is that it was the creation of a madman. But Helen believes that such an analysis serves only to shield people from believing that a holocaust could happen to them in their own society. An appraisal of Hitler's mental health, Helen says, is less important than an examination of the historic forces at play and the ways Hitler was able to manipulate them.

"As soon as the war was over," Helen told me, "I began to read about what had happened since 1933, when my world closed. I read and read. How did the S.S. state develop? What was the role of Britain, Hungary, Yugoslavia, the United States, France? How can it be possible that the Holocaust actually happened? What was the first step, the second step? What are people searching for when they join fanatical movements? I guess I will be asking these questions until my last days."

Demonizing the enemy was prominent in the early days of the Bosnian war in Yugoslavia. Everywhere we went in the former Yugoslavia, we asked, "What was the first thing you noticed that indicated your country was heading for trouble?" There are many root causes of that war, but we were interested in how a people accustomed to living together could be made willing to go to war against each other.

The most frequent answer we heard was that political leaders began to blame the problems of the society on one group. When economic hard times come, if people cannot get what they need — a job and safety for their family — because of their ethnic group, the dynamic for anger and fear of anticipated terror can be created. Strain between individuals begins to tear at the fabric of society.

An individual or a nation's identity as victim is most dangerous. As Julie Mertus says in her book *Kosovo: How Myths and Truths Started a War:* "Real or imagined, these stories shape our understanding of ourselves as heroes, martyrs, triumphant conquerors and humiliated victims. The most dangerous identity is that of victim. Once we see ourselves as victims, we can clearly identify an enemy. Steeped in our own victimhood, we no longer feel bound by moral considerations in becoming perpetrators." Revenge becomes possible. "We had to do it," the victim rationalizes about any crime.

I saw this happen to friends on all sides of the war in the Balkans. Women accepted the logic and no longer criticized the acts of their military. While stating that they were opposed to killing and other horrid acts, they would tell us, "We understand what drove them to it. We could no longer take such humiliation and degradation." Once started, the frenzy of war is difficult to stop. And even when stopped, by treaty or some other international act, the war comes home, as the women must live with the men who, having loosened the bounds of their morals, may continue their violent behavior at home and in the community if anything does not go their way. So the story is not finished.

How did the blacks in South Africa hold themselves as victims in such a way that they did not pay back all the violence they had endured during the many years of apartheid? Partly the answer was that they exposed their own violence to a critical light. The philosophy of the black leaders as well as the culture as a whole must also have made significant contributions to the people's ability to not focus on resentment and retribution, but rather to work on forgiveness and reconciliation.

The process of creating the enemy in the Balkans was slow and involved many complex factors. In Serbia, it was the Croatians and the Moslems who were the other — the cause of the problems. In Croatia, it was the Serbs and the Moslems. The others were fired from key jobs as police officers, schoolteachers, and other professional positions. Not because they were the last hired, not because their job was no longer necessary, but because of their ethnicity. A person of the favored group was hired in their place. Isolation and anger and suspicion built between the groups. Milosevic went to Kosova/o in 1990 and heard from the Serbs there how they were being abused by the Albanian majority. He saw how his power could be increased if he played the Serb nationalist card in Kosova/o, as well as wherever there were Serbs. Lies were spread, and guns were distributed in the Krajina, which was in Croatia, but had a Serb majority, and where Bosnian Serbs controlled the public machinery. "If only we could get rid of those people, we would be better off. We will take care of our own." This is the nationalistic logic of ethnic cleansing, and war.

When you have an other and you choose to blame a nation's troubles on them, you create the conditions for nationalism and social insanity. Nationalism encourages a society to do everything in the interests of the dominant group; the other is made to serve that group's goals. This kind of thinking is at the root of white supremacy movements, which hold that white people should maintain control of economic or political units. It also leads to a country or group's looking out only for its own interests, ignoring the impact of its policies on others.

Nationalism is very different from patriotism. There may be only a hair's difference in definition, but there is whole world of difference in consequence. Patriotism involves pride and working for the progress of one's own nation or group; nationalism uses pride to cause people to work *against* the interests (economic, life, health, or access) of another group. A white person who is a patriot may say, "We can do better than live by racism," while the nationalist says, "This is a white country, and the whites should make the rules."

In the Balkan region during the 1990s, I have seen the enemy mentality operating in a most destructive way. When some group is declared by the society to be the enemy, it skews all relations, even with friends from that group. Kosovar ethnic Albanian women had made good friends with Serb women. At a certain point, as the war came closer, members who supported violent strategies in the KLA began to kill members from their own group who maintained friendships with Serbs, or were seen in Serb businesses, or even talking with Serbs. It became dangerous to build bridges to the other. This was very painful for men and women on both sides. The young people who formed the Postpessimists worked to keep their membership multiethnic; they went to great lengths to maintain those relationships. They knew better than to be open, but also better than to give up good friends. Suspicion is a pernicious disease and a major aspect of social insanity. This aspect of rabid nationalism is necessary in order to create war.

I trace my interest in nationalism and social insanity back to my childhood in Idaho, when I frequently accompanied my father on his trips around Idaho's Magic Valley. He supervised farms for a Dutch land company, and we would drive around from farm to farm, talking together, eating potatoes freshly dug from the ground — raw, sliced with Dad's pocket knife, and salted from the shaker he kept in the glove compartment for just such moments. As we passed a group of low-lying army barracks just outside Paul, Idaho, he would often get sad. He explained to me that these were the prisons, politely called "internment camps," where people of Japanese ancestry were held during World War II.

My father would invariably say something like, "When bad times come, people become frightened and do things they would never do in ordinary circumstances. Governments even do things against their own laws. In bad times, some people become more generous, think more about other people's needs as well as their own, act as leaders for sanity. Others become selfish and greedy, thinking only of themselves or their group. Some leaders lead in very bad ways, so they can maintain their power. They may have ideas that really hurt other people — especially those who are weak or outside the mainstream of society."

We have known serious social insanity in the US: lynchings conducted by whole communities (including burning entire black communities such as Rosewood, Florida; and white riots against Mexican Americans in Wastonville, California); the rounding up and imprisoning of 110,000 Japanese Americans in World War II (over 60 percent of whom were US citizens); the scapegoating of progressives and liberals in the McCarthy period; ethnically targeted riots focused on blacks, native Americans, Latinos, gays, or any disenfranchised group.

Returning home from the former Yugoslavia, I couldn't help noticing how the insecurity of US citizens was being manipulated and social insanity whipped up by demagogues and political opportunists. Here, it is called "culture war." In the economic restructuring we are undergoing, services to the poorer sector are vanishing in our winner-take-all economy. Immigrants, gays, various racial and cultural groups are seen as the other. Leaders can use the targeting mechanism to whip up policies against the interests of the other group. The common good is lost.

No period of social insanity is quite like another; but in such times there are certain predictable manifestations of the terror just below the surface. Some of the signs of social insanity are:

1 An increase in random street violence against the target groups

1 Increased polarization in communities

2 Yellow journalism, which fans the insanity

3 Political opportunism, using hateful rhetoric to get votes or attention

4 A sense of urgency that we simply do not have the time to arrive at a national (or group) consensus — that decisions must be made quickly

5 Social and/or legal constraints on dissent

6 Legal, civil and human rights are ignored

7 The rise of vigilante groups

8 An increase in military and police abuse of target groups

9 A rise in all-male groups with a macho focus and training, and pseudo/military activities.

We must face the possibility that a society in the early stages of social insanity can resist the attacks for only so long. When the system breaks down, it becomes vulnerable to opportunistic infections; massive abuse and genocide are possible. In such times, some people and groups will work only in the interests of their family, their company, or their ethnic group, no matter what the cost to the community. Looking out for one's own group rather than the common good is one response in social insanity. And we walk around in our daily lives as if nothing is happening around us — even though we can all smell the stench of fear. The dynamic of inaction is in force in epidemic proportions.

Policies of nationalism turn neighbor against neighbor and build a climate of increasing suspicion and fear. Social insanity almost always is misplaced, and for good reason. In Yugoslavia, for instance, the IMF ordered the government into economic restructuring — cutting back on social, education, and health services to release more money to pay the interest on the World Bank loans. Economic good times were beginning to sour. Rather than point the finger at the excessive borrowing of Tito, or at the manipulations of the international monetary community in forcing structural adjustment, the Serbs and the Croats began to focus social discontent on ethnic minorities, the other. The Croatians decided to move for independence for their relatively rich country with such a rush that they put aside any concern for what this would do to Bosnia and Kosova/o. Ultimately, the wildfire of social insanity spread through the less educated, the rural populations, the more economically marginalized. And so, citizens were drawn into a war that no one knew how to stop.

Our social connection is very fragile. As we move toward the year 2000, the shadowy forces from deep within our societies are rising. We are all feeling the same impacts of economic restructuring — less money for social services, education, health care. Until there is active rebellion, cuts will continue. For legislatures, the bottom line is money; for communities, it is community cohesiveness. The test for each individual is and will be, will we have the courage to work for justice fearlessly, nonviolently, maintaining respect for the right for dignity in the life of each creature we encounter? We must not let our fear of violence conquer our passion for change. The key is how to change without violence.

The most important social act is to strengthen existing institutions and build new ones that can reach across divisions, and can guard the rights of all individuals and groups in the society. Government and common institutions must be made effective in solving problems. The dissolution of society's mechanisms to manage conflict in an orderly and transparent manner creates the fuel for social insanity. The job of government is to provide for safety and order for competing groups in the society. If that breaks down, groups organize to provide for their own safety and interests.

While no society is immune to these forces, democracy has elements that mitigate against social insanity. Democracy has many important features, but surely one is the knowledge that when you lose in a struggle, you know that the loss is temporary, and that you have possibilities for redress and change. A party may lose in an election or court case, but there are other elections, and appeals of lower court decisions to a higher court, with broader allegiances. This flexibility in institutional life is important in fighting the wildfire.

The most powerful antidote to social insanity is community: people knowing each other through time, acting together, with all their strengths, differences, and vulnerabilities. Human beings are the agar plate on which the bacteria of social insanity grow — or fail to grow. We will be strong as a community to the degree that we know, protect, and honor a wide variety of people in our community, their perspectives, concerns, and gifts. Each of us helps create the environment in which history occurs.

As we work for change, nonviolence is the most substantive change we can work for; when we work for change in a nonviolent way, we hold fast the means to both a specific goal and the broad goal of a less violent world.

In any frightening situation, the press are also suffering shock, and are often unable to think flexibly. They take the words from the most authoritative source, which often seems to be a governmental or industrial representative, often someone with a vested interest or far from the scene. The press often become narrowly focused on the dramatic phenomena, and don't report on the alternative forces. Increasingly, rich and powerful corporations hire neighborhood people to form groups, to sit at tables in the community, and to confuse the picture in the media. Complexity is lost.

But there are always people working for nonviolence and calm. For example, hundreds of people heard about the bombing in

Oklahoma City and came immediately to help: rescue workers and communications people; choirs and performers; masseuses to help the rescue workers; counselors and pastors; and even cooks. Everyone can do something. In the Los Angeles uprising, an African American woman saw the beating of a white truck driver on television. She got in her car and went to the scene, stopped the beating, and took the driver to the hospital. When people reach across their isolation, new possibilities for creative change are born.

There are always people ready to act for decency, and there are many more who will act when someone else leads the way. In Tuzla, Bosnia, an ethnically mixed city, the mayor, a Muslim, went to a crowd that had begun menacing Serb shopkeepers after a particularly harrowing Serbian artillery attack. He looked out at the furious crowd and said, "Anybody who wants the house of a Tuzla Serb must take mine first." Often, if one person sets the tone for the entire context, others find courage and decency for themselves.

In Australia, Henry Reynolds wrote a book (*This Whispering in Our Hearts,* Allen & Unwin, 1998) chronicling humanitarian white immigrants who stood up and demanded justice for the Aborigines. He noted their distancing self-righteousness, and their defeats as well as their victories.

Do not be afraid to act; you have many allies. The media will not be able to take its focus off the horror to tell about the alternative acts of decency. Newspapers will report the words of authorities, and will not come looking for community resistance to violence perpetrated by authorities. It is probably often to the humanitarian's advantage not to be noticed by the media, as that would serve to organize critics and repression. But the lack of these stories in our cultural memory means that others do not have access to models for their own action. By acting against the terror, you are the best antidote to social insanity. Know that you are never alone — but it may take a while to find the others who are agents of healing.

When my father and I drove past the site of the internment camp, he regularly gave me this advice: "Each generation has bad times while they are on the earth. Live so that you can be generous and courageous in bad times; you will have more fun with your friends and will feel better about yourself. Your community will benefit if you work for the common good, rather than simply for your own interests. And bad times always do come to an end. When good times return, people remember who helped in the community and who didn't. Shame is not as much fun as pride."

Each moment of our lives is a destiny-creating moment; each of us plays a part in creating the atmosphere we live in. We have the freedom to make choices that can make a difference. Having taken action once, one is more inclined to act again. We met so many people in the former Yugoslavia who wished they had taken more seriously the threat seen in demonizing others, had spoken up, and acted against ethnic hatred and social insanity when they saw them building.

Life is always a balancing act — we need time to observe and time to act; we need to be receptive as well as creative, sometimes choosing to accept the world as it is, and other times working to reshape it. No matter what happens in history, it is important that we act from our healthiest, life-affirming self. Then, at least, when history moves on, we can be proud of ourselves for how we cared for life — *all* life, not just our group. And besides, as my father said, "It's more fun." Surely hatred is not fun. It takes an incredible amount of energy to hate someone, or even to maintain isolation from the other in this small and complex world of ours. Closing the distance and developing relationships based on respect for the life and piece of truth in the other is dynamic and rewarding — even if that other is disagreeable.

Chapter 18

How I Keep Going

PEOPLE FREQUENTLY ask how I keep going in this work
for social change. Occasionally, I detect an attitude from others that I should settle down to a "real job" and leave working for a better world to the young and naive. At other times, I sense
a note of wistfulness in the tone of their questioning. How do I pay
my bills and afford the time and travel expenses? Still others seem
to know personally the disappointment and disillusionment that
comes while working with groups of people in a political context:
they wonder how I manage to stand up to these difficulties, which
often drive other sensitive people out of social change work. The
most frequently asked question is, "How do you keep your hope
alive?"

Of course, times come when I lose my way in this work. I, too,
get sucked into the deep swamps of sorrow, confusion, despair, and
not knowing what to do next. Betrayal and defeat have occurred
more often than I wish. It's the little deaths in life that are difficult.
Times and people change. Sometimes I am able to flow with those
changes, and sometimes I'm not. And the contrast between the
sparkling integrity I see in the eyes of people working for positive
futures, and the barbarism that sometimes dominates reality, is dis-
heartening.

I remember feeling especially low in Sarajevo in 1996, six
months after the Dayton peace accords, while staying with people
who had put their lives on the line to live in a diverse city. I was
surrounded by bombed-out buildings and destroyed sewage treatment facilities, and NATO armed forces were everywhere. It was
heartbreaking. And returning from Macedonia in 1999, where I did
humanitarian work to aid Kosovar friends, I found controversy
swirling around me every time I gave a talk on my work.

At other times, I have also been the subject of controversy, but
never so intense as in the International Hotel, when I could not
even cross Grant Street; one side was with the hotel (and the

People's Republic of China), and the other was with the landlord (and coincidentally, the government of Taiwan). I do not thrive in such a charged environment, but I have learned to keep my head down and continue my work. I have a support group which helps me think through what criticisms to accept and how to handle all conflict.

In 1984, when the Sixth Street Park was being demolished to get the city spruced up (that is, to get the poor out of sight) for the Democratic convention, it was a particularly complex time in my inner life. I had been asked by Mahantji to come work in India cleaning the Ganges River, and my financial and love lives were in disarray. I lived on Anderson Street, a three-block street up a hill, but one night I accidentally turned up Andover Street, a two-block street. I got to the top of Andover and my house was not there. I stopped the car. How could my house have vanished? My love had vanished, my park, my job, and now my house. I was in such bad emotional shape that it actually, in that moment, seemed possible that a house, in fact a whole block, could disappear. Finally, I pulled myself together and found my way home. I only tell you that story to illustrate how upset I was. I had lost my way. The wind had stopped blowing my sails.

In that moment of discouragement and depression, I did not possess the internal resources to make a decision about what to do next. I knew I needed to remake my life, but I lacked the self-esteem and the insight. Finally, in desperation, I called five of my most trusted friends and asked them to come to help me. I promised that I would do what they advised. Only in this way would I have the commitment to do what they would suggest.

When we gathered that night, I introduced them to each other, and then I poured out every detail of the morass I found myself caught in. I talked about my feelings of depression, of anger about the park, of abandonment by my lover, and the details of my financial situation. I shared that Mahantji had requested that I come to India, but that I was not confident enough to take on that task just now. I answered all their questions. Then I said, "OK, that's it. Now you know as much as I do about my mess. I'm going into another room to watch television. You decide what I should do. I will do whatever you suggest to the best of my ability. Come and get me when you are ready."

From the back room, I heard them laughing and wondered what they were saying. Finally, they called me back into the living room. "You will leave for India on January 10. Tomorrow, you can begin cleaning your life up by cleaning your car." (They later said that they wanted to give me something doable on the first day.) "We want you to take seriously your life as a social change worker. When you return, we suggest you find work that gives you the flexibility to do your work for the world." They also gave me a certificate that I could use to eat at each person's house once a week in the event of financial hard times. They didn't want me to starve to death.

This push was what I needed to get going. I cannot imagine that on my own I could have grown enough in my sense of myself to begin the work in India. Idaho girls just don't think of themselves as possessing enough wisdom, courage, or chutzpah to do something like clean up the Ganges River. Support like this has been an important part of my work for the past fifteen years.

I am part of a support group some friends and I started over ten years ago. We meet once a month for three hours. Each of us is involved in work for social change, and we all help each other when we can. Carol R. works as a social worker with families where abuse is a factor, Carol S. raises funds for human rights work, Bev teaches and does photography, Rita is a nurse and does nonviolence training and human rights work, Nonnie does community organizing around fair trade issues, and Amy has various social change projects. We have had men in the group, but not just now. We maintain contact with many people who have been in the group and moved away.

One example of how we work together to support each other's social goals: Rita became concerned some years ago that demonstrations about Central America were tending toward violence. She brought her concern to the group. We brainstormed and decided to create a leaflet reminding people of the agreements of nonviolence for the demonstration. Someone helped with the writing; another found a free way to duplicate the small leaflet. Whenever a member of the group went to a demonstration, she would carry some leaflets to pass out. Rita's concern became our concern.

Support takes many forms for our group. When Rita had hepatitis, one group member each day fixed Rita a meal. Our support group packed all the bundles bound for Yugoslavia. Each meeting, we discuss each person's work and give advice. Their critique of my work has been essential. They watch when I need to rest; they know my weaknesses and keep check on them. Basically, we share a lot of love. The human spirit needs a fair amount of compassionate, committed tenderness in order to maintain high-quality work and hope.

A side advantage is that through helping the other members with their work, I have a sense of involvement in many other campaigns. Rita keeps me apprised of her work in the medical system; Carol R. shares the effects of cuts in social services. Through helping Carol S. with her work on affirmative action, I am able to contribute to that issue in ways I otherwise could not, given my other commitments. Nonnie and Bev came to India one year, and took great photos that have helped in the work there.

In the early days, some of us went to jail together to work against nuclear power or the nuclear weapons development facility at Livermore. We have called ourselves the "Department of California Corrections" (after all, we are trying to correct California, aren't we). We joined hundreds of others similarly organized into affinity groups, usually with interesting names. We committed civil disobedience together. Members of the group who could not join us in jail acted as support: answering phone calls, feeding my cat and chickens, watering the garden.

The key to social change, day in and day out, is *support*. The gift of the antinuclear power movement was how the large group was organized into smaller decision-making and strategy-determining groups. We each found our way into affinity groups. In my case, our support group formed itself into an affinity group; others bonded with the people in their nonviolence training groups. Each group consisted of people doing civil disobedience and those who were supporters. This form of organizing showed an understanding of the necessity of support, accountability, and personal friendship in social change work.

I have been in jail sixteen or seventeen times, nearly all for civil disobedience. I sat in the middle of a road, crossed a line, or climbed over a fence. Each trip to jail has been a real learning experience, starting with my first demonstration for equal employment at the San Francisco Sheraton Palace Hotel in the early 1960s. Each time, I have felt an increasing degree of freedom, knowing I have survived a degree of the worst punishment my society has to give out.

My first arrest at Diablo Power Plant (imagine a nuclear power plant built on an earthquake fault!) was an organizing disaster. Hundreds of women were locked up in a large warehouse. We tried to work as affinity groups, with a representative going from the affinity group to the "reps council." As I remember, the group did not have enough trust to allow this process to work. One of the worst parts of being locked up is that your life is out of your control. You wake up when someone tells you to, eat strange food, and the day passes with little to do. Adults do not easily take to being out of control. So it is important to work on ways to build trust.

In later jail experiences, friends and I decided to adopt organizing elements that might help minimize the fear and build trust and calmness into the experience. Several members of our group sent out notices that the Diablo Canyon Civil Disobedience Educational and Cultural Committee was organizing classes and workshops for our time in jail. Frequently, several hundred women would be in jail together, with the same number of men in a separate facility. We suggested that people prepare classes to make the best use of our time together. Classes in exercise, tai chi, and Yoga, watershed maintenance, and nuclear physics. People told about trips to faraway places, which for a short time took us outside the confines of the jail.

Often while in jail, we had special events like a fashion show, a parade on Gay Pride Day (I was the cheerleader, twirling a baton made from the handle of a broom), talent shows, and other spontaneous events. This opened a tremendous well of creativity. People hate being shouted at by guards or organizers all day, so we started to make announcements by passing notes through the meal lines. Morning and night, we would have several people walk through the hall, stopping to talk with each person. "What's going on with you?" If they were not well, we had a list of health workers from among us — doctors, nurses, accupressurists, and massage specialists — as well as people specializing in various forms of counseling and therapy, if they needed to talk about upset feelings. We could send the kind of health worker the person wanted.

One of the most difficult things about jail for some people was the absence of addictive substances, so various twelve-step programs held meetings. Usually, we would be housed in a gym or tent, with hundreds of women in a small space, sleeping on narrow cots. Naturally, people got tired of being in a crowd all the time. Snorers like me were singularly unwelcome. Conflict-assistance people were also needed. All this support made the time in jail useful and manageable.

Realizing how difficult it was for a group to have to depend upon the guards for their every need, we planned a few other aspects. If people had food they did not want, it would be turned over to a committee, which could pass it out to people who got hungry at a time other than meal times. People who had extra blankets, or who were being released, gave their blankets to a committee, which kept them for people who were cold. A lounge area was put together with extra cots and books and magazines for everyone to use. The guards also enjoyed this area during the long nights they had to watch over us.

Occasionally, a group of us would be sent to the regular jail. For instance, after the second Diablo Canyon demonstration, the judge gave us the option of paying a fine of several hundred dollars or going to jail for three months. About thirty of us did not want to support the budget of the county, and so took the option to going to jail. We had a hearing before the judge before formal sentencing. Each of us was given time to speak to the judge directly about our motivation and concerns about nuclear power. The speeches took all afternoon. People brought pictures of their children and talked about the world they wanted for them. Others brought facts about nuclear power and the threat it posed. The judge asked us to come back the next day for sentencing as they prepared the jail for us.

The next day, I was finding my seat in the courtroom when the judge began his speech. "Ladies and Gentlemen: When I was given this assignment, I thought you were criminals, that you were interested in causing trouble, and I felt you deserved the longest period of imprisonment possible. But I heard what you said yesterday. Last night, I could not sleep. I respect your motives. Therefore, I am reducing your sentence from three months to two weeks." This is not a verbatim report, but what I remember.

There were sixteen women in our side of the jail, and about the same number of men. The other prisoners had been told we were "riot girls," and they were prepared not to like us. But, as we got to know them and see the situation they were experiencing, we realized that the jail officials were violating laws in their treatment of the prisoners. So we started visiting the law room, where we looked up prison law and wrote papers to the court exposing these conditions, or asking for remedies for the other prisoners.

As these petitions on behalf of the other prisoners started reaching the court, someone in the system decided we were not being rehabilitated and could be released early. As we were on our way out, the guards decided to single out a couple of women for special sentencing. They would be kept, while all the rest of us would dance free. It is important in social change that no one be isolated for special good or bad treatment. So we all sat down. We were all going out, or none of us were going. We sat for over an hour, but finally we were all released. When you are together as a group, you have tremendous power.

If authorities are in some way able to divide a group, it is very difficult to maintain power. Support is the key. An interesting sidelight to this particular arrest is that they must have been doing research, as the men were subjected to television all day and night, whereas the women could turn the TV on or off anytime we wished. We rarely watched TV, as we had so many other interesting things to do. We told stories every night: our spiritual histories, our class histories, our sexual histories. We had classes and exercise every morning. A caring group, committed to each other, emerged. Our schedule was lots better than TV. It was clear when we got out that the men had been punished more than we had.

There is, of course, another kind of support that is essential in social change work: financial support. In the late 1970s, after the Sixth Street Park, I needed to find work that allowed me large periods of time away from home for performing tours, lectures, and cleaning up the Ganges. At the time, I was running a furniture store and teaching. I needed a way to make money that allowed me to come and go. After surveying all the possible jobs, I settled on taxi driving.

I loved driving a cab, but after three years, coworkers in my social change work began to wish that I could devote full-time to my work for the world. A friend, David, asked if I could meet him for breakfast one day. He announced that the think tank I was part of had put together a group of funders who would support me if I would agree to stop driving a cab. I have an inexpensive lifestyle, so the amount of money they pledged was sufficient. This arrangement has continued with little change for over fifteen years.

I write these supporters a letter on my birthday in August, reporting on the work of the past year and sharing my plans for the next year. One of the funders, Barbara, is a close friend and knows my work habits, what I am working on from week to week, and the amount of work I get done. If anyone in the support circle has questions, they can ask her, and she vouches that I am working. She has said that the group wouldn't mind if I went to the beach for two or three months for a vacation, but that is not my way. I am a slow, steady, relaxed worker. I am rarely busy.

Another tradition I have established is a public accounting each year on my birthday. I invite all my friends to a potluck dinner. Usually sixty or so people attend. I ask them not to bring friends I may not know.

First, I have my guests introduce themselves to the group, as they may only have heard about each other. Then we eat, and I have the delightful experience of watching my friends find and enjoy each other. Later in the evening, I sit down with everyone gathered around me and take about half an hour to speak about my life. I talk about the victories of the past year and the difficulties. Then, I talk about the year I see coming, and share as openly as possible the concerns I have for the next year. I share frankly about the help I anticipate needing.

With friends, I run a small NGO, Crabgrass. We have a board of directors, which meets twice a year and gives us advice. We also have a volunteer staff that carries on part of the work. Support comes in so many forms. Ann works on selling the products we bring back from nonnationalistic women's groups in the former Yugoslavia; Tova, Jan, and Nonnie help with bookkeeping and organizing; Diane and Sarah take care of mailing the newsletter; Susan and Amy maintain the mailing list; Emily works on graphics and formatting the newsletter; and Barbara does editing, and works on specific projects in Yugoslavia. Other volunteer staff members work from time to time as needed.

Our staff and board meetings start with a check-in to personalize our work in the context of our lives. We talk about what's happening in our lives, so our knowledge of each other is not limited to our work. We sometimes have "Cs and Cs" (criticisms and complaints), so we can clear the decks before starting on new business. Usually, people make complaints on themselves if they know they have messed up or hurt another member. We can take a few minutes to work on the conflict. If an issue is more serious, we schedule more time.

Since there is a high degree of intuition in my work, it is very helpful to discuss the work with peers and get their advice and perspective. Catherine Porter, who has been my partner in the India work for ten years, has been valuable as a thinker and ballast in what are sometimes difficult waters. One year, in a meeting with the head of the Ganga Action Plan, I said some outrageous thing. Catherine came in quickly with her typical, "Well, I wouldn't say that." Where I am short on niceness, she is long. And we delight in talking about pepperoni pizza and sushi when we tire of Indian food.

Teamwork is deeply satisfying to me, and many ideas have been improved by work partners. Many ideas are thought to be crazy at first — I've gotten used to that. But as people explore an idea, as they shape it and work with it, they can often see some merit. Occasionally, a staff or board member goes on an international trip for a project, so she can see it up close.

Projects in our own community involve many others. A community has evolved around our work, and the sense of teamwork is usually a joy. Occasionally, we have conflict that either a member of our community or a counselor helps us with. Conflicts are natural in a growing, risk-taking, changing organism.

Many social change workers have formed NGOs and support themselves in unique ways, like selling goods made by people they work with, or writing grants. Entrepreneurial social change is a growing field. People simply find something that needs work, and begin the work. Some people have day jobs and do their work for the world in evenings or on weekends. I have been able to help others form support circles for economic sustenance. These people are so committed to their work that nothing will stop them from doing it. I believe that support circles are a liberating way of doing social change work. We are not required to fit our work into funding guidelines, and do not find it necessary to inflate what we are doing to attract attention in order to get money. If Johnny Appleseed had had to write grant proposals, or had had to get media attention in order to get funding, he would have planted many fewer trees.

I wish that each community were able to support its own social change worker. This person would not be someone we all agreed with; rather he would be someone whose perceptions and intuition we trusted. The community could ask the person to visit places it was concerned about, and report back what she learned, and suggest ways to participate as partners in what is happening there. If no meetings were taking place about a new development (like the Gulf War), the social change worker would gather us together and facilitate the discussion of action plans. Maybe the community social change worker would not be limited to one cause, but would have a general perspective; reading, thinking, attending conferences, and writing broadly. Maybe he would encourage leadership in the community on specific issues, and mentor the young people longing to become activists. In Cambridge, Massachusetts, the city has a position called Peace Commissioner. Our friend Cathy played that role in the community when we were there, and we appreciated her work with violence prevention in the schools.

I guess that's what I am — a community social change worker. Since there is no exact model for my work, I am always trying to find a description for it. I report to specific groups what I find in the world and what I think. In this complex world, gathering information firsthand from people you can see and touch is better than relying on the media to give us cues as what to do to help a situation. With that information, the community can do what the members want to do. I have developed connections to specific communities in the San Francisco Bay Area that I work for and with, as well as other communities outside the area: Bellingham, Washington; University of New Hampshire; Heart Politics people in New

Zealand and Australia; University of Western Sydney in Hawkesbury, Australia, and Lismore, Australia; and, of course, the former Yugoslavia and India.

Spirituality is very controversial in social change. I'm not sure why. Surely, all social change workers must keep their spirits tuned up in ways that support their work. However, at gatherings of social change workers, this is the hottest topic. Some say that spiritual groups leach off energy from social change; that vast periods spent sitting, praying, or meditating could be better put to social change work. Others complain about the divisive effect in campaigns of people using a social change project to proselytize for their religion or ideas. Still other voices say that spirituality is a personal aspect and should not be brought into the public sphere.

My own spiritual nourishment comes from many sources. I have a meditation practice that I began in the late 1970s. I designed this practice, because I needed to remain centered in kindness for the world, in spite of the confusing and fear-provoking news. Some people tell me that they stop reading the newspaper because of the effect of the news on their sense of the world. I also notice that my steadiness is negatively affected by the way the media spin the news toward the terrible. I read two newspapers every day, a national paper and a local paper. Sometimes I find myself chuckling, sometimes crying.

But I take all the input from the newspapers, e-mail, and other media to my time of meditation. I call to mind the earth as if I could hold it in my hands and look at it up close. My eyes wander over the surface; they "touch" the oceans, mountains, rivers, and deserts. As I move my attention from continent to continent, I contemplate what I know about what is happening in that place. When my concern rises for a place undergoing war, catastrophe, suffering, I call to mind all the people there longing for peace and a good life; all the people working against war, working for the common good. I may know people in that place. I send them my best wishes. "May you be happy and have a fulfilling life. May you have what you need. I send you my best wishes." Then I ask myself, "What can I do to help the earth and her people thrive?" I sit quietly waiting for that life spirit to send inspiration.

When I first started this practice, I pledged to ask this question each day for ten years, and if nothing came to me by then, I would stop. But soon ideas began to occur to me. Sometimes it is a small idea — "Call your sister." Other ideas come, like going to Yugoslavia to find out how people in the US could be helpful in their situation. There is something within me, and I believe in all people, that, when tuned into the common root system of life, knows what to do. As projects develop, this time of meditation helps keep me calm, steadily moving toward the goal of working for life in all its dimensions.

Another source of spiritual inspiration is exercising creativity and imagination, as well as participating in appreciating the acts of creativity by others. Musical performances touch that inspirational place. I particularly like folk music. Theater helps me think in new ways. Art pulls my consciousness along. My imagination is engaged, and I can see new alternatives in the future. I find going to cultural performances where I know the performers wonderfully inspirational. Large events or television don't do it for me. Hope is a muscle. There is something so enlivening in the act of creation; in a social environment, the impact is magnified.

Children's growth is a special antidote to hopelessness for me. I frequently talk to school groups and relish the interaction. I remember a second grade class in Albany, California. They had asked me to come at the completion of their unit on India. I was impressed with the thoroughness of their education. After I showed my slides and finished the talk on India, the teacher introduced the idea that I worked on social change. She asked the students what, if they were to work on social change when they grew up, would they like to work on. Many hands shot up. They called out: alcoholism, war, child abuse, hunger, homelessness, girls being thought of as less than boys, angry parents, no place to skateboard. They went on for some time. They are thinking, as are all of us, of things that could be better.

Finally, the teacher said, "Now, Fran Peavey is going to have to leave. If you have any questions, ask them now, because this is your last chance. When she is gone, I will not be able to answer your questions." A young man who had been sitting up front and who had been a little wiggly, thrust his hand into the air. The teacher called on him. "Omar." "Do you need any help?" he asked earnestly. "Yes, Omar, I do need help. Study hard, because there is a lot of fine work waiting for you. Thanks for thinking of that question."

Laughter is a spiritual discipline from which I draw nourishment to keep me walking calmly amid great suffering. When I was a comedian, I thought a lot about the difference between healthy and unhealthy comedy. I tried to practice what I came to call "compassionate comedy," which occurs when you are laughing at yourself and your group, not in a down, laughing *at* way, but more of an inclusive laughing *with*. This is to be distinguished from condescending comedy that allows the one who is laughing to pretend to be superior to those whom he is laughing at. Compassionate comedy also does not put oneself down. It does not rest upon distance, but upon our commonness for its comedy and for its relief.

My work as a social change worker is akin to that of an artist, in that I work from inspiration. Sometimes, I can help create experiences that allow the participants (including myself) to see things differently. One of my greatest joys in life was a party that I held the second year I was working in Varanasi. I wanted to thank all the people who had assisted me in my work that year. I invited everyone — college professors, the cook and her family, the foundation members and their families, the people who cleaned my room and drove me to my appointments — to a party with chocolate pudding, slides of Ganga, and socializing.

We all sat together and introduced ourselves by sharing something in our lives that gave us joy. Our cook, her husband, and children are of the untouchable caste. This aspect is irrelevant to me, but means a lot in their system. Those children saw their father, who is a gardener at the university, sitting in the same room on the same level with professors. Did Georgia O'Keefe ever have such joy with a painting as I did that night?

I remember I said, "I came to this work through the work of Martin Luther King Jr., who modeled much of his work after Mahatma Gandhi. So in a sense, I am your grandchild. In our work for civil rights, we had a song that meant a lot to us, which I would like to teach you tonight." My friend Virendraji had added a special verse about cleaning the river. Then we sang "We shall overcome" (in Hindi), concluding with a verse "We shall clean the river" (again in Hindi).

Writing poetry also nourishes me. Often when I enter my small writing castle in the morning, I am so overcome with what is happening in the garden outside my window that I must start with a garden poem. My small garden bulges with life: raspberries, a fig tree, an apple tree, a pear tree, an apricot tree, a plum tree, many flowers, a veggie bed, and a small pond with goldfish that have babies from time to time. My first spiritual home was in the forest, and now my garden is a source of inspiration. I am learning to love tides and oceans. Whether the vast expanse is water or sand, the immenseness and consistency fill me with awe. Life, in general, seems to call to my life; creative gardening helps me touch the glorious renewal of life from season to season.

I attend a church because of my ancestors. It was Protestant prayers and songs that brought them across the ocean, across the plains and mountains, to Idaho. I participate in my lineage sitting in church. I am aware of the need for those prayers and songs as I go across the ocean into places where my spirit sometimes needs fortification. For years, I found my spiritual home in Quaker Meeting for worship, but I finally experienced the need to sing. Music is an important sustainer of my soul, so I searched for a place with the best singing in the Bay Area. I now call Metropolitan Community Church my spiritual home. I have a linguistic problem when asked "what is your religion?" I cannot identify with one religion exclusively. I cannot say "I am a Christian," if by saying that, I mean I am not a Buddhist or Hindu or Jew. My god has many names and is everywhere.

I am happy worshipping, as I occasionally do, in a Jewish synagogue. The old Hebrew prayers are also a part of my heritage. When I am in India, I frequently go to Sankat Mochan Temple with Mahantji at night. I sit on a step to the side of the temple, while he does his *puja* (worship). I watch hundreds — sometimes thousands — worship with him. That god of his temple is Hanamanji — the God who removes obstacles. I feel that my God is there.

One day, I said to Mahantji that I was not very attracted to Hanamanji. I wondered how he felt about that. "Fine," he replied. "Are you drawn to any Hindu God?" "Yes. I always feel happy around Ganesh" (the elephant god who is a remover of obstacles). So Ganesh became my Hindu God. I am frequently given statues of Ganesh, and as we travel, temples to "my Hindu God" are pointed out.

I experience spiritual support in many ways beyond organized religion. One year, I needed a sabbatical, so I applied to the Bunting Institute at Radcliffe College in Cambridge, Massachusetts, for a fellowship and received the Bunting Peace Fellowship. It was a fine honor and gave me a chance to withdraw from day-to-day work for a year, to write, to think, and to pray. Before leaving the Bay Area for Radcliffe, I went to anyone I had any unresolved conflict with and did what I could do to work out the issues between us. I didn't want anyone resisting my return home. I wanted to have as clean a slate as possible. My goals for my sabbatical were to work on my next ten years of work in social change and to research water. I also set the goal of learning to kneel.

I read a book, *An Interrupted Life*, by Etty Hillesum, a Jewish woman killed in the Holocaust at the age of twenty-nine. She set a goal to learn to kneel and pray. That stuck with me, and I have had that goal for a few years. Once when I was alone in Thailand, I tried to prostrate myself in prayer at a Buddhist temple. I didn't feel authentic, and I try to honor the spirit that is mine by staying in the wide range of me that is real. My Protestant backbone does not seem to submit easily to kneeling in prayer, but I thought it might be a useful inner skill to be so supple of spirit. I wanted to understand the inner experience of surrender. So I tried to find that place of authentic kneeling within myself during this year of reflection.

Etty Hillesum worked for a Jewish organization in Amsterdam in the late 1930s and early 1940s. She knew what was happening to her people. What Etty saw was also what I perceived in Sarajevo — the capacity of humans for creation of unspeakable horror. While on my sabbatical, from time to time I would go to my office at the university, close the door, and try to kneel. Of course, physically I could kneel, but I wanted to authentically kneel. I wanted to feel surrender inside and express it outside. I wanted to find inner kneeling. I would stand at my desk and begin to move to the sofa, where I anticipated I would kneel and pray. But as I got close to the sofa, I would fall out of touch with myself and start pretending I was going to kneel. Then I would stop. That wasn't good enough. I didn't want to be a pretend kneeler. I needed to really kneel in surrender to awfulness.

That year, a friend loaned me a lovely house in a forest on a creek in Maine. Every week in the fall, I drove up to this house. The next door neighbor was cutting down the trees on his property, so he could have a boat storage lot. It made me sick to think of all those trees being cut down.

One day, there was a bad storm. I went outside to survey the damage the next day. The tree right on the border of the neighbor's lot had tipped over in the wind. There it lay on the ground, its roots reaching wildly into the air. I walked to the tree and knelt immediately. The tree knew the same thing that I had felt in Sarajevo, and that Etty had known in Germany decades earlier: human beings are capable of horrible, horrible acts. Now I can kneel anytime I want. I have surrendered to this very nasty reality. And I feel I work with more energy and clearness of purpose.

My sabbatical also focused on developing a metaphor for thinking about social change using water. So often, social change workers think in militaristic terms — strategy, conquering, winning, losing. Maybe, if we look to more natural phenomena for how to think about our work and how to do it, we will find new ways. I want to be so like water that I can fit into any vessel, flow anywhere, move with the grade, not only in my own way. Think like water! Fluid. Not limited by ideology, concepts; fresh in every moment. I wish to think and act like water — powerfully working with other drops of water to wear away resistance drop by drop. Wear away the stones on which poverty and suffering rest. Always looking for the deepest way to flow, and to allow the world to flow through me. Cleaning, sparkling, bubbling. Think like water!

My family offers support in many ways. My brother, Art, and three sisters, Ann, Dorothy, and Susan, occupy a variety of political positions, most of which are somewhat different from mine. But our love, connection, and support of each other are not altered by our opinions. We share something more important. My nieces and nephews often teach me exactly what I need. Some of the next generation pulled me out of the Payette River when the boat I was in capsized. Another time when I experienced a profoundly painful loss and went through a very difficult time, my nephew, Aaron, wrote a sweet letter from college on e-mail titled "We're here for you."

> *Dear Fran,*
>
> *I am sorry to hear of your current situation… Our hearts are with you, and we are here to support you in any endeavor you decide to pursue. Will be thinking of you and hope that we can see each other in the near future.*
>
> Love,
Aaron

The emotional, intellectual, and moral support I draw from my intimate relationships is awesome to me.

Support circles, support or affinity groups, families, boards, or crisis decision-making groups — they all make social change work. Of course, working with people has its difficulties, but working without them is worse. It is axiomatic that working with people involves differences, conflict, and sometimes betrayal. Some people grow and change; some people don't. The social forces of greed work on social change workers as well as industrialists. Childhood suffering has its damaging effects on the ego.

Social change workers may have more than average problems with their egos. Seeing and feeling the pain of the world is a very difficult emotional experience. A sense of urgency frequently creeps into our work (after all, people are dying, aren't they?), and that may cause us to want to shortcut careful, tender care with the people with whom we work. When the situation is desperate, it is often even more important to work slowly and carefully. Excellence in social change work is so important, because we are always trying to build people's confidence in themselves and their fellow human beings, so that life will appear to be worth saving.

I notice that when I have been in the news, I sometimes lose touch with my goals and myself. While many people working for social change think only of the benefits of media attention, I do not necessarily think being in the media automatically moves our goals forward. Especially when the group is young, or the people in the group are newly together, media attention can (1) alert your opposition to the need to organize against you, (2) start grabs for attention and power within the group, (3) isolate the spokesperson or leader in a way that destroys her focus on the goals and relationship to the group. I think it is much more important to keep my own social context informed about my work and the thinking that arises from that work. I believe that communicating to people in person is the most powerful form of communication. So I usually do not seek out media that would dilute or cut up my information in ways that do not do honor to it. Fortunately, I do not need media coverage for funding or my ego.

When I was working with Sixth Street Park, one of my jobs was to take journalists to the park, introduce them to the staff, and help them understand the story of the park. A reporter from the *Wall Street Journal* asked for my help in getting the story of the park. I took her to the park, and she spent a long time talking with the staff. Later, she offered to take me to lunch, so I could help her with some of the background facts. I jumped at the chance to "do lunch" on the *Journal*.

The next day, when the story came out, I was featured more prominently than the park staff. Some outrageous and funny comments I had made were in the article. Vicky, the secretary in the office I worked out of, called me in the morning and said that the producer from the Johnny Carson Show had called and wanted me to be on the show. I brushed this information off as a joke by my comedy partner, Charlie. Vicky called back a few minutes later, saying that the people in the office had discussed it and thought I should take the number and call the man back. They did not think it was a joke. I returned the call, and it was not a joke.

Minutes later, a family member called to say that my Uncle Frank, vice president of a large construction company, had called my aunt, the former director of the US Mint, asking if I could possibly be the Fran Peavey in the center section of the front page of the *Wall Street Journal*. "Yes," my aunt replied. "Mary, why is it that the two of us with all our prestigious jobs have never been on the front center section of the *Journal,* and this young upstart niece working with poor people is there?" I called Charlie to tell him these funny stories. My head, and especially my ego, were spinning.

Charlie got the joke. After hanging up from me, he called Vicky, pretending to be the producer of the Merv Griffin Show. Vicky called me back. "Now it's the Merv Griffin show. He says 'Don't sign with Johnny Carson until you talk to me!' " The Johnny Carson show was very tempting for a budding comedian. Maybe this could be my Big Break. Oh! I was full of myself. It didn't take me long to recover and think about the effect of making light of the park and the people there. The producer refused to have any of the park staff go on with me. He flattered me with how wonderfully candid and funny I was. I may be the only comedian who ever refused Johnny Carson.

The attachment to doing good is an equally dangerous trap for the ego of social change workers. We all want to be thought of as good people. This is folly, and offers many possible opportunities for delusion. We all do and are good and not so good. If we are attached to being good, we will not be able to risk that concept. Sometimes we have to make a choice of bad alternatives. Whatever is good in one time has evil embedded in it as well. Our work uses up the earth's resources, and carries an ugly underbelly. The more we deny that there is a dark side to our work and our characters, the more we are attached to our goodness, and the more vulnerable we are.

Attachment to being good people as social change workers may separate us from other people — the ones who write the computer programs, clean the offices, and teach the children — who often are doing very good work. We need people in all places who think of themselves as social change workers, and to the degree that we occupy that niche exclusively, we create obstacles to other people adopting that identity. We are neither good people nor bad people. Both constructs are made up, a fantasy. The illusion does not serve anything except our need to recover from negative self-images that were given to us by punitive and simple-minded people, wedded to a delusional lifestyle. I am not good or bad; I'm just doing my job as well as I can. Good people often do bad things. Me, too. There is no permanent category for people; we are just minute-by-minute finding our way among the shadows, doing the best we can, and, we hope, cleaning up the messes we make as we go along.

There is often unexpected support for our work that buoys our spirits. Once, just before we were to leave for the Balkan region, I promised that when we returned I would take my partner away for a night at a bed-and-breakfast inn to celebrate her birthday. I called a friend who ran such a place. She had promised us that we could have a free night there someday; now was the time — I hoped. "No,

I have rented the place out full-time. Sorry," She said. She recommended a friend of hers. I called her friend, and I liked the sound of the place until I asked how much it would cost. I don't go to such places much, so I had no idea what to expect. When she said $130, I was blown away. "What does that include?" I inquired incredulously. "Maybe you want to call other places," the woman suggested. "No, I guess I'll have to find the money for this one, because I don't have the time to call around. I leave for the former Yugoslavia in a couple of days and have no time to make calls."

"What did you say your name was?"

"Fran Peavey," I replied.

"Oh, for you it's free. I heard you on the radio talking about your work in Yugoslavia, and I wanted to send in something, but I couldn't write your address down fast enough. This way, I can support you to recover from your work. It would be my joy."

Thus, my friendship with Penny and James Livingston of Cricket Cottage began. I go there from time to time, paying what I can, to rest and get away from the phone and the responsibilities at home.

Working for social change is a lot like riding a bicycle; sometimes it's all you can do to stay upright, other times the wind is so strong or the grade so steep that you cannot help but slip backwards. Sometimes it is important to stop peddling the bike. Get off and think about things. We don't have to work until we drop from sheer exhaustion. We can set the bike down and rest. I find it is particularly important to be rested in order to do nonviolent work honoring all the people involved in the struggle. In the I-Hotel, I sensed that if we could all get some rest, our work, our sense of dignity, as well as our sense of humor would improve. We will get back on the bicycle, there is no doubt about that, for there is no joy so great as flying for the common good.

In my work, I have known moments that can only be termed as betrayal. This is part of working with people. The I-Hotel involved times when groups worked secretly from their own goals, and we were exposed to dangerous and upsetting times. When a member brought a handgun to a scary meeting, I was alarmed — partly because of the physical threat I feel from guns, and partly because if it had been used, I would have been associated, without my knowing it, with a violent group. Trust had been broken. I have come to think that next to life itself, trust is the most precious thing.

Several other groups have floundered when one person decided that she was the kingpin, and no one else had a right to be critical or have any voice in the affairs of the group. We continually have to fight for democracy and transparency in groups, and sometimes we lose. The struggle is hard, the losing even harder. I had to leave a group when they decided to accept funds from the National Endowment for Democracy, a CIA-front organization. I could not agree to that, so I was forced to leave a group that had been an intellectual and a spiritual lifeline for me. More regrouping, new ways of working; I maintain the old friendships, but with a fresh sense of identity. Throughout the life of a social change worker, it may be that different groups move in and out of the role of workmates. With each disruption of a community, I have had to take time to re-evaluate my life and work, and find new avenues to do my work. Sometimes I have had to make different friends.

Another aspect of support is the nourishment I derive through supporting others, personally or in their social change work. Seeing myself as one cell in a large dynamic social body gives me a particular joy. I appreciate the opportunity to give cash or care to individuals, groups, or organizations. I try to pass on any positive information that reaches me about the work of others. Our support group and Crabgrass occasionally give awards for admirable work that comes to our attention. Recent award recipients have been the mayor who spoke up against skinheads who were becoming powerful in his town; a Tibetan refugee in America who has worked steadily to help other refugees; a black woman who regularly cooks food for homeless people in her neighborhood in Oakland; a Native American who works with Indian young people to end the hatred of others. We simply send a letter of appreciation "for service to humanity"; sometimes we are able to enclose a little bit of money, too.

In fact, I find giving support as satisfying as receiving it. A key question whenever confronted with suffering is, "How can I support you?" Sometimes the question is so challenging that people do not know how to respond; sometimes individuals or groups can identify something simple that they need; sometimes support will be more complex. If the request is beyond my abilities, it is hard, but it is better to say no in that moment and free others from that expectation of me.

The need for support may be a natural one that we share with other animals. One day, I was walking through the Stanford University campus with a friend when I saw a crowd of people with cameras and video equipment. They were clustered around a pair of chimpanzees — a male running loose, and a female on a chain about twenty-five feet long. Inquiring of several people from the crowd, I learned that the male was from Marine World, and the female was from one of the animal laboratories at Stanford. The scientists were introducing them to each other, trying to get them to mate. They had invited the press to view the event.

The male was eager. He grunted and grabbed the female's chain and tugged. She whimpered and backed away. He pulled again. She pulled back. Watching the chimps' faces, I began to feel sympathy for the female. Suddenly, the female chimp yanked her chain out of the male's grasp. To my amazement, she walked through the crowd, straight over to me, and took my hand. Her hand felt rough but strong. She led me across the circle to the only two women in the crowd, and she joined hands with one of them. The four of us stood in a circle. The chimp had recognized us and reached out across all the years of evolution to form her own support group. We all need support from others who understand our position, who can empathize with us.

Mahantji has taught me many lessons about social change. When I first started to work with him, I frequently would say something like, "This is so exciting." Mahantji would caution me that if I relied on what was exciting as a criterion for what to do, I would soon burn out and be unable to find the long-term energy to continue this work year after year, decade after decade.

I replied, "Well, if I don't decide what to do by what speaks to my passion, what will I use to know what to do?"

"Do your duty, do what you can do, do what you think will be effective toward your goal," was his wise reply. I have come to value this perspective. Capitalism, with its emphasis on hype and selling, is so woven into my cultural fabric that I need to watch carefully so that it doesn't skew my work, especially in cultures that are not so involved in these aspects of our economic system.

There are times of discouragement. Sometimes it seems that we are losing more than winning. In the winter of 1992, I returned from India with deep doubts. We had received the first results from the water-testing kits. The fecal coliform count was in the tens of thousands. Little did I know that the figure was actually ten times higher, because we found out a year later that the laboratory assistants were multiplying incorrectly. For the water to be healthy to drink, the World Health Organization says the count should be 200. It was upsetting — an understatement — to learn just how ill my grandmother was. On my final visit to the river that year, shit was floating on the surface of the water, since the electricity was off and the pumps were not working. Raw sewage was flowing into the river at every possible juncture. I had never seen so much shit floating on my dear Ganga — or had I forgotten how bad it was in the beginning of our work? The small group I had taken with me for my farewell journey was quiet as we floated along in the boat. It was one of those spiritual moments when the will is toughened. But not before it sinks to the lowest depths of despair.

Perhaps my own intestinal battles added to my misery. I am as careful as I can be, but still I had three parasites when I returned that year. I gathered trusted advisors around me to tell them what I had learned. One friend, Naomi, asked a question: "Why don't you work on something where you can be successful?" I found some answer in the moment that got me off the hook that night, but for the next three or four days I was plunged into deep questioning. Social change is not one of those instantly gratifying kinds of jobs. Could I work harder or smarter in order to be successful in cleaning Ganga? We have had successes with the river, but success is hard to claim and harder to measure. There is still so much more work to be done.

Then, I thought about how I could find a project that promised to be successful. But in these dark days, when environmental and human rights are under threat everywhere, I could not figure out how to tell in advance what would be successful. There were many times when I was learning to walk that I fell, many times I nearly drowned in my early days of swimming, and I did not catch or hit the ball in my early days of playing softball. There are many moments of failure in a full life. Sometimes I think I should write a book, "Parking Lots I Have Helped to Build," in which the story of the failures of Sixth Street Park and the I-Hotel could be recounted, honoring the defeats that were part of those efforts. I now think mostly of the victories I see from those times, but there are also failures. I cannot be afraid of failure, or I will not be able to take risks; I am only afraid I won't be able to laugh about it when it's over. What I have spent years building may be destroyed overnight, but I choose to continue building. I will give the world my best, even though I know the reward for that is only more work and a load of criticism.

Sometimes it is hard to understand what real success is. Success may be an illusion anyway, as is failure. Ultimately, after all this grappling with discouragement and despair, I have concluded for this moment that I aim to be effective. I give my best. I try to learn how to improve my work. I work hard, but I do not have control. I am not called to be successful, but to be faithful. Faithful to my heart, to my love. Faithful to my friends.

My vision of strategy is not based on a military vision of complete control of the process as well as the ends. I see a vision of water meandering along, finding its way. In some moments, I see myself rowing a boat with many others, my colleagues rowing from their perspective in building the future. I row on the left, as strong and clear as I can. Others are rowing in other directions from their sense of what is best. The direction of the boat will be a mixture of all the forces acting on it — and the boat may go in a combination of several directions at the same time. The future is going to be a mixture of the goals of all of us rowing on the left, and the goals of those rowing on the right, as well as those rowing in other directions — backwards, up, and down. I row for human rights and environmental restoration. I do not row against another force. The river will blend the forces, and the boat will move. Sometimes it seems that history is moving more toward goals that I do not appreciate. I just keep rowing. What else can I do?

Postscript

Letter to Social Change
Workers

IN THE DARKEST time of the year, a letter from enthusiastic
young women social change workers arrives in my mailbox.
They have some questions they would like to ask me, as a mentor and longtime social change worker. This letter sits on the desk
for days unattended.

I've been laid up with an infected foot for three months, unable
to walk out of my house, incapacitated in this season of many social
opportunities. I cannot get up and go, so I tend to sit and think. The
undertow of my personal life, as well as the sorrowful life of the
world, plays itself out in the theater of consciousness until I pray for
unconsciousness. When one is able to move and go out into the
world with one's work, it is easy to ignore the suffering one carries
deep inside.

"What can I tell these bright, enthusiastic young women? Shall
I share what it is like to be in my mid-fifties and see so much of
what I have worked for being destroyed by the market economy?
Now, everyone is so involved in their careers, it's difficult to organize meetings for anything except emergencies. If a specific change
is really successful, the Next Generation does not even know that
things were not always that way. For the young, the high ground
that we fought so hard for is now the valley on which they stand;
they define the status quo as the enemy. As they set new goals for
themselves, young women deride us older feminists. "We don't
want to be like you old fashioned feminists. We see a new woman
whom we will become." They seem to forget that many sisters and
mothers fought for this ground they now take for granted. All of
this is as it should be.

Besides the temporariness of our victories, there's also the
invisibility that we must contend with. Even those occasional victories that we have in a life of social change become invisible in

history. The role of any individual so merges into the total picture that it's hard to remember exactly what one's contribution was. So often we work in cooperation with many other people, and whatever is created is a group success. The most profound social change is a collaborative act.

Not only is our work invisible, but it is also often incomprehensible. I remember as a young woman having to deal with knowing that my mother would never understand my work in the world. Even now, when I say that I must travel to India to help clean the Ganges River, friends envision that I take a sieve and stand in the river collecting the feces. When I explain that mostly I sit in meetings, work with staff, write letters and position papers, and encourage everyone along the way, that does not sound like work to some of them.

Maybe the young women who wrote the letter have not yet grown accustomed to the fact that their college classmates are probably earning five to ten times as much as social change workers do, and thereby have access to vacations, owning their own homes, and the joy of being able to give generously. We get used to all these little problems of social change work, until one has to sit week after week and think about work. That small self, that selfish and self-centered ego that has been ignored so long, begins to kick and scream.

The ego, so identified with what we do as being our claim to value, begins to demand attention in the painful reflection of the darkness. With few external sources of reward available to the social change worker, is there any security for the needy ego? And then there are the inevitable sequences of betrayals, defeats, and criticisms one has had to endure. It all rolls around inside. Should I tell these young social change workers about all the internal suffering that is the legacy of the life of social change? I do not want to discourage them.

Mixed up with all of this individual suffering is the awareness of the horrible suffering of the human beings for whom we campaign. The historical and moral imperatives compel action, but progress is slow and painful. Even though for many years we worked for justice in Central America, those dear people still do not have a real peace or justice. Now, no matter how much I care or how many hours I work, my friends in Yugoslavia are still being killed. Every day's e-mail brings me news of atrocities. I have worked for the rights of poor people in San Francisco my entire life, and yet more homeless people died on the streets of San

Francisco last year than all the years before. Sometimes it's just too hard to cope with the intense suffering that I must carry in my being. Tears come to my eyes, as I face my helplessness in the streets of my city as well as in the Balkans. The newly homeless refugees and the long-time homeless of my city share the pain that cuts straight through my heart. Seventeen years I have worked on cleaning the Ganges River in Varanasi, and still the largest killer of children in the city is waterborne disease. We have had successes, but the overall task is enormous. Shall I tell the young women about the sense of futility and helplessness that a social change worker must learn to cope with, and yet strive for excellence and success in every campaign, every meeting, every human connection and piece of writing?

At this moment, a friend from my affinity group arrives for a visit. Our affinity group, composed of women working in social change either in our home, neighborhood, in our paid work or as a volunteer, has been meeting for fourteen years. We meet monthly to remind one another of our social dreams, and to help each other in any way possible.

We have helped members with weddings, divorces, funerals, and commitment ceremonies. We have urged members to step out of social change for a while to rest and get a fresh perspective; carried food to members who are ill; and listened to each other's troubles with partners, children, parents getting old and dying, jobs, money, and tomato plants. It is my experience that what made the difference between those of us who were able to sustain a life of social change through the years and those who gave up with discouragement in their twenties was our organizing a strong support system to carry us through the rough waters.

"How are you doing?" my friend asks. There's nothing like old companions in the struggle for social change. They know me so well, having seen me in frightening situations, in intimidating moments, and through the valley of the shadow of uncertainty. They have learned how to criticize and how to love.

My friend sits in the rocking chair, and we talk the afternoon away. I tell her about all my doubts and my suffering. She listens respectfully, offering a few suggestions from time to time. We talk about a project she's working on, and I listen, having long ago learned that the goal of communication is not to fix, but to really listen and drink deeply of the other person's life.

And then, we begin to remember how we first met each other in jail, because we had climbed over a fence at a nuclear weapons facility. My initial impression of her was that she was a jerk; her first impression of me was that I was erratic and confused. We laugh as we remember the many campaigns, the difficulties, the times we have disagreed with each other and with others, the battles we have won and the ones we have lost. But then, as we look at those campaigns from this distance, there were learnings and small victories even in the bitterest of compost heaps. My, how we have grown and changed. The camaraderie we have enjoyed through time is a sweet balm in the darkness.

"I'm making some chili for my family late next week. Would you like me to bring some by?"

"Sure, I love chili."

The darkness of the season and the darkness of my soul are still with me. In fact, even when I'm working now, I'm aware of the morass of suffering I carry with me. When one is a social change worker, one rarely works where there is no intense suffering. Only our internal sense of excellence in communication and caring and the camaraderie of our allies makes a life of social change bearable. It is the support of others that makes social change work. Redwood trees, those tallest of all living things, maintain themselves upright by spreading their shallow roots and intertwining those roots with the trees and plants all around them. The renewal of the spirit is essential as we walk in the river of history. We rarely have the sense that, as individuals, we have achieved much, but then we never know how we have changed the flow of the river by standing steadfastly in it. In social change, success is measured as much by faithfulness and quality of interaction as by achieving specific goals.

Most of all, I would want young people interested in social change to know that I welcome them into this field of human endeavor and wish them well in their pursuit of social change. If I do not meet you in this life, it will be my loss.

Some time ago, I wrote a piece that comes to me now:

IF

If you can keep focused on your task while all around you there is chaos;

If you can maintain a simple lifestyle while all around you people are consumed with consumption and amassing wealth;

If you can remember your true task in the face of funding guidelines;

If you can remember that people opposite you in any struggle have divided hearts and that part of each heart longs to work for the common good;

If you can work for positive social goals without becoming self-righteous or sanctimonious;

If you can determine when you have done enough work and allow yourself to rest and play without guilt,

If you can remember to be proud of yourself, your traditions, and your people even while working to change some aspects inside yourself or your culture;

If you can remember that all around you is support for you and your work even though that support may not always be visible;

If you can remember that no abstract principle is more important than life itself;

If you can keep your intimate relationships as well as your garden a blossoming nourishing home for your soul;

If, among the brokenness of life, you can find shards of hope and lift that hope up to the masses in a way that inspires them to dream anew;

And if you can keep your sense of humor while facing suffering and devastation and still cry at the sorrow of this world and of our time;

Then you can be a social change worker, my friend, and I guarantee there is no greater love, no more meaningful life available in humanity. You will find joy in almost every day, and peace as your head falls onto the pillow each evening. Each of us can do so little to preserve life in our lifetime; but that we do our little part is important. It is all we can do. Making history is not a science, but a genuine mystery with components of passion, truth, and delusion all mixed together in a convoluted pendulum of time. History may or may not judge our work kindly, we do not have control; but we can rest easy in the assurance that we have done our best with what we knew.

Fran Peavey
January 1, 1999

Index

drug addiction 90
Dubois, Mark 297
Dubrovnik 232, 251, 343
duty, war and 220, 229
Duvall, Mrs 40
Dwiedi, Urmila 190

early adaptor and early majority types 305
Earth Summit 6, 208
earthquake fault lines 135–6
ebonics 19
economic development schemes 84
Edinburgh 152
education
    India 175–6
    Thailand 159–60
egos, social change and 372–4
Einstein, Albert 100, 308
El Hilal 267, 274, 275, 277, 278
Ellis, C.P. 21–2
emergency services, nuclear disaster and 119
emotions, social change and 296–9, 322
environmental degradation 200–11, 296–7, 301
Evers, Medger 54
eviction campaign 63–79
    Thailand 160–1
expectations, behaviour and 314–15

facilitation 307
faith 378
family, support from 372
    see also Carpenter, Grandmother; Peavey family
FBI 71
fear 95
    nuclear weapons and 119–28, 149–50, 153, 216, 292
    obstacle to change 292–3, 342–4
    preying on 101–13, 134
feel good politics 1
feelings, about nuclear weapons 120–4
Feinstein, Dianne 98, 115
financial support 364
    see also support systems
fish 48, 202
fluidity in thinking 371–2
food additives 56
food distribution, Kosovo 276–8
Food Quality Protection Act 209

Food System 68, 71
forest conservation 48, 301
Forni, Captain 88
fortune telling 150–1
free speech 50
Friends of the Ganges 171
friends, hope and 358–60
Fuller, Alia 120, 123
Fuller, Bob 119–20, 122

Gandhi, Indira 153, 176
Gandhi, Mahatma 176
Gandhi, Rajiv 177, 178
Ganga Action Plan 177, 178, 181–99, 365
Ganga, cleaning it 168–99, 305–6, 307, 308–9, 338, 359–60, 377–8, 384
Gay Pride Day 362
gay rights movement 23–4, 362
    Harvey Milk murder and 113–15
General Motors 205
genocides 212–21
Gilligan, Dr James 245
Glendinning, Chellis 120
Glide Memorial United Church 80–99
Godfather 84, 90–1, 96
Goldman, Emma 50
goodness, egos and 374
Goops, The 41, 43
Graham, Bill 336
Great Britain 141
Green, Bailey 196
Green, Tova 236, 245
Greenham Common 142
groundwater contamination 186
group processes, dangers of 101–13, 314–39, 344–5
guilt
    individual and collective 215
    survivor 116
Gulf of Tonkin 54, 344
Gulf War 145, 222–32, 343
Gurdjieff community 115
Guyana 104–13

Hammad, Mr 191
Hardin, Lakota 332
Hartsough, Jan 260–77
hate 330–4, 344
heart politics 1
    key concepts 2–3
    see also connectedness
Heck, Alfons 348–9

trees, love for and identifying with
29–31, 327
trust 375
Truth and Reconciliation Commission
22–3
Tudjman, Franjo 244, 320–1
Turkey 212
Tutu, Archbishop Desmond 165
Tuzla 356
Twin Falls, Idaho 28–48, 50, 168

UCK 259, 260
Ugly American, The (Lederer) 9
Ungsongtham, Prateep 160
UNICEF 269, 274
United Nations Environment Programme
6
United Nations High Commission for
Refugees (UNHCR) 261, 262, 267,
274, 275
United Nations Human Rights
Commission 214
United States of America 156–7, 285
untouchables, US society and 88
Upadhyay, Dr S.N. 172, 185

Valja 272
Varanasi 152, 155, 157, 163, 169–99, 307,
384
Vietnam War protests 50–1, 54–9, 213,
294, 340–1, 346–7
violence 245, 319–21, 354
street people and 84, 86, 93–4–5
virtual connections 335–6
Vjosa 261, 268, 271, 277, 278
voting 56
Vukovar 243
Vula, Mrs 263–7, 279

Wall Street Journal 373
war, self doubt and 221
individual and group actions against
222–33
rape and 234, 243
water 44
think like 371–2
water testing 180–4
Waterford, Helen 348–9
Watsonville 203
Westmoreland, General 213
Whispering In Our Hearts (Reynolds) 356
whistle blowers 108
White, Dan 107, 112–15
wilderness 45
Williams, Cecil 95, 98, 104, 109
women
Albanian 254
pessimism of 154
wars and 228, 236–42, 246–57
Women In Black 249–50, 342
Woodward, Susan 245
World Bank 177
World Conference for Women, China
317, 337
World Council of Churches 164
World Food Program 274, 276
World Health Organisation (WHO) 274
worship 369–72

Yip, Mr 64
Yugoslavia 1, 22, 102, 146, 293, 294, 320,
342–4, 383
Bosnian crisis 234–57, 326, 336–7,
350, 356
Kosovo crisis 258–87

Zagreb 239, 243
Zaporah, Ruth 246